MW00783897

Fighting for the Higher Law

AMERICA IN THE NINETEENTH CENTURY

Series editors:
Brian DeLay, Steven Hahn, Amy Dru Stanley

America in the Nineteenth Century proposes a rigorous
rethinking of this most formative period in U.S. history.
Books in the series will be wide-ranging and eclectic, with
an interest in politics at all levels, culture and capitalism,
race and slavery, law, gender, and the environment, and
regional and transnational history. The series aims to
expand the scope of nineteenth-century historiography by
bringing classic questions into dialogue with innovative
perspectives, approaches, and methodologies.

FIGHTING FOR THE HIGHER LAW

Black and White Transcendentalists
Against Slavery

Peter Wirzbicki

PENN

UNIVERSITY OF PENNSYLVANIA PRESS

PHILADELPHIA

Published by
University of Pennsylvania Press
Philadelphia, Pennsylvania 19104-4112
www.upenn.edu/pennpress

Printed in the United States of America on acid-free paper

1 3 5 7 9 10 8 6 4 2

Library of Congress Cataloging-in-Publication Data

Names: Wirzbicki, Peter, author.
Title: Fighting for the Higher Law : black and white
    Transcendentalists against slavery / Peter Wirzbicki.
Other titles: America in the nineteenth century.
Description: 1st edition. | Philadelphia : University of
    Pennsylvania Press, [2021] | Series: America in the nineteenth
    century | Includes bibliographical references and index.
Identifiers: LCCN 2020020792 | ISBN 9780812252910
    (hardcover)
Subjects: LCSH: Antislavery movements—New England—
    History—19th century. | Transcendentalism (New
    England)—History—19th century. | African American
    abolitionists—History—19th century. | Transcendentalists
    (New England)—History—19th century. | United States—
    Intellectual life—1783–1865.
Classification: LCC E445.N5 W57 2021 |
    DDC 326.8097409034—dc23
LC record available at https://lccn.loc.gov/2020020792

CONTENTS

Introduction   1

Chapter 1. Transcendentalism in Black and White   23

Chapter 2. The Latest Forms of Infidelity   62

Chapter 3. The Cotton Economy and the Rise of
    Universal Reformers   102

Chapter 4. Fugitive Slaves and the Many Origins of
    Civil Disobedience Theory   142

Chapter 5. Heroism, Violence, and Race   178

Chapter 6. A War of Ideas   219

Epilogue   258

Notes   265

Index   317

Acknowledgments   323

Introduction

There was no high, no low, no masters, no servants, no white, no black.

—Frederick Douglass

In August 1844, Frederick Douglass was traveling through central New England, part of the so-called Hundred Conventions tour, when he arrived in Northampton, Massachusetts. He had only escaped from Maryland slavery six year earlier. Since then, Douglass had become one of the abolitionist movement's most valuable lecturers, working for the Massachusetts Anti-Slavery Society by retelling his experiences of slavery throughout the state—in rural hamlets such as Acton, respectable villages such as Groton, and burgeoning industrial towns such as Lowell.[1] To be an abolitionist, in the 1840s, was to almost always be despised and ostracized, but to be a black abolitionist—and a fugitive slave to boot—was to be exposed to near-constant hostility and danger: rowdy audience members threw rotten vegetables at Douglass, railroads and hotels refused him service, and sometimes mobs tried to rush the stage. Northampton was no different; Douglass remembered the treatment that he received as "harsh and repellent." Friends of his would long keep as souvenirs the rocks that proslavery roughs had thrown at him when he tried to speak at the Northampton Town Meeting.[2]

As was often the case when he was on an antislavery speaking tour, Douglass spent the night with supporters. This time, it was with the Northampton Association, a utopian socialist community that had existed since the early 1840s. The contrast with the rest of the town could not have been greater. "Here," he remembered, "neither my color nor my condition was counted against me."[3] The community was stark and simple—amid a tangled forest on the outskirts of town was a single "brick building which the communists had now converted into a dwelling and a factory" and in which they lived and worked together. Douglass was struck that in the Association, black abolitionists such as David Ruggles and Sojourner Truth lived and worked side by side with educated and "well-to-do in the world" white men and women. Truth had a similar impression. Leaving New York, she had originally hoped to move into A. Bronson Alcott's community at Fruitlands but instead decided that the "accomplished, literary, and refined persons [who] were living in that plain and simple manner" at Northampton would make better comrades.[4] Ruggles described the members as "endeavoring to live out the sacred principles of HUMAN EQUALITY."[5]

Fifty years later, Douglass, recalling his visit to the Association, wrote of the fervent climate of intellectual and moral debate—"the period was one of faith, hope, and charity; of millennial foreshadowing." New ideas percolated through the spartan community—"the air was full of isms," he remembered, including abolitionism and socialism. In addition, Douglass remembered "transcendental-ism" as one of these intellectual movements that marked the Association.

There were many reasons Douglass associated Transcendentalism with these Northampton abolitionists. The Association had been inspired by the example of Brook Farm, the Transcendentalist commune founded by George Ripley in West Roxbury. One of the leading members of the commune was Charles May, who was the brother-in-law of the Transcendentalist philosopher A. Bronson Alcott. The original circular advertising the community had been, in the words of one historian, "dominated by Transcendentalist idealisms" about the duty to develop individual personalities and promote the union of manual and intellectual labor.[6] And, most telling, William Adam, a leader of the Northampton Association, had come to join after Wendell Phillips, the abolitionist orator, had lent him a copy of the famous Transcendentalist journal the *Dial*, inspiring his interest in joining a commune.[7]

But, given much of our popular understanding of antislavery politics and Transcendentalism, it can still be hard to imagine Douglass, America's greatest abolitionist—a former slave who had wrestled his master to submission, escaped from brutal slavery, and just dodged brickbats—serenely talking about airy Transcendentalist abstractions of the "oversoul" around a fireplace in the New England countryside. Writers such as Ralph Waldo Emerson, Margaret Fuller, Henry David Thoreau, and others were developing the intellectual movement of Transcendentalism by combining idealist metaphysics from Germany, Romantic poetry from England, and a new theology that emphasized personal and subjective religious experience. While Transcendentalists occupy a central place in our intellectual and literary histories of the antebellum years, we have long been told that their political vision was obtuse, self-indulgent, and irresponsible. One of the most famous historians of the twentieth century set the popular tone by declaring that the Transcendentalists' "headlong escape into perfection left responsibility far behind for a magic domain where mystic sentiment and gnomic utterance exorcised the rude intrusions of the world."[8] But here, in a commune in the Connecticut River Valley, the rough-and-tumble world of abolitionist agitation was finding a welcome home in the empyrean romanticism of Transcendentalist philosophy. In fact, as we will see, there was nothing unique or strange about abolitionist radicals in the Northampton Association reading and debating Transcendentalism with Frederick Douglass.

The philosophy of Transcendentalism and the politics of abolitionism, in other words, were mutually reinforcing. They helped create each other. A typical New England radical understood their philosophical and spiritual commitments in the language of Transcendentalism and their political commitments in terms of abolitionism. This book examines why this was so: how an intellectual and ideological alliance between antislavery reformers and Transcendentalist philosophers was created, how Transcendentalism articulated deep moral and philosophical assumptions that encouraged antislavery activity, and how, in exchange, abolitionist politics helped shape the form that Transcendentalist ideas would take. No less an authority than Emerson himself—who once told Lucretia Mott that "I got some leaves out of *your* book"—testified to the way that abolitionist ideas spread into Transcendentalism.[9] And, as the examples of Douglass and Truth illustrate, black abolitionists were important figures in this intellectual and ideological exchange. If Transcendentalism provided a language with which to understand a broad critique of antebellum American society, abolitionists, especially black abolitionists, helped aim that critique squarely at slavery and its Northern apologists.

In 1855, one of Douglass's allies, the white minister and Transcendentalist Thomas Wentworth Higginson, made an important observation about how abolitionism had shaped New England culture. "Without the anti-slavery movement, our literary men would have been what the literary men of England in the last century were, a slavish race," he told the New England Anti-Slavery Society. "They would have been . . . a race of time-servers and little men."[10] Higginson was correct: by forcing a number of New England intellectuals into the political arena, the antislavery struggle left indelible marks on their thought and, in turn, on the broader culture of New England and America. Accepted wisdom has too often seen political concerns over slavery as marginal to what came to be known as the American Renaissance—the literature, philosophy, and art of the antebellum North.[11] In contrast, Higginson thought that the

abolitionist struggle shaped almost every aspect of Transcendentalism. Ruminating on the relationship between Transcendentalism and abolitionism, Higginson was specific. "It is possible," he wrote toward the end of his life, "that
those seemingly vague and dreamy times might have communicated to those
reared in them too passive and negative a character but for the perpetual tonic
of the anti-slavery movement."[12] Transcendentalism—ethereal, subjective, and
Romantic—needed the righteous fire of a concrete political fight in order to
avoid dissolving into what Herman Melville mocked as its tendency toward an
"opium-like listlessness of vacant, unconscious reverie."[13] This book centers abolitionism in the story of American Transcendentalism.

But if Transcendentalism needed the ballast of abolitionism, the reverse
was also true: the antislavery movement drew tremendous energy from the philosophic and ethical commitments that Transcendentalism encouraged. If, as
one historian has declared, there was an "inner Civil War"—a conflict that
took place as much at the level of philosophy and moral values—so too was
there an inner life to abolitionist politics that Transcendentalist ideas helped to
create.[14] Characterizing radical New England were deep structures of thought
and styles of moral reasoning of which Transcendentalism was the philosophical expression and abolitionism the main political expression. Participants at
the time were well aware of this close relationship between the philosophical
impulses of Transcendentalism and the political rebellion of abolitionism. Abolitionists became used to being tarred as "transcendental reformers."[15] On the
other side, when the leading Transcendentalist, A. Bronson Alcott, sat down to
write the history of Transcendentalism, it turned out to be as much a story of
abolitionists such as Wendell Phillips and Elijah Lovejoy as literary figures such
as Emerson and Thoreau.[16]

If abolitionism was a cultural and intellectual movement as well as a political one, then this means that black abolitionists—crucial members of the anti-
slavery crusade—helped to shape and create New England intellectual life. The
black abolitionist Lewis Hayden fought alongside white Transcendentalists to
free fugitive slaves, William C. Nell participated in "conversations" led by his
friend A. Bronson Alcott, and the African American doctor and activist John S.
Rock debated race and racism with Theodore Parker, the Transcendentalist
minister. As a teacher and mentor to the newly emancipated in South Carolina,
Charlotte Forten sought to realize the Higher Law vision in the fertile soil of
the Reconstruction South.

At all stages, black activists reminded white Transcendentalists that American slavery was not abstract or foreign. They told firsthand stories about the

horrors of slavery and argued for the best way to end it. White Transcendentalists thus shared an intellectual community with African American activists who brought issues to their attention, criticized them when they repeated racist tropes, and helped to introduce ideas that would frame their thought. At its best, Transcendentalism was open to hearing the experiences of people such as Hayden and Nell and integrating stories like theirs into conceptions of freedom and morality that they were developing.

This tradition of mutual influence continued. In the twentieth century, as historians have long recognized, black intellectuals mined New England Transcendentalism for inspiration to understand their own place in American society and their resistance to its injustices. When W. E. B. Du Bois famously described the African American experience as that of a soul irrevocably split between an American and black self, he reached for the term "Double Consciousness" from an Emerson essay. Thoreau's "On Civil Disobedience" became a crucial text justifying nonviolent resistance during the civil rights movement, directly influencing Martin Luther King Jr. himself. In fact, one of King's most famous quotations, destined to be prominently displayed in Barack Obama's Oval Office, is in fact a paraphrase of Transcendentalist Theodore Parker's lesser-known claim that "I do not pretend to understand the moral universe; the arc is a long one. . . . And from what I see I am sure it bends towards justice."

Despite this, relatively few historians have asked what black activists at the time thought about Transcendentalism, and even fewer have asked what Transcendentalism might have learned from black intellectuals. This is a crucial question to help us understand not only the nature and development of antebellum black thought but also the meaning of Transcendentalism itself. Black thinkers participated in Transcendentalist clubs, attended Transcendentalist meetings, and organized politically alongside them. In fact, black thinkers in the antebellum North had a long engagement with many of the famous European intellectuals who also influenced white New England Transcendentalists. For black Transcendentalists such as William C. Nell, then, it was easy to embrace an intellectual movement that had such similarity to the styles of thought to which they were already accustomed.

Black activism, leadership, and testimony shaped what we might call the political unconscious of Boston radicalism, helping to set the tone of debate and the scope of action. Black intellectuals were often in the avant-garde, pushing white intellectuals to take bolder stances on questions such as the role of violence in the movement and the importance of political equality in the North.[17] In addition, of course, black intellectuals engaged in direct and self-conscious intellectual activity, writing books, giving lectures, and engaging the public. Often this was in direct alliance with white Transcendentalists: black New Englanders attended Transcendentalist reading clubs and "conversations," asked white Transcendentalists to speak to their own intellectual clubs, and read and discussed works by thinkers such as Samuel Taylor Coleridge and Ralph Waldo Emerson. When intellectual pursuits gave way to political resistance, these black thinkers raised money with famous Transcendentalists, spoke alongside them, and fought and bled next to them.

Intellectual History in the Open Air

This book is an intellectual history of the New England abolitionist movement, a study of the ideas and thinkers that influenced it. But there is an argument about ideas and about intellectual history in my method. Too often, intellectual historians have treated intellectuals as existing in a rarified world of pure ideas, texts, and abstractions. But, as John Dewey pointed out one hundred years ago, this dualism—ideas up here and action down there—only serves the interests of those in society most invested in defending the status quo by preventing the application of ideas to life. Transcendentalists, more than anyone, knew that an idea "may prove well in the lecture-room, yet not prove at all under the spacious clouds and along the landscape."[18] So this book seeks to take seriously the traditional history of ideas—texts, arguments, writers—while simultaneously examining how those ideas left the page, so to speak, went out in the open air, and rambled around in the world of people and things. This method thus troubles the assumption that there was a simple or stark division between an intellectual movement such as Transcendentalism and an activist movement such as abolitionism. Between an abstract idealism that treats ideas as purely autonomous and a reductive materialism that sees them solely as reflecting some "true" economic or social reality lies a form of intellectual history that can both be attentive to the internal logic of ideas and ask how they are in dialogue with social and economic life. Or, as Emerson said, with much greater grace, "the inmost in due time becomes outmost."[19]

Doing an intellectual history in the open air means looking far and wide for ideas. While some Americans had the privilege to be able to write long books, have their lectures published, or edit a newspaper, many more did not. These traditional sources—books, newspapers, and sermons—will always be an important source for intellectual historians, and they form the backbone of this book. But if we want to understand the ideas of a wider democratic cast of characters, we also have to mine less traditional sources—long the domain of social or cultural history—for insight into how other Americans thought about political and philosophical issues. Thus, I also look at newspaper advertisements, activist training materials, and other unexpected sources, searching for evidence of intellectual production. Doing so, I hope, does not mean abandoning the attention to the specificity of ideas that marks intellectual history. Rather, looking broadly for evidence instead democratizes our understanding of intellectual life, demonstrating, as the early Transcendentalist James Marsh once wrote, that "every man . . . has his metaphysics."[20]

Men and women who participated in abolitionism did not artificially distinguish between ideas and action; in fact, they often described how the very act of participating in antislavery politics became an intellectual event. This is what the black historian William C. Nell was suggesting when, in 1850, he described his work in the antislavery Boston Vigilance Committee as "a school indeed."[21] James Freeman Clarke, a Transcendentalist-turned-abolitionist, expanded on Nell's point: "How many radical problems in statesmanship," Clarke wrote of the antislavery struggle, "in political economy, in ethics, in philosophy, in theology, in history, in science, came up for discussion during this long controversy."[22] In organizations such as the Boston Vigilance Committee, white Transcendentalists listened to the experiences of ex-slaves, and free black abolitionists worked side by side with some of the most famous intellectuals of the day. Antislavery fighters, black as well as white, adopted slogans and styles of thought from Transcendentalism, while Transcendentalists appealed to examples drawn from slavery to illustrate their abstract arguments. "Abolitionism," as one leading antislavery paper declared, "is itself an American form of metaphysics."[23]

We can see the outlines of a more open intellectual world when we notice how a wide range of Americans—poor as well as wealthy, black as well as white, women as well as men—used Transcendentalism. Transcendentalist and abolitionist ideas were received, repurposed, and remade by a wide range of people. For instance, there is Thomas Sidney, a black orphan from the streets of New York, who, having raised himself up to become a schoolteacher, stays up late educating himself about European philosophy and helping to introduce the Romantic thought of Coleridge to black New York. In Lowell, a "mill girl" named Lucy Larcom, who will one day write poetry dedicated to Emerson, shudders in horror that the cotton that passes through her hands was picked by enslaved workers. In New Bedford, one might walk into a black church and hear Jeremiah

Sanderson, a barber during the week and preacher on Sunday, whose sermons cite Transcendentalist heroes such as Emerson and Parker. Or consider Caroline Putnam and Sallie Hollie, lifelong friends and living companions, devotees of Margaret Fuller and Emerson, who moved to Lottsburg, Virginia, after the Civil War to open one of the most successful schools for freedmen. To some degree, this is a story of reception, of ordinary New Englanders taking the ideas, slogans, and inspiration from a philosophical movement and adapting them to their lives and their struggles. But this is not simply a history of reception; everyday Americans also created the ideas that would be refined and popularized by famous intellectuals. Ideas trickled up as much as they trickled down.

Writing a more democratic intellectual history, one that "lives in the open air and on the ground," as William James urged, means locating ideas more in the public, seeing how they are less the personal domain of famous thinkers and more how they exist in common, becoming a shared bank of ideas.[24] An idea that remained the private property of one person, by definition, would struggle to be widely influential or historically important; only ideas that exist in the commons matter in these ways. As an example, think about a term such as "elevation," which was central to black abolitionist culture but also used in similar ways by white Transcendentalists. Seeing how keywords traversed groups such as this suggests that both were reading similar sources (in this case, European Romanticism and Unitarian writings on self-culture), and both were part of a shared discourse of politics and ideas that united self-development with radical politics. Thus, I pay close attention to particular and popular words and phrases commonly used by reformers, believing them to be evidence of an intellectual history in common.

Paying attention to the physical and geographic places of intellectual production is another way to demonstrate how ideas developed in common spaces shared by many people. Ideas develop out of real interactions that occur in physical spaces. The places in which ideas develop are sometimes traditional—churches, universities, and newspapers—but sometimes unexpected: activist meeting rooms, street protests, and jail cells. Studying the records of attendance at intellectual and activist meetings, as well as mapping out overlaps in social worlds to determine who was in dialogue with whom, reveals that trying to put activists and intellectuals in hermitically sealed boxes such as "Transcendentalists" or "abolitionists" is quixotic. It was very common for individuals to attend an abolitionist meeting one day, a socialist lecture the next, and a Transcendentalist "Conversation" the third. When, in 1850, Frederick Douglass wrote to Emerson asking for a review copy of his new book, for instance, this act spoke volumes about the intellectual community that the famous escaped slave considered himself part of.[25] Thus, this book pays particular attention to who was speaking to whom—who the Adelphic Union invited to speak to them, who the Town and Country Club invited into membership, and who spoke on stage with which intellectuals. And concrete geography mattered too: it was not coincidental that Massachusetts, where the anxious inheritance of the Puritan conscience collided with the newfound wealth of the cotton importers, was the home to particularly uncompromising abolitionists and reformers.[26]

But if outer spaces mattered, so did inner ones, and central to my method will be to examine shared ideas of selfhood and individuality. Transcendentalism helped articulate the shared "background" intellectual and moral assumptions about selfhood that helped birth the Northern antislavery impulse. Demonstrating this means examining, in part, the theories of the self that united the two movements, a recurring theme in this book.[27] This is not to say that I will be claiming insight into the true nature of the inner lives of Emerson, Garrison, or William C. Nell. Rather, when we talk about the history of the self, I am interested in the way that certain historically specific and shared ideas, languages, and assumptions provide a background for how people inhabit the world, a set of frameworks that, in the words of one philosopher, forms the "horizons within which we live our lives" and gives us models for selfhood.[28] It is exactly from within these historically structured frameworks and background moral commitments that we make sense of—and occasionally revolt against—our place in the world we inhabit. I use the term "ethos" to describe how the specific and well-articulated philosophical ideas of intellectuals, as they are shared and repurposed in more open common spaces, helped form background imaginations that structured abolitionist selfhood. And these background frameworks and ethoses are historical artifacts, shaped by shifting economic patterns, political exigencies, and cultural trends. I am thus interested in how things such as industrialization, shifts in Christian piety, Northern racism, partisan politics, and other forces shaped the new Transcendentalist moral background in which abolitionism grew.

Looking for intellectual history in the open air allows us to see that people did not neatly separate their lived experiences of Transcendentalism and abolitionism. Converting to one often meant converting to the other. Moncure Conway, for instance, was a Virginian-born slaveowner and budding proslavery racial theorist. But one day, by accident, he stumbled upon an Emerson article that precepted a spiritual and moral crisis. Soon he had moved to the North, befriended Emerson and Thoreau, joined the most radical abolitionists, and dedicated himself to women's suffrage. Emerson had brought him to Garrison.

When we do not artificially distinguish between ideas and action but instead ask how these ideas operated in the real world, looking at how they percolated and formed a "background" ethos, we can see that people did not necessarily experience Transcendentalism and abolitionism as separate. Instead, it is better to understand the movements as linked at a deep level by a shared culture and orientation of activism, what I am calling a Higher Law Ethos.

The Higher Law Ethos

Holding together the selfhood of antislavery Transcendentalism was a Higher Law Ethos, their central contribution to the American radical intellectual tradition. This was a distinctive orientation toward radical politics: nonconformist, rooted in a critical and idealist philosophy, privileging the sanctity of conscience over expediency. It was well suited for democratic dissent. The Higher Law Ethos, no doubt, built on values with long histories in American life, including Quaker ideals of the Inner Light, republican and Lockean beliefs in the right to revolution, and long-standing commitments to natural law.[29] But abolitionists faced a new political reality: as one of the first generations of Americans living in a democracy, they quickly realized that just because they had no king or corrupt courtiers in Massachusetts did not mean an individual was free. In fact, as Emerson was aware and as Alexis de Tocqueville demonstrated, many of the tools that furthered democracy—such as the popular press and partisan politics—also, ironically, encouraged conformity and the silencing of moral issues such as slavery. But abolitionists never abandoned democracy. Instead, in the hands of Transcendentalist theory and forged with the stern alloy of antislavery politics, these older traditions were transformed into something new: a full-throated philosophical and existential defense of nonconformity and disobedience in a democratic culture. They would thus reenergize democracy by embracing individual nonconformity within it. Born in antebellum America, the Higher Law was a political and intellectual orientation that would have a lasting influence on American and global radical traditions. Echoes of it would reappear everywhere from American labor organizers to Gandhi's India to King's civil rights movement.

The Higher Law rose out of the experience of moral rebellion that they lived as abolitionists and theorized as Transcendentalists. It grew as they sought justification for political behavior that contradicted and negated the dominant values of the society. Part of the Higher Law was philosophical: before they could articulate it, they had to reject forms of metaphysics, epistemology, and theology that they believed encouraged moral passivity and conformity to social norms. The Higher Law, for instance, contained a radical humanism that led to a social critique: abolitionists responded to the new world of markets and the expanded division of labor by demanding that one act and think about a moral question not as a "farmer, or a professor, or an engineer" but first of all as a human being with a conscience, rejecting the social roles that the market created for us. And part of the Higher Law was aesthetic and existential: by rejecting the role-playing of market life, the Higher Law demanded that one approach politics and social life in a way that would express something "higher," more "spiritual," less personally compromising than mainstream forms of political engagement. Their politics was thus rooted in what one historian has called the "infinite individuality" of Romantic thought, a self whose finite political struggle took strength from its communion with some infinite totality.[30] Thus, a longing for the Absolute, what Higginson called "a yearning for the ideal," an existential desire for reunion with the Oversoul, could go hand in hand with the most useful and concrete political struggles.[31] Put together, the Higher Law Ethos could impart a political vision that lived in what William James called "the strenuous mood." This was not a self-indulgent or passive worldview but one that faced injustice with a straight back and fire in its eyes, whose "infinite and mysterious obligation from on high" gave it a stern and uncompromising energy.[32] In the simplest sense, the Higher Law taught them how to be unpopular, how to retain their political and moral convictions in the face of friends who ostracized them, mobs that roamed the Boston streets, and ministers and politicians who used all the powers of social authority to silence heterodox opinions.

The diversity and contradictions in Transcendentalist philosophy have sometimes obscured their political influence. One Transcendentalist famously described the movement as "a club of the likeminded . . . because no two . . . thought alike."[33] There was, no doubt, an often-bewildering diversity within the Transcendentalist movement, a porousness to its intellectual boundaries. If Emerson and Thoreau came to doubt the special nature of Christianity, other Transcendentalists thought they were renewing Christian belief. There was a socialist wing—led by George Ripley and William Henry Channing— alongside thinkers such as Thoreau who tended toward a proto-anarchist individualism. Some Transcendentalists, such as James Freeman Clarke, were interested in a careful study of German idealist philosophy. Many others tended toward a mysticism that threw around names such as Schleiermacher, Schiller, or Kant more for their academic prestige than because they truly cared to understand the intricacies of these metaphysical systems. Confusing matters, ideas, and impulses often traveled between wings of the movements, frustrating any attempt to clearly define factions. This bagginess imparted a certain prejudice against systematic thought among the Transcendentalists; "nature hates calm system makers," Emerson wrote in his journal.[34] There was even a proto-Pragmatic pluralism to how writers such as Emerson and Higginson celebrated the wild spontaneity of nature against philosophers' vain attempts to impose a totalizing order over the world.[35]

Transcendentalism was an imperfect set of ideas. It was premised on a sort of vulgarized Kantianism whose assumptions of a separation between subject and object would be soon rejected by both Pragmatists and the Transcendentalists' more immediate philosophical successors among the late nineteenth-century Hegelians. For some good and many bad reasons, scholars in today's transnational moment are often uncomfortable with how Transcendentalism ended up wedding itself to a romantic sense of American identity. Some, though certainly not all, white Transcendentalists held views of African Americans that drew on discredited and reprehensible notions of nineteenth-century racial science. There are plausible, though I believe flawed, interpretations of Transcendentalism that condemn it for privileging personal expressions of righteousness over the properly political task of public engagement and democratic compromise—a self-congratulatory gang of narcissistic Beautiful Souls or, in the words of Irving Howe, "despots of conscience."[36] It is true that Transcendentalism, in the hands of the more mystically inclined, could descend into what Hegel once called "rapturous haziness," the undisciplined attempt to gain philosophical and spiritual wisdom through the sheer force of will and intuition, to jump the queue into true knowledge and God's grace without doing any of the hard work of earning it.

Still, there is an appealing Romanticism to Transcendentalist democracy that can be separated from these elements, and that constituted the core of the Higher Law Ethos. When I started this project, I was struck by how beautifully out of sync Emerson's politics of enthusiasm were in the age's neoliberal consensus. It was no coincidence that the philosopher of an "infinite hope for mankind" fell out of favor in an era that declared, with Margaret Thatcher, that "there is no alternative" to market capitalism.[37] In a disturbing parallel with Thatcher's capitalist realism, the academic left had largely rejected the Transcendentalists' spirit of nonconformist humanism and social optimism. As the philosopher Richard Rorty pointed out twenty years ago, leftist academics may have thought they were being radical by ditching the democratic idealism of people such as Emerson, Whitman, and Dewey in favor of the tragic pessimism of Poe or Melville. But the declining fortunes of nineteenth-century Transcendentalists were one small example of the larger victory of a contemporary politics of pseudo-leftist cultural despair, the rise of a "spectatorial, disgusted, mocking left" that dismissed the Transcendentalists' optimism, their exuberant humanism, and their celebration of open-ended democratic possibility.[38] Critique replaced hope. As I discovered the many interactions between black abolitionists and white Transcendentalists, I became convinced that this rejection of the spirit of antebellum reform was a mistake, that it was movement that had more to offer to scholars of civil rights and African American history than is generally accepted.

Transcendentalism is difficult to define partly because of the contradictory ways it manifested itself. There could be a vitalism, an unconscious energy, even a rough embrace of something raw and Dionysian in Transcendentalism. Writers such as Emerson, Thoreau, and Fuller saw their project as ripping away the comfortable veil that masked life, facing their naked aliveness square on, and reveling in the few solitary glimpses of the infinite that penetrated the fog of everyday life. Think of Emerson wishing for thinkers who had "lived a life passed through the fire of thought" or Thoreau escaping the quiet desperation of bourgeois blandness into the wildness of primal nature. Yet at the same time, Transcendentalism was yoked to a philosophical idealism that demanded the stern command of the mind over the body, the spirit over the material, and the moral over the practical. At its best—the feminism of Fuller, the existential ethics of Emerson, the environmental writings of Thoreau, or the democratic poems of Whitman—this was no contradiction, and Transcendentalism could embrace the doubleness, balancing precariously but productively between the rough embrace of the world and the serene self-contemplation of the otherworldly saint. For lesser thinkers, however, this logic led not to Thoreau's fantasy of tearing apart a woodchuck with his teeth but to a retreat into the honeydewed anesthesia of spiritual solipsism. At a deeper level, American Transcendentalism drew on seemingly competing existential desires for personal transcendence and for communion with the immanent Godhead. On one hand, the dream of the mountaintop, Thoreau atop Katahdin, the absolute freedom of the sacred self, a leap into the infinite, a heady disdain of the particular or contingent; on the other, a fantasy of the boundless ocean, a dissolution of the self into the universe, Emerson's invisible and impersonal eyeball entering by osmosis into the warm waters of the oversoul.

Its political impulses can seem just as contradictory. Transcendentalism elevated spiritual integrity and personal authenticity over political engagement,

believing that one could not blindly adopt one's inner personal codes from outside moral or political imperatives. And yet its practitioners were inevitably attracted to radical politics, seemingly drawn into the orbit of abolitionist,
feminist, and socialist politics against their will. It had universalistic elements
but also reveled in the irreducible singularity of each individual. Born with the
goal of renewing religious faith, it served as a halfway house for future unbeliev-
ers. They worshiped individuality—the infinite potential of each person—
while often rejecting forms of political and economic individualism that seemed
to undermine the full flowering of personality. Thus, it could be both a highly
individualistic movement and also give birth to some of the first homegrown
socialist intellectuals in America. Emerson was not kidding when he declared,
"With consistency a great soul has simply nothing to do."[39]

Transcendentalism's legacy reflects these contradictions. On one side there
is the antidemocratic Nietzsche, the devotee of Emerson; on the other, Gandhi,
Tolstoy, and King, influenced by Thoreau. Black nationalists from Alexander
Crummell to Edward Blyden to Marcus Garvey drew on the language of Emerson, but so did white capitalists such as Henry Ford and Andrew Carnegie, who
turned the humanistic radicalism of self-reliance into a crude capitalist self-
justification. If Emerson towers over nineteenth-century American literature, it
is his namesake, Ralph Waldo Ellison—an equally imposing figure in twentieth-
century literature—who perhaps best understood the conflicting legacy of
Transcendentalism. Ellison's high regard for Emerson did not prevent him
from creating one of the greatest satires of the Transcendentalist mind-set in
Mr. Norton, the naive Northern philanthropist who counsels that the Invisible
Man read Emerson, even as he is himself incapable of openly confronting the
messiness of the Jim Crow South. The two most prominent philosophers to use
Emerson in recent thought are probably Cornel West and Stanley Cavell, men
who shared little besides a brilliant eclecticism that has left their work outside
of the traditional academic disciplines.

It is one of my contentions, though, that, through the fog, we can still identify certain core philosophical assumptions that united Transcendentalists and
abolitionists and constituted the core of the Higher Law Ethos. One is a critical
style of thought that rejected instrumental logic (what they called "Understanding") in favor of a more moral and dialectical style of thought ("Reason" in
Transcendentalist terminology) that was capable of autonomously determining
its own moral ends. There was a boundlessness to Transcendentalist Reason,
which refused to be hemmed in, as Understanding might, by the narrow consis-

tency of syllogisms, means to an end logic, or the false comfort of "common sense."[40] A second important aspect of Transcendentalism was a politics of idealism that demanded that society be judged not by what did or had existed (what Elizabeth Cady Stanton called "tyrant custom") but by what *should* exist.[41] As James Russell Lowell put it, "The real will never find an irremovable basis till it rests on the ideal."[42] Transcendentalists and abolitionists shared that beautiful naïveté that leads people to be sincerely outraged that the ideals of the Declaration of Independence are not actually upheld in American society. A third was a personal ethics that expected people to live by the "Higher Law," a law that commanded personal judgment based on ultimate moral duties, not particular professional or social duties or roles. Transcendentalist epistemology, which emphasized the universal ability to experience inspiration and to access divine truths, encouraged a democratic and egalitarian approach to moral problems since everyone from the greatest intellectual to the humblest washerwoman was capable of channeling and expressing Reason's boundless truths. Their sense of human potential pushed them away from antisocial forms of liberalism and toward notions of freedom as personal development or, as Margaret Fuller described it, freedom as "the growth of individual minds, which live and aspire, as flowers bloom and birds sing."[43] Finally, there was a political style that demanded a "heroic," even foolhardy, self-expressive politics rather than narrow expediency—there was a reason that Transcendentalists wrote paeans to John Brown rather than William Seward.

This Higher Law Ethos that they helped created traversed political groupings between and among Garrisonians, "political abolitionists" who voted for the Liberty Party, and even hold-out Democrats and Whigs. Garrisonian abolitionists—who considered the Constitution an immoral compromise with slavery and who were drawn to an anarchist belief that all governments relied on violence and coercion—provided a great deal of moral and personal energy to the world of New England radicalism. But Garrison's influence was far greater at an intellectual and moral level than it was at a practical electoral level. Relatively few grassroots abolitionists felt the need to definitely choose whether they were followers of Garrison, Gerrit Smith, or Salmon Chase. In the same way, the Transcendentalist philosophical imagination mattered to far more than simply those who attended their meetings or read the *Dial*. Transcendentalism and radical abolitionism are important because they articulated the deep moral assumptions of the radical impulse, but this impulse was manifested and made real by many individuals who did not necessarily accept every part of their platforms. This book describes, then, the birth of a moral and political imagination, an ethos, not the platform of any party or sect.

The Virtues of Idealism

Historians have often missed the close relationship between abolitionists and Transcendentalists because they have favored pragmatic or commonsense theories of political democracy. In doing so, they have missed the virtues of political idealism that the Higher Law created. Historians once fiercely debated the relationship between the antislavery impulse and Transcendentalism because they saw it as key to understanding the moral imagination of antebellum reform.[44] Ironically, past generations were very aware that, as Stanley Elkins said, "the abolitionists . . . duplicated the intellectual pattern of the Transcendentalists."[45] But they made these connections, as Elkins himself did, to show the supposed dangers of both movements. During the Cold War, the Transcendentalist reformers became proxy victims of the liberal war on political utopianism. Thus, in the anticommunist *Partisan Review*, men such as Lionel Trilling sided with the ironic skepticism of Hawthorne over the wide-eyed Emersonian will toward moral perfection.[46] Later, for scholars such as Stanley Elkins, the affinity between abolitionism and Transcendentalism—both "men without responsibility"—was considered the best evidence for the anti-institutional recklessness and excessive individualism of antebellum reform.[47] But perhaps the most popularly influential writing in this regard was Robert Penn Warren's essay on the legacy of the Civil War, which saw the abolitionists as classically tragic figures whose admirable courage and righteousness grew "so distempered by impatience" that they became proponents of violence and intolerance, their Transcendentalist individualism corrosive of the institutions of American life that perhaps could have kept the nation together.[48] Warren's argument, building off Elkins, was conservative even if it did analyze the cultural and political importance of Transcendentalism with an ethical probing and psychological depth that later analyses largely lacked. Scholars of this generation introduced the question of the relationship between the moral and psychological context that produced Northern reformers and the strategies and forms of abolitionist practice that developed, even if they did so in order to condemn the abolitionists for embracing the antinomian disregard for institutions that they supposedly learned from Transcendentalists. Given this strand of argument, it made a certain sense for later historians, in the wake of the civil rights movement, who wished to rehabilitate abolitionism to either deny that Transcendentalism had played a role in the development of antislavery or, more commonly, simply ignore Transcendentalism, which largely faded as a concern in history departments.[49] While recent historical studies have cast interesting light on individual Transcendentalists' political activity, there has not yet been a sustained attempt to address the positive impact of Transcendentalism on the whole of American reform or one that that asked seriously about the relationship between Transcendentalism and black abolitionists.[50]

While the reputation of abolitionists has obviously improved, skepticism still remains about the effect of Transcendentalism and the Romantic imagination on antebellum abolitionism and reform. Emerson's attitude toward fugitive slaves, one recent study declares, had a "satisfying clarity" but was premised on a self-indulgent rejection of the moral claims of the Union and of political compromise.[51] In another recent history of Romantic Reformers, Transcendentalist-inspired reform is presented as inspired by noble ideals but marked by an excessive individualism, a moralism that could turn judgmental, and a utopianism that, when frustrated, became violent and self-destructive.[52] Many historians and political philosophers are skeptical of the Higher Law Ethos as well. Thus, even one of the most brilliant analyses of antebellum political thought declares that ideas such as the Higher Law "carry with them well-recognized risks of anarchic moral narcissism."[53] One result is that work on American political thought often feels comfortable ignoring or downplaying the Transcendentalists and abolitionists—assuming that they have little to offer an American political tradition that instead roots itself in the balance and moderation of the Scottish Common Sense School or the epistemological humility of the Pragmatists.[54] By ignoring or decrying the Transcendentalist influence on antislavery practice, it has become easy to erase the contribution that abolitionists made to American democratic and radical thought, to treat them as simple moralists or saintly "prophets," not strategic and philosophically informed actors responding to the new realities of antebellum democracy.

Abolitionists would have agreed that they did politics in a unique way. But to them, there was a great deal of pragmatism to the anti-pragmatism in the Higher Law Ethos. For instance, in 1853, Wendell Phillips dedicated a whole speech to respond to what were, even then, common critiques of the abolitionists: that they were too "fierce" in their language, they appealed to "feeling" rather than "reason," and they had "hurried in on childish, reckless, blind, and hot-headed zeal." This speech is partly interesting for including one of Phillips's most warm celebrations of Emerson: "his services to the most radical antislavery movement have been generous and marked." But more to the point, Phillips laid out a theoretical defense of how the impulses toward idealism and utopianism, the boundless Romantic imagination, and the Higher Law Ethos were necessary to capture the attention of a public that would otherwise ignore the inconvenient antislavery message. Politicians such as Daniel Webster, Phillips pointed out, thought of slavery in terms of "the chess-board of the political game," where preexisting political interests dueled it out, horse-trading and bargaining on the premise of expediency, compromise, and reasonableness. Phillips believed that the defining problem of antebellum America was conformity: "the press, the pulpit, the wealth, the literature, the prejudices, the political arrangements, the present self-interest of the country, are against us." Thus, all the pieces on Webster's chessboard looked the same. Since politicians would only respond to the "present convictions of the people," all the Madisonian virtues of civility, compromise, and reasonableness simply disarmed the unpopular abolitionists all while lending an air of respectable realism to their more mainstream enemies.[55]

The abolitionists, then, had to create a political interest—to turn millions of Northerners into a powerful force of antislavery "public opinion" so that even the most cynical politician would be forced to cater to them. And to do this, to conjure up an antislavery political force, required thinking differently about politics than a Webster would. It required them to appeal to an ideal over the heads of their society, some higher values not yet apparent on Webster's political chessboard: the future, the human race, Truth, conscience, or, simply, the Higher Law. Moreover, abolitionists needed a politics of imagination; they could not let their vision be hemmed in by reality as they had experienced. "Do not," Phillips told his audience, "set down as extravagant every statement which your experience does not warrant."[56] Phillips returned again and again to the need for a politics of feeling, of enthusiasm rather than dry logic—"there are far more dead hearts to be quickened, than confused intellects to be cleared up."

At the end of his speech, Phillips explained how the abolitionists' political style paid off: all of this abolitionist enthusiasm was beginning to shake public opinion, to create the space for cautious and responsible politicians to advocate their policies. He was correct. There had long been antislavery political sentiment in the country, but Phillips and the other abolitionists were radicalizing it, creating room for antislavery politicians by building an antislavery public opinion. Abolitionists were helping to generate the conditions that would lead to the rise of an antislavery North, to Lincoln, to the victory of the Republican Party, and, eventually, to the abolition of slavery.[57] Thus, in 1863, Phillips would boast with some truth that Abraham Lincoln "is a growing man, with his face

Zionward. . . . But how does he learn? Why did he grow? Because we watered him."[58] Historians love to cite Max Weber's description of politics as "the slow and difficult drilling of holes into hard boards." But in America, it first took the moral enthusiasm of the abolitionists, what Weber dismissed as the "ethics of commitment," to make Lincoln's "responsible" politics possible, to soften, in a sense, the hard boards.[59] This, then, is the story of how, thanks to Transcendentalists, black radicals, and other idealists, abolitionists learned to speak the language of the Higher Law and, in the process, helped create the political conditions that would overthrow slavery.

Making a Higher Law

The story of the abolitionization of Transcendentalism (to coin an ugly phrase) begins in a surprising place: not tranquil Concord, Massachusetts, but in the bustling streets of downtown Manhattan. Meeting in church basements and lyceum halls, a group of young black activists read and politicized the poetry and prose of the English Romantics, especially Samuel Taylor Coleridge, the first major Anglo-American proponent of Kantian metaphysics. The 1830s were exciting times, as European ideas echoing from the Lake District of England or Konigsberg, Germany, were being picked up by Americans throughout the young republic, shattering philosophic assumptions that had dominated elite intellectual life since the Revolution. Among New York and Boston black activists, a style of thought was being born that united Romantic thought with antislavery commitment. These black thinkers—the subject of Chapter 1—were adopting Romantic ideals of freedom as self-development, rationality as more than instrumental logic, and political struggle as rooted in idealism and utopianism. Crucially, they were the first to explicitly use ideas such as these to combat slavery and racism.

Meanwhile, in New England, white Transcendentalists such as Theodore Parker and Ralph Waldo Emerson were initially converted to abolitionism thanks to a shared interest in religious reform. Abolitionists, contrary to some narratives, derived much of their moral energy from their hostility, rather than loyalty, to the established churches. They found allies in the Transcendentalists, who were determined to resist the "pale negations" of established religion, disgusted at a church that was politically conservative and spiritually dead, simultaneously silent in the face of the monstrous injustice of slavery and unable to respond to the deep spiritual yearnings of New Englanders with anything but a self-satisfied repetition of formalistic doctrines. As I show in Chapter 2, there was tremendous affinity between the Transcendentalists' and abolitionists' critique of antebellum Christianity and close ties to their proposed reforms.

It was in their challenge to capitalism that one can best see Transcendentalists and abolitionists channel a wide-ranging democratic impulse. Building off the observation that black abolitionists were deeply interested in the utopian socialism preached by Transcendentalists, Chapter 3 explores the abolitionist economic agenda, challenging the notion that abolitionists generally operated within the ideological space of capitalist free labor. Abolitionists, both black and white, were closely tied to a variety of Romantic and utopian critics of the marketplace. The Transcendentalist impulse toward positive freedom and dislike of materialism contributed to a sense that Americans need not be satisfied with the unwilled anarchy of the marketplace. Their model of the self, which sought an integral unity of inner self with outward communities, was produced, in part, in rebellion against the encroachments of capitalist selfhood—the materialism, buffered individualism, instrumental reason, and amoral egoism of market life.

Transcendentalist ethics also inspired the abolitionist development of civil disobedience theory. In 1850, Congress, with the conspicuous aid of some of Massachusetts's most prominent politicians, passed the Fugitive Slave Law, which increased the power of the federal government to capture and return fugitive slaves. Black Americans, of course, had long been disobeying laws intended to capture fugitives, but their activity now gained prominence and national attention. Chapter 4 demonstrates how, along with famous white intellectuals, black activists helped to articulate a theory of civil disobedience that would prove to be one of their most lasting contributions to American political philosophy. Transcendentalism provided a language while abolitionism provided a context for a set of ideas that stressed one's personal obligations to transcendent moral obligations over any man-made legal duties. The "Higher Law" became a symbol for both civil disobedience and all the best qualities of the soul, threatened by unjust slave laws, the lures of cotton wealth, and the stifling conformity of bourgeois society.

The willingness of some abolitionists and Transcendentalists to dabble in nineteenth-century racial science demonstrates the limits to their vision. As the 1850s progressed, as Chapter 5 shows, abolitionism gained popularity and mainstream acceptance but began to lose some of its utopian and critical edge. This became most apparent as relationships between white and black abolitionists frayed as many white abolitionists became attracted to nineteenth-century theories of racial science. Abolitionists learned that they could attract white New

Englanders to their movement by framing the abolitionist struggle as a cultural struggle between North and South. Doing so allowed abolitionists to tap into strong currents of New England regionalism but did so at the cost of alienating many black supporters, who were marginal to such cultural politics. It is a sobering reminder of the ubiquity of racialized thinking in the nineteenth century that even radical social movements can be captured by ideas whose origins lie in the very injustice they are combating.

Still, there was some energy left in the Transcendentalist egalitarian imagination. Many scholars have assumed that the first cannon shot over Fort Sumter abruptly ended the romanticism of the antebellum years. These older narratives often framed the Northern war effort as nonideological, uninterested in political ideals such as antislavery or equality, and only unintentionally revolutionary. Certainty the Civil War, which converted former disunionist abolitionists into fierce patriots and forced even the most idealist philosophers to consider the metaphysical worth of howitzers, changed the nature of Northern radicalism. But Transcendentalism, as Chapter 6 shows, remained a crucial part of what Northerners called the "war of ideas." Transcendentalists and abolitionists fought to ensure that the Northern war effort remained devoted to a set of high moral and political principles, marrying the newfound bureaucratic pragmatism of the war effort to a moral idealism that emphasized the importance of emancipation and equality to the purposes of the war.

These black and white thinkers transformed both the culture of nineteenth-century America and the nation itself. Abolitionist strategies—from petition campaigns to mass meetings to civil disobedience—would become standard for later radical movements. Transcendentalism helped bequeath a vision of democratic individuality that has become central to American political norms. In the era of nation building, they were central figures in the ideological move to associate the meaning of American nationalism with devotion to transcendent values of liberty and equality, rather than race or descendent. By uniting philosophical and political idealism, they modeled how later political struggles could combine radical action and thought.

CHAPTER I

Transcendentalism in Black and White

Every year, on the Fourth of July, the young black men of the Hamilton Lyceum in New York City met for their most important lecture of the year. The tradition had begun several years earlier when a group of teenagers, including the future abolitionist leaders Alexander Crummell and Henry Highland Garnet, "resolved, that while slavery existed we would not celebrate the Fourth of July." Instead of patriotic speeches or parades, the day "was devoted to planning schemes for the freeing and upbuilding of our race," Crummell remembered.[1] Since the mid-1830s, Crummell and Garnet had helped to create a series of black intellectual organizations in New York that organized lectures, created libraries, and discussed everything from British poetry to the *Amistad* captives. And so, on Independence Day 1844, as the fireworks and drunken revelry of the white celebration echoed outside, Crummell rose to deliver the yearly address to the somber crowd, titled "Necessities and Advantages of Education Considered in Relation to Colored Men."

Though only twenty-five at the time, Crummell was already a leader among the burgeoning community of young black intellectuals in Manhattan. He had been raised among abolitionist activists and had received the best education available in the segregated North. After brief stints at schools in New Hampshire and Upstate New York, he had returned to New York City and attempted to enter the clergy. After a struggle with the white-dominated hierarchy, he had finally been ordained an Episcopalian priest. Later, he would become well known as a controversial advocate of Liberian emigration, of the "talented tenth" ideal of black leadership, and, half a century later, as a mentor to a young W. E. B. Du Bois. By the time Du Bois met him, Crummell was a white-haired patriarch—a man of "simple dignity and an unmistakable air of good breeding" leading the African Episcopal Church. Describing Crummell in the 1840s,

Du Bois imagined a tall and thin man with a distant self-confidence, holding to a spiritual striving that could withstand even the bigotry of the antebellum church and a sincere if sometimes overly serious demeanor: "he wrote his sermons carefully; he intoned his prayers with a soft, earnest voice."[2]

On this particular July afternoon, Crummell's lecture was on a topic near and dear to his heart: the way in which education and intellectual development would aid the elevation of free African Americans and contribute to abolitionism. It was an opportunity to both discuss his theory of pedagogy and, even more, his vision of black intellectual life under the conditions of racism and oppression. From a cosmopolitan set of sources—New England Transcendentalism, British Romanticism, German idealistic philosophy, and traditions rooted in the black Atlantic—Crummell outlined a political sensibility that would not just change the way black thinkers conceived of their political life but would help to shape all forms of Northern abolitionism. It was an important statement of the philosophical and metaphysical basis of the Higher Law Ethos that came to dominate American abolitionism.

If slavery denied black people their freedom, Crummell told the crowd, Northern racism attempted to destroy their dignity and their sense of inner worth. The consequences for many black men were dire. The white vision of black men was one in which they were reduced to "mere instruments," tools in the hands of slaveowners or racist politicians. If this racist order had its way, black men might internalize these ideas, accepting a degradation of their consciousness and loss of their self-worth. Denying them education and discouraging them from considering themselves as worthy of self-creation, white people sought to force them back onto the only thing left to develop a subjectivity: their physical senses and the arbitrary outward circumstances of a segregated and impoverished life. "He who relies upon his senses for his well being, degrades himself; takes the first step downward toward the brute," Crummell wrote.[3]

Underlying Crummell's concern for the state of black education was a philosophical, even metaphysical, critique of American racism. Black men would have to reject not just the racism of white America but also the system of thought that underlay its treatment of African Americans, a philosophy that encouraged people to define their inner lives by the external experiences they had lived through. Crummell feared that theories and practices of the self that privileged the importance of sensory inputs to the creation of ideas, opinions, and habits (such as those associated with British empiricism) risked eliminating the characteristically human ability to freely determine one's own moral and political fate. Stuck in conditions determined by racist white Americans, African Americans needed some transcendent source of selfhood beyond the world as it existed around them. Crummell thus believed that actual freedom began when people were able to reject the determinism of physical effects. "Sense is the proper element of the mere animal, in its search after pleasure. Spirit, reason, and a moral nature, are the fountains of excellence to man."[4]

It was in the cultivation and use of these parts of the human mind that black men would "elevate" themselves and reject white racism. In doing so, Crummell argued, black men would be able to reject "condition, place, power, and all the mere <u>outward</u> circumstances of life."[5] A black person would need to be radically, transcendently free in his internal self before he was capable of becoming politically and socially free in the wider world. In this light, it is easy to dismiss Crummell as a naive individualist. But if we listen closer, we realize that, for this young idealist, individual development and freedom were means to an end. The Transcendent faculties of thought, moral sensibility, and reason were required not only to grant individuals free will but also to allow them to *act* politically, to conceive of and fight for a world not purely determined by the circumstances of history as given. Crummell was articulating a crucial part of the Higher Law Ethos: it did not just matter *what* an individual thought; it mattered *how* they thought and what mental paths they took to discover a political truth. Radical politics, he believed, required modes of thinking—especially intuitive "Reason" and an idealist theory of knowledge—that allowed and encouraged people to criticize the values of a racist and unjust society.

Crummell's idealism explicitly shared many assumptions and influences with the burgeoning Transcendentalist movement in New England. Ending his lecture, he included a lengthy quotation from Ralph Waldo Emerson's first major antislavery piece, the famous "Address on Emancipation in the British West Indies." Since Emerson's address was first given on August 1, 1844 (and Crummell's a month earlier), we have to assume that Crummell went back and added this section to his lecture notes. Perhaps most interesting was the hand underlining with which Crummell underscored Emerson's description of the Haitian revolutionary Toussaint L'Ouverture. "The intellect," Crummell underlined in Emerson's essay, "that is miraculous! Who has it, has the talisman: his skin and bones, though they were of the color of night, are transparent, and the everlasting stars shine through, with attractive beams." Here Emerson's belief in the universality of humanity based on shared ability to receive the influx of intellectual inspiration linked up with Crummell's vision of an ascendant transnational African race whose education would prepare it for both moral and political freedom and, as the example of Toussaint suggested, maybe revolution.

In this lecture, as well as countless other speeches and writings, men and women such as Crummell, Thomas Sidney, William C. Nell, and Charlotte Forten were creating black Transcendentalist thought. Black Transcendentalists used many of the same assumptions and intellectual influences as white Transcendentalists but centered much earlier and with more consistency than their white colleagues on racism and slavery. They were doing this in intellectual clubs—such as New York's Phoenixonian Literary Society and Boston's Adelphi Union—and in journals and newspapers, side by side with unknown fugitive slaves and next to world-famous white intellectuals. Abolitionists had to learn how to think about politics in new ways in order to overcome the years of political and ideological inertia that sustained slavery; Transcendentalism in the hands of black thinkers helped them do this. These black thinkers sought inspiration from German and British Romantics, people such as Friedrich Schiller, Samuel Taylor Coleridge, and, through them, the German philosopher Immanuel Kant. Black intellectuals were on the forefront of thinking through how these new styles of idealist philosophy could contribute to the abolitionist struggle. To understand their thought, we must consider Transcendentalism not as something cloistered among a select group of white intellectuals in Concord but as a living philosophy, one constantly being renewed and produced by those who spoke its language and seized on its ideas.

The black embrace of Transcendentalism is a reminder that antebellum black intellectuals played a central role in the history of American thought. Black thinkers were engaging with many of the broad philosophical assumptions that marked early nineteenth-century idealist philosophy: the belief that human life involved the conscious use of reason to order and fix society; that real knowledge was critical; that truth was gained through movement, struggle, and becoming; and that true freedom was about self-development, not being left alone. Influenced by British, French, and German philosophers, these were the moral and political assumptions that have historically inspired radical social movements. To see black thinkers in antebellum America in dialogue with this same tradition is to appreciate that black abolitionists were intellectually sophisticated radicals in touch with revolutionary philosophical and political thought.

Weapons of the Mind

The best place to begin a study of antebellum black intellectual life is in the intellectual clubs—such as Crummell's Hamilton Lyceum—that sprouted up in the early part of the nineteenth century. Rivaled only by the black church, these clubs were crucial institutions of community and intellectual development, an essential component of what one historian has called "the early black public sphere."[6] In Philadelphia, New York, Boston, and throughout the North, free blacks were creating intellectual clubs that served as valuable places for education and self-improvement, sociability, and the development of political consciousness. Most combined lectures, reading rooms, debates, and theatrical performances. Among the forty-five that we can recover in the written record, a small sampling includes the Female Literary Society in Philadelphia, the New York Garrison Literary Association, the Pittsburgh Theban Society, the New Bedford Debating Society, and the Young Men's Mental Improvement Society in Baltimore.[7] As one observer in New York City boasted, the various literary organizations were "institutions of which we may well be proud . . . we can refer to them as evidences of the literary taste existing among us."[8] Some of them, no doubt, were short-lived, while others, such as the New York Phoenixonian Society, which was well into its sixth year in 1839 and boasted a substantial library, were enduring.[9] By the time of the Civil War, they had spread all the way to the Pacific coast, with California boasting the San Francisco Literary Institute.[10]

Black intellectual clubs assumed many forms. Some were libraries, funded through donations from members or endowed by a white philanthropist. In 1821, according to the *New York Journal*, a library was "about to be established at Boston, for the exclusive use of people of Color."[11] Others, such as the Female Literary Society, in Philadelphia, were places of intellectual and moral uplift, where members exchanged poems and letters with each other, helping to form bonds of community and solidarity.[12] Boston's Adelphic Union sponsored a lecture series that competed with the most prestigious in the city, attracting famous scholars and activists (both white and black) to speak before integrated audience. Sometimes organizations focused on more quotidian educational matters, helping to spread literacy and basic math skills to the black population in the antebellum city. Thus, the Boston Mutual Lyceum, which was organized in 1833, gave classes on reading, writing, and math, as well as debating topics such as "what are the best means to adopt, to remove the prejudice which exists against the people of color?"[13]

For black Northerners, these private clubs were necessary because they were largely excluded from public intellectual life, "denied usual facilities for mental cultivation," in the words of William C. Nell.[14] Boston's school system was segregated until 1855, and Harvard would not graduate an African American student until the 1860s. White-run lyceums and libraries regularly excluded blacks. Nell reported that in Boston, "large audiences in Lyceum lectures have been thrown almost into spasms by the presence of one colored man in their midst."[15] In 1845, white allies Ralph Waldo Emerson and Charles Sumner created a controversy by boycotting the New Bedford Lyceum on account of its segregationist policies, evidence of the continued prejudice of lyceums even in a Quaker and abolitionist stronghold.[16] The one intellectual institution to which African Americans did have sporadic access was the press, as William Lloyd Garrison's *Liberator* and other antislavery newspapers sometimes published their writings. But even this venue had limits: in 1854, Samuel R. Ward, who had run a short-lived black newspaper in Boston in the 1850s, complained of a type of paternalist abolitionist who "a thousand times would . . . rather see us tied to some newspaper that represents us as being about mid way betwixt slaves and men, than to see us holding up a bold front, with a press worthy of entire freemen."[17] Starting in New York City, with *Freedom's Journal*, black abolitionists thus created their own independent newspapers.

From small towns such as Schenectady to bustling metropolises such as Manhattan and San Francisco, these clubs were crucial in framing the intellectual aspirations of black thinkers in the antebellum republic. Most of the important black abolitionist leaders were involved in one of these intellectual clubs, including Frederick Douglass (a member of the East Baltimore Mental Improvement Society while still a slave), Maria Stewart, Alexander Crummell, James McCune Smith, Samuel Ringgold Ward, and William C. Nell. They were increasingly political organizations, in which black thinkers pioneered a combination of philosophical and intellectual debate with political organizing. It is in these clubs that we can see the development of a black Transcendentalist intellectuals.

Thomas Sidney and the "Spiritual" School of Philosophy

Before the rise of black Transcendentalists, though, the Scottish Common Sense School was the dominant philosophical system in these black intellectual clubs. For instance, in 1828, William Whipper gave a speech before the Philadelphia-based Colored Reading Society, arguing that black men had to pursue "Scotch Philosophy." Whipper was drawn to the Scottish vision because he saw it as encouraging black men "to exercise, and by exercising to improve the faculties of the mind."[18] The Scottish School was dominant among American elite and anchored the curriculum at most American colleges—including Harvard and Princeton in the antebellum years.[19]

As its name implies, the Scottish Common Sense School preferred the concrete, the tangible, and the straightforward rather than abstract and airy concepts associated with French and German thought. The Scottish School had developed partly as a way to salvage John Locke's epistemology, the idea that we start life with minds like blank slates and develop everyday knowledge from what we see, hear, taste, feel, or smell around us. David Hume and others had started demonstrating that despite Locke's own desires, this "empirical" method could lead others to a radical skepticism. Lockean principles could develop into materialism, fatalism, and amoralism, as personal ethical standards seemed to lack external validation beyond one's own experiences and collective political values were held hostage by received power and tradition. In response to these concerns, the Scottish School put up bulwarks, declaring certain things such as causality, moral benevolence, intuition, and the existence of a self to be inherent principles of human existence, without which social and religious life would be impossible. They breathed an egalitarian spirit into Aristotle's old *Sensus Communis*, holding it to mean that all people had the capacity for reasoned discussion rooted in their mutual capacity for common sense. At the same point, there was a certain skepticism of abstract philosophy in the Scottish School, a tendency to assume where others debated. As Thomas Carlyle sneered, the Scottish philosophers "let loose Instinct, as an indiscriminating ban-dog to guard them" against Hume's skeptical conclusions.[20]

Like any abstract theory, Common Sense moral philosophy could lend itself to multiple political interpretations and uses, some moderate and others quite radical. Some historians have pointed to the Scottish-inflected education that James Madison received at Princeton as the origin of the Constitution's emphasis on balance, moderation, and the encouragement of compromise.[21] And most famously, the Declaration of Independence's promise of "self-evident" equality seems to owe much to Jefferson's reading of Scottish thinkers, who had commonly used that phrase.[22] It seems clear that the democratic optimism of Jefferson—his belief that a "ploughman" could make the same or even better moral judgments as a "professor"—developed from his reading of Scottish philosophers such as Thomas Reid and Francis Hutchinson. And William Whipper seems to have believed it could be used to demonstrate black intellectual achievement.

But as early as the mid-eighteenth century, some critics had disagreed, perceiving limitations to the Scottish Common Sense School's philosophy and politics. Eighteenth-century radical Dissenters in Great Britain, such as James Burgh and Richard Price, had argued during the French Revolution that Locke and his contemporary Scottish defenders could lead to political conformity and the abandonment of human agency and freedom.[23] And the Scottish School's appeal to "common sense" to get out of philosophical jams had outraged German idealists such as Kant and Hegel. Both criticized the Scottish School for its lack of philosophical rigor, for assuming the reality of exactly those things that were the duty of the philosopher to prove—the existence of the self, the validity of our senses, and causality itself.[24]

And American Transcendentalism would be born out of an extension of these critiques against the Scottish School. Thus, in his more polemical moments, the Transcendentalist Theodore Parker came close to blaming all modern ills, including slavery, on the moral philosophy of John Locke and his Scottish followers, whose "sensualism" was responsible, according to Parker, for generations of moral relativists and apologists for unjust social systems.[25] According to Parker, the epistemology of Locke and all philosophers who had swum in his wake had no space for moral values, since in Locke's system we can only "know" what our senses perceive, and this left no place for transcendent values such as justice, equality, dignity, and freedom, which were not experienced by the senses of smell, touch, or sight.[26] These critiques of the Scottish School were not always nuanced or even fair. Both Locke and many Scottish thinkers such as Francis Hutchinson and Thomas Reid had been desperate to preserve space in their conception of the human self for morality, critical thought, religious belief, and altruism. In truth, the Transcendentalist's caricatured vision of Lockean philosophy as materialistic and robotic was really a more appropriate response to the French philosophes, atheists such as Helvetius and Holbach, or the crass utilitarianists around Jeremy Bentham who had taken Lockean principles to their materialistic extreme.

And so by the 1830s, an avant-garde of American thinkers, partly under the influence of German thinkers such as Kant, had joined in the rejection of the Scottish School. In New England, in particular, a group of young white intellectuals, dissatisfied with the influence of Locke and the Scottish School on the Unitarian Church, were advocating German and French thought in response. They read Samuel Taylor Coleridge's *Aids to Reflection*, especially focusing on the influential introduction penned by the University of Vermont scholar James Marsh. By the early 1830s, some had dug back to Coleridge's main source of inspiration—Kant—as Frederic Henry Hedge did in the *Christian Examiner*.[27] They absorbed the theology of Friedrich Schleiermacher, who had sought to synthesize post-Kantian metaphysics with Christian experience. James Freeman Clarke and Hedge introduced the writings of other European Romantics, such as Goethe, Schilling, and Victor Cousin, to American audiences. Meanwhile, at Harvard, Karl Follen, a scholar of Fichte and Schiller who had fled Germany because of his democratic politics, was introducing students to the idealism of post-Kantian German philosophy. These white scholars eagerly read Thomas Carlyle, who viciously attacked the Scottish School and Locke in his famous essay, "Signs of the Time." By 1836, writers such as Emerson, Alcott, and Brownson went beyond simply describing German thought to creating their own classic works inspired by it.[28]

The rebellion of the white Transcendentalist generation against Locke and the Scottish School is well known; less appreciated is how black intellectual clubs were fomenting a similar rejection of Scottish styles of philosophy at the same time. Two essential nodes of black intellectual production in the antebellum North contributed to the black abolitionist embrace of Transcendentalism. The group of black intellectuals clustered around the Adelphic Union in Boston was geographically closest to Concord and the world of white Transcendentalists. They would make important contributions, especially in the 1840s and 1850s. But the move toward a black Transcendentalist politics was first pioneered in New York City, where the circle of black thinkers and activists around the Phoenixonian Society (later the Hamiltonian Lyceum) played the pivotal role. The evolution of their thought mirrored and in some ways preceded the white Transcendentalist rebellion against Locke and the Scottish School.

In New York, the two main figures were Thomas Sidney and Alexander Crummell. They had attended the New York "Classical School," along with future leaders such as Henry Highland Garnet, James McCune Smith, and Samuel Ringgold Ward.[29] But the defining moment in their intellectual journey occurred in 1835, when Sidney, Crummell, and Garnet were invited to attend the Noyes Academy, a school founded by New England abolitionists in Canaan, New Hampshire. Soon after the three black New Yorkers arrived, they discovered that the school—like similar attempts in New Haven and elsewhere—had incurred the wrath of racist New Englanders. As Crummell remembered, "fourteen black boys with books in their hands set the entire Granite State crazy!"[30] Despite brave resistance by Garnet—who set the other boys at work molding bullets—a mob soon descended and, on August 10, dragged the school into a swamp, ending their brief experiment with New England education.[31]

Though the mob had succeeded in destroying the school, it had inadvertently given Crummell, Sidney, and Garnet a political education they would never forget. All three would be radicalized by the event, which would inspire their later nationalist and revolutionary politics. If their experience in New Hampshire politicized them, they learned to express that political commitment in philosophical terms at the Oneida School, in Upstate New York, where they later enrolled. At Oneida, they studied, among other things, "metaphysical tests" under Beriah Green, as well as Romantic poetry.[32] Green's Oneida Institute emphasized ethics and philosophy, courses that Green, the "Professor of Mental and Moral Philosophy," taught. Inspired by the British poet Samuel Taylor Coleridge's ideas, Green taught Crummell and Garnet that Reason— "that same clear, certain, unerring light throughout the Universe" was how Green described it—was a portal to God, a manner in which God's truth was replicated and republished in the individual conscience. In fact, Green developed a sort of abolitionized version of the British poet, in which Coleridge's notion of the power of intuitive Reason underlay the antislavery project.[33]

Fortified by Green's teachings, Sidney, Crummell, and Garnet returned to New York City to form the core of a black intellectual club named the Phoenixonian Literary Society, later rechristened the Hamiltonian Lyceum.[34] The Phoenixonian Society appears to have coexisted with the Phoenix Society, which may have effectively functioned as the same organization. The Phoenix Society had been founded in 1833 in order to educate "colored people in Morals, Literature, and the Mechanic Arts," according to its early constitution.[35] It was one of the most prominent such clubs in the black North, serving as the direct inspiration for a similar society "for moral improvement" that existed among the black residents of New Bedford.[36] A generous donation from the white philanthropist Lewis Tappan had endowed the society with a library and school that met regularly.[37] When that society was dissolved, the Phoenixonian Society incorporated many of its members and, it seems, its library.

For the young black intellectuals of New York, the club's regular gatherings served two purposes: to discuss how to elevate their race and to learn about famous Romantic poets and practice their own art. They would plot how to sow insurrection in the South and, on the same day, read poems about the "captive's dream of Liberty" that they had written while leaving room to discuss the poetry of Milton and Wordsworth.[38] The very language used to describe these "rash but noble resolves," where members would pledge to "start an insurrection and free our brethren in bondage," betrays the influence of the Romantic imagination.[39] Nor did their interest in poetry distract them from politics. In 1839, they organized a public reading and "exhibition" to raise funds for the *Amistad* captives.[40] When discussing their intellectual life, black thinkers in New York often reached for martial metaphors, as when they described James McCune Smith's education as a development of the "the weapons of mind, into the *Intellectual Arena*, in defense of the welfare and interest of his people."[41]

Of the New York Romantics, Sidney is the least well known but best exemplifies the shift toward Romanticism that occurred among black intellectuals in the 1830s. His personal story was as remarkable as his intellectual journey. Born an orphan, he distinguished himself at an early age for his precocious intellectualism. Nathaniel Rogers, the quirky New Hampshire abolitionist, declared Sidney to be, at age seventeen, "an accomplished scholar, an elegant declaimer, a graceful orator" who could outshine many Boston "patricians" in eloquence.[42] Sidney, a brilliant but impatient student, tangled with older members of the black leadership in New York, such as the editors of the *Colored American*, who admitted he was a "penetrating" speaker and "undoubtedly, one of the most talented youth of the age" but condemned him as "extremely imprudent."[43] When Sidney gave an antislavery speech that seemed to promote slave insurrection, the editor declared him "learned and eloquent, but . . . irrelevant and bloody."[44] After his experiences in New Hampshire and the Oneida Institute, Sidney became the schoolmaster of the New York Select Academy, where he taught "Natural Philosophy" to black youth.[45] He was also the corresponding secretary for the Association for the Political Improvement of People of Color in New York City, putting his political commitments to use.[46] His colleagues would long remember the influence that Sidney had on them, and he would serve as a sort of symbol of black intellectual achievement. Fifteen years after his death, Samuel Ringgold Ward would list him as one of the pieces of evidence "sufficient to contradict any disparaging words concerning the *modern* Negro."[47] According to Crummell, Sidney was proficient in classical history; could read Latin, Greek, and Hebrew; was starting to learn German and French; and was especially attracted to Romantic British poets such as Coleridge and Wordsworth.[48]

In the summer of 1840, Sidney abruptly died, leaving a hole in the Phoenixonian Society from which it would never fully recover. His mysterious death at twenty-three was a tragedy for the fledging community of New York black intellectuals and probably explains his relative absence among historical accounts of black thought. But it did produce a fascinating eulogy by Crummell that is a crucial source for understanding Sidney's thought and the development of antebellum black intellectual life.[49]

Sidney, as Crummell presented him, was a philosopher, interested in the same questions of epistemology and ethics that were animating New England Transcendentalists. "It was in metaphysical investigation he chiefly delighted," declared Crummell. Sidney had studied the "two great schools of Philosophy— the Sensual and the Spiritual." By age sixteen, he had "read and paid much attention to Locke," what Crummell meant by the "Sensual" (since all knowledge came from the senses), but, like the New England Transcendentalists, soon rejected it in favor of the "Spiritual" school of philosophy.[50] This rejection of Locke's philosophy would be replayed throughout New England intellectual life.

More important even than the genealogy of Sidney's beliefs were the reasons given for his rejection of Lockean empiricism. Here Crummell explained that Sidney rejected "sensualism" because of its inability to foster the type of individuality and principled behavior that he wanted. "Spiritual" philosophy, on the other hand, had a boundlessness to it, providing "insight into our own spiritual consciousness, that we might admire the mysterious framework of our own being," thereby increasing "our regard and reverence for human nature." Crummell's description of Sidney's metaphysics, as well as the consequence they had for his political beliefs, maps almost perfectly onto the Transcendentalist framework. He rejected Locke because he wanted to affirm the divinity of the individual man, believed the mind powers to be independent of what nature and the external world imprinted onto it, and saw the ability of man to approach godliness as related to a set of ethical imperatives—"the active agents of Right and Holiness."

Sidney's philosophy was also tightly linked to his politics. Of this, Crummell was clear. His mind was not "mere abstract speculative thought. It was practical in the highest degree." Like a good idealist, he dealt in first principles— ideals—but then pushed to realize them in political activity. Sidney claimed that "what I have brought forward . . . are fundamental principles, and the measures I have proposed, according to the course of nature will most certainly at some time have to be acceded to." Ideals such as equality, justice, and righteousness were not simply abstract but were goals to be realized in abolitionist political struggle.[51] Along with Crummell, he dreamed of leading a rebellion of Southern slaves, wiping away a monstrous injustice with one heroic act of righteousness.

The description of Sidney's "spiritual" philosophy as a contradiction to the Lockean "sensualist" school of "mental science" suggests that Sidney was reading the English poet Samuel Taylor Coleridge's influential *Aids to Reflection*, which helped introduce Kantian metaphysics to American audiences. Coleridge had studied Kantian philosophy and interpreted the German philosopher as someone whose system was better suited to protect religious faith than those derived from Locke. Coleridge was one of the most important reference points in the early black press, and his writings were often reprinted in *Freedom's Journal* and especially in the *Colored American*, the paper Sidney would have been most frequently reading.[52] Frederick Douglass would begin his 1855 autobiography, *My Bondage and My Freedom*, by quoting the British Romantic.[53] Many white abolitionists, such as Samuel May Jr., who helped to publish some of Coleridge's poems for the first time in American presses, were also strongly influenced by the British poet.[54] Crummell was obsessed with Coleridge, quoting him throughout his long life. In James Marsh's words, "instead of adopting, like the popular metaphysicians of the day [defined as Locke and the Scottish Common Sense School philosophers], a system of philosophy at war with religion, and which tends inevitably to undermine our belief in the reality of any thing spiritual . . . [Coleridge] boldly asserts the reality of something distinctly spiritual in man."[55]

A series of essays by a black abolitionist in 1839—quite possibly Sidney himself—demonstrated how black thinkers in New York were using Coleridge to think philosophically about politics. In September 1839, the *Colored American* began publishing a series of philosophical texts called "The Reflector" by an African American going by the name "Long Island Scribe."[56] The author listed their address as Newtown, New York (now Elmhurst in Queens). The name "reflector," it seems, is a reference to Coleridge's *Aids to Reflection*. Across the essays, Long Island Scribe attempted to demonstrate that inherent in human life was our ability to reason and think: "the *power to think,* includes the *power to originate thought.*"[57] Here we see black thinkers embrace one of the central tenets of American Kantianism—that the human mind is a creative organ capable of more than simply repeating and republishing the sensory inputs it has received. But Long Island Scribe was interested in this notion because such a view of the mind, he claimed, was essentially egalitarian. "The constitution of mind," he declared, "is *universally identical.*"[58] The example the author used to prove the equality of the human mind—he argued that "the inhabitants of Central Africa" would be just as capable of reasoning as any European—illustrated the political importance of his metaphysics. In a later piece, he argued that "Colored Americans" were trained to only consider their immediate perceptions and never to reflect and evaluate their conditions.[59] Too many black Northerners were inattentive to their condition, and the result was that "only about one in ten of the five hundred thousand free colored Americans are abolitionists."[60] Thinking properly, for the Long Island Scribe, was an abolitionist act.

By thus defining his own metaphysics as spiritual rather than sensual, Sidney was joining Coleridge and Marsh in rebelling against the most common and popular forms of philosophy in the Atlantic world, those associated with John Locke and other British thinkers. Starting in the late eighteenth century,

critics of Locke, especially in Germany and France, had charged him with holding a reductive and mechanical view of human consciousness, as well as ignoring the reflective powers of the mind. American Transcendentalists were united
in seeing Locke's tendency to root knowledge in our senses as leading to a mechanistic, amoral world. Writing to his sister, who apparently had asked advice for
works on "mental philosophy," Thoreau described the Lockean and Common
Sense philosophers as having "squeezed the infinite mind into a compass."[61]
And Emerson had nothing but disdain for the "skeptical philosophy of Locke,
which insisted that there was nothing in the intellect which was not previously
in the experience of the senses."[62]

To many Americans, the philosophy of the German Immanuel Kant
seemed to offer Americans a surer ground for religious and political truth than
Lockean skepticism. Kant became so popular among New England reformers
that Lydia Maria Child complained to a friend about the endless stream of
bearded men in the 1830s constantly trying to engage her in discussions about
the German philosopher.[63] Kant had argued that you could think of the world
from one standpoint, where the world appeared as "phenomena," as our experience is constituted by our senses, laws of cause and effect, and awareness of time.
But at the same time, Kant argued, there were limits to our ability to calmly
observe the world in this manner, and the standpoint of phenomena did not
necessarily tell us about "noumena," or "things-in-themselves," which we could
not directly know with our senses. In a sense, Kant's epistemology was both
humbler than Locke's—as he was arguing that our experience of "phenomena"
did not actually give us pure insight to what was "out there"—and, in another
way, more ambitious because, for the exact same reason, it seemed to reserve a
greater space for truths that "transcended" mere everyday sensual experience.
This was well illustrated in his theory of mind, where an individual could simultaneously think of herself in the "world of senses," her consciousness determined by physical necessity *and* as a free member of the "intellectual world," in
which her consciousness freely determined moral laws that it then followed.
Integral to Kant's philosophy was the idea that the mind is not a blank slate but
instead is constituted by certain structures that allow it to order and understand the sense material it receives. The human mind could even discover
knowledge without empirical evidence by uncovering the Holy Grail of Kantian philosophy, truths that were simultaneously a priori (they did not require
empirical evidence) and synthetic (they added to our store of knowledge). Kant
and his followers held, therefore, a view of the mind that was much more active
and powerful than Locke's.

Julia Ward Howe—the abolitionist author of the song the "Battle Cry of Freedom"—articulated well how Kant's seemingly abstract set of ideas about the mind and our sources of knowledge could inspire radical politics. In a philosophical autobiography that she wrote, Howe remembered reading the German philosopher as the key moment in her political awakening. Previous philosophers had taught her that our ideas of justice had to be limited by the empirical world, what currently existed. Since there was no really existing world of pure justice, these philosophers had "led me to look upon wrong and suffering as permanent institutions." But "in Kant's writings I heard the eternal 'Thou Shalt' in its trumpet tone of victory." In other words, for Howe, Kant's moral philosophy and his transcendental metaphysics inspired her to reject the moral passivity and political quiescence that she had inherited from other philosophers (unnamed but presumably empiricists in the Lockean tradition). This happened, she claimed, because Kantian moral philosophy encouraged "a sense of enfranchisement," whereby human judgment could critique "all the phenomena of experience." Howe thought that "women especially" were trained by a sexist society to "glide through life under the influence only of its surface impressions" and thus needed Kant's philosophy of critical judgment to encourage them to seize control of their life from "indifferentism."[64] She even wrote poetry in honor of the German philosopher ("the fixed ideal, the everlasting hope").[65]

Kant is notoriously dense and difficult to read, and few white Transcendentalists understood the German philosopher well. The first translation of the *Critique of Pure Reason*, only published in English in 1838, by Francis Heywood, was famously hard to follow. M. D. Meiklejohn's second version, published in 1855 in hopes of being clearer, was barely more comprehensible—"beyond making out," as James Elliot Cabot remembered.[66] One consequence was that Kantianism in America, in the antebellum years at least, was as much about what Americans wanted to see in the German philosopher as what was actually there in the original text. Americans relied heavily on British interpreters such as Samuel Taylor Coleridge, who had filtered his understanding of Kant's noumenal realm through the writings of Christian mystics such as the Quaker George Fox. Americans thus tended to synthesize Kant's metaphysics with Christian theology, believing that the German philosopher offered a surer footing for religious belief.[67] More than a rigorous philosophical system, Americans inherited from Kant an unfocused impulse toward idealism and mental dualism and a vague suspicion of the body and the senses.

This was largely because Americans—and in this they were not unique—were less interested in the rigidly rational elements of Kant and tended toward the Romantic interpretations of his philosophy. Kant himself was strictly ratio-nalistic but, when combined with burgeoning religious and artistic develop-ments, inadvertently helped lay the groundwork for what we think of as the Romantic movement. The British Romantics—particularly Coleridge and Carlyle—shared a hostility to the frigid utilitarianism that seemed to dominate British society and drafted Kant into their war against what they saw as a coldly mechanistic Anglo-empiricist philosophy derived from Locke. In America, es-pecially, Kant was seen as a Romantic celebrant of the mind's power as opposed to the supposed materialism of Locke, a dichotomy that, it was true, was fair to the philosophical complexity of neither Locke nor Kant.

In other words, Sidney and Crummell were not alone in their interests in "mental science." Rarely have debates about epistemology and theories of the mind garnered such wide audiences as they did in the 1830s and 1840s in Amer-ica. As one 1840 commencement speaker told the graduating class of the Mount Saint Mary College, the "temper of the times" was a rejection of the "gross and sensual system of the last century to purer and more spiritual doctrines."[68] The speaker, Eugene Lynch, went on to give a popularized version of the debate be-tween the "sensual" and the "spiritual" schools of epistemology. Francis Lieber, one of the most important political theorists of the Civil War era, began his 1838 *Manual of Political Ethics* with a defense of human free will and mental auton-omy.[69] In Liberia, ex-slave colonists read in the *Liberia Herald* about the intrica-cies of John Locke's theory of self. The editor determined that "Mr. Locke's observations upon this subject appear hasty."[70]

This widespread philosophical and even cultural debate—between what was perceived as a Lockean "sensual" and a Kantian "spiritual" theory of the mind—spoke to an anxiety, common in antebellum society, that materialism was overwhelming Americans' spiritual obligations, that, in Thomas Carlyle's words, "men are grown mechanical in head and in heart."[71] Colonial-era Calvin-ism may have been gloomy, but it at least evinced some encounter with the mys-teries of life and death, some awareness of people's need for emotional and spiritual depth. Calvinist rigor was now giving way to either a sunny but shallow Unitarianism or an anti-intellectual evangelicalism. At the same time, in the in-dustrial towns springing up throughout New England, the ageless rhythms of agriculture were being replaced by the artificial steam whistle and timetable of the factory floor. "We live in a transition period," Ralph Waldo Emerson de-clared, "when the old faiths which comforted nations . . . seem to have spent their force."[72] Perhaps as a rejection of the materialism that surrounded them or one last desperate search for something fixed and permanent beyond the maelstrom of emergent modernity, pamphleteers and lyceum speakers became obsessed with distinguishing between philosophical systems, between those that relied on materialism and the senses (with roots in Hobbes, Locke, and Hume) and another that left space for what Emerson called "the power of Thought and of Will."[73] Thinkers such as Emerson, Theodore Parker, and Alexander Crummell found in this celebration of idealism a way to preserve their moral dignity in a world seemingly overrun by a gray reductive materialism.

The Abolitionist Romantic Self

Alexander Crummell was, along with Thomas Sidney, a crucial figure in the development of this style of black Romantic philosophy. His father, Boston Crummell, had been an important activist in New York City, and Crummell had attended school with Sidney, James McCune Smith, and Samuel Ringgold Ward before entering the church. Thanks to the abolitionists at Oneida, the professors at Cambridge University, and his own tireless work, he would become one of the most important black intellectuals of the nineteenth century. With Sidney he shared a love of the British Romantics, especially Wordsworth and Coleridge, whom he had read at the Oneida Institute. After Sidney's premature death, he took the lead among the New York Romantics articulating an abolitionist idealism in a series of speeches and sermons.

One of Crummell's great contributions to black Transcendentalist politics came in his appreciation for intuitive non-instrumental forms of reasoning. We can see this in his embrace of one of the key aspects of antislavery Transcendentalist imagination—the boundlessness of thought. Crummell described this style of thinking as "intuition," "that penetrative quality, which is as much moral as it is intellectual, which leads the mind, as by a flash, to the very centre of its subject."[74] Describing the mind of the abolitionist Thomas Clarkson, for instance, Crummell quoted Coleridge and then argued that "the logical faculty is not strongly developed in Clarkson's writings. Like most Reformers he perceives truth as by intuition; and without the labor of severe ratiocination."[75] Crummell had used similar language—celebrating the "spontaneous exercises of Reason"—in his eulogy on Sidney.[76] For Crummell, spontaneous Reason and "intuition" were virtues that were as moral as they were intellectual, more spiritual than logical. Crummell's "intuition" indicated a way of thinking about thinking that transcended the limited instrumental logic of Anglo-American empiricism. At about the same time, in Emerson's famous *Self-Reliance*, the white Transcendentalist

THE REV. ALEXANDER CRUMMELL.—[See Page 288.]

Figure 1. Alexander Crummell as a young Episcopal minister. Courtesy of Miriam and Ira D. Wallach Division of Art, Prints and Photographs, The New York Public Library, Astor, Lenox and Tilden Foundations.

was celebrating a similar set of intellectual virtues, defining a self-reliant person as one who "knows that to his involuntary perceptions a perfect faith is due" and elevating "whim" as the preeminent source of truth.[77] For Emerson, whims were brief flashes (like Crummell, he sometimes compared them to lightning strikes) in which a deep truth was unveiled to the thinker. "A glimpse, a point of view," Emerson described this form of thought, "that by its very brightness excludes the purview—but no panorama."[78] Emerson and Crummell considered these short bursts of inspiration and enthusiasm—semi-secularized versions, perhaps, of the fleeting moments of grace experienced by the Calvinist devotee—to be better sources of knowledge, more reliable epistemological moments, than strenuous systematic thought. Counterintuitively, Emerson declared that the highest form of Reason "never *reasons*, never proves, it simply perceives."[79]

Neither Crummell nor Emerson believed that by celebrating "whim" or "intuition," they were completely abandoning standards of accuracy or judgment. As Emerson wrote, "I hope it is somewhat better than whim at last, but we cannot spend the day in explanation," and Crummell argued that intuition was useful exactly because it was more likely to lead to "accuracy and correctness."[80] What the two shared was a theory of how the mind worked, how it best came to moral and even epistemological judgment. Crummell's insight here is that often our minds know more than we are able to articulate or prove logically. Knowledge was something gained by adopting a position of openness, a spiritual and moral receptivity, what Emerson called the "perpetual openness of the human mind."[81] Truth was not found, they argued, in labored deduction or the accumulation of external facts. Like Coleridge's embrace of "imagination," Crummell's "intuition" linked the human mind to "an echo of divine self-understanding."[82] There were deep reserves in the human mind, Coleridge had taught, that were not necessarily obvious even to the subject themselves, wells of prereflective spiritual and intellectual vitality. It was the British poet, after all, who introduced the term "subconscious" to the English language and who had argued that true philosophy was about listening to that which "lies beneath or (as it were) behind the spontaneous consciousness."[83] Thus, in a Coleridgian moment, Thoreau could sum up Transcendentalist psychology: "the unconsciousness of man is the consciousness of God."[84] The position of Emerson or Crummell thus was not an anti-intellectual rejection of reason but a celebration of a deeper wisdom hidden from immediate reflective consciousness, one derived from the deep self. Lacking the secular language of Freud or modern psychiatry, both interpreted this unconscious energy in religious or spiritual terms as either the voice of God (Crummell) or evidence of the Oversoul (Emerson) speaking to the individual conscience. Part of what makes the vision of Crummell and Emerson so distinctly modern, though, was their awareness of the depths and complexities of the human subject, whose inner world could not be reduced to our immediate consciousness, sensory perceptions, or even our surface sense of our self.

We can understand Crummell's evocation of "intuition" as a contrast with "ratiocination" by putting it in the context of Transcendentalist philosophy, particularly the distinction Transcendentalists made between Reason and Understanding.[85] As Crummell showed with his citation of Coleridge, it was the British poet who had popularized the distinction in America between Reason and Understanding as two competing forms of thinking, though its roots were in German philosophy going back to Hegel and Kant. As Kant had explained in his *Groundwork of the Metaphysics of Morals*, "understanding" was a mental faculty tied to the body—it took the raw material of the senses and made it into something intelligible—while "reason" was more "spontaneous," able to create "ideas" and the only human faculty capable of determining its own moral ends and was thus the source of moral freedom.[86] Hegel would expand this division between *Verstand* (Understanding, which held to the principle of identity) and *Vernunft* (Reason, which alone was able to use the negative dialectic to progress through contradictions), and continuing through Weber and the Frankfurt School, this distinction has remained a central part of Continental philosophy.[87] If antebellum Transcendentalists did not always grasp the full intricacies of Kant's method, they eagerly jumped on this distinction between narrow, problem-solving, and instrumental Understanding and dialectical, unifying, spontaneous, and "genius" Reason.[88]

This concept of Reason, derived from German idealists, was unique in many ways to Transcendentalists in this period of American intellectual life and crucial to their political development. To his brother, Emerson wrote that "the distinction of Milton[,] Coleridge and the Germans between Reason and Understanding [was] philosophy itself."[89] It was key to the Transcendentalists' boundless style of moral and political thinking. Coleridge had defined Reason a bit as Hegel had *Geist*, as uniquely both individual subject and divine object. In other words, the inward faculty of Reason both provided evidence of God and, at the same time, *was* God, or at least His divine echo—the "highest faculty of the soul," Emerson described it.[90] Reason was more poetic and abstract, more spiritual and moral, better able to weigh competing ethical claims and best experienced in moments of divine inspiration and intuition. Even when used in secular contexts, Reason was the faculty that gave individuals access to moral truths, and it was the linchpin that made one's pursuit of the ideal possible, allowing individuals the ability to reach out of the world of material necessity into the realm of moral and spiritual freedom. Without Reason, you could not imagine or know what the ideal society should look like, much less compare it to the degraded society of the real.

By embracing this German idea of Reason, Romantics such as Crummell were rejecting the British tradition of empiricism, which had instead defined reason as "reckoning with consequences"—simply a formal process with which people intelligently sought to achieve an end determined by arbitrary and uncontrollable desires. What Transcendentalists called the "Understanding"—narrow and pointed means-to-an-end logic—could be like this, a slave of the passions, but never Reason, which was more active, more ethical, capable of determining one's own ends, and more far-reaching. Emerson called Understanding "that wrinkled calculator" and said that it served two masters: "Custom and Interest."[91] Emerson's twinned critique of conformity and greed thus could not be separated from his broader opposition to the type of narrow mind dominated by Understanding that produced these vices. Like an observer confronted with a Rubin vase who can either see faces or a vase but never both at the same time, our mind can see and appreciate the logic of Reason or that of Understanding, but using one often precludes the other. "The power by which man contemplates the Necessary, the True, the Good, or, what we call absolute truth," Emerson wrote, "stands in wonderful antagonism with the power by which he apprehends particular facts, and applies means to ends."[92] Thus, those who habitually used the means-to-an-end logic of the Understanding risked experiencing a sort of parallax shift in their ethical judgments, a moral degradation that culminated in losing their ability to Reason. As Emerson reported in his *Divinity School Address*, "there is no doctrine of the Reason which will bear to be taught by the Understanding."[93] It was exactly this style of thought that Crummell was referencing when he commended Clarkson and Sidney for perceiving truth by intuition and not through forced reasoning.

Crummell's Romanticism and the development of black intellectual clubs deepen our understanding of later African American intellectual history. Crummell is well known for two facets of his thought. On one hand, as an advocate for black emigration and the creation of black colleges, he was an early voice in the history of black nationalism. As one scholar has noted, the black nationalism of Crummell was the product of "European romanticism and cultural nationalism."[94] But Crummell, who throughout his life was a fierce advocate for black education, is perhaps best known for the tribute paid to him by

Du Bois in his classic *The Souls of Black Folk*. Du Bois saw Crummell, whom he had met at Wilberforce University, as both a quiet example of black learning and dignity and an exemplar of the "talented tenth" idea. To see Crummell's intellectual biography as shaped by these black intellectual clubs and in a transatlantic world of Romanticism deepens our understanding of the early roots of black radicalism.

Romanticism, as a broad body of thought, was influential throughout the black Atlantic. Especially in the francophone Atlantic, many black intellectuals were participating in the broad set of philosophical and artistic impulses that marked early nineteenth-century Romantic thought. Just as black Americans jettisoned the conservative politics that sometimes accompanied it in Europe, intellectuals in Haiti used Romanticism for radical ends. In Haiti, the so-called *cénacle* of Ignace and Emile Nau and the Ardouin brothers was inspired by Victor Hugo, Alexandre Dumas (who was partly of Haitian descent), and others to publish a series of political journals, histories, and poems.[95] Haitian poetry, observed one abolitionist paper, "often sounds very like the echoes of Lamartine or Victor Hugo," two French Romantics known for their revolutionary sympathies.[96] These followers of "Haitian romanticism in social thought" were largely responsible for the revolt of 1843, an event that Haitian historians proudly note preceded the European revolutions of 1848, normally seen as the clearest political manifestation of Romanticism as a body of thought.[97] Even in the antebellum South, where blacks were rarely afforded the ability to participate in intellectual or political dialogue, Romanticism helped shape political aspirations. Among the free Creole population of New Orleans, a heady mix of Romantic impulses, the memories of the French and Haitian revolutions, and native thought produced liberal tendencies that would culminate in one of the most radical bastions of egalitarianism in the Reconstruction South.[98]

The Adelphic Union

In the early 1840s, Alexander Crummell began a period as a semi-itinerant minister, traveling between congregations in New Bedford, Providence, New Haven, and Boston.[99] Years later, he remembered that "my removal from New York to Boston seemed to me a transition from the darkness of midnight to the golden light of a summer morning." Likely, after fifty years, Crummell was romanticizing a bit. But the young intellectual would have had many reasons to find Boston, which he saw as "the very Mecca of American culture," an intellectually exciting place.[100] Perhaps he thought this because the same impulses that drew Crummell to Romantic philosophy and away from Locke were leading many white Bostonians toward a new style of thought influenced by the same German and French sources. These white intellectuals began meeting in what became known as the famous Transcendentalist Club in 1836.[101] That year, when Emerson published *Nature*, Orestes Brownson published *New Views of Christianity, Society, and the Church*, and A. Bronson Alcott published his *Conversations with Children on the Gospels*, which has become known as Transcendentalism's *annus mirabilis*, when American thinkers began to meaningfully create an intellectual tradition of their own. But if the Transcendentalist Club, home to Emerson, Theodore Parker, A. Bronson Alcott, James Freeman Clarke, and other white intellectuals, has gotten a tremendous amount of scholarly attention, another club, founded just three months later, would have an equal impact among black intellectuals and would develop in ways that were similar to the Transcendentalist Club. On March 10, 1840, Crummell spoke before this black club, the Adelphic Union, on the "position, relations, and duties of the free people of color."[102]

The Adelphic Union Library Association was one of the most fascinating intellectual clubs, black or white, that developed in the antebellum North. Few organizations, then or now, brought together such a fertile mix of thinkers: radical African Americans, many of whom were born in slavery and had little formal education, along with elite white intellectuals to debate scientific, cultural, and political ideas. Formed after a meeting on December 11, 1836, the Adelphic Union soon rose to become the most prominent intellectual institution among New England African Americans.[103] It developed partly by incorporating the rival black intellectual societies in the city, including the Young Men's Literary Debating Society and the Thompson Literary Debating Society, which had both been active in 1836.[104] Thanks to a donation from Abner Forbes, the Union had started with a substantial library, which the members augmented by seeking donations from around the country.[105] On January 2, 1837, the *Liberator* advertised the "introductory," the first of a series of scientific lectures in Boston, the beginning of the Adelphic Union. "All persons who feel interested in scientific improvement" were invited.[106] Over the next ten years, the Adelphic Union would grow into a community center, library, debating club, political organization, and amateur theater. The leadership, which included John Hilton, Benjamin Bassett, Thomas Cole, and, most important, William C. Nell, was entirely black, though white Bostonians sometimes overcame their prejudices to attend the lectures, a testament to the Adelphic Union's success.

Meeting in the Smith School House, the Adelphic Union's main task was to run a series of lectures. Nell and the other black leaders, who were in charge of curating the lectures, consciously choose the speakers list, making the Union an expression of their own political priorities and intellectual aspirations. Introductory lectures become annual traditions, and in 1838, the Adelphic Union had that year's first speech—given by the Garrisonian Edmund Quincy—printed up as a pamphlet for sale.[107] Many of the speakers were white, including such notables as Sylvester Graham (of cracker fame), the economist Amasa Walker, the feminist Angelina Grimké, and the leadership of Boston abolitionism.[108] Unique among local lyceums, the Union encouraged both black and female speakers. Indeed, a number of black intellectuals used the Adelphic Union as an entryway into public life. The most famous speaker was Frederick Douglass, who lectured there on antislavery activism in January 1844, when he was a little-known fugitive still legally owned by his Maryland masters.[109] William C. Nell spoke at least three times, often on the purpose of black education. New Yorker James McCune Smith, former member of the Phoenixonian Society, spoke in 1845, suggesting that the Union attracted black intellectuals from around the country.[110] Lesser-known black Bostonians, such as Thomas Cole, who occasionally wrote for the *Liberator*, and John Fatal, a day laborer who lectured on the "Nipnet Indians," also spoke before the Union.[111] Nell would point out that, while black led, the Adelphic Union always welcomed white speakers and attendees, while white schools and lyceums refused to return the favor. Part of the purpose of the Union was to build social links between black activists. In 1845, for instance, William C. Nell wrote an apologetic note to Robert Morris, concerned that he had "appeared rather severe and as if personal towards you" after an event.[112] A main purpose of the "Society" was to build bonds between black activists, and Nell wanted to ensure that he had not undercut that goal.

The black leadership of the Adelphic Union shaped the lectures, even those given by white speakers, to ensure their concerns were addressed. The black leadership gave introductions to white speakers, providing black thinkers opportunities to set the tone for the day's lecture. In 1844, for instance, the Transcendentalist Theodore Parker wrote in his journal about his lecture in front of the Adelphic Union, recording that "when Mr. Nell announced me, and that, too, as *a friend of mankind*, the negroes applauded. I was never so much gratified but once before."[113] Most important, the black leaders chose whom to invite, signaling their appreciation for a particular thinker by nominating that person for popular "Introductory" lectures. This honor generally went to well-known abolitionists. There was a "Lecture Committee" that comprised various black leaders, including Nell, Charles Battiste, and Thomas Cole, who made the relevant decisions about speakers.[114] The board, for instance, wrote to Wendell Phillips in 1843 to inform the aristocratic abolitionist that they "unanimously made choice of Wendell Phillips as the very best one to deliver their Introductory" lecture for the season.[115] Likewise, in 1845, Nell wrote to Charles Sumner, frantically scrambling to find a replacement for a speaker who cancelled at the last minute.[116] White speakers adjusted their talks to meet the expectations and interests of their black audience. When Sumner gave a lecture on the Constitution, the future senator went back and wrote in the margins the following notes to himself, circling each one: "3/5s of all persons," "slaves escaping," and "right to petition." In other words, he reminded himself to mention and emphasize those aspects of the Constitution relevant to black listeners in the age of the Gag Rule.[117]

The Union may have started with a mandate to discuss natural science, but it quickly morphed into an association interested in more political and philosophical issues. In the first lecture year, for instance, seven of ten identifiable addresses covered topics in the natural sciences, including "anatomy" and "electricity."[118] In fact, in its early years, the members of the Adelphic Union often referred to their organization as a scientific one. In the original meeting, the members dedicated a "literary and scientific society," with the hopes of addressing the problem that "not a sufficient degree of interest has been shown among us in anticipating the want of a practical Scientific institution."[119] In the first year, the only notable abolitionist to speak was Wendell Phillips, and even he chose a seemingly apolitical scientific theme: "Properties of the Atmosphere."[120]

By the end of the Adelphic Union's existence in the mid-1840s, however, the Union's lectures were much more self-consciously political. From 1845 to 1846, the last years for which we have good information, only one out of sixteen lecture topics was about natural science, while speakers were more likely to discuss historical, social, or political topics (nine out of sixteen of the lectures). Not only were speakers focusing on obviously political themes, such as "Duties of the American Citizen" and "Freedom of Speech and Inquiry," but the Union was inviting notorious radicals and controversial speakers—men and women such as Theodore Parker, Wendell Phillips, Maria Weston Chapman, and Angelina Grimké.[121] While the Adelphic Union had always framed itself as an organization dedicated to fighting racism, increasingly, the speakers were men and women who were explicitly known (notorious in some cases) as abolitionists. It is also worth emphasizing that the Union was willing to invite white women speakers to address a mostly black and male audience, a quite shocking thing to do at the time. William C. Nell admitted as much when, writing to

invite Maria Weston Chapman, he acknowledged that "this is somewhat an un-
usual, though not an unprecedented request," but "Miss. Grimké" had already
lectured to the Union.[122] This move to a more political understanding of itself
seems like a rebuke to some earlier white patrons, such as Edmund Quincy, who
conceived of the Union entirely in terms of individual uplift ("we do not assem-
ble to plot political changes," he told the Union in 1838).[123]

    This shift to a more political and less scientific intellectual life may echo a
broader cultural tendency, as scientific thought was becoming specialized and
technical. Benjamin Franklin's model of the small artisan-inventor was becoming less and less relevant to most lay Americans' experiences. More important,
though, with the rise of scientific racism, black intellectuals were growing wary
of mainstream science. Discussing scientific racism in 1839, the *Colored American* sadly acknowledged that "we had hoped for much from science" but were
disappointed as scientists seemed only interested in "popular applause."[124] The
turning away from science was also consistent with a Romantic disdain for the
type of instrumental logic embedded in the world of specialized science. Even
Thoreau, for instance, frequently criticized modern science as "almost as inhuman and wooden as a rain-gauge" and worried he would be laughed at by any
professional scientific organization because he cared about "science which deals
with a higher law."[125] In fact, black thinkers connected these concerns, arguing,
as the historian Patrick Rael has put it, that racial science "denied man's capacity and duty to 'elevate' those parts of the human character that could be developed: the mind and the morals."[126]

    It is remarkable how many Transcendentalists spoke in front of the Adel-
phic Union. The first and perhaps most important Romantic speaker was Alexander Crummell himself.[127] Unfortunately, the text of this speech has been
lost, but it was only after the black New York Romantic addressed the Adelphic
Union that the New Englanders began reaching out to local Transcendentalists. The black audience heard twice from Theodore Parker, a man whose heretical religious opinions had ostracized him from most white churches. Other
members of the famed Transcendentalist Club who spoke in front of the Adelphic Union included James Freeman Clarke, Karl Follen, William Henry
Channing, and Caleb Stetson. Lecturers who attended A. Bronson Alcott's
"conversations" included John Sargent and S. K. Lothrop. Transcendentalists
were demonstrating their antislavery political commitments, and black intellectuals were returning the favor with an appreciation for Transcendentalism.

    Karl Follen was a particularly interesting Transcendentalist speaker before
the Adelphic Union whose presence indicates the mutual and reinforcing af-

finities between black intellectuals, German idealism, American abolitionism, and the European left. Years after Follen's early and tragic death, William C. Nell would fondly remember his speeches to the Adelphic Union, recalling the "lamented" professor's appearances in an article in Frederick Douglass's *North Star*.[128] In Jena, Germany, Follen had helped lead the German democratic nationalist student movement. As a student, he had publicly advocated tyranicide, an awkward position to find himself in when a friend, Karl Ludwig Sand, assassinated a reactionary German writer. Sand, the assassin, lost his head, first metaphorically in a fit of mental illness, then in reality, when the Prussian state executed the hapless student. The incident provoked, among other things, a conservative reaction against liberal and nationalist thinkers in Germany, which may have led to Hegel's famous statement in the *Philosophy of Right* that "the rational is real and the real is rational," widely seen as a defensive attempt to placate the newly emboldened censors of the Prussian state. Follen, meanwhile, fled to Paris and then America. Recruited to be a professor of German languages at Harvard, his political life changed when he came upon David Walker's *Appeal*. Soon the scholar of Schiller and Goethe was helping to lead the Massachusetts Anti-Slavery Society and becoming a lonely voice from the Harvard establishment to support what his colleagues saw as the outrageous fringe of "ultraists" in the abolition movement.[129] As a Harvard professor of Germanic languages, he was a central intellectual figure for the early Transcendentalists, who were becoming obsessed with everything German, and was an early member of the famed Transcendentalist Club. He helped introduce the philosophical idealism of Victor Cousin, Schiller, Fichte, and Kant to America. Although he died in 1840 (William Lloyd Garrison named a son after him, as did the abolitionist father of famed architect Charles Follen McKim), Follen provided an important early link between European democratic radicalism, antislavery activism, and Transcendentalism.[130]

It was no coincidence that the Adelphic Union embraced Transcendentalism at the same time the club was becoming increasingly political. A brief return to Transcendentalist metaphysics can explain how they were laying the groundwork for a politicized selfhood. One key to Transcendentalist ideas about politics lay in their seemingly abstract belief that there was a doubleness to the human subject, torn between competing worlds of Reason and Understanding, the divine and the human, the ideal and the real, the numinous and the phenomenal. You can understand something of the doubleness that fascinated Transcendentalists—the tension between the inner and outer—by thinking about the seeming paradox of what we mean when we say something

like "I am in a bad mood because I am hungry." On one hand, Transcendentalists believed, it seems clear that we exist like everything else in the world of
cause and effect (hunger causes our mood to sour). But we are also aware that we
have part of our consciousness that seems more free, which can, as it were, stand
above this part of our self and observe our hunger and bad mood (the "I" in the
sentence). Are we the mood? Or the "I" observing the mood? To a large degree,
to be self-conscious is to be conscious *of* our self. We seem split between a part of
our self that is unfree, shaped by circumstance and physical necessity, and a part
of our self that is, at bare minimum, at least free enough to observe and com-
ment on that lower part of the self. William James would call this the distinction between the Transcendent Ego and the Empirical Ego—the strange fact
that, when we look inward, we are both the "knower" and "the known."[131] Confusing matters, of course, was the fact that the Empirical self is not purely derived from the external world; instead, as Coleridge had taught a generation of
American thinkers, our inner life and even unconscious itself can become an
object of observation. Still, the Transcendentalists believed, in the higher self
(Transcendental ego) lay freedom and autonomy, the possibility of exerting
power over the material sensations that shape our consciousness.

Transcendentalists were very nearly obsessed with this doubleness, with
the experience of this duality. Thoreau, ruminating from the banks of Walden
Pond, summarized this sense of internal twoness: "I only know myself as a
human entity; the scene, so to speak, of thoughts and affections; and am sensi-
ble of a certain doubleness by which I can stand as remote from myself as from
another."[132] In his sermons, Crummell returned over and over again to his belief that a Christian lived a double life. On one hand, "Man has an <u>inner</u> life
which determines his spiritual qualities." But "so too he has an <u>outer</u> life," by
which he is known to the public.[133] Likewise, Emerson's masterpiece essay "Experience" is a brilliant examination of that strange sense of being a spectator to
your own consciousness, the balance between our moods and temperaments
that constitute our windows on the world and some rude sense of an internal
self that observes and struggles to grasp ahold of these slippery and fleeting
states of consciousness. Fuller would sit and stare at her writing desk, wondering whether she was the person holding the pen or the person observing the
body holding the pen. Walt Whitman was alternately inspired and horrified by
the realization that there was a "real Me" that stood "untouch'd, untold, alto-
gether unreach'd," below his own capacious ego.[134]

The solution, and what became the key to their politics, was to demand a
dialogue between parts of the self. Freedom occurred, the Transcendentalists

thought, in the fertile mix of the given and the willed, the dialogue between a physical reality that shapes us and our consciousness that is free to shape itself. As Emerson wrote, good thinking lay between abstract consciousness—"the thin and cold realm of pure geometry"—and raw "sensation." He called this "the equator of life, of thought, of spirit, of poetry."[135] Fuller agreed: a consciousness who "remains imbedded in nature" would never understand the meaning of life, but nor would one who was so self-absorbed that they ignored the beauty and divinity that nature reveals.[136] While they always emphasized the importance of the higher parts of consciousness to compensate for society's dismissal of it, they still demanded a dialogue with the empirical world, a constant to and fro between these components of the self, an embrace of thinking as the two-in-one of a consciousness that was both observer and observed.[137] Through this doubleness, they thus avoided both the narrowness of a mechanical psychology and the self-indulgence of an idealism that would never realize itself in concrete action. Thoreau immersed himself in the sounds, sights, and animal life of Walden Pond. Emerson embraced the whims of his subconscious, the hidden wisdom found in the dark "chambers and magazines of the soul."[138] Whitman sang of the dusty open road, the joyful solidarity of mingling with rowdy crowds and haughty citizens of the street.

To think freely, then, for Transcendentalists required one to experience the world in all its bright and complex glory and then reflect on what one has learned, to open up a dialogue between the experiencing-self and the reflecting-self. This was more than simply the passive amalgamation of empirical and a priori knowledge sitting side by side in lumps next to each other; in the open dialogue between the self-that-experiences and the self-that-reflects, a sort of chemical reaction occurred, changing how you saw the knowledge created by both. Thoreau was convinced, for instance, that he saw beauty and meaning in the landscape of rural Massachusetts that others missed, exactly because he could view the growing oaks and rocky soil of New England through the lens of boundless consciousness—Reason—while his quietly desperate neighbors dully experienced it through the passive lens of Understanding. The problem, he believed, with "inhuman" and supposedly apolitical science was that it stopped at simply accumulating facts, which focused on "outward things merely" and did not link these facts to the "subjectivity" of human life.[139]

Thus, one way to think about Understanding—that form of logic and thinking that Emerson and Crummell so disdained—is that it is an unfree form of thought because it is bounded by our self-as-an-object, by the empirical ego. When Crummell worried about a mind shaped by things and the senses, this is what he was concerned about. Let's say you experience a physical sensation—hunger, for instance. And all do you is ask yourself, "How can I fulfill that desire?" Your mind may still have work to do—to figure out the means to satisfy that end. But you are not reflecting on that desire and you have, in a sense, simply turned your mind into a passive tool of that arbitrary sensation. Freedom, instead, requires that the higher part of the self—the self-as-subject— can apply Reason and morality to judge those facts. Reason, in a sense, was thinking that occurred when the Empirical Ego dialogued with the Transcendental Ego, when the self could act as a subject of itself, while Understanding was a form of thought that stopped at the Empirical Ego, which only took what was given to it by arbitrary nature and did not reflect on or examine those facts.

The phrase that Emerson would coin to describe this tense but productive psychological split between Reason and Understanding would have a long afterlife. He called it "double consciousness," a term that, famously, W. E. B. Du Bois would pick up to describe the phenomenology of the African American experience. For Du Bois, this Emersonian term would capture the "two-ness" born by living through the eyes and assumptions of others, as well as the creative tension created by a division between a spiritual African self and a materialistic American self.[140] Du Bois would emphasize, to a greater degree than Emerson, both the psychic costs of such an internal division, as well as the privileged existential position it granted African Americans. Under the conditions of racism, this doubleness was experienced as "two warring ideals in one dark body," a sort of internal self-alienation. But black Americans also had, Du Bois believed, a divine mission, offering America redemption by promising to reconcile these two contradictory aspects of the American self, to tame the cruelty and materialism that Du Bois saw as endemic to white America.

The Transcendentalist embrace of double consciousness—the productive play between abstract Reason and concrete Understanding—was the key to their politics. In the early 1840s, Emerson wrote two essays that captured how his epistemology and psychology shaped his politics: "Man the Reformer" and "The Conservative." In both, political orientations developed from prior psychological and philosophical commitments. The conservative, as a stock figure, sides with the empiricist commitment to facts, the fatalism of material life, history, and Understanding; the reformer lives in the Transcendentalist virtues of consciousness, hope, willpower, and Reason. A good reformer, of course, is aware that the reality to which the conservative constantly appeals cannot be ignored. But the reformer, Emerson believed, sees the given world as the starting point and seeks to use the powers of the human mind—consciousness, ethics, and morality—to remake that world. As Fuller said, "No true philosophy will try to ignore or annihilate the material part of man, but will rather seek to put it in its place, as servant and minister to the soul."[141] The doubleness of American Transcendentalism, its demand for a dialogue between experience and consciousness, fit well with a black radical tradition that understood well that it could not passively accept what Emerson called "the actual state of things" as given to them.[142]

Black abolitionists seemed particularly likely to appreciate the political values in Transcendentalism's message of double consciousness. For many, Transcendentalism offered a message of political hope, a sense of the power of their autonomy in the face of the seeming insurmountable injustice of antebellum America. Frederick Douglass, for instance, interpreted Emerson as an advocate of social hopefulness, a rejection of the pessimism of belatedness. The Transcendentalist evoked a hope in a world that we can imagine, a faith held even in the face of an empirical world that gives only despair. In his *North Star*, Douglass ran Emerson's line that "it is a mischievous notion that we are come late into nature; that the world was finished a long time ago. As the world was plastic and fluid in the hands of God, so it is ever to so much of his attribute as we bring to it."[143] Here, Emerson's command in *The American Scholar* that each generation must reexamine the truths of the world becomes a rallying cry that we are able and obligated to change it.

William C. Nell and Charlotte Forten
as Early Black Transcendentalists

No black thinker played a larger role linking Transcendentalism with abolitionism than the printer, activist, and historian William C. Nell. Born on December 16, 1816, to a free African American from Charleston, South Carolina, named William Guion Nell and Louisa Marshall, a Brookline native, Nell grew up free in Boston. He always resented his inability to visit "near and dear relations, unless at the risk of fines and imprisonment," who still lived in the South. Nell repeated too often, however, that he was "unable to trace my genealogy back to slavery" to be able to deny that he felt a distance from the less educated escaped slaves.[144] Like other African Americans born free in the North, he was torn between solidarity with Southern slaves and a certain pride in his free birth and better education. He always vacillated between pride in his hometown, where he would eventually discover an abolitionist community that embraced him, and an intense biting anger at the compromises of the city's rulers. His life exemplified the chasm between

William C. Nell

Figure 2. William C. Nell, leader of the Adelphic Union and "charge" of the Town and Country Club. Collection of the Massachusetts Historical Society.

the ideal of revolutionary Boston, the "Cradle of Liberty," and the reality of mercantile Boston, home to the Cotton Whigs and textile barons. Nell had difficulty finding stable work, as the usual employments attractive to ambitious and intelligent youth were closed to black men.

As if to prove wrong the racists who would not recognize his academic achievements, Nell actively cultivated the persona of the scholar and intellectual. By the early 1840s, he was the leader and most outspoken advocate of the Adelphic Union. He was also the driving force behind inviting such Transcendentalists as Theodore Parker, William Henry Channing, and others to speak in front of the black intellectual club. In addition to his leadership in the Adelphic Union, Nell had long and lasting connections with important Transcendentalists. In the 1850s, he served as a deacon in Theodore Parker's 28th Congregational Society and often attended Parker's lectures with Lewis Hayden and others.[145] He attended A. Bronson Alcott's conversations, discussing "Social Life" with a group of Transcendentalists, including William H. Channing, Charlotte Dall, and Alcott himself.[146] Nell was drawn to Ralph Waldo Emerson as well. He likely first met Emerson while working in the Town and Country Club in the late 1840s. In 1852, Nell mentioned in a letter to William Lloyd Garrison that he had heard Emerson speak and "appreciated" his lecture while implying a familiarity with Emerson's speaking style.[147] Referring to Emerson as one of the "ever-to-be-honored friends of equal rights," Nell was particularly grateful for Emerson's appeal against segregated lyceums, a cause dear to Nell's heart.[148] In 1857, Nell began selling seven different "lithographic Prints" of various "Champions of Freedom," including an image of Emerson, along with abolitionist mainstays such as Garrison, Phillips, and Gerrit Smith.[149]

Transcendentalism may have a reputation for individualism, but in Nell's hands, it seems to have become a way to solidify friendships based on shared devotion to black "elevation." The relationship between William C. Nell and the New Bedford black abolitionist Jeremiah Burke Sanderson was a particularly close and intellectually stimulating friendship premised, in part, on their shared interest in Transcendentalism. Sanderson was a barber in 1840 when he met Nell and became more involved in abolitionist activities.[150] Throughout the early 1840s, they exchanged a series of passionate, almost daily, letters on everything from the state of abolition, the racial prejudice that they had encountered, and the means of elevation. Sanderson would even name a son after Nell. Like Nell, Sanderson became interested in Transcendentalism and when, in 1848, he began preaching, his sermons were laced with quotations from "Emerson, Carlyle, and Theodore Parker."[151] Like Nell, Sanderson, who had been arrested trying to desegregate the New Bedford Railroad, was particularly moved by Emerson's support for the desegregation of the New Bedford Lyceum, writing to Frederick Douglass that "my heart reverenced" Emerson's "noble rebuke of the injustice."[152]

For Nell and Sanderson, "elevation" was a keyword that denoted a whole project of individual and communal self-development. Although deriving in many ways from unique black sources, the elevation impulse bares some comparison to the German ideal of *bildung* or the Unitarian value of self-culture. Historians have long debated what exactly black leaders meant when they called on their followers to "elevate" themselves. Was the call for "elevation" evidence of conservative capitulation among black elites, who pushed an emerging bourgeois sensibility of personal striving, restraint, and self-improvement on their working-class followers? Or was elevation understood to be a communal value, as the whole community raised its standing in the world?

During the heyday of the Adelphic Union, the meaning of "elevation" became more political and less oriented solely toward individual goals. The history of organizations such as the Adelphic Union, with their roots in transatlantic engagement with post-revolutionary Haiti and radicals such as David Walker, should dispel any idea that these sets of ideas were apolitical.[153] A person who lacked the ability to elevate oneself, black intellectuals feared, was condemned to second-class citizenship. Writing to attain clemency for Washington Goode, a black sailor condemned to death in 1849, John Hilton, a leader of the Adelphic Union, sought clemency for Goode on the grounds that he "belongs to a race against whom a cruel prejudice paralyzes his efforts at self-improvement, shuts the halls of lyceums against him, banishes him to separate schools . . . and deprives him up the best means of education."[154] Black statements of the period consistently linked the theme of elevation to the issue of slavery.[155] Benjamin Roberts's short-lived 1853 newspaper, the *Self-Elevator*, explicitly linked elevation to political equality. After denying that he wished to "engage in political strife" or to "be identified with sectarianism in any form," Roberts explained that his project was the "General Improvement among the Colored People." This was partly about fighting for more employment opportunities and training. But the end result, Roberts was clear, would be "the elevation of the colored people to the common position with other citizens in our great community."[156] The term "elevation," then, captured a wide range of personal, political, and moral aspirations.

It is worthwhile to consider the black celebration of elevation in conversation with Emerson's call for "self-reliance." After all, Nell and other black boosters of the Adelphic Union were not the only people calling for the elevation of individuals in ways that suggested a complicated interplay between economic self-improvement, Romantic striving for fullness, and political commitment. In arguably the most famous American essay ever, Emerson's *Self-Reliance*, the white Transcendentalist celebrated the individual who sought to stand apart from society in spiritual if not physical terms. Such a developing celebration of one's own faculties Emerson called, among other things, "elevation."[157] Emerson's essay, which would be read and referenced by black leaders throughout the antebellum period, was consistent in many ways with black ideas of elevation, even sharing many of the contradictions of the black elevation ideology. Just as black boosters of elevation would often be interpreted as accepting the logic of capitalism, so would Emerson's essay—despite his claim that "the reliance on Property" demonstrated a lack of self-reliance—be misread by generations of robber barons as nothing but a philosophical justification for the capitalist virtues. Just as the elevation ideology balanced the need for individual self-growth with communal regeneration, so Emerson, throughout his life, tried to rebut accusations that his philosophy was simply one of selfishness.

Fundamentally, *Self-Reliance* shared with the elevation boosters a concern for the limits that individuals faced in their search for full self-development. And while commentators then and now tend to focus most on the external limits that Emerson criticizes—social pressure to conform, small-minded moralism, or unthinking religious belief—he was in reality as concerned with the internal limits that people place on themselves: instrumental logics that master your conscience, foolish consistency to past opinions, or the fear to heed the whims and instincts that reveal divine truth better than a dogged scientific reason ever could. Fundamentally a text borne out of an encounter with modernity, *Self-Reliance* is the product of a world in which the older foundations of self-making (religion, tradition, culture, and even stable philosophical truths) have all demonstrated their inner emptiness and in which individuals are forced back on themselves to understand their naked existence as needing a process of eternal becoming in order to match the dizziness of modern life. Similarly, the black call for "elevation" demanded a change in inner orientation as much as an accumulation of knowledge. For theorists such as Crummell and Nell, "elevation" was a process intended to give black men and women the inner resources to survive in a racist world, both the knowledge required to succeed and the inner confidence to face the constant racial hostility of the antebellum North.

It should be no surprise, then, that abolitionists frequently spoke of "self-reliance" to describe their political and social goals. Within years of the 1841 publication of Emerson's famous essay, for instance, Henry Clapp Jr. (still in his earnest abolitionist phase and not yet the bon vivant bohemian he would become) could declare that "anti-slavery has no lesson which it teaches so plainly as the great lesson of *self-reliance*."[158] But it was black abolitionists who most productively adapted Emerson's language. In 1848, Frederick Douglass took to the *North Star* to complain of the spirit that "robs us of all manly self-reliance" while calling for greater black participation in abolitionism and in elevation movements.[159] A black newspaper published in Canada declared that "our motto must therefore be self-reliance," a trait the editors defined as the development of the free black community and emancipation in America.[160] After immigrating to Liberia, Alexander Crummell often deployed the term in his religious and political sermons, an interesting example of how the term traversed the Black Atlantic.[161] And in 1865, J. Sella Martin told a British audience that his time with newly liberated slaves had taught him that the length and severity of slavery meant that the freedpeople could not be expected to instantaneously "spring into habits of self-respect and self-reliance."[162] As late as 1894, John Mercer Langston, who had met Emerson while serving as the dean of the Howard Law School, had "Self-Reliance[,] the Secret of Success," serve as the epigram in his autobiography.[163]

The point is that when black boosters of the Adelphic Union celebrated elevation as the key to personal and communal empowerment, they were participating in and contributing to the same broad conversation about the relationship between individual fulfillment and social regeneration that Emerson was in *Self-Reliance* and Thoreau was in *Walden*. When Charles Reason, the first black professor in an American college, told a black audience in Boston that elevation was dependent on an appreciation for "the proper dignity of man," he was echoing Transcendentalist claims on behalf of sanctity of the individual self.[164] Or perhaps Transcendentalists were echoing the claims of people such as Reason. The elevation ideology has to be seen as part of a Romantic interest in creating a heroic individual, one that could never be reduced to mechanistic or degraded visions of the self and could stand proud and determined against oppression. Black boosters were primarily concerned with ways that social oppression—racism, unemployment, and, above all, slavery—reduced people's ability to develop their true potential. Emerson himself was not blind to the ways that social arraignments were capable of limiting the self, singling out, along with love of property, narrow-minded churches and self-serving politicians. Soon, he too would come to understand slavery as the preeminent threat to individual flourishing in America.

Charlotte Forten also demonstrated the close black engagement with Transcendentalism. When Forten moved to New England as a precocious teenager, Nell's model of the intellectual activist was immediately appealing to her. Forten, who came from one of the wealthiest and most distinguished black families in the North, only moved to Massachusetts in 1854.[165] Unable to find a desegregated school in Philadelphia, her father had sent her north, where she stayed with Charles Lenox Remond's family in Salem and befriended Nell, a frequent visitor to the house. Forten was perpetually torn between the conflicting lures of respectability and radicalism, between a desire to live as a refined Victorian middle-class lady and her commitment to racial justice and antislavery, which kept putting her in the company of bohemians and revolutionaries. Mediating these interests, combining her antislavery commitments with her intellectual curiosity, was her interest in New England Transcendentalism, which blossomed during the 1850s.

Starting in 1854, when she moved to Salem from Philadelphia, Forten immersed herself in the world of New England Transcendentalism. As often as possible, she attended the Salem Lyceum, which fed her a heavy dose of Transcendentalism and abolitionist radicalism.[166] She read James Freeman Clarke, talked with feminist and Transcendentalist Caroline Healey Dall, often attended Theodore Parker's church, and visited his house to talk with him and examine his library. She was particularly drawn to Emerson.[167] She read *English Traits*, "which I very much like," as she put it; heard him lecture on topics as diverse as "Beauty" and "France"; and even compared other speakers negatively to Emerson. In her journal, she mentions attending at least five different lectures by him and reading his work at six different times.[168] Her Transcendentalism and abolitionism were intertwined; in one mundane but telling example, she reported running into Wendell Phillips and talking politics with the abolitionist at an Emerson lecture.[169]

Like her white Transcendentalist friends, Forten was a pastoralist, spending evenings walking by herself through the fields and hills outside Salem. But to see her pastoralism as contradictory to her politics would be a misjudgment. Like Thoreau, Forten saw a radical political argument in every clear blue sky. In a poem that she wrote for the graduation of the State Normal School in 1856, she claimed that selfish, greedy, and ambitious people suffered because "the voice of Nature is by them unheard. They see no beauty in the wavering trees."[170] Critics have noticed how she often juxtaposed pastoral scenes of unspoiled nature with images of how slavery degraded the country.[171] Just as Thoreau, confronted with the degradation of Boston authorities who returned Anthony Burns, took solace in the purity of the waterlily rising out of the muck and decay, so Forten, in her journal, turned from describing the worst of slavery with images of the natural beauty that surrounded her. "A beautiful day," she wrote in 1854, as a fugitive slave was kidnapped off the streets of Boston. "The sky is cloudless. . . . How strange it is that in a world so beautiful, there can be so much wickedness, on this delightful day, while many are enjoying themselves in their happy homes, not poor Burns only, but millions besides are suffering in chains."[172] Nature, whose boundlessness Forten saw as both spiritual comfort and a majestic judge, stood in stark contrast and silent condemnation to the white Bostonians who would sell themselves to the slave power. Even in moments of joy—as when she began a story about the impact of the Emancipation Proclamation by noting the "deep blue sky, with soft white clouds"—Forten came back to imagery that evoked limitless nature.[173] For Forten, slavery took the place of factories or railroads, as disturbing signs of modernity gone awry, what Leo Marx called "machines in the garden," which disrupted her pastoralism and her Romantic "relatedness" with nature, rupturing her ties to the natural world and highlighting the spiritually draining aspects of a slave system premised on such inhumanity.[174]

Nell and Forten were not alone; many black intellectuals in antebellum America read and admired canonical Transcendentalism. James McCune Smith read and cited Emerson, taking from the philosopher a sense that racial characteristics were not essential but contingent and capable of development.[175] H. Ford Douglass quoted from Emerson's essay *History* on the nature of laws in order to condemn American slavery.[176] A black correspondent for the *Anglo-African*, writing in 1862, declared that anyone who wondered why they were fighting the Civil War needed only to study the words of prominent abolitionists and "muse over the philosophy of Emerson."[177] Frederick Douglass was appreciative of Emerson's antislavery work and used Emersonian themes in his famous lyceum lecture, "Self-Made Men."[178] Edward Wilmot Blyden, the black emigrationist leader, quoted Emerson's belief in the superiority of "moral sentiment" over the "influences of climate" to explain why Africa "will furnish a development of civilization which the world has never yet witnessed."[179] James Monroe Whitfield wrote a poem in tribute to "Self-Reliance."[180] Robert Morris, the pioneering black lawyer in Boston, kept a tattered copy of an 1845 newspaper clipping of an Emerson speech his entire life.[181] Ednah Dow Cheney would long remember the words of an anonymous enslaved South Carolinian who had stumbled upon an antislavery Emerson speech in 1856 and "told how they had been an inspiration and a strength to him ever afterward."[182]

In the pages of black newspapers and publications, Transcendentalism spread. The rise of a black print culture gave African American intellectuals the ability to control their own intellectual message for the first time. Frederick Douglass's papers were especially attuned to Emerson, often using quotations or epigrams of his to fill in spaces on the pages (a common practice in nineteenth-century papers). Douglass pointedly defended Emerson's abolitionist credentials. In 1855, the black abolitionist published an article detailing Emerson's history in the movement in order to rebut a *New York Evening Post* article that had called Emerson a "recent anti slavery man."[183] Douglass's papers often ran selections of Emerson's writings—as they did on February 25, 1848, when they reprinted a passage from *Nature*.[184] Douglass even wrote to Emerson in 1850, asking for a review copy of Emerson's *Representative Men*.[185] In 1854, Emerson contributed a poem—"On Freedom"—to an anthology intended to raise money for *Frederick Douglass' Newspaper*.[186] In 1855, that same paper reported on his lectures—remarking that "to the mind of such a man as Mr. Emerson, the merely *visible* part of things has very little interest . . . showed, with his own *unique* richness of ideas, the real foundation of slavery."[187] Douglass seemed like a particularly avid reader of Emerson, but he was not the only black editor to reprint the Concord Transcendentalist. The South was, generally speaking, not fertile territory for Transcendentalists, but the *New Orleans Daily Creole* must have had a Transcendentalist editor. Not only did the editors reprint selections from Emerson, but they even were reading *Walden*, Thoreau's masterpiece, which was received so poorly in the white press.[188] In 1856, when Thoreau was still largely ignored among white Northerners, the *Daily Creole* chose to reprint Thoreau's famous description of a battle between ants.[189]

The Adelphic Union stopped meeting in 1847. Nell accepted Frederick Douglass's offer to assist with a new paper to be published in Rochester, New York, and the absence of the energetic leader largely doomed efforts to continue the Union. Meanwhile, a rival intellectual club formed in 1845, the Young Men's Literary Society, headed by Isaac Snowden, kept alive the mission of the Adelphic Union while siphoning off members.[190] Although the Literary Society kept a lower profile than Nell's Adelphic Union, it lasted at least until the fugitive slave crisis and continued to be a link between African American intellectual life and political activity. The Young Men's Literary Society was particularly active in the fight to desegregate the Boston public school system.[191] Increasingly, though, black abolitionists were encountering white Transcendentalists in the very institutions of abolitionism. Perhaps they no longer needed separate organizations where they would invite Transcendentalists to speak. Abolition was becoming Transcendentalized and vice versa.

CHAPTER 2

The Latest Forms of Infidelity

If slavery seemed abstract to some white thinkers, it was a brutal fact to Lewis Hayden. Born in Kentucky, his master sold his parents away from Hayden at a young age. His mother was bought by a man who wished to sexually abuse her. When she refused his entreaties, she was beaten and jailed and soon descended into what Hayden called "crazy turns." Suicidal, she tried to kill herself and once assaulted Hayden himself, hoping to spare him, perhaps she thought, a lifetime of slavery. In occasional moments of lucidity, she would pull Hayden close and whisper about the horrors she had seen. Having sold his parents, Hayden's master then swapped Hayden himself for a pair of carriage horses. Long afterward, he would bitterly remember this insult. Given a chance to examine the animals that his master valued more than him, he "walked round them, and thought for *them* I was sold!"[1] Yet Hayden's sufferings weren't over. His first marriage ended in tragedy when his wife and young son were sold to Henry Clay, the world-famous Whig politician who soon sent them "down the river."[2] Years later, from the safety of Boston, he would shudder thinking about his long-lost child—"I can never bear to think of" his son, he confided to Harriet Beecher Stowe.

Hayden could never be repaid for his loss, but he did, in his own way, get revenge on Clay. Years later, the ex-slave would lead one of the most remarkable and famous violations of the Fugitive Slave Law, a law that Clay had helped to pass. Clay probably did not know, as he sputtered in rage on the Senate floor about "people not of our race" who had stymied the enforcement of the law, that his own heartless sale of Hayden's wife and son had set in motion the events that brought Hayden to Boston to lead resistance to the law.[3]

Sometime in 1844, Hayden met a white man named Calvin Fairbank and his partner Delia Webster. Of abolitionist sympathies, the two had been secretly assisting fugitives. Testing him out, Fairbank asked Hayden—working at this point as a waiter in a hotel—why he wanted his freedom. "Because I am a man," Hayden responded without missing a beat, and Fairbank at once began to plan a way for his escape.[4]

Soon, Hayden and his new wife, Harriet, were on their way to the North, eventually ending up in Boston. There he would become a community leader—a prominent activist, leader in the Prince Hall Masons, clothing salesman, and eventually a Republican politician. During Hayden's escape, though, Fairbank and Webster had been caught and imprisoned. Penniless and in a foreign city, Hayden nonetheless took it upon himself to raise the money to "buy" his own freedom, thus emancipating Fairbank. For help, Hayden turned to a white Transcendentalist: James Freeman Clarke, who invited the fugitive to speak before his congregation. Through Clarke, Hayden received a $29 donation from Theodore Parker, another white Transcendentalist.[5] The ex-slave and Clarke would develop a lifelong friendship and working relationship.[6] As late as 1888, Hayden could be found visiting Clarke and writing personal letters to him and his wife.[7] Hayden would also have a close working relationship with Parker, especially in the 1850s, when they collaborated in the Boston Vigilance Committee to protect slaves.

It was probably through his connection to Clarke that Hayden soon found himself in Walden woods, working with the leaders of Transcendentalism. The local abolitionist society had invited Hayden to speak before the 1846 celebration of the anniversary of British emancipation in the Caribbean. The talk took place in what the *Liberator* described as the "best of all groves" in the Concord woods: right by the famous Walden Pond.[8] Thoreau was almost certainly present, and one historian has speculated that it may have been this rally that convinced him to write up his recent experiences with tax refusal and submit it to *Aesthetic Papers*, the essay that we have come to know as *On Civil Disobedience*.[9] Thinking about the meaning of his own freedom, one can imagine Thoreau thrilling to the ex-slave recounting, "what a glorious thing liberty is," as Hayden did. The speakers on this clear August day combined the famous and obscure: Ralph Waldo Emerson spoke before the unknown Hayden.[10]

It is easy to assume that there was little connection between the hard struggles that marked Hayden's life and the privileged white Transcendentalism of Concord dreamers. But Hayden's story in Boston blurs these lines. When the antislavery activist Thomas Wentworth Higginson later wrote that abolitionism had saved Transcendentalism from being too "vague and dreamy," perhaps

Figure 3. After escaping from Kentucky slavery, Lewis Hayden opened up a successful clothing business in Boston, helped lead the protection of fugitive slaves, and eventually became a Republican politician.
Courtesy of the Ohio History Connection.

he was thinking about moments like this, when thinkers such as Thoreau and Emerson were forced to face, head on, individuals and stories from the slave South.[11] Whether or not white Transcendentalists such as Emerson wanted to "avert their eyes" from slavery, as they are sometimes accused of doing, because of black radicals such as Hayden, they were forced to constantly confront its terrors.[12] In fact, black abolitionists such as Hayden, William C. Nell, and others had close connection with many antebellum Transcendentalists, helping to politicize and radicalize them.

In the daily encounters of abolitionist activism, antislavery radicals and Transcendentalists met each other. They were both movements of the fringe, associated with radical outcasts in New England society. Little illustrated this better than John Quincy Adams's irascible reaction when he was subjected to a "stream of transcendentalism," given by a guest preacher at his otherwise respectable Unitarian church. Taking to his journal, he diagnosed the cultural problem: "a young man, named Ralph Waldo Emerson . . . starts a new doctrine of transcendentalism." Like some perverted Pandora's Box, out rushed all the misfits of New England society: "Garrison and the non-resistants, abolitionists, Brownson and the Marat democrats, phrenology and animal magnetism, all come in, furnishing each some plausible rascality as an ingredient for the bubbling cauldron of religion and politics."[13]

"Plausible rascalities." Adams tempered his annoyance with a certain world-weary indulgence toward these deluded idealists. Others were less patient. They saw Transcendentalism and abolitionism as linked to a breakdown in gender and racial hierarchies. Transcendentalists were thrown in with the "odds and ends of creation," as one journalist described them, along with "female lecturers," "blacks," abolitionists, and other outsiders.[14] Another hostile paper would describe the audience of a Wendell Phillips lecture as a "straggling audience of unsexed women, wondering negroes and long-haired transcendentalists."[15] Along with the intense fear of racial and sexual disorder that these accounts demonstrate, they show the degree to which Transcendentalism was linked with marginalized figures—feminists, blacks, "Marat democrats," religious enthusiasts, and, most of all, radical abolitionists.

There is another aspect of Hayden's story worth considering. His owner, the man who had sold him, had been a minister, one Adam Rankin, who had "said in the pulpit that there was no more harm in separating a family of slaves than a litter of pigs."[16] When Hayden addressed the Concord crowd, a reporter noted the conspicuous absence of the town's "orthodox minister," scared away by the possible association of the event with William Lloyd Garrison. The religiously heterodox—such as the plebian Universalists and the bohemian Transcendentalists—instead dominated the event. The linkages between Transcendentalism and abolitionism cannot be understood outside of the context of their shared rebellion against proslavery and mainstream forms of Christianity.

Both Transcendentalism and abolitionism gained social power, in part, because they were experienced as rebellions against mainstream forms of religious life. Abolitionists had originally hoped to work within the established evangelical churches, but as they realized how hostile most sects were, they increasingly looked elsewhere to unorthodox spiritual movements such as Transcendentalism for support. While many abolitionists continued to draw on Quaker, Unitarian, and other Christian forms of belief, the movement as a whole helped to undermine, rather than support, traditional religious authority in the North. Likewise, while it is true that Transcendentalism developed out of the desire to reinvigorate the Unitarian faith, it quickly became the first popular American intellectual movement that broke free of the confines of the Church. Abolitionists and Transcendentalists participated in the strange dialectic that characterized much Protestant reform: attempting to defend piety from the corruption of manmade idols, they undermined the actual existing churches and its authority. The problem with the mainstream churches was that they were, in a sense, not religious enough: they channeled and controlled the spirit of religious searching rather than allow it to inform political struggle. In their attitudes toward religion, one can see an important component of the Higher Law Ethos: their democratization of the infinite, a desire that politics be rooted in some set of spiritual values higher than the everyday, yet still not controlled by any priest or authority.

It was, for radical New England, an era of fervent experimentation, as the collapse of religious authority contributed to a more general cultural democratization—the "bubbling cauldron," as John Quincy Adams had called it—of antebellum American reform. Interpretations that view them as moralistic bourgeois reformers miss the democratic enthusiasm—what Irving Howe called their "mood of expansiveness"—the utopian fire and, at times, the wonderful oddity of abolitionist and Transcendentalist thought in the 1840s. Once liberated from church control, their boundless style of thinking gave their movement a centrifugal energy that spun out into women's rights, food reform, Non-Resistance, peace movements, tax refusal, and everywhere else that an enthusiastic and enflamed conscience might go.[17] As Transcendentalists and abolitionists increasingly encountered each other as allies in these various movements, they forged personal and intellectual connections that drew the two groups closer.

Transcendentalism and Abolitionism
Against Orthodoxy

From the start, the contemporary fights over abolition and slavery formed a crucial backdrop for Transcendentalist literature. In "Prospects," the eighth chapter of his 1836 book *Nature*, Emerson prophesied about the future reign of Reason. While currently, Emerson wrote, "man applies to nature but half his force," there were portents of a coming better day, chiefly religious reforms but also "the abolition of the Slave-trade."[18] Even Orestes Brownson, who often personally clashed with abolitionists, in his 1836 book *New Views on Christianity, Society, and the Church*, declared that in the coming future, "Man will shudder at the bare idea of enslaving so noble a being as man."[19] At a purely rhetorical and aesthetic level, almost every canonical Transcendentalist text, from *Self-Reliance* to *Leaves of Grass*, relied heavily on imagery from the fights over slavery that abolitionists such as David Walker and Garrison had forced into the public sphere. At deeper conceptual and philosophical levels, abolitionism and Transcendentalism soon became linked.

But sympathizing with abolitionist martyrs from the safety of their Concord parlors did not necessarily mean the Transcendentalists wished to accept the perils of antislavery activism themselves. While black Romantics in New York and Boston always centered slavery in their thought, white Transcendentalists did not—at least at first. Theodore Parker remembered that he had barely noticed the 1835 mobbing of Garrison because "I was so lost in Hebrew, and Grecian, and German metaphysics."[20] Emerson's early antislavery utterances in the late 1830s were cautious—at this stage, he was probably closest to the position of his former Unitarian mentor, William Ellery Channing, whose 1835 book *Slavery* condemned the peculiar institution but distanced himself from the vehemence and intolerance of Garrisonian abolitionists. Emerson's library records indicate that throughout the 1830s, he was reading extensively about slavery—including works by abolitionists such as Abbe Raynal and Thomas Clarkson.[21] His bravest act in support of abolition was probably when, while still a minister at the prestigious Second Church, he opened his church doors to radical Garrisonians to speak before his congregation.[22] But both Emerson and his friend Margaret Fuller largely refused to publicly identify with the abolitionists during this period. James Freeman Clarke, an important white Transcendentalist who would later become a prominent antislavery preacher, served as a Unitarian minister in Kentucky in the 1830s. While in the South, he professed his dislike of slavery but praised the rival colonization movement and declared the principles of Garrisonian abolitionists to be "false, and the consequences of their efforts evil."[23] William Henry Channing, who would also one day become a radical abolitionist, was, in the 1830s, "bitterly prejudiced against the Abolitionists," perhaps on account of their virulent attacks on his uncle, William Ellery Channing.[24] In 1834, the young Channing joined the Cambridge Antislavery Society, a moderate rival of Garrison's that reflected the genteel moralism of the Harvard elite.[25] As late as 1840, abolitionist Edmund Quincy attended a meeting and was outraged to see the Transcendentalist minister Theodore Parker—not normally one to conceal his opinions—refuse to take sides in a discussion on slavery. "Alas!" Quincy complained, "How long & difficult is the route by which a Unitarian minister is transformed into a Man!" Later, when Parker finally threw his lot in with the abolitionists, Quincy interpreted it as a rejection of "Emersonian" aloofness.[26] And Maria Weston Chapman worried that, in the 1830s, "hundreds of young persons have made him [Emerson] their excuse for avoiding the anti slavery battle."[27]

The irascible Transcendentalist Orestes Brownson contributed to the abolitionists' distrust of the Concord set. Brownson was a difficult and argumentative man who had climbed from New Hampshire rural poverty into the center of New England intellectuals. His whirlwind religious career had already swept him through Congregationalism, Universalism, and Unitarianism and had, for now, deposited him among the Transcendentalists (Lydia Maria Child joked that Brownson "seems to stay in any spiritual residence a much shorter time than the New Yorkers do in their houses").[28] But Brownson happened to be in his Transcendentalist phase when, in 1838, he started a high-profile feud with the abolitionists by writing a scathing review of an antislavery book. Although he claimed to dislike slavery, Brownson attacked abolitionists' vitriolic language, their "exceedingly narrow and crude" publications, and denied that Northerners had moral grounds on which to attack Southern slavery.[29] He earned himself, of course, a stinging rebuke from the *Liberator*, which declared him a "Judas-like personage . . . notorious by his treachery to the cause of freedom and humanity."[30] Brownson's hostility to abolition, like almost everything else in his life, was sui generis, and in fact, many other Transcendentalists personally disliked him. Within a decade, he had forsaken his earlier Transcendentalism and, swinging from one religious extreme to the other, finally settled on

Catholicism, becoming the most prominent voice for Catholic conservative organicism in American life. His conversion, in October 1844, a coup for the embattled American bishops, removed the only real anti-abolitionist from the cadres of Transcendentalism.

As Brownson's example illustrates, a certain amount of the early distance between the movements can be chalked up simply to personality conflicts. Margaret Fuller remembered finding the abolitionists "so tedious, often so narrow, always so rabid and exaggerated in their tone."[31] During the 1830s and early 1840s, white Boston abolitionism was dominated by the "Boston Clique," a small group including Garrison himself, Wendell Phillips, Maria Weston Chapman, Edmund Quincy, Lydia Maria Child, and Francis Jackson. Other than Garrison, the Boston Clique came from wealthy backgrounds. Bitter, in many cases, about the social ostracism their abolitionism had brought them, they developed a tight insider dynamic that brooked little criticism. Some, especially Quincy, were capable of nasty racist outbursts, and few were socially comfortable around the working-class and middle-class adherents of their movement. Nor did they promote black abolitionists or introduce them to their inner circle. To some degree, Transcendentalists were, at this early stage, just another rival group competing for followers and public attention. Julia Ward Howe was later embarrassed at how hostile she had been to both Emerson and Fuller, remembering that, at an early run-in with Emerson, she "thought that he was only a more charming personation of Satan" and that she dismissed with a sneer his gentle suggestion that she befriend Margaret Fuller.[32]

Nor were Transcendentalists always easy to love. Perhaps it was no coincidence that one of Emerson's most famous poems is "The Sphinx," as there was a certain distant mystery to the personality of antebellum America's greatest intellectual. He often felt awkward at social events and disliked political confrontations. He was capable of the most passionate and private grief but would project a detached serenity that sometimes bordered on insensitivity—as when he seemed to suggest that the death of his beloved son did not "touch me . . . falls off from me, and leaves no scar." Both Thoreau and Fuller were transformed by their friendship with him but also ending up feeling disappointed, as if he would pull back when they got too close. One young visitor recalled that "one always felt in Emerson's society that there was an invisible barrier between yourself and him."[33] It is easy to imagine how Emerson's seeming aloofness might have infuriated men and women who were risking their life for a great cause. Although Emerson came to admire Garrison immensely, they were never warm personal friends. To be fair, coincidence and farce played a role in the early abolitionist distrust of Emerson: there was a reactionary theologian at Andover named Ralph Emerson, who signed a number of anti-abolitionist petitions in the 1830s. This Ralph Emerson incurred the public wrath of Maria Weston Chapman, earned himself a column in the *Liberator*'s "Refuge of Oppression," and confused abolitionists at the time and has almost certainly confused historians, who easily mistook the Andover theologian for the Concord idealist.[34]

There were exceptions to the social frigidity that existed between white Transcendentalists and abolitionists in the 1830s. In 1838, the *Liberator* reprinted and praised Emerson's letter to President van Buren protesting the treatment of the Cherokee tribe.[35] The most prominent individual to link the movements was Lydia Maria Child, who became one of the most important intermediaries between the two worlds. An accomplished novelist before she entered the abolitionist movement, Child was a personal friend of many of the early Transcendentalists (she mentored a young Margaret Fuller) and curious—if sometimes skeptical—about the religious reforms they suggested. "Circumstances afterwards made me acquainted with the transcendentalists," she wrote toward the end of her life, "and I attended some of their meetings, where I saw plenty of fog with rainbows flitting over it."[36] This description of Transcendentalism as abstract and airy, with occasional bursts of profound truth scattered throughout, was a common and enduring view of Transcendentalist writing. Child's series "Letters from New York," which appeared in the *National Anti-Slavery Standard* in the early 1840s, frequently quoted Emerson, along with a series of other Romantic heroes such as "Wordsworth . . . Herder, Schiller, and Jean Paul."[37] Samuel J. May, Garrison's close associate and early member of the abolitionist inner circle, also had intimate connections with Transcendentalists, in this case A. Bronson Alcott. May's sister married the Transcendentalist philosopher—explaining why their daughter Louisa would sport the middle name May—and Alcott became an early supporter of the Massachusetts Anti-Slavery Society. Too concerned, however, with mapping the psyche of the universe to pay rent, Alcott leaned heavily on the financial resources of his abolitionist brother-in-law (it was people such as Alcott who inspired the joke that Transcendentalists were a "race who dove into the infinite, soared into the illimitable, and never paid cash"), so perhaps this particular intimacy strained the Transcendentalist-abolitionist alliance as much as it helped it.[38]

But the early tension between Transcendentalism and abolitionism was not simply personal. Another source of conflict was that Emerson, like Thoreau after him, detested cheap moralizing and often adopted the cocky pose of the anti-moralist rebel in his writings, with a certain bohemian contempt for the hypocrisy of the prudish New England middle class. Emerson surely wanted to shock his audience when, in *Self-Reliance*, he urged readers to follow even those impulses that came from the devil. But he was making a real point: an honest relationship to the universe and to one's self, he believed, was a more important ethical task than conforming to outside rules of right and wrong. This anti-moral stance obviously sometimes put Transcendentalists in conflict with the abolitionists' strident moral crusade. In a widely cited passage in *Self-Reliance*, Emerson wrote that "if an angry bigot assumes this bountiful cause of Abolition ... why should I not say to him 'Go love thy infant; love thy wood-chopper ... never varnish your hard, uncharitable ambition with this incredible tenderness for black folk a thousand miles off."[39] With typical Emersonian psychological acuity, he was suggesting that, while abolition is a just cause ("bountiful"), many activists were attracted to such a pure moral crusade exactly because it's obvious righteousness shielded them from their own anxiety, granting them a false moral pride that silenced the uneasiness in their souls. Throughout his life, Emerson would be drawn to thinkers who adopted a certain devilish amoralism; he preferred honest rogues to the cant of insincere reformers. For instance, though he was embarrassed by his friend Thomas Carlyle's racism and elitism, he still admired the Scottish writer's sincere disdain for the "rosepink sentimentality" of many British reformers.[40] Rather than be morbidly obsessed with guilt, as some historians have suggested, Transcendentalists such as Emerson were concerned that an elevation of simplistic morality risked the creation of not just hypocrites but also profoundly shallow people who thought that the crooked manifold of life's struggles could be solved by unthinking obedience to some external tablet of moral codes.[41]

Of course, Emerson was not a nihilist opposed to moral judgment. Instead, to Transcendentalists, the internal state of political actors and the motivations that drew them to political commitments were as important as the actual content of their politics. Abolitionists, Emerson feared, started from the position of solving an outward and social evil and then twisted their internal compass to meet those external demands, when true ethical behavior did the opposite. Because he so valued the integrity of these sparks of what he would come to call the "Oversoul," the grand oceanic spirit of the universe, Emerson embraced the idea that all of one's impulses, even the dark ones, should be heeded. "Good and bad," he wrote, with premonitions of Nietzsche, "are but names very readily transferable to this or that; the only right is what is after my constitution."[42] Philosophically optimistic, Emerson assumed that those impulses, manifestations of the Oversoul in us, would generally lead to good but considered obedience to them the most important ethical task. Eventually, by the 1850s, abolitionists would embrace the value of self-expressive politics, synthesizing abolitionist moralism with Transcendentalist interest in spiritual and aesthetic expression. But during the 1830s, unable to combine these two impulses—one bordering on narrow-minded moralism and the other on self-indulgent narcissism—white abolitionists and Transcendentalists seemed largely separated.

And so a common critique that many early Transcendentalists made of abolitionism was that it was a "partial" reform, aiming only to emancipate slaves and not to fully remake individuals by developing their true selves. Thus, Alcott criticized William Lloyd Garrison and Wendell Phillips for wanting only "a Revolution in the state" and not a "monumental Reform," which would entail, he seemed to think, the creation of an entirely new species of American, one walking proudly in the light of pure Reason.[43] Thoreau made a similar argument for why he kept his distance from the official abolitionist organizations (because they did not allow for the full exposition of his individuality), and in a famous letter rejecting an offer to join the utopian community of Brook Farm, Emerson privileged personal growth over social regeneration.[44] Understandably, abolitionists saw this attitude as the self-indulgent logic of the comfortable seeking excuses for their own apathy. Still, it is crucial that we remember that Alcott and Emerson considered abolition to be a fundamentally good cause; they simply worried about the path that individuals took to get there. Transcendentalists did not believe in a wholesale rejection of politics—most would eventually be conspicuously involved in the antislavery fight—but demanded a politics that did not demean the individual activist, one in which personal growth and social justice coincided. As Transcendentalists came to move toward the abolitionist movement, one of their distinctive traits was their desire to reconcile these two demands: to find a form of self-expressive politics that united private individual concerns about personal integrity with public action against a political evil.

An Abolitionist Theology

Abolitionists and Transcendentalists first allied together in earnest during a fight for religious freedom. If the two sides had maintained a certain tense distance in the 1830s, they began to come together based on their fight against the so-called Standing Order, the tight nexus of power between the Congregational and Unitarian Churches and the state government—the still-living remnant of the old Federalist Party's political base that existed even after formal disestablishment. In the mid-1830s, Boston was riveted by the lengthy court case of Abner Kneeland, the editor of the free-thought journal the *Boston Investigator*. State prosecutors had charged Kneeland with blasphemy based on his pantheistic religious beliefs, his support for the socialism of Robert Owen, and his articles advocating birth control. He would gain the distinction of being the last American jailed for the crime of blasphemy.[45] In his defense, both Transcendentalists such as Emerson, Theodore Parker, and George Ripley and abolitionists such as William Lloyd Garrison signed a petition asking for Kneeland's sentence to be commuted. The *Liberator* declared that his imprisonment for expressing his beliefs was "a disgrace to the Commonwealth of Massachusetts, and a proof of the corruption of modern Christianity."[46] Garrison was, in fact, only repaying Kneeland. In 1830, when Garrison was first getting his antislavery crusade off the ground, he could not find a church to speak in. It was a foreshadow of things to come that it was only the free-thinking Kneeland who provided Garrison with a forum before his Universalist Society.[47] It was not lost on abolitionists that Kneeland's prosecutor, State Attorney General James Trecothick Austin, had been one of the conservatives who had publicly defended the mob that had lynched the Illinois abolitionist Elijah Lovejoy.[48]

As the Kneeland case suggests, abolitionists were in near-constant conflict with the mainstream churches. True, the Massachusetts Anti-Slavery Society had initially hoped to work within the churches. As Garrison remembered it, "instead of seeking a controversy with the pulpit and the church, they confidently looked to both for efficient aid to their cause."[49] And in the 1820s and 1830s—especially in the Old Northwest—evangelical impulses contributed significantly to the rise of immediatist abolition. But in New England, abolitionists soon discovered what black abolitionists had long known: mainstream Northern churches were bastions of white supremacy that depended on the donations of merchants and eagerly catered to the racism of their laymen. The "American Church" was, according to Daniel Foster, "deeply dyed in guilt, in respect to the enslavement" of the African race.[50] Prominent ministers—men such as Nehemiah Adams, a famous Boston Congregational minister who wrote a series of pro-Southern books, and Moses Stuart, the Andover theologian who defended the Fugitive Slave Act—would be among the abolitionists' fiercest critics.[51] Even Unitarian Churches—which today enjoy a reputation for having been antislavery—were often quite reluctant to address slavery. While William Ellery Channing, perhaps the most important early Unitarian minister, eventually espoused a cautious abolitionism, his successor in the prominent Federal Street Church, Ezra Stiles Gannett, was supposed to have declared,

"The Mission of Unitarianism to slavery is silence."[52] When abolitionist John Burleigh wrote that he would trust the clergy to run an antislavery organization as much as he would trust "the hands of slaveholders themselves," he expressed a common abolitionist anticlericalism.[53] Black abolitionists agreed. "The hostile position of the American church and clergy to the cause of oppressed millions at the South, and their complicity with the Southern church," a Colored Citizens Convention resolved in 1858, was responsible for "perpetuating the horrible system of American Slavery."[54] William C. Nell was particularly outraged at Rev. Nehemiah Adams, calling the Boston Congregational minister's support of slavery to be "sentiments revolting to humanity."[55]

Ultimately, as Garrison himself pointed out, abolitionists were forced to distinguish between the institutions of the church—what he called "all the great, controlling ecclesiastical bodies and religious denominations in the land"—and the content of Christian faith.[56] "The religious forces," Garrison discovered, "on which they had relied were all arrayed on the side of the oppressor."[57] Abolitionism, Garrison believed, had to jettison these outward forms of Christian life and instead rely on the inner spirit of religion, the "essential part of Christianity," the living faith in a loving God, the "spirit of Jesus," and a Bible "construed on the side of justice and humanity."[58] This abolitionist sense of the difference, even tension, between the existing phenomenal church, represented in real institutions run by men and even the specific words of the Bible, and the underlying spirit and idea that supposedly created it mirrored the Transcendentalist division between a "transient" church of men and a "permanent" church of the spirit.

Some abolitionists went even further, beyond attacking the institutions of the church to assault the foundations of Christianity itself. This was perhaps already implicit in Garrison's privileging of politics over orthodoxy. And as early as 1833, the abolitionist had disapproved of adding biblical citations to antislavery texts, as doing so would imply that "the rights of man depend upon a text."[59] But others went further than even Garrison would. With curt simplicity, Nathaniel Rogers, the ornery New Hampshire abolitionist, declared that if it were true that Jesus Christ had never spoken against slavery, then the Messiah "*didn't do his duty.*"[60] The black minister Rev. J. W. Lewis, from Maine, expressed a similar attitude, declaring that "should Gabriel come into his room with a parchment containing the Fugitive Slave Law, signed by the Almighty, he would believe he was no longer God."[61] Henry C. Wright, the abolitionist minister, took this position to its logical conclusion when, confronted with the possible proslavery implications of some Bible passages, he proclaimed that "the

Bible, if Opposed to Self-Evident Truth, is Self-Evident Falsehood."[62] By 1858, Wright could publish a pamphlet with the incendiary title "The Errors of the Bible Demonstrated by the Truths of Nature" that, while not atheist, drew from both Transcendentalism and earlier Paineite skepticism.[63] The philosopher Charles Taylor has called Wright an example of how intense piety and egalitarianism, developing out of Christianity itself, could bounce back and actually strengthen "the moral credentials of unbelief."[64] Even Wendell Phillips, whose personal religious beliefs remained relatively traditional, bluntly told an audience that, if they wanted to be better abolitionists, then "you should not go to church," as the vast majority were proslavery.[65]

Thomas Wentworth Higginson's expulsion from the ministry illustrates well the tension between abolitionists and church authority. Higginson, who was well connected and good-looking, made a point of cultivating the dashing style of an impulsive and chivalrous Romantic rebel. Just graduated from Harvard Divinity School, he had accepted a position at the Unitarian Church in Newburyport, Massachusetts. From the start of his ministerial career, he had been interested in social reform—his ordination sermon was given by none other than William Henry Channing, known at the time as a socialist reformer (Higginson was connected to the Channing family through his marriage to Mary Channing).[66] Although his congregation contained many wealthy ship owners, Higginson began to condemn slavery, determined to be a "preacher who is a man, and not a machine."[67] To that end, he preached against slavery, accepted the nomination of the Free Soil Party for political office, and, worst of all, invited the hated Theodore Parker to preach a guest sermon.[68] When he bucked the town's Whig establishment by inviting Emerson to speak before the Newburyport Lyceum, he further alienated his wealthy congregation.[69]

Finally, in 1849, some of Higginson's powerful parishioners revolted. It was the "well-to-do merchants" in Higginson's congregation who led the charge, entirely open about the fact that it was his "position as an abolitionist they could not bear." In September, the rich minority threatened to all withdraw funds at once, and Higginson resigned rather than see the church destroyed. One suspects that the headstrong Higginson was happy to demonstrate his haughty superiority to the stuffy "intellectual drudgery" of the declining seaport town.[70] But he was hardly the only minister to lose his position on account of his antislavery opinions, and most did not have family money to fall back on. J. G. Forman, for instance, a Congregational minster from West Bridgewater, was hounded out of his ministry by "persons of wealth and influence in the community" after he gave an antislavery sermon.[71] Most ministers, abolitionists charged, responded to pressures of this sort with a timid careerism that silenced whatever concerns they had about slavery.

Transcendentalists, meanwhile, were at this time mostly known as religious radicals, attacking the authority of the clergy and the underlying assumptions upon which much of their religious authority was based. They were some of the first in America to absorb the writings of David Strauss and other writers in the German Higher Criticism movement, which subjected the Bible to historical and philological scrutiny, leaving them skeptical of the miracles recounted in even the New Testament (Unitarians had already begun questioning the Old Testament). Emerson himself had left his prestigious Unitarian ministry when he came to believe that "the theological scheme of redemption" was impossible.[72] And so in his *Divinity School Address*, the lapsed minister contrasted the sincere belief inspired by nature, divine laws, and the ideas of Christ with the formalism, pedantry, and reliance on the person of Christ found in mainstream Christianity. Humans, Emerson suggested, had originally created institutions such as churches and rituals to get them closer to God, but then they had started worshipping not God but those institutions! Jesus, on the other hand, Emerson told the 1838 graduating class at Harvard Divinity School, was simply a man who allowed God's spirit to speak through him in a pure and unmediated way, just as anyone could if they listened to the voice of nature and their own sparks of genius. Emerson's speech denied the specially supernatural essence of Christ (or, more accurately, claimed that the divinity that marked Christ could be found in all of us if we were only open to it), suggesting instead that believers would be better suited to search for God in their own conscience, in the beauty of nature, or in the boundless impulses of Reason.

If Emerson's *Divinity School Address* hinted at what Transcendentalist heresy would sound like, it was Theodore Parker's 1841 sermon, "A Discourse on the Transient and Permanent in Christianity," that truly laid it bare, scandalizing the Boston establishment. Huxley to Emerson's Darwin, Parker was blunt where Emerson had been circumspect. Given as part of the induction ceremony for Charles C. Shackford on May 19, 1841, Parker's sermon was a bold salvo against the Orthodox and Unitarian intellectual establishment intended to distinguish between the "accidents" of Christianity—the various sects, dogmas, and doctrines that men seemed determined to fight over—and the "substance" of religious truth, which he claimed was universal. Parker condemned the obsession with both the contemporary structures of the church and with the words of the Bible itself. Most courageously, Parker questioned whether Christ had any uniquely supernatural characteristics at all. Jesus, Parker argued, had simply been an especially profound man, "the organ through which the Infinite spoke," and his statements should be accepted because they were "immutable truth," not because Christ had made the dubious claim to be the son of God. An appeal to the authority of either the Bible or Christ's supposed supernatural essence diminished the obvious truth of his statements and undermined authentic faith by forcing a believer to accept a questionable logic instead of a direct and honest relationship with God. The sermon, which scandalized the Unitarian establishment and led to Parker's near-isolation among fellow clergymen, made his name synonymous with religious radicalism.[73] Unitarians, organized on the congregational model, could not formally discipline Parker as long as his own West Roxbury flock supported him, but other ministers could refuse to exchange pulpits with him, preventing him from spreading his heretical beliefs to their congregation and denying Parker a valuable source of rest. If polite Boston shuddered at Parker's name, William C. Nell and other black thinkers, as we have seen, eagerly invited him to speak before the Adelphic Union.

Still, if the Transcendentalists such as Parker and Emerson took a bit of pleasure shocking buttoned-up Boston with their frank skepticism of the New Testament and other Christian traditions, they were adamant not to be confused with the open atheism and materialism common among French and German intellectuals. Instead, Transcendentalists envisioned a selfhood that would be open to what was spiritually valuable in nature without retreating back into superstition and blind faith. Out of this combination came a new view of selfhood, one that emphasized openness and connection to an outside divinity— but a depersonalized, abstract, and sometimes frustratingly intangible Godhead. At a religious level, this manifested in rejecting the sacred nature of the Bible but still looking for meaningful religious communion with the forces of the universe. As Margaret Fuller said, an open blue sky "preaches better" than any minister or Bible ever could.[74] Having eaten the poisoned apple of Enlightenment rationality, they could not go back to a belief in superstitious forces, religious rites, traditions, or, in many cases, even a personal God. But still seeking some emotional connection with the universe, they tended toward metaphors of sunlight or deep water, forces that tended to resist clear and direct observation but evoked a sense of mystery and awe. Hence, one of the Transcendentalists' favorite words—"influx"—which they took from the Swedish theologian Emanuel Swedenborg, captured something of the openness of the Romantic self to the all-pervasive spiritual ether that surrounded them. Readers, it is true, could be excused if they never could quite put a finger on what exactly was "influxing" into the soul of the Transcendentalist—at various times, it would be "the ALL" or "the one" or, Emerson's favorite, "the oversoul." But it was the very lofty abstraction of this Oversoul—"the universal beauty, to which every part and particle is equally related"—that encouraged an implicit egalitarianism.[75] The Oversoul could not quite be owned by anyone or any institution (this would limit its universality), even as its spirit pervaded every fleck of dirt in nature and shone in the inner bosom of even the humblest person. Transcendentalist cosmology, then, was a bit paradoxical: flat, homogeneous, but conspicuously still enchanted time and space.

Armed with these Transcendentalist assumptions, a recognizable antislavery theology could thus develop, one that rejected many outward forms of Christian doctrine and discipline, such as ministerial authority and the sanctity of the Sabbath, while still retaining a sense of the sacred in political life. The authority of some puffed-up Harvard-educated minister had no special spiritual worth, but the causes of equality and human dignity always did. Both Transcendentalists and abolitionists sought to respiritualize a world that seemed to have been conquered by cotton, compromise, and formalisms. When the *Liberator* pointed out that "those who appear to care least for that which constitutes the real essence of religion, are most fearful lest its outward forms should not be sufficiently respected," it was echoing common Transcendentalist complaints about the hollowness of modern worship.[76] Garrison's anti-Sabbatarian campaign illustrated both the distance that Garrison had traveled from the evangelical abolitionists (defending the Sabbath had been one of the Tappan brothers' most important political interests) as well as the degree to which he was approaching Transcendentalist religious assumptions.[77] While taking on the clerical establishment in order to restore steamboat, railroad, and mail service on Sunday, Garrison, like Transcendentalists, attacked a rule of the church not because he did not believe but exactly because he *did* believe, more so, he claimed, than those who used the state to enforce religious doctrine. The hostile newspaper that sneered that Garrison seemed to "wish for *more Sabbath*, not less," inadvertently explained the radical position better than Garrison himself did.[78] While anti-Sabbatarianism developed out of a concrete need of the abolitionist movement—Sunday was the only day that most working people could come to abolitionist meetings—it also reflected a real theological position. Claiming that the Sabbath was a leftover from "Jewish" superstition, anti-Sabbatarians argued "Christianity knows nothing of a holy day, but only a holy life."[79] Just as Fuller, Emerson, and Alcott asked their followers to expand their religious vision—seeing divinity in quotidian experiences, not just in the formal rites of the church—Garrison argued that every day should be a time for Godly living, not just Sunday.

And so white Transcendentalists and abolitionists began collaborating on questions of religious reform, especially anti-Sabbatarianism. As early as 1838, Maria Weston Chapman, never one to praise lightly, sent a copy of Emerson's heretical *Divinity School Address* to William Lloyd Garrison, indicating her approval.[80] The Rev. Samuel J. May, one of Garrison's first and most loyal supporters, kept a theological commonplace book throughout the 1830s and 1840s in which he engaged extensively and sympathetically with the arguments of Transcendentalists, including Parker, George Ripley, and James Freeman Clarke. He was particularly attracted to how they defined miracles not as the stoppage of Newtonian laws but instead as the constant presence of God in one's conscience and in the beauty of nature.[81] By 1849, Garrison's own religious beliefs were close enough to the Transcendentalists that when his son—Charles Follen Garrison—died at a tragic young age, he had Theodore Parker officiate at the funeral.[82]

In 1840, both abolitionists and Transcendentalists were prominent attendees at the Chardon Street Convention, a characteristically disorderly meeting of Boston's religiously and politically heterodox, whose official purpose was to discuss the reorganization of the American Church. The call for the Chardon Street Convention (technically the "Church, Society, and Sabbath Convention") grew out of conversations held between Transcendentalists and abolitionists at a Non-Resistance meeting in 1840.[83] Emerson, a prominent Chardon Street attendee, famously described the eclectic audience at Chardon as "madmen, madwomen, men with beards, Dunkers, Muggletonians, Come-outers, Groaners, Agrarians, Seventh-day-Baptists, Quakers, Abolitionists, Calvinists, Unitarians, and Philosophers."[84] Chaired by abolitionist stalwart Edmund Quincy, the convention brought together Transcendentalists such as Emerson, Fuller, Thoreau, and Parker with abolitionists such as Garrison, Maria Weston Chapman, and Quincy. Although the convention came to no official conclusions and wrote no official reports, it did illustrate a common interest of the parties in attacking the special status of Sunday and reorganizing the church.[85]

The most concrete result of the Chardon Street Convention was the "Bible Convention," held on March 29, 1842, as a follow-up. Meeting in the Masonic Temple, a smaller group of religious dissenters discussed the "credibility and authority of the Scriptures of the Old and New Testaments." The meeting debated a resolution declaring that the Bible should "be judged like every other book by the light of the present hour."[86] The highlight, by Emerson's account, of the Bible Convention was the mechanic Nathaniel H. Whiting, a sort of plebian Transcendentalist, who denied that the Bible—but a "meager and very questionable *record* of miracles, said to have been wrought hundreds and thousands of years ago"—could be a proper basis of religious faith. Instead, Whiting, one of many working-class New Englanders touched by Transcendentalism and abolitionism, advocated truths that were "intuitive to the soul."[87] The call for the convention, signed by two thinkers known primarily as Transcendentalists (Emerson and Alcott) and two activists known as abolitionists (Maria Weston Chapman and Edmund Quincy), further demonstrated the growing alliance between these worlds on matters of religion.[88]

Throughout the 1840s, abolitionists and Transcendentalists continued to collaborate on the anti-Sabbath campaign. In response to abolitionist agitation, conservatives had formed the American and Foreign Sabbath Union to fight to retain laws that protected the Sabbath.[89] In 1848, Garrison, Theodore Parker, and a number of likeminded allies called for a convention that would answer the newly invigorated clergy.[90] Daniel Ricketson, Thoreau's good friend, was the secretary, and a series of abolitionists, from Garrison to Lucretia Mott to Maria Weston Chapman, were in attendance. Parker called for the Sabbath to be converted from a day of superstition to one of "religious, moral and intellectual culture, to social intercourse."[91] The speakers made no secret that anti-Sabbatarianism was intended to help the abolitionist movement. Selling a human being, the bearer of a divine soul, abolitionist Henry C. Wright pointed out, was the most commonplace of activities, and the major religious journals would not make a peep as long as it was done on a Monday. But sell a bag of grain or a railroad ticket on a Sunday and those same newspapers would breathlessly declare that you had violated a fundamental law of God.[92]

Both Transcendentalists and Massachusetts abolitionists inhabited a transitionary place in the story of American secularism. Although they fought to remove all preferences given to particular religions and resist the ability for the state to interfere with faith, they did so because they thought this would renew authentic religious belief, not protect disbelief. They believed their religious vision was more expansive than that of most traditional churches, which narrowed the moment of worship to the time of Sunday and the place of church. These orthodox churches, one Transcendentalist complained, "believed in a God who worked occasionally, or semi-occasionally in the world's affair; who stole into his house of earth by the private door of miracle."[93] Taking the Puritan logic of their ancestors one step further, Massachusetts radicals pushed to make the entire world equally sacred, but they did so by stripping the rites, traditions, and legal status of Christianity of any uniquely special power. Christianity, in Henry C. Wright's language, was "an all pervading, omnipresent principle of life," not a "religion of time and place."[94] Thus Garrison attacked the distinction between "sacred and secular acts," upon which the worship of the Sabbath was based, because he argued that this separation implied that everyday actions, especially political struggle, could not be sacred.[95] Likewise, for Transcendentalists, it was demeaning to God to locate Him only in a superstitious ritual or the authority of one class of people because the whole universe equally demonstrated the presence of God, whose being exuded throughout the spiritual ether of existence. Thus, Thoreau could, counterintuitively, declare that holding to the Sabbath was a sign of "infidelity," since it implied that God *only* manifested Himself on Sunday.[96] Their God was one of radical immanence, whose presence could not be limited to specificities such as the Sabbath or the clergy—"God put the whole of himself into every atom of the world," as the second-wave Transcendentalist O. B. Frothingham declared.[97]

Looking for God everywhere, they may have unintentionally prepared the way for those who would see Him nowhere. It was Emerson who saw this best, asking "what is this abolition & non-resistance &temperance but the continuation of Puritanism tho' it operate inevitably the destruction of the church in which it grew."[98] By elevating all of existence to an equally holy level and thereby eliminating the *specially* supernatural nature of the clergy or the Sabbath, Transcendentalists and abolitionists were stripping away the crutches of mystery and authority that sustained the traditional Protestant worldview, hopeful that believers would thus be able to walk on their own two feet on a pure and rational religious path. But a future generation, raised without the traditional halos of sanctity around the church, clergy, and rituals of Christianity, would find that the Transcendentalists' abstract pantheism had paved the way for the disenchanted world of secular modernity, where all existence was equally accessible to the probing tools of science. In Transcendentalist terms, by making the universe equally accessible to the illumination of divine Reason, they had inadvertently opened it up to a dissection by human Understanding. As William James pointed out in his classic *Varieties of Religious Experience*, by taking the view that the entire universe is equally supernatural, a system such as Emerson's "surrenders . . . easily to naturalism."[99] Trying to save New England from a deterministic naturalism, Emerson may have actually simply provided a different route to secular modernity, one paved in gentle Transcendental ethereality rather than materialist skepticism.

Antebellum black political thinkers were acutely aware of the ways that Christian institutions could buttress slavery and racism. Much of their suspicion of mainstream white Christianity came from their experiences in slavery. The brutality of Frederick Douglass's master became worse after he converted to

Methodism, as he could "find religious sanction for his cruelty."[100] In this light,
Lewis Hayden's distrust of the white clergy is not surprising, given his experiences with his master.[101] And even Northern clergy were not free from the influence of slavery, as Alexander Crummell discovered about the Episcopalian
Church; he was denied entry to the General Theological Seminary because the
church did not wish to alienate Southern donors.[102] Even Northern blacks who
had never experienced slavery resented the way that most white churches were
complicit with proslavery politicians. Charlotte Forten, for instance, believed
that "the churches and ministers are generally supporters of the infamous system" of slavery.[103] Samuel Ringgold Ward, who had the unique experience of
serving as a black pastor to a largely white congregation, still condemned the
white churches for "the contempt they all alike maintain towards the Negro"
and their preference for quiet harmony over justice.[104]

Jeremiah Sanderson's experience as an itinerant antislavery speaker was
typical of many black abolitionists' encounters with the white church. Writing
to his good friend William C. Nell, he explained what had happened when trying to lecture in Sharon, Massachusetts. "I have applied to some of the Deacons
and Ministers and find that I can get no Sympathy from them." Only one minister, "a Mr. Philips," even deigned to explain his reasons: a debate about slavery
"would have the effect to alienate the attention of those who were seeking to
know Christ." Sanderson pleaded with Mr. Philips in vain that a true Christian
should care about injustice and suffering. Philips's Christianity, he concluded,
"has no humanity in it, no Sympathy with the suffering and oppressed, and
such is the character of the 'religion' of the present age generally."[105] To the degree Sanderson had positive interactions with white churches, they tended to be
among the radical and iconoclastic "come-outers." In 1842, for instance, he
wrote to Nell about a meeting he had with the "Primitive Methodists" in Lowell.
They were eccentric, he admitted, but "they are liberal . . . not regarding names,
are independent, not connected with Slave-holding Churches," and had invited
him to speak on slavery.[106]

In fact, some black intellectuals began criticizing Christianity itself, even
as manifested in black churches, doing so in language that was similar to how
white Transcendentalists attacked their churches. Frederick Douglass's belief
that slavery was sustained by "too much religion . . . the people were too rever-
ential God-ward to be honest man-ward," went beyond attacking the structures
of the church, seeming to reject the otherworldliness of belief itself.[107] In 1837,
the Philadelphia Association for the Moral and Mental Improvement of the
People of Color, a black intellectual club, went as far as to publish an open let-

ter, claiming that "the different persuasions of our religious assemblies [have] been the very instruments used against us, for perpetuating our degradation, by keeping us divided."[108] It was William C. Nell, with his strong connections to religious radicals such as Theodore Parker, who took the lead among Boston blacks. In 1848, a controversy erupted in the pages of the *North Star* over the issue of having segregated churches and the general position of the black clergy. Nell took a hardline anticlerical position, criticizing the "large numbers of colored Clergymen, Deacons, and lay members" who had stood in the way of black "elevation," often because of their dedication to sectarian religious dogma. In good Transcendentalist language, Nell reminded his audience that "religion teaches us to recognize God in all things. Every moment of our lives we are in the temple of the Creator." He went on to locate the presence of God, with premonitions of Whitman, in a list of His manifestations throughout nature: "mountains that lift their heads above the clouds—the boundless ocean, the roar of whose waves chant from shore to shore." The implication was clear: since God's presence was everywhere, there was not a need for a specially ordained clergy unless it was assisting the political needs of the community. Nell went on to relate the minutes of a meeting of black Bostonians in which they had compared the anti-intellectualism of "colored ministers of the gospel" to slaveholders.[109] Though obviously the black church was not tainted with proslavery attitudes the way white churches were, its power was challenged by some black intellectuals, who found its religious vision narrow, sectarian, and anti-intellectual.

Women's Rights

The centrifugal energy of Transcendentalist ideas, which were already spinning out into abolitionism and religious reform, played a crucial role in the emergence of a feminist intellectual life in New England. While Emerson was dodging the various bearded enthusiasts announcing themselves at his Concord doorstop, expecting an ear for their utopian schemes (and, of course, a warm meal), his friend Margaret Fuller was leading her famous "Conversations," another place that brought together Transcendentalists and abolitionists. Fuller's Conversations are famous as early expressions of antebellum feminism. Semi-structured discussions of pre-circulated themes, the Conversations were one of the first opportunities for middle-class women to discuss religious, philosophical, and historical issues away from male oversight.[110] Among the attendees were a number of women—most notably Lydia Maria Child and Ann Terry Phillips—who were already associated with the abolitionist movement. Fuller, as was appropriate for a friend of Emerson, was a fascinating tangle of contradictions: she had an intellectual pride that could drive away many but was also capable of wounded sensitivity; in her personal life, she was a radical nonconformist and individualist, but in her spiritual vision, she was intoxicated by the possibility of unity and communion with the universe. Her personal charisma was legendary, but she seemed lonely even among fawning friends. She was, at this point in her life, sympathetic to the cause of abolitionism but disdainful of what she saw as the narrow-minded fanaticism of many abolitionists.[111] So, for instance, in 1840, when Maria Weston Chapman asked her to devote a conversation to abolition, she demurred, saying that "my own path leads a different course and often leaves me quite ignorant of what you are doing."[112] But if the Conversations did not explicitly deal with antislavery, it quickly became clear that the Transcendentalist humanism infusing her feminism was pushing her followers toward abolitionism.

The Conversations helped to instill a sense of intellectual independence and self-confidence that women would draw upon in the antislavery movement. In the Conversations, Fuller would push back whenever women suggested that they labored under essential disabilities, constantly reminding the audience that "we should hear no more of repressing or subduing faculties because they were not fit for women to cultivate."[113] Ednah Dow Cheney, who would become an abolitionist and women's rights activist, remembered that after Fuller's Conversations, "perhaps I could best express it by saying that I was no longer the limitation of myself, but I felt that the whole wealth of the universe was open to me."[114] Cheney saw the Conversations as crucial moments in her politicization. Like abolitionism, Transcendentalism offered women both communities beyond the dull solitude of the home and ideas that they could use to challenge the patriarchy that dominated their lives.

The women's rights movement largely grew out of the experience of female abolitionists such as Maria Stewart, Lucretia Mott, Maria Weston Chapman, and others who were realizing that sexual oppression was as real as racial oppression and that the same conservative figures who opposed their rights were standing in the way of black emancipation. As Margaret Fuller herself acknowledged, "there is a reason why the foes of African slavery seek more freedom for women."[115] Both abolitionism and Transcendentalism struggled against the authority of the same traditional religious leaders who were trying to silence women. Transcendentalists, especially, offered a vision of human dignity available to all who could Reason, regardless of race or gender. The logic of abolitionist egalitarianism pushed its adherents to dismantle all hierarchies, including those in the family. Perhaps most important, the everyday experiences of both abolitionist activism—which mobilized thousands of women to act politically—and Transcendentalist intellectual life, which invited them to discuss and reflect on their own spiritual lives, encouraged women to challenge male authority.

Even before Fuller, black women had been some of the first in Boston to begin speaking and organizing as women. For all the attention that historians have given Fuller's Conversations, few have pointed out that the black Afric-American Female Intelligence Society well predated Fuller's Conversations. Like Fuller, the Afric-American Society sought to give Boston women, in this case poor black women, an opportunity to develop independent intellectual lives. And black women, especially the religious leader Maria Stewart, were groundbreakers in addressing public audiences of mixed genders well before it was common for white women to do so. Stewart had worked with David Walker and then William Lloyd Garrison while becoming one of the first major female antislavery orators. The widow of a successful black businessman, Stewart was defrauded from her inheritance by a group of unscrupulous white merchants. Two years later, in 1831, she had a religious awakening, made a public profession of belief, and began lecturing on political and religious themes. Her public career was meteoric. After quickly breaking ground as the first black female intellectual and abolitionist, she left Boston after three years in the spotlight and did not publish new material again until 1879.

Stewart developed a particular version of the elevation ideology intended for black female audiences. She shared Fuller's concern that women had few options outside the home; for black women, that meant little other than mindless drudgery in the kitchen or laundry. As such, Stewart claimed, black women were becoming identified with their tools rather than their spiritual selves. Like Transcendentalists who tended to juxtapose humans' soul with material objects, Stewart was concerned that black women be more than simply creatures "compelled to bury their minds and talents beneath a load of iron pots and kettles."[116] At its core, Stewart's philosophy, like Fuller's after her, was an attack on the idea that women had no place to grow beyond the confines of traditional female roles. If Fuller's audience was concerned with the boredom and emotional emptiness of the life given to middle-class white women, Stewart's was more concerned with the dehumanization inherent in low-wage work, with how living your life as a hired "hand" did not speak to your soul or brain.

Had white Transcendentalists been listening to Stewart, they might have recognized a kindred spirit. More traditionally religious than white Transcendentalists, Stewart was still deeply concerned that members of her audience were unable to demonstrate their "noble and exalted faculties" because economic necessity or social conformity limited their potential.[117] Stewart anticipated Emerson's complaint about the intellectually stifling effects of the division of labor when she pointed out that one consequence of menial employment was that "continual hard labor deadens the energies of the soul, and benumbs the faculties of the mind."[118] She consistently argued that the activities required of black women were not conducive to the creation of the habits, skills, and moral traits that would constitute a godly existence. Stewart was obviously not a follower of Transcendentalism, a movement that did not yet really exist when she was active. But the elevation ideology of which Stewart was an able proponent shared a number of intellectual and existential concerns, including an interest in developing the moral and spiritual capabilities of adherents and a Romantic desire toward a full life. She illustrated, better than Emerson himself, the "democratization of the sublime" that was the Transcendentalists' core project, her hope for the spiritual growth of black Boston mirroring Emerson's demand that all peoples become "flecked with divinity."[119] Years after she moved out of Boston, William C. Nell would remember her "holy zeal" and moral fortitude.[120]

As white women followed in Stewart's footsteps and began addressing "promiscuous" audiences (those with male and female members), the abolitionist movement quickly became associated with a radical sexual agenda. By the mid-1840s, Fuller herself began to shed her skepticism of the abolitionists. In her landmark 1844 essay *Woman in the Nineteenth Century*, she lauded abolitionists as the party that "makes, just now, the warmest appeal in behalf of woman."[121] For Fuller, there were deep reasons why women's rights, antislavery, and Transcendentalism formed a mutually reinforcing triangle. She saw parallels in how nineteenth-century patriarchy treated women "as if she were a child, or a ward only," with how white Americans thought of black people. In a provocative passage, she suggested the political power of her Transcendentalist idealism: "If the negro be a soul, if the woman be a soul, appareled in flesh, to one Master only are they accountable. There is but one laws for souls, and if there is to be an interpreter of it, he must come not as man, or son of man, but as son of God."[122] Here, Fuller's Transcendentalist theology—which, like Emerson and Parker, held that every person could channel the same divine spirit as Jesus and thus become, in a sense, the son of God—brought together an abolitionist and feminist message on the common grounds of a divine humanity. For neither women nor black people could be defined by their phenomenal appearances (the "apparel" of their flesh) and instead had a core dignity that transcended such arbitrary external markings. Certainly, this radical privileging of the spirit over the flesh contained the possibility of erasing important distinctions (however the Oversoul may have seen black people, the American population saw them with black skin). But for Fuller, it anchored a politics of radical dignity, in which each person had the right to grow and prosper in a way that reflected the divinity of their soul.

Fuller waffled between holding that there were physical and emotional differences between men and women and a radical humanism that denied such differences. At times, she seemed to embrace a Romantic essentialism that held there to be fundamental differences between men and women. At other times, though, she held that the core of a human being was a Transcendental soul, some aspect of the self that could not be defined by something as petty and arbitrary as their body or outward condition. Like Emerson, this was partly experienced as a sense of doubleness. "How is that I seem to be this Margaret Fuller?" She asked as if some essential part of her was standing apart from the physical "being who now writes," watching in bemusement and confused distance from her own self.[123] If her empirical self was a woman, this higher and mysterious "spirit uncontainable and uncontained" in her could not be hemmed in by such a category. This tension between a radical universalism and essentialism would reappear in some white Transcendentalists' ambivalence about racial science.

The development of Caroline Healey Dall, one of Fuller's disciples, illustrates well how feminism, abolitionism, and Transcendentalism all mutually reinforced each other. As a girl, Dall had been particularly close to her father, grateful that, unlike others in her family, he had encouraged her to read and seek an education despite her gender, and she forever credited him with instilling a sense of intellectual independence in her. But he also had a controlling temper, was a conservative Whig with business investments in Mississippi, and was rabidly opposed to abolitionism. In 1841, she began attending Fuller's Conversations, reading Emerson, and defending Theodore Parker's unorthodox theology. From Parker, she took a sense of the poverty and frivolity of the life given to middle-class women and began yearning for a higher education and purpose. Moreover, under the influence of her new abolitionist friends, she began slowly moving to the left. When Dall took her first steps toward abolitionism in 1845, writing an antislavery article for the *Christian World*, a newspaper edited by James Freeman Clarke, her father was outraged.[124] He wrote a letter "full of remonstrances" in response. As Dall began protecting fugitives while her father hosted Daniel Webster, tensions rose even more. He refused desperate requests for money from the new mother, demanding that she give up contact with abolitionists and threatened to disinherit her, writing that abolitionist activity was "the worst thing that is possible for you to do except <u>murder.</u>"[125] She continued her work, though, eventually becoming an important feminist speaker.

Dall was not the only woman for whom Transcendentalist ideas both encouraged her abolitionist principles and solidified devotion to women's rights. Sallie Holley was a student at Oberlin when she befriended a fellow student named Caroline Putnam. Their intense friendship bloomed over shared interest in religious reform and antislavery radicalism. By 1850, Sallie was writing to Caroline about attending an Emerson lecture and being amused at the hypocrisy of the "chivalry" of her town, which would put up with Emerson's "ultra radical views" (she saw Emerson as a radical abolitionist) only because he had the blessing of the bigwigs of the local Athenaeum. The next year, Holley became an agent for the American Anti-Slavery Society, touring throughout New England, Pennsylvania, and New Jersey on behalf of Garrisonian antislavery. Through her abolitionist contacts, she got to know William Henry Channing, attended Theodore Parker's church, and sat in on Alcott's "Conversations" when in Boston, always faithfully reporting back in long letters to Caroline. She eventually declared herself a "Theodore Parker Unitarian."[126] She was so devoted to the memory of Margaret Fuller that, between abolitionist commitments, she made a pilgrimage to Manchester, New Hampshire, to talk with Fuller's mother. Holley and Putnam, neither of whom married and who spent the bulk of their lives living together, even visited Walden Pond together to see the landscape "on whose banks Thoreau *hermited*." Holley, in fact, came to deeply admire Dall, meeting her at the same Women's Rights Convention (in 1855), in which Emerson spoke.[127] Well in the 1860s, the two would travel to small towns through the rural North, lecturing in cold Methodist meeting houses and small libraries to raise money for the abolitionist cause.[128] After the Civil War, Caroline and Sallie moved to the South, operating a school for freedmen and braving the threats and scorn of reactionary Virginians to educate former slaves.

Non-Resistance and the Transcendentalist Imagination

If Transcendentalists and abolitionists shared some deep concerns about religious reform and women's rights, more contingent national political issues were also drawing them together. One of the issues propelling Emerson and Thoreau closer to the abolitionist movement was their shared outrage over the treatment of black sailors. After Nat Turner's 1831 rebellion, Southern elites, fearing slave revolt, had turned their attention to Northern black sailors, many of whom they (rightly) suspected of bearing radical antislavery and egalitarian ideas. Free in the North yet treated as slaves in the South, black sailors personified the contradictions upon which the antebellum nation uneasily rested. In a clear violation of the Constitution, Southern states had passed a series of laws banning black sailors from entering their states and imprisoning and even enslaving those who did come. This issue outraged a surprising cross section of Massachusetts society: blacks and abolitionists for obvious reasons, merchants who disliked the disruption of their crews, and proud Yankees who saw it as a threat to Massachusetts sovereignty and pride. Emerson summed up the sense that these imprisonments threatened New England when he complained that "the deck of a Massachusetts ship was as much the territory of Massachusetts, as the floor on which we stand. It should be as sacred as the temple of God."[129]

Especially galling was what happened when Massachusetts sent a delegation to South Carolina to negotiate the matter in 1844. When Samuel Hoar, a prominent judge and politician (and father to the anti-imperialist Senator George F. Hoar), arrived in Charleston, he found the state government, headed by future secessionist James Henry Hammond, to be completely uncooperative. Hoar and his daughter Elizabeth only barely survived when a mob threatened to burn down their hotel and they were forced to flee the state.[130] New Englanders were outraged at the insult to an official Massachusetts delegation. A mass meeting of black Bostonians assembled at the Belknap Street Meeting House, declaring the new laws "alike unconstitutional and atrocious" and constituting a war on Massachusetts and the North more generally. They created a small committee, including William C. Nell and John T. Hilton, to write to prominent British abolitionists warning them of the threat to black British sailors.[131] Transcendentalists were particularly upset as Hoar happened to be a neighbor of Emerson, and Elizabeth, who had attended Margaret Fuller's Conversations, had even been engaged to Emerson's brother. The unwillingness of Massachusetts politicians to complain vigorously alienated Massachusetts abolitionists even more from the Whig Party. Whig senator Rufus Choate, when confronted with the issue of black sailors being abducted, had refused to make an issue out of it, fearing that it would threaten the possibility of a new tariff, which the textile industry desperately needed.[132] Now, after Hoar's near-lynching, elites again seemed unwilling to act. In his journal, Emerson fumed that "Boston merchants would willingly salve the matter over."[133] Emerson's outrage, it was true, was based as much on his sense of wounded Massachusetts pride at the servile complicity of the leading Massachusetts men as compassion for the black victims.

Meanwhile, other national developments were deepening a sense of pessimism about the state of national politics. Southern repression made the region nearly wholly inaccessible to abolitionist propaganda. The Gag Rule had, for much of the 1830s, silenced abolitionism in Washington, D.C. Worse, the 1842 Supreme Court case *Prigg*, authored by Harvard professor and Supreme Court Justice Joseph Story, seemed to foreclose the possibility of Northern states protecting fugitive slaves and suggested the possible nationalization of slave codes. In this context, the Garrisonian argument about the limitations of the U.S. Constitution gained an audience beyond even the core of his committed supporters.

But it was the annexation of Texas and the subsequent Mexican War that truly cemented the Transcendentalist turn toward radical abolitionism. Margaret Fuller, now writing for the *New York Tribune*, ceased all criticisms of Garrison and declared the act the most "wicked" done by any nation.[134] If the treatment of Hoar brought the arrogance of slaveholders home to Concord, the annexation of Texas and the Mexican War illustrated the haplessness of too many Northern politicians, a "sniveling and despised opposition, clapped on the back by comfortable capitalists," as Emerson called them in the *Massachusetts Quarterly Review*.[135] Even conservative Whigs opposed the annexation of Texas, both on the grounds of traditional Whig skepticism of territorial expansion and, for some, for antislavery reasons. But not wishing to antagonize their Southern business partners, their resistance was half-hearted, as they purposely tried to avoid mentioning slavery in their arguments and resisted mobilizing public opposition.[136] "A despair has crept over the Whig party," Emerson wrote in his journal, as the debate over Texas annexation heated up.[137] The caution of most supposedly antislavery Northern politicians stemmed from a basic contradiction in their strategy. Most voted against the declaration of war, but, fearing a repeat of the debacle of 1812—when Federalists had nearly destroyed their party after seeming unpatriotic—they nevertheless voted money for supplies and troops. This stance, of course, pleased nobody. The Wilmot Proviso, championed by Northern politicians as a way to prevent the spread of slavery to newly conquered lands, passed a divided House of Representatives but failed in the Senate. It was this series of events that led John G. Palfrey, an aspiring Massachusetts politician and old mentor of Emerson, to write his influential *Papers on the Slave Power*, attacking those who were "cottoning" to slavery in the North.[138] His book helped both to popularize the term "Slave Power" and to indict the Northern Whigs who Palfrey accused of being junior partners in the South's crimes.

It was in this context that a young Henry David Thoreau decided not to pay his taxes in July 1846 because he wished to avoid complicity with "the present Mexican war."[139] Thoreau was not the first of his circle to refuse to pay taxes for political reasons; a young Charles Stearns was jailed in 1840 for refusing to support the militia, and A. Bronson Alcott had briefly done the same in 1843.[140] Thoreau, more so than his friend Emerson, had always been close to the abolitionist movement. Raised in a family with close connections to abolitionism, among his earliest writings were salvos in support of abolitionism. In 1844, he wrote a positive review of Nathaniel Rogers's *Herald of Freedom* in the Transcendentalist journal the *Dial*.[141] Thoreau admired how Rogers, a leader of the proto-anarchist "no-organization" abolitionists in New Hampshire, gruffly thumbed his nose at all forms of authority, including slavery, capitalism, the clergy, and, it seemed, God Himself.[142] Many of Rogers's ideas about the sovereignty of the individual conscience and suspicion of organized politics would be echoed in Thoreau's famous *On Civil Disobedience*.

It is illustrative that the first major antislavery actions taken by both Emerson and Thoreau were negative: Thoreau refusing to pay his taxes, Emerson refusing to speak before a segregated lyceum. As Massachusetts taxes funded an army that extended slavery, and the political demands of a slave nation seemed to invade the North, white Transcendentalists' political concerns were centered on anxiety about their own complicity as much as concern for slavery's victims. In the 1830s, Emerson had thought of slavery as an external and far-off evil and was slightly skeptical of those who obsessed over it. But by the early 1840s, he increasingly saw how New England was involved in slavery. As he wrote in *Man the Reformer*, "The abolitionist has shown us our dreadful debt to the southern negro."[143] Complicity became a key concept as Emerson and Thoreau saw that, even though they could not see the lash or whips of the peculiar institution themselves, slavery was interrupting their ability to live moral lives.[144] Abolitionism increasingly appeared as a way to cleanse their lives, polluted as they were with the foul stench of slavery. This had contradictory consequences: on one hand, the impulse to question one's complicity in a slaveholding society revealed to New Englanders their own personal stake in slavery. On the other hand, it was an ethical vision that was primarily concerned with the white New Englanders' moral purity, not the sufferings of black Southerners. In one extreme version of this logic, Emerson would declare that he valued the moral purity of one white Northerner over the welfare of 1,000 black slaves.[145] It was a portent of some of the uglier racial logic that would infect the thought of many white Transcendentalists in the 1850s.

Thoreau's ideas in *Civil Disobedience* were equally inspired by Transcendentalism and the Non-Resistance movement, a form of Christian pacifism associated with Garrison and other abolitionists. A sign of his growing radicalism and utopianism, Garrison had advocated his own Christian proto-anarchism in the late 1830s. Similar in many ways to later ideas elaborated by Tolstoy, Garrison and allies such as Henry Wright, Edmund Quincy, and Maria Weston Chapman held that all forms of government, as well as other institutions such as the police, the army, and, obviously, slavery, that rested on physical force were immoral and illegitimate, invalidated by the New Testament injunction against resisting evil. And so Garrison led a group of dissidents away from the American Peace Society, a more mainstream organization dedicated to international arbitration and cooperation, to form the New England Non-Resistant Society in 1838. The new society proclaimed against voting, taking oaths, serving on juries, holding office, joining the army, or in any other way helping to sustain a government that "rests on the life-taking principle" and therefore had no moral authority.[146] Along with slavery and government coercion, they condemned the death penalty, dueling, and other forms of public and private violence. Non-Resistants even went so far as to agitate against donations to the Bunker Hill Memorial, as it violated their pledge to avoid "all celebrations in honor of military or naval exploits."[147]

Although black thinkers did not take the lead on issues of peace or Non-Resistance, many were supportive of these causes. In 1839, a group of black citizens was interested enough to request William Lloyd Garrison lecture specifically on his theories of "non-resistance, peace, women's rights, government, political action, and the Sabbath," and his views were received with "entire satisfaction."[148] William C. Nell and his friend Jeremiah Burke Sanderson were also supportive of the Non-Resistance movement. In 1841, Sanderson wrote to Nell thanking him for having sent Non-Resistant literature. "The more I think and read of those excellent principles," Sanderson told Nell, "the more firmly I am convinced of their Heaven born origin. . . . I am a non resistant in theory." Sanderson admitted, though, that his "natural feelings" might resist practically living out this nonviolence in all situations.[149] Like many black abolitionists, Sanderson and Nell refused to condemn using violence to protect fugitive slaves, as Garrison did.

Central to Non-Resistant ideology was the idea that conscience was higher than immoral governments. Transcendentalists, skeptical of the power of the masses and of governments, responded warmly to this argument. A. Bronson Alcott, then known as a Transcendentalist educational reformer, joined the New England Non-Resistant Society in 1839, seeing it as the ultimate expression of Transcendentalist self-reliance, as "an assertion of the right of self-government," and as proof of the inherent divinity at the core of every individual.[150] Attending his first Non-Resistant conference, in 1839, Alcott predicted the coming end of governments, as "an individual is more mighty than church or state."[151] Emerson was likewise warm to the idea, albeit with more reservations, seeing in Non-Resistance a faith in the individual and celebrating Garrison's direct and principled positions, "the weapons of a great Apostle."[152] Theodore Parker, George Ripley, and William Henry Channing were among the prominent Transcendentalists to attend the second convention of the Non-Resistant Society.[153] Parker admitted, in his journal, that he did not entirely agree with the Non-Resistants but respected their "spirit and upward tendency," probably a good description of Emerson's feelings as well.[154]

Non-Resistance illustrated how close to Transcendentalist ideals of self-expressive politics many abolitionists already were. Non-Resistance, the abolitionist Edmund Quincy argued in a remarkable 1840 essay, was fundamentally about personal self-discovery, as "the heart's desire of a true non-resistant is to learn the laws of his own nature." These inner urges, if pure, were God's law, in whose image man was made. Thus, to disobey manmade law and follow these urges were "the only condition of safety and happiness." Once a Non-Resistant had learned to follow God's law within, he or she "rigorously applies these laws to all the institutions by which he [or she] is surrounded—whether those institutions claimed a Divine origin or not." One would be hard-pressed to come up with a better summary of the model Transcendentalist political actor, one who examined political institutions from the standpoint of what his or her own nature—which, properly understood, was coterminous with "the Divine mind"—dictated and not what social norms or past precedent laid down as right.[155]

The Non-Resistant attitude explains, to a large degree, the relative ease with which Garrisonians jettisoned the markers of antebellum political respectability. While some abolitionists, such as the quirky Lysander Spooner, sought to smuggle antislavery into the Constitution or debated the exact and intricate meaning of this or that Founding Father's statements, a surprising number of Massachusetts radicals simply ignored the Constitution. To abolitionists such as Garrison, slavery was not just wrong because it violated the technical details of some manmade document—the way that expanding your garage might violate a lien on your property. Slavery was wrong in a fundamental, heaven-defying, absolute manner, regardless of what any law or Constitution said. This skepticism of the Constitution united Transcendentalists with Garrisonians. As Thoreau would write, "The question is not whether you or your grandfather, seventy years ago, did not enter into an agreement to serve the devil . . . but

whether you will not now, for once and at last, serve God."[156] To continue to
respect the Constitution, they argued, meant that you accepted that the laws of
man would bound your political imagination, even if you could somehow include antislavery into the framework of those laws. The Non-Resistant position,
on the other hand, gleefully threw out such constraints, demanding that the
state be judged by abstract ideals and, if it failed, asking individuals to withdraw
their allegiance. This skepticism of the Constitution was so associated with
Transcendentalism that in 1848, when Garrison and Phillips were petitioning
the Massachusetts legislature to embrace peaceful disunion, the *Boston Daily
Evening Transcript*, a hostile newspaper, mocked the move as "Political Transcendentalism."[157]

The combination of Transcendentalist religious heterodoxy, Non-Resistant
expressive individualism, and the general democratic enthusiasm of antebellum
life imparted a quirkiness to abolitionist politics that critics were quick to sat-
ire. Public conventions were generally "free speech" meetings, which meant
that everyone had the right at some point to speak. Not a few meetings were
derailed by unrelated topics and the bugbears of particular activists, those
whom Lydia Maria Child lovingly described as "sincere and zealous workers,
but who have no balance-wheel in their machinery."[158] For instance, abolitionist meetings tended to collect eccentric figures such as Silas Lamson, who was
convinced that "saints should dress in white raiment and wear long beards" and
carry "long, crooked scythe-snaths." Lamson could often be seen at Boston
wharves, his white robes flapping in the wind, preaching antislavery to amused
sailors.[159] It was not uncommon for entire afternoons—as was the case in one
1848 convention of the American Anti-Slavery Society—to be taken up debating "metaphysical" questions, in this case whether slaveholders were actually
"human beings," given their immoral activity.[160] Nor was the speaker's platform
always restricted to the terrestrial. In one 1855 meeting, speakers debated a message John Orvis (former Brook Farmer and future member of Marx's First International) claimed to have received from the "spirit world," advocating "a new
Union . . . for universal liberty."[161] There followed a lively debate about whether,
according to the rules of the meeting, the chair could recognize speaking to
those who were not, in the technical definition of the word, alive. Stephen Foster checked the rules carefully and earnestly reported back that "we have no
right to extend our sphere beyond the human race" while Garrison disagreed,
siding with the free speech rights of the incorporeal. "The spirit," Garrison declared, "was entirely in order."[162] It was, perhaps, not that surprising that the
back row of abolitionist meetings often featured snickering "rowdies" enter-

taining themselves by occasionally throwing invective (or rotten eggs) at the stage. If inefficient and, no doubt, at times a bit ludicrous, abolitionist styles of politics can be seen in the proud tradition of prefigurative activism, attempting to enact in the very structures of their own institutions the type of democratic and inclusive society for which they fought.

"Practical Transcendentalism"

By the mid-1840s, abolitionists and Transcendentalists were increasingly collaborating. One of the first signs of this growing rapport was the relatively friendly treatment that Lydia Maria Child had given to Transcendentalism in an 1841 article in the *National Anti-Slavery Standard* (though she did admit that "imitations of Transcendentalism are unquestionably the most contemptible form of affectation and sham").[163] Abolitionist papers often ran Transcendentalist texts—as when the *National Anti-Slavery Standard* ran the length of Emerson's *Man the Reformer* in 1841.[164] Abolitionist editors used quotations by Transcendentalists to fill in empty space, helping to create a Transcendentalist common sense among their readers. In 1844, Emerson finally gave a stoutly antislavery address at the Concord celebration of West Indian emancipation. Sitting next to Emerson on the dais, as the Transcendentalist finally publicly cast his lot with the abolitionists, was a black abolitionist whom the newspapers misspelled as "Fredric Douglas."[165] Abolitionists were thrilled, and Emerson soon found himself bombarded by invitations to speak at antislavery events. John Greenleaf Whittier even publicly attempted to recruit Emerson to a leadership role in the Liberty Party.[166] A year later, Concord was the site of a small abolitionist controversy when the local lyceum banned Wendell Phillips from speaking. In the ensuing fight, the conservative curator resigned, and Emerson and Thoreau, supporters of Phillips, were elected.[167] By the end of the decade, Emerson was a regular at antislavery rallies, speaking alongside Garrison, Wendell Phillips, and other abolitionist stalwarts.[168] Emerson was a coveted speaker at abolitionist meetings because he appealed to a crowd that was not instinctively radical, helping to legitimize antislavery ideas. As Charles Sumner wrote him in 1851, "You have access to many, whom other Anti-Slavery speakers cannot reach."[169] Conservative papers, such as the *Boston Advertiser*, took to tarring the Free Soil Party as antigovernment abolitionists, based on the fact that Emerson seemed to be canvassing for Free Soil candidates.[170] In 1854, Emerson contributed a poem "On Freedom"—a meditation on poetry's ambivalent ability to

Figure 4. William C. Nell sold this lithograph, which shows how Transcendentalists such as Emerson and Parker were seen as antislavery leaders. Collection of the Massachusetts Historical Society.

inspire the enslaved—to Julia Griffith's project *Autographs for Freedom*, meant to raise money for Frederick Douglass.[171] Meanwhile, Margaret Fuller, although she had moved to New York City, was becoming more and more interested in the issue of slavery and, as a literary editor at the popular *New York Tribune*, gave a glowing review to Frederick Douglass's new autobiography. In 1846, Fuller fully committed herself to being associated with the abolitionists, submitting an essay for the Garrisonian periodical, *Liberty Bell*.[172]

Most remarkable was the conversion of Theodore Parker to abolitionism. Known first and foremost as a religious heretic, he was already probably the most hated man in Boston and had little to lose when he first spoke out publicly against slavery in 1841. But it was not until 1845, with the annexation of Texas, that Parker became entirely identified with the cause. Parker was not a lovable man—by most accounts, he was cold, vain, and capable of holding grudges for years. After the controversy around his "Transient and Permanent" sermon, he embraced his role as a persecuted martyr with a bit too much enthusiasm. But both his fellow Transcendentalists and abolitionists respected him for his courage and intellectual gifts, and he became a vital link between the increasingly allied worlds. His marriage was unhappy, and one suspects that he transferred some of that energy into an increasingly frantic work and activist life. Continuing to write on philosophical and theological matters, he threw himself into antislavery activism, becoming one of the most prominent Boston abolitionists. Two years after diving into abolitionism, in 1847, Parker helped organize a private meeting, bringing together some of the most prominent Northern radicals—they informally called themselves the "Council of Reformers." Stalwart Garrisonians such as Wendell Phillips, Maria Weston Chapman, and Garrison himself joined political abolitionists such as Charles Sumner and the Liberty Party editor Elizur Wright as well as the leading lights of Transcendentalism, including Emerson, Alcott, James Freeman Clarke, and William Henry Channing. They discussed the "general principles of Reform" and for six hours had a "spirited conversation . . . on all the great Reform subjects of the day." But slavery was fast becoming the most important issue. As Samuel May, an attendee, reported of the meeting, "I am more than ever convinced that the Anti-Slavery Reform carries all others with it, and that its triumph will be theirs."[173]

One legacy of the increased interaction between abolitionists and Transcendentalists that Parker was helping to orchestrate was the new journal, the *Massachusetts Quarterly Review*, which began publication in 1847. Emerson wrote the editorial address, in which he hoped the new journal would have the "courage and power" to address the questions of socialism, nonresistance, and slavery.[174] Emerson and Parker offered the editor position to a young Charles Sumner, who turned it down, and so Parker ended up doing the bulk of the work, including writing a series of mammoth articles about slavery and theology.[175] From the first issue, the *Quarterly Review* was far more concerned with slavery than previous Transcendentalist journals, such as the famous *Dial*. Thomas Wentworth Higginson, writing to his mother, crowed that the *Quarterly Review* would "come down on Slavery and War like a thunderbolt."[176] Parker wrote on the Mexican War, Richard Hildreth published a series on the legal status of slavery, Henry I. Bowditch published on the constitutionality of slavery, and James Birney wrote on the right to petition.[177] As the example of Birney, the former presidential candidate of the Liberty Party, demonstrates, the journal was especially open to supporters of political abolitionism, those who, unlike Garrison, believed in forming third parties to advance the abolitionist agenda.

This same alliance between Transcendentalists and abolitionists gave birth in 1848 to the Town and Country Club, a sort of reading room and intellectual club in Boston. Emerson took the lead, describing in his journal how a literary "assembly room" could be developed: "by a little alliance with some of the rising parties of the time, as the Socialists, & the Abolitionists, and the Artists, we might accumulate a sufficient patronage to establish a good room in Boston."[178] The resulting Town and Country Club was a veritable who's who of Boston radicalism, including Garrison, Sumner, Parker, Wright, Samuel May, Emerson, Thoreau, Thomas Wentworth Higginson, and even John Orvis, the editor of the labor newspaper the *Voice of Industry*. For the next few years, it would be a vital link connecting Transcendentalism, abolitionism, and socialism before disbanding in the early 1850s.

By 1849, William C. Nell—while never an official member—had attached himself to the Town and Country Club. He was the "charge" of the club, a sort of librarian who maintained the books and the reading room.[179] It is likely that he never asked for admittance, probably because the dues were too expensive for the perpetually underemployed Nell. There is no record of his membership being discussed, though it is clear that the club was open to African Americans. Emerson, at least, was on record saying (in regard to Frederick Douglass) that "with regard to color . . . I am of the opinion that there should be no exclusion. Certainly if any distinction be made, let it be in the colored man's favor."[180] Most likely, Nell, who volunteered at a lower wage in order to take the job, wanted the opportunity to interact with some of America's most famous intellectuals. "The Cream of <u>American</u> and foreign Literature cover the Tables," he boasted to a friend. And he was clearly a participant in the intellectual discussions, writing to a friend that "I can assure you I glean much valuable information from the different circles."[181] Nell was proud of his connections. He bragged to his friend Amy Kirby Post about how much "it would please you to meet here and share the Society of Ralph Waldo Emerson, A. Bronson Alcott, and Literary men of various shades."[182] In fact, Alcott even served as a job reference for Nell, who began advertising himself as a freelance "Copyist, Accountant, Collector, and Business Agent."[183]

Nell would continue to act as a personal link between black abolitionism and Transcendentalism. In late 1840s and early 1850s, Alcott, whose varied and frantic philosophical quests had left him perpetually on the brink of poverty, began a series of "Conversations," with which he hoped to support his long-suffering family. These events (literally) brought into conversation radical abolitionists such as Parker Pillsbury, Transcendentalists such as Emerson and Thoreau, and Free Soil politicians such as Charles Sumner and James Russell Lowell. And, by 1851, black abolitionists in the figure of William C. Nell joined. In 1851, Alcott apparently invited Nell, whose name appears on the list of attendees.[184] And it was probably thanks to Nell that Alcott's Conversations were publicized in Douglass's *North Star* in 1850, more evidence of the interaction between black abolitionists and Transcendentalism.[185] Nell continued going to Alcott's Conversations, remarking in a letter to a friend about one he attended in December 1852.[186] These conversations were often held in the room of the Town and Country Club, and the fact that Nell was listed as an official participant suggests that he also functioned as an informal member of Emerson's club. Unfortunately, record keeping was spotty, and any intellectual contributions Nell may have made were not recorded. Nevertheless, his presence, along with that of other radical abolitionists in the Transcendentalist debating society, illustrated well the increasingly close ties between the movements.

The broader public, especially the hostile press, noticed the increased connections between Transcendentalism and abolitionism, appearing both baffling to common sense and threatening to the comforting stability of Massachusetts institutions. As the *National Anti-Slavery Standard* complained in 1841, "Transcendentalism being something new, strange, and unpopular ... therefore it was deemed good policy to prejudice the public mind by representing abolition merely as a lure to transcendentalism."[187] The *New York Herald*, Gotham's mouthpiece for racist populists, noted as early as 1845 that "we find the transcendental philosophers and social reformers of all classes, such as Ralph Waldo Emerson and William H. Channing," in the abolitionist movement.[188] Hostile commentators saw both movements as evidence of the breakdown in traditional hierarchy. Conservatives, such as the Methodist preacher James Porter of Lynn, Massachusetts, condemned Transcendentalism, abolitionism, freethinkers, and come-outers as akin to the "infidels and revolutionists in all ages" and as threats to Christianity, social stability, and the institution of marriage.[189] The association of both Transcendentalism and abolitionism with French Jacobinism was actually quite common, as when a Boston newspaper predicted that "our transcendental philosophers" would soon inspire an upheaval to rival the Reign of Terror.[190] James Henry Hammond, in his famous letters to William Wilberforce, seemed to conflate Transcendentalism with all of democratic modernity, declaring, with ahistorical confidence, that its destructive spirit had been "first concentrated to a focus at Paris" during the Revolution and was now leading the spirit of abolition.[191]

Anti-abolitionist activists quickly discovered that associating abolitionism with Transcendentalism was a good way to discredit it in the minds of many Americans. In 1850, a meeting of the American Anti-Slavery Society in New York was mobbed by the notorious Capt. Rynders and one "Dr. Grant," who appropriated the lectern to give a rambling speech, likely lubricated with cheap whisky, denouncing "your wild speculations in view of transcendental negro elevation."[192] In fact, when moderate abolitionists were concerned about Garrison's radicalism, they attacked him as standing too close to the "transcendental reformers who are running stark mad with the wildest and most bewildering vagaries."[193] And by the 1850s, white Southerners would increasingly attack abolitionism as a product of Transcendentalism. One of the more bizarre attacks on Transcendentalism came from Robert Knox, one of the racial obsessives inspired by the new schools of racial science. Transcendentalism, he claimed, was only attractive to the "Slavonian" mind, and the popularity of "the metaphysics of Fichte, Schelling, Hagel [sic] among South Germans" (and not Anglo-Saxons) proved that "the Caucasian family" was not unified but had racial divisions and hierarchies within it.[194] In 1857, Governor McWillie of Alabama, in an inaugural address, called for Southern defiance against the "transcendental[s] of the higher-law school," who, he explained, must be "crushed out by force, and strangled in their own blood."[195]

Thus, by the end of the 1840s, on the eve of the passage of the Fugitive Slave Act, Transcendentalism and abolitionism were increasingly linked movements in the public mind. None of the major Transcendentalists, by the mid-1840s, had failed to come out in support of abolition. Pretty much every major Transcendentalist with the possible exception of Margaret Fuller, who was now living aboard, had become involved in practical abolitionist activism. Meanwhile, many of the values of Transcendentalism—its idealism, its religious heterodoxy, its utopianism, its distaste of "expedient" logic, and its preference for a "universal" reform that would remake individuals—were becoming part of abolitionism's basic language. By 1848, even A. Bronson Alcott, never one to be accused of being overly practical, was boasting that "<u>Transcendentalism</u>, from being almost purely metaphysical, and thus beyond the reach of the common people, is becoming more practical and, by including the facts of every day life, begins to attract the attention of practical men. It has a <u>state and Church now to build</u>."[196]

CHAPTER 3

The Cotton Economy
and the Rise of Universal Reformers

In December 1843, the Friends of Social Reform in New England began circulating a call to unite the region's nascent socialist movements. Decrying the "Tyranny of Capital" and the associated degradations of chattel slavery, women's subordination, and "all forms of bondage," it called for a convention to be held at the end of the month to discuss social reforms, especially those offered by the French socialist theorist Charles Fourier. Adopting the principles of "Association," the call argued, would elevate the "toiling masses," so that each individual could achieve his and her full destiny.[1] It was signed by members of a variety of currently operational socialist communities, including members of the Northampton Association and the famous Brook Farm. Alongside the names of these well-known white socialists was that of the young black activist William C. Nell, one of only seven people from Boston to sign the call.[2]

Characteristically disorganized, the meeting that followed, during the week after Christmas, did not keep attendance, but descriptions of it noted the presence of abolitionists. Emerson attended, remarking simply in his journal that he had seen his friend A. Bronson Alcott, whom he saw as the socialists' true leader (an opinion likely not shared by the socialists themselves).[3] On the business committee were stalwart white Transcendentalists such as William Henry Channing and George Ripley, along with a newcomer to the Boston reform scene, a young fugitive slave named Frederick Douglass.[4] Scholars have made much of the fact that Douglass had disapproved when a fellow antislavery lecturer named John A. Collins had tried to mix abolitionism and socialism earlier that year.[5] But the presence of the young black abolitionist at this convention suggests that Douglass's opposition to Collins's mix of socialism and abolition had been strategic, not ideological. In concrete terms, the convention accomplished little besides the passage of three resolutions. Emphasizing their interest in peaceful reform, the convention condemned the oppression of women, distinctions based on "caste," and, above all, the "establishment of a MONEYED FEUDALISM."[6] Abolitionists, including William Lloyd Garrison, were prominently in attendance prompting the *Present*, a socialist journal edited by Channing, to declare that this movement was realizing that the "universal principles of Freedom and Human Rights apply to the serfdom of wages as well as to that of chains, to the oppressions of White and Black alike."[7]

Likely the emphasis that Boston socialists put on connecting the cause of the slave to that of broader American life interested the black abolitionists who attended. Nell's friend Douglass later wrote that he was attracted to utopian socialism because its adherents also tended to be abolitionists.[8] Personal friendships also drew Nell to socialism. Especially prominent was George Benson, a member of the Northampton Association, whom Nell knew through Benson's brother-in-law, William Lloyd Garrison, and Henry W. Williams, the general agent for the *Liberator* with whom Nell had collaborated in his campaign to desegregate the Boston public school system.[9] It seems that the meeting converted Nell to Fourierism or at least led him to appreciate its supporters. In the coming years, he would invite a number of prominent advocates of Fourierism, including Henry Clapp Jr. and William Henry Channing, to speak before his black lyceum, the Adelphi Union.[10] Socialists, in other words, were omnipresent in the abolitionist circles of Boston.

In other words, it was extremely common, almost a default position, for Boston abolitionists to question the marketplace. George Fitzhugh, the reactionary proslavery ideologue, was only exaggerating a bit when he wrote that "the abolitionists are all socialists and communists."[11] None other than Frederick Douglass himself remembered that, though he was primarily concerned about slavery in the 1840s, he had "a strong leaning towards communism as a remedy for all social ills."[12] From Wendell Phillips to Theodore Parker to Horace Greeley, prominent antislavery advocates often expressed sympathy for socialist ideas. Historians, though, have often missed this ideological affinity, instead sometimes even going as far as painting abolitionists as proto-capitalists.[13] They have missed how, in the 1840s, many black and white abolitionists began a campaign, imperfect and halting but real, to unite antislavery and anticapitalist politics in New England, calling for "universal," "impartial," and "consistent" reform. The unique political economy of antebellum New England—in which textile elite were increasingly reliant on purchasing cheap cotton from the slaveholder class—contributed to this alliance. To challenge the slaveholders meant also to challenge their "cottonocracy" allies in Boston banks and counting rooms.[14] "Cotton thread holds the union together," Emerson complained, and abolitionists were determined to break that thread.[15]

It was Transcendentalism that helped to create this ideological connection between abolitionism and socialism. The Higher Law Ethos drew on a long tradition of idealist philosophy that envisioned mankind as capable of being able to impose a rational and moral order onto the unwilled chaos of the given world; this politics of idealism drew them especially toward socialist and anticapitalist politics. Transcendentalists, through people such as George Ripley, William Henry Channing, and A. Bronson Alcott, played central roles in the creation of the utopian socialist movement in New England. They helped push New England reformers to take seriously issues of poverty and exploitation. In fact, Nell may have met some of the important white Transcendentalists for the first time at this socialist convention. More important, though, Transcendentalists provided a language and philosophical critique of market life that would reverberate throughout the nineteenth century. Markets and industrial capitalism warped people's minds, they believed, encouraging greed and instrumental thought among the rich while reducing workers to degraded tools of another's will. The fact that Northern men defended both slavery and capitalism was a prime example, Transcendentalists thought, of life lived by the lower laws of psychological hedonism and the dominance of "dead" traditions over morality. And so it was exactly on the domain of a Romantic critique of the marketplace—pioneered in America by Transcendentalists—that many abolitionists began developing their own way to think about a politics that could link the oppression of the enslaved worker with the exploitation of the wage worker.

The 1840s were politically fertile years for the development of the ideas of universal reform, as the combination of abolitionist egalitarianism and Transcendentalist idealism pushed the reform community into increasingly radical and utopian positions. The new alliance between Transcendentalists and abolitionists was beginning to bear fruit. As one abolitionist paper declared, the "Anti-Slavery movement in America . . . begun with no aim beyond the extinction of chattel slavery, [has] gradually discovered itself at odds with war, with the system of free-labor, (so called,) with the enslavement of women, with the church."[16] These American Romantic reformers formed socialist organizations where they debated Hegel and Fourier, condemned slavery, and welcomed freedpeople. Appropriately, the New England reform community responded warmly to the great outbursts of revolution in Europe in 1848. As Parisian workers marched for "work and wages" and demanded the emancipation of slaves in the French West Indies, Boston reformers believed they had found kindred spirits. Inspired by a transatlantic exchange of ideas, New England abolitionists connected their struggle against the American slave power with the French and British workers' fight for democracy and socialism, adopting strategies and arguments from Europe to meet their needs.

The Cotton Economy

It should be no surprise that radical abolitionists were critical of Northern capitalism. Every day, in the workings of New England industrialization, they would have seen evidence of slavery's long shadow. The entire thrust of New England economic development—going back at least to the War of 1812—had seen the New England industrial region and the Southern cotton states become more and more entwined. Historians are increasingly becoming aware that there was one economic system that relied on the labor of both free and enslaved workers to produce cotton, textiles, factories, and dividends.[17] To posit completely separate modes of production—a Northern capitalism and a Southern slavery—is to distort what the antebellum economy looked like to Boston abolitionists.

During the first half of the nineteenth century, economic development transformed New England into a bustling financial and industrial center. The New England countryside became the site of grand experiments in industrialization, the creation of a proletariat, and urbanization. This entire social transformation was made possible by one single commodity: cotton—what Wendell Phillips called the "fibre that bound Massachusetts and Carolina together."[18] The mythical ages of gold and iron, celebrated by classical poets, had passed, Karl Marx quipped, and the Atlantic world was entering the decidedly unheroic "cotton age," in which the commodity was "one of the central pillars" of bourgeois society.[19] Marx considered cotton produced by American slaves to be crucial to the rise of capitalism. This is why, in *Capital*, a mature Marx would conclude that "the veiled slavery of the wage-labourers in Europe needed the unqualified slavery of the New World as its pedestal."[20] Though the sociology of the South Carolina plantation and the Massachusetts mill town was very different, cotton framed both as processes of exchange and production in which slaves picked cotton in the South and white workers spun it into cloth in New England, making economic growth possible. Boston capitalists got rich buying and selling raw cotton as well as by converting it, in their factories, into textiles.

Then, to complete the cycle, many of the finished textiles were sold to the South as "negro cloth" to clothe the very slaves who had picked the cotton. As the Scottish travel writer George Combe, collecting data on Lowell, noted, "The southern slave states afford the great market for the manufactures of New England."[21] By the late 1840s, Boston consistently received about 40 percent of the cotton bales consumed by the country. In 1849, for instance, 270,693 bales of cotton were unloaded in Boston harbor, comprising roughly 44 percent of the cotton consumed by American manufacturers that year.[22] In 1845, an estimated 20,710 workers were employed in the 802 mills operational in the state.[23] While Massachusetts was the largest economy in New England, taking the region as a whole, cotton played an even larger part: on the eve of secession, New England's consumption of Southern cotton would rise to an estimated 800,000 bales, employing about 30,000 workers (roughly 9 percent of the workforce) and $30 million of capital investment.[24]

Industrial capitalism in the North and slavery in the South, then, were linked in a tight embrace that had both economic and moral consequences. As New England mills avidly consumed cotton, Southern planters moved westward into Louisiana and Texas in order to meet the demand, bringing their slaves with them. The New England cotton economy was so entangled with slavery that, in 1832, Massachusetts politician Rufus Choate admitted to a friend that Northern industrialization had caused an "increased value of slaves" in the South, a development that he hoped would eventually lead the slave region to abandon its resistance to protective tariffs.[25] Hidden in Choate's defense of New England industrialization were the stories of thousands of borderland slaves sold away from their families and sent to the South as their "increased value" dictated their sale to the cotton-producing states. Exactly such a tragedy befell Lewis Hayden, still a Kentucky slave when Choate was a congressman, who would be forever haunted by the memory of his infant child sold away from him by Choate's political partner, the famed senator Henry Clay.[26]

The shift from merchant to industrial capital altered the political and ideological assumptions of Boston's ruling class.[27] The importance of cotton to the wealth of this Boston elite led them to begin to take more cautious views on the issue of slavery, even inflecting their nationalism with an acceptance of slavery. Although their general outlook was that of Burkean conservatives who disliked democratic populism, they had originally inherited a Revolutionary-era disapproval of the institution of slavery. During the Missouri Compromise debates, even Daniel Webster had led a group of citizens to introduce a memorial against the spread of slave states. Significantly, Webster's political transition away from free trade and to an embrace of industrialization roughly coincided with his growing reluctance to publicly criticize slavery, as he and the Boston elite forged close links to Southern slaveowners. As merchant Stephen Phillips explained, in "our commercial intercourse with the ports of the slave-holding States . . . it [is] almost impossible for those who continue in the trade, to exonerate themselves from an actual, a direct, a constant participation in the support of slavery."[28] As Henry Adams later drily noted of his New England home, as industrialization proceeded, "the Rights of Man occupied public thoughts less, and the price of cotton more."[29]

More profoundly, Northern industrialization had changed the very way that the Boston elite thought. The rise of the factory system was linked to the domination of an instrumental style of thought, one that weighed costs and benefits, means and ends, with a bloodless rationality. Transcendentalists came to believe that the intellectual influences that dominated Boston elite life—the conservative wing of the Unitarian Church, Edmund Burke's dislike of abstraction, John Locke's epistemology, and Scottish Common Sense benevolence— all were particularly congenial to the psychic demands of the industrial elite. The rejection of Calvinist gloom fit in well with the optimism of an expanding and prosperous bourgeoisie, while the rationality of the Unitarian religion mirrored the predictability they sought in their business transactions. When Emerson quipped that Boston Unitarianism represented "the best diagonal line that can be drawn between Jesus Christ and Abbott Lawrence," he captured the widespread sense of the affinity between elite Unitarianism and the market.[30] The ethical vision of Unitarianism and the Scottish School—while providing a legitimizing veneer of virtue—was not so demanding or rigorous as to seriously question the underlying economic or political order. Their benevolence was not dishonest or insincere. But it had its limits, as the abolitionists quickly discovered—limits that were informed by their conservative readings of British philosophy. From Locke, Burke, and the Scottish Common Sense philosophers, Boston Unitarians took a general distrust of abstract political ideas, preferring the concrete, the knowable, and the accumulated wisdom of the ages as embodied in current institutions.

It was the political issue of tariffs that had finally cemented the moral surrender of the Boston elites. The textile industry could compete with British imports only by maintaining a protective tariff, effectively taxing the rest of the nation to subsidize New England manufacturing. New England's need for a tariff put it in a weaker position vis-á-vis their Southern trading partners, who did not care whether Massachusetts, French, or English factories spun their cotton (in 1850, for instance, while the vast majority of cotton entering Boston came from the South, its 195,076 bales only comprised about 11 percent of Southern cotton, most of which went to Europe).[31] New England industrialists, in other words, needed Southern cotton more than Southern planters needed access to the New England market. Much of antebellum domestic politics could be explained by the fact that Northern capitalists needed the federal government to impose tariffs, protect copyrights, charter banks, and build improvements, leading them to a generally nationalistic outlook, while Southern planters did not need those things and instead eyed with unease a federal government that they might not always wholly dominate. Abolitionists would soon criticize the increasingly desperate concessions that Northern Cotton Whigs would make in order to win the votes of Southern Whigs for new tariffs.

Boston capitalism, in summary, relied heavily on trade with Southern slave-owners, and the entanglement of slavery and capitalism in the constitution of elite power defined the politics of the era. Not only would the rich withhold from abolitionism the financial aid they generously gave to temperance, missionary, and colonization causes, but they would actively conspire to silence the movement. Moreover, elite moral cowardice on the issue of slavery called into question the whole array of intellectual and psychological structures that abetted the Boston elite worldview. The wealthy and respectable would be at the front of the mobs that attacked abolitionists in the street—Elihu Burritt called these mobbings a simple "business transaction," just "one piece of silver paid for Southern trade."[32] Elite churches, grown fat on the donations of merchants, would ban all but the most milquetoast discussions of slavery. As Margaret Fuller noted, socialists, abolitionists, and Transcendentalists all shared this same enemy: a hypocritical and narrow-minded industrial elite. "Disgusted with the vulgarity of a commercial aristocracy," Fuller wrote of the younger generations, "they become radicals; disgusted with the materialistic workings of 'rational religion,' they become mystics."[33]

Abolitionists and Capitalism

This economic history explains a central part of abolitionist rhetoric: their constant and bitter attacks on the Boston capitalist elites. They saw the merchant elites as among those who, alongside the churches and the federal government, provided essential Northern backing for proslavery policies. Garrison had originally wished to distinguish himself from the labor movement, and in a widely

cited (probably overcited) article in the first issue of the *Liberator*, he had pointedly separated himself from the class consciousness of the early Workingmen's
Party. But this article was written when Garrison still hoped to appeal to the
traditional constituencies of moral reform movements: ministers and wealthy
patrons. As he radicalized in the mid-1830s, once it became clear that the mainstream churches, universities, and merchants would fight abolitionism tooth
and nail, he became much more critical of the marketplace and more supportive
of social reorganization.[34] By the mid-1840s, the abolitionist leadership realized
that their constituency would not be the respectable merchants who might
fund overseas missionary work but instead a much more populist constituency
who were interested in a ten-hour day. Theodore Parker was one among many
abolitionist leaders who believed that the movement drew from the middling
class, while the rich and the educated joined the desperate poor in the mobs
that tried to silence it.[35]

The 1840s, as labor recovered from the Panic of 1837, were a particularly
fertile time for collaboration between abolitionists and representatives of the
New England working class. Spokesmen for socialist organizations began appearing in antislavery meetings, and abolitionists such as Garrison became
more interested in socialist communities, often speaking before them, as he did
at the 1844 Convention on the "Reorganization of Society" in Northampton.[36]
While Garrison remained primarily concerned with slavery, he largely abandoned the hostility he once evinced against labor reformers and implicitly acknowledged the overlap between abolitionism and labor reform by running
articles and notices about working-class and utopian socialist events in his paper. Socialist papers such as the *Harbinger* and the labor press such as *Voice of
Industry* advertised abolitionist conventions and ran favorable articles on abolitionist activity. Labor leaders put antislavery planks in their lists of demands, as
the New England Workingmen's Association did, when its fourth plank demanded that the government "abolish all slavery, by connecting the obligation
to cultivate, with the right to own land."[37] The antislavery *Liberator* returned
the favor, publicizing the activity of land reform and labor reform activists. Beginning in 1844, dissidents from the Democratic Party and representatives of
the labor unions formed the labor-oriented Workingmen's Party. The *Liberator*,
normally quite hostile to any political parties, reported meetings of the organization, including printing at length the resolutions of the party.[38] Throughout
the 1840s, in fact, the preeminent abolitionist paper announced various
working-class meetings and events, as it did in June 1845, publicizing a meeting
devoted to "the elevation of the producing classes and industrial reform and the

extinction of slavery and servitude in all their forms."[39] The *Liberator* advertised the organization of socialist clubs, such as the New England Fourier Society, headed by Transcendentalist George Ripley.[40] The placement of these
advertisements suggests that labor and socialist leaders expected that the abolitionist readers of the *Liberator* would be sympathetic to their cause. In 1845, the
New England Workingmen's Association even nominated the abolitionists
Wendell Phillips, William Lloyd Garrison, and Theodore Parker to be delegates
to a labor convention in New York City.[41]

The phrase "Universal Reform" became a rallying cry that denoted a politics that included justice for the slave as well as for the Northern worker.[42] The
Hopedale Community advertised itself as a "Universal Reform Association"
while William Lloyd Garrison took to praising colleagues' devotion to "the
cause of Universal Reform."[43] The term even makes an appearance in the *Communist Manifesto*, where Marx and Engels protest that scientific socialism was
not "invented, or discovered, by this or that would-be universal reformer."[44] Increasingly, thus, New England abolitionists incorporated critiques of the wage
system in their thought. Thomas Wentworth Higginson considered himself "at
least a halfway socialist for life," and Parker rejoiced at the arrival of Fourierism,
"because I think our present form of society is irrational and unchristian . . .
trade (in the main) is robbery."[45] In the late 1840s, Higginson barnstormed on
behalf of the ten-hour day, teasing his businessman brother that he had just addressed an "infuriated Torchlight convention of the plainer classes."[46] Even
after the Civil War, Lydia Maria Child wrote to a friend that the socialist "Fourier was a great prophet of the future. I am convinced that this troublesome
knot of employers and employed can never be disentangled except by some process of association which shall apportion some manual labor to all, and some
culture and recreation to all."[47]

Black abolitionists were not of one mind about the role of white workers in
their movement, but some eagerly hoped to make common cause. William
Powell, the New Bedford black leader, was one of many abolitionists who believed that the logic of slavery threatened the freedom of white Northern workers as well as Southern slaves—"if it is right to enslave black men in *South
Carolina*, under the United States Constitution, then it is right to enslave white
laborers in *Massachusetts*," he told a meeting of "Colored Citizens" in the seaport town.[48] Speaking of the prospects of the abolitionist movement, Charles
Lenox Remond declared that "the poor white man is as interested in its promotion as the black man . . . the slave is a wronged man, and the poor white man
who pays his taxes to support Slavery shown his relation to the infernal sys-

tem."[49] On the other hand, Samuel R. Ward could savage both the commercial elite who supported slavery and also condemn the "very low origin" of anti-abolitionist Americans, implying that aristocratic England treated blacks better than Republican America because of their wealth and superior culture.[50] If Ward sometimes baited anti-abolitionists as "low, degraded persons," he also noticed attempts to improve the lives of white workers and praised government intervention "between the employer and the employed, [that] led to the adoption of many very important improvements," for the British working class.[51] More common than expressing direct solidarity with the workers was the rhetorical strategy employed by John S. Rock: viciously attacking the Northern rich. "The educated and wealthy class despise the negro," he told a Massachusetts audience, "because they have robbed him of his hard earnings, or, at least, have got rich off the fruits of his labor; and they believe if he gets his freedom, their fountain will be dried up." If black thinkers generally emphasized the moral degradation of the proslavery rich, rather than focus on their economic exploitation of workers, this did not prevent some, as Rock did, from eventually determining that "the interest of the laboring classes is mutual" and looking forward to the day when white and black workers might work together.[52]

One indirect way that abolitionists expressed their skepticism about the market and its connection to slavery was in their consistent anti-urbanism. They argued that the ideological conquest of slavery could be best seen in its dominance of the politics of certain cities, Boston prominent among them. When discussing why the North supported slavery, Emerson declared that material self-interest accounted for why in "the seaboard, and in great thoroughfares . . . the Northern merchant or manufacturer exchanges hospitalities with the Southern planter, or trades with him, and loves to exculpate himself from all sympathy with those turbulent Abolitionists."[53] Theodore Parker was more specific, arguing that the "slave power depends on the four great commercial cities of the North—Cincinnati, Philadelphia, New York, and Boston."[54] J. Sella Martin had a similar view of the geography of Northern racism, optimistically telling a British audience that "there was no feeling hostile to the negro in the North, except on the seaboard of the Atlantic."[55] The patrician Josiah Quincy, former Federalist mayor, traced the moral decline of Boston to the expansion of cotton profitability and the subsequent rise of the positive good theory of slavery in the South. "A like change," Quincy argued, "contemporaneously, came over the free States, in certain localities, where cotton-spinning and cotton-weaving began to be a source of wealth, and consequently of political power." In case any of his listeners doubted his point, Quincy continued,

"Boston became one of these localities . . . and of course became identified with the cotton-spinning and cotton-weaving interests."[56]

While Boston did slavery's bidding, the New England countryside, especially the burgeoning mill towns, was antislavery. Outside of Boston, as James Freeman Clarke wrote, people were "not corrupted by direct commercial transactions with the South," and so antislavery assumptions still held strong.[57] Even textile industrialist and Cotton Whig Amos A. Lawrence admitted, in a private letter, that "we are more slavish here in Boston, than in the country."[58] Industrial centers such as Springfield, home to John Brown during the 1840s; Worcester, where Thomas Wentworth Higginson reported workers reading abolitionist tracts to each other as they worked; and Lowell, home to John Greenleaf Whittier, were centers of radical antislavery activity.[59] New Bedford, despite being a seaport town, remained orientated toward the whaling industry—and since it did not sell a significant amount of sperm oil in the South, there was greater abolitionist radicalism there than in Boston.[60] Geography, as is normally the case, indicated class, as proslavery Boston was far wealthier than the antislavery and industrial hinterland. As Higginson summed it up, "radicalism went with the smell of leather," referring to the aprons worn by the shoemakers of Lynn and Abington, a class he saw as particularly drawn to religious and political revolution.[61] The abolitionist sense of political geography seems to have been largely correct. For instance, in 1842, supporters of the fugitive slave Latimer presented a massive petition to the state legislature. After a comprehensive canvassing campaign, they were able to get roughly 10 percent of the population of Lowell, 16.5 percent of Lynn, and 21.5 percent of Concord to sign their petition. A paltry 7.4 percent of Boston signed.[62] Antislavery parties likewise tended to do relatively poorly in Boston compared to their performance in the state's interior. Transcendentalist pastoralism and anti-urbanism, then, were linked to the widespread belief that—as Thoreau wrote—when it came to slavery, there were two sides: "the party of the city, and the party of the country," with only the latter having any moral authority.

Given the geography of cotton and the ways that it connected Boston to slavery, criticisms of the city became one of the most popular ways for black thinkers to articulate their rejection of the Boston Associates and the cotton economy. Not wanting to give Southern propagandists ammunition, they rarely focused on the suffering of the Northern worker, which they probably found underwhelming compared to that of the slave anyway. But Boston's blacks were profoundly alienated from their city and especially criticized its economic elites' complicity with slavery. Charles Lenox Remond, for instance, declared that

"Boston remains a base conservative city, and Massachusetts a base conservative State."[63] Henry Highland Garnet attacked the city's self-identification as a center of revolutionary liberty. "Now, Boston was called the cradle of liberty," he told a British audience. "If it were the cradle, they had managed to rock the cradle so hard that it had killed the baby."[64] And William Wells Brown went so far as to tell a British audience that "the slave is just as much a slave in the city of Boston" as in South Carolina.[65]

United by their distaste for the Boston rich, in the 1840s, black and white abolitionists increasingly framed their antislavery message in language familiar to labor organizers. While the *Liberator* ran notices of meetings of workers, it was Elizur Wright's *Chronotype* that really exemplified the growing affinity between these movements.[66] Wright's paper, which was a daily unlike Garrison's biweekly offering, was arguably more influential in antislavery circles by the late 1840s. Wright had long hoped to ally the workers' movement and the antislavery cause—spearheading a campaign for the abolitionist Liberty Party to fight on behalf of the ten-hour workday—and opened his paper up to debates on socialism and abolitionism. In his journal, Emerson noted that his family "read the vivacious little Chronotype, eating rebellion with our daily bread."[67] Wright published regular columns by the Boston Union of Associationists along with his own work opposing the Fugitive Slave Law and supporting the Free Soil Party.[68] In a typical editorial, he quoted one "W.G.C.," who thought that America "must have slavery abolished at the South, that Socialism may get an entrance."[69] Wright was also a regular speaker at labor and working-class rallies.[70] When the *Chronotype* was folded into the *Commonwealth*, Wright, who remained the editor, continued to advocate for workers, even betraying his own class of newspaper editors by supporting a strike of New York City journeymen printers.[71]

Workers at the Lowell mills demonstrated how labor politics, abolitionism, and Transcendentalism could all blend to create an oppositional activist culture. At age eleven, Lucy Larcom entered the mills, working as a "doffer," running between the spinning frames and changing the bobbins, before eventually working her way up to become a spinner. Years later, she would remember with some disgust the dull monotony of the "buzzing and hissing and whizzing of pulleys and rollers and spindles."[72] Smuggling into the factory books of poetry and philosophy to entertain and educate herself, she began to write for the famous *Lowell Offering* and soon was following the well-worn philosophical path of reading first Locke, then Coleridge, and then finally embracing Emerson and the Transcendentalists.[73] She would one day write a poem to Emerson— "doors hast thou opened for us, thinkers, seer!"[74] And when the antislavery

poet Whittier took her under his wing in 1843, she became committed to abolitionist politics.

According to Larcom, workers at the mills understood their moral and
economic entanglement with slavery. Years after she left the mill, she wrote a
poem about work in the Lowell factories. A main character in it reflects on the
fact that "for our daily bread, we, who must earn it, have to suffocate the cry of
conscience."

> When I've thought,
> Miss Willoughby, what soil the cotton-plant
> We weave, is rooted in, what waters it,—
> The blood of souls in bondage—I have felt
> That I was sinning against light, to stay
> And turn the accursed fibre into cloth
> For human wearing. I have hailed one name,
> You know it—'Garrison'—as a slave might hail
> His soul's deliverer. Am not I enslaved
> In finishing what slavery has begun?[75]

Larcom's poem illustrates the way some "mill girls" saw how cotton linked the
oppression of the slave with their own working conditions—"enslaved in finish-
ing what slavery has begun."

Larcom was not alone in noticing antislavery opinion among the workers
who turned the slave-picked cotton into textiles. As early as 1835, a number of
Southern leaders became outraged to discover that in Lowell, a town they considered within their affective embrace because of its economic ties, workers were
organizing abolitionist societies.[76] In 1845, the labor press proudly noted that the
line of mill girls in Lowell who signed an antislavery petition was "more than a
mile" long.[77] In fact, the fame of the relatively apolitical *Lowell Offering*, which
was managed by paternalist local ministers, has probably concealed some of this
antislavery radicalism. Larcom remembered that the mill girls were "unanimous
on the antislavery side."[78] Harriet Robinson, a friend of Lucy's, was only a teenager when she helped lead a strike in 1836.[79] She remembered reading newspapers—
including the *Non-Resistant, Liberator*, and even the Transcendentalist *Dial*—with
her coworkers.[80] As if to weave together all the threads that tied together resistance to the cotton economy, Harriet, who later married William Robinson, a
prominent Free Soil journalist who went by the name "Warrington," attended
an antislavery "sewing society" at Emerson's house in 1857, probably organized

by Emerson's wife. Lucy, who would remain Harriet's lifelong friend, was impressed that she had been "a-gossiping to the house of the Seer."[81]

Transcendentalist Theory

It was no coincidence that some factory workers were drawn to Emersonian philosophy. Transcendentalism was closely linked to ideas about criticizing the marketplace. As Emerson joked, referencing the area in Boston where banks tended to congregate, "the view taken of Transcendentalism in State Street is that it threatens to invalidate contracts."[82] Transcendentalists, of course, had started their rebellion with an assault on the mainstream Unitarian Church, and given the church's close connection with the economic elite, Transcendentalists soon widened their charge to encompass an attack on the power and authority of the Boston rich. There were clear affinities between the emerging capitalist self and Lockean and Scottish Common Sense philosophy. Locke and thinkers of the Scottish Enlightenment were themselves crucial figures in the development of free trade and capitalist doctrines. And in the hands of Locke's more materialistic followers, a buffered possessive self would develop out of empiricist ethics (which defined morality through one's individual experiences of pleasure and pain) and easily morph into *homo economicus*, the instrumentally rational maximizer of their own economic utility. American followers of the Scottish School such as the Cotton Whigs disdained what Adam Smith had called the "man of system" a person who has the hubris to try to instill an overarching rational logic on the self-moving system of society.[83]

The American Transcendentalists, though, were quintessential "men of system." Their ethics posited a rational and spiritual subject, one who could critique existing historical and social arrangements by the light of a critical moral and rational logic.[84] They demanded a reassertion of human agency over what Theodore Parker called the "accidents of human history."[85] As followers of German idealist philosophy, perhaps an inclination toward socialism was inscribed deep in the intellectual DNA of Transcendentalism. The rationalist and critical philosophies of Kant, Schilling, and Hegel were closely associated with the simmering revolutionary energy that churned beneath the surface of absolutist Europe.[86] As early as 1843, Friedrich Engels was arguing that the rise of communism in Germany was the product of the "philosophical revolution" of Kant and, of course, Hegel.[87] The most famous product, of course, of this connection between German idealist philosophy and revolutionary traditions would be Karl

Marx, whose early debt to the philosophies of Hegel and Feuerbach is well known. The internal logic of New England Transcendentalism, inspired as it was by these same Continental philosophers and growing in similar economic conditions, drew its adherents to a parallel, if less militant, criticism of capitalism.

For New England thinkers, though, it would be the early essays of Thomas Carlyle, the acerbic British writer, that both introduced many of the themes of German philosophy to America and served as foundational texts for the emerging Transcendentalist critique of the marketplace. In his extraordinarily important 1829 essay *Signs of the Times*, Carlyle described industrial mechanization as the source of all that ailed British society. All of England, he charged, from its religion to its philosophy, its politics to its art, was becoming dominated by materialism, instrumental logic, and the colonizing mentalities of the marketplace. The dark mysteries of the human soul, the awe of God's presence, and the ancient problem of the relationship of man to his fellow men: modern thought treated all of these mighty questions of the human experience like math problems, to be dissected by the cold tools of science and utilitarian logic. Carlyle linked this cultural and economic philistinism to the reigning philosophies of Locke and the Scottish School, whose epistemologies had fashioned the human mind into a machine, simply inputting sensual experiences in one end and cranking out a finished product of thoughts and opinions from the other. *Signs of the Times* was most concerned with the spiritually deadening values of the modern age, but its use of industrialization as both a metaphor and a symptom of this disorder demonstrated the manner in which many Romantic intellectuals would come to view capitalism.[88] Before his rightward turn was consolidated, then, Carlyle was widely associated with his criticisms of the marketplace and defenses of the British working class. His essay *Chartism*, whose language on the "cash nexus" would find its way into Marx's *Communist Manifesto*, was one of the first serious intellectual critiques of capitalism that most New England intellectuals had ever read.

From their earliest influences, then, Transcendentalists connected their philosophical rejection of English and Scottish empiricism with concerns about the excesses of the marketplace. And so, it wasn't just the "socialist" wing of the Transcendentalists who criticized capitalism. Even among those Transcendentalists not associated with George Ripley, the logic of their ideas pushed them to see market life as lower, limited, and unjust. For instance, in *Self-Reliance*, a text too often misread as the philosophical rendering of the impulses of possessive individualism, Emerson cautioned that "the reliance on Property, including the reliance on governments which protect it, is the want of self-reliance." Greed and excessive concern for material comfort exemplified an unhealthy displacement of one's inner genius onto external goods, crutches that prevented self-development.[89] In fact, a theme that runs throughout Emerson's writings, from his earliest political writings of the 1840s up until his Civil War–era speeches, was his association of property with passivity, cowardice, and moral betrayal. The duality that suffused so much Transcendentalist philosophy reappeared as a criticism of the material world that seemed to dominate not just the spiritual world but even the ethical and political worlds. "Things are in the saddle," he famously wrote, "And ride Mankind."[90] Emerson was no communist, but he would have heartily approved of young Marx's sense that capitalism strangled the inner true life of man in the process of producing external material things. Throughout the 1840s, he would list socialism as one of the great reform movements that was a sign of a better day ahead. "As long as our civilization is essentially one of property, of fences, of exclusiveness," he declared, "it will be mocked by delusion. Our riches will leave us sick; there will be bitterness in our laughter; and our wine will burn our mouth."[91]

Emerson's distrust of property was tied to broader themes in his thought: his celebration of self-creation and his linked rejection of the dead weight of traditions and the inheritance of the world as given. These two impulses—skepticism of property and his ethics of infinite personal becoming and creation—were linked at a metaphoric level: in *Representative Men*, the "party of property" stood in for those in American society most tied to a traditional religious and existential worldview, to the unthinking defense of orthodoxy and conformity. But at a more concrete level, Emerson described conservatives as those who defended "the interests of dead labor—that is, the labor of hands long ago still in the grave, which labor is now entombed in money stocks, or in land and buildings owned by idle capitalists."[92] Here, property—described in the terms of the classical labor theory of value as the crystallization of past labor—becomes a literal embodiment of the accumulated and crushing traditions that the self-reliant person must overcome. Emerson's distrust of "dead" property fit in well with his larger argument in *Self-Reliance* and elsewhere that mankind suffered a loss of existential courage when it "postpones or remembers" rather than lives unreflexively in the present.[93] While Emerson's vision for the future remained stubbornly individualist, his language brings to mind Marx's dictum that capitalism was the domination of "dead" congealed past labor (capital) over living present labor and that "in bourgeois society, therefore, the past dominates the present."[94]

If Emerson's critiques of the market were always a bit detached, uttered with a certain well-fed disdain for the hustle and bustle of State Street, Thoreau was living his rejection of the market's comforts in the untamed wood of rural New England. For Thoreau, capitalism and industrialization colonized the soul, imprinting a set of values and habits onto the self that were hostile to a good life. Even more than Emerson, Thoreau became obsessed with the manner in which modern industry was dehumanizing his neighbors, mechanizing their mental and physical life. Thoreau's criticisms of the market were fourfold: first, in echoes of Marx's arguments about alienation, Thoreau argued that the modern division of labor was demeaning to the producer, turning individuals into rote automatons with no "poetic" sense left to their work.[95] Second, Thoreau suggested that these types of employments and the manic search for wealth degraded the mind, so that our "very intellect shall be macadamized," splintered into separate components and no longer capable of an integral relationship with the world. The lathe operator learned how to perform that function but never to question what it would mean to live a good life when he was not turning the lathe.[96] The habits of mind created by the market—its greed, instrumentality, and cautious prudence—discouraged those virtues that led to a good and heroic life. Third, modern industry created artificial desires in people, pushing the latest ridiculous fashion from Paris on Americans who bought luxury goods simply to impress others, encouraging people to live outside themselves, and orienting their sense of the good toward social approval and status. And finally, uniting all of Thoreau's criticisms was his sense that there was a fundamental contradiction between the pursuit of wealth and living an examined and ethical life. "The ways by which you may get money," he concluded in his bitter essay *Life Without Principle*, "almost without exception lead downward."[97]

In a broadest sense, then, Emerson and Thoreau were upset that capitalism and industrialization seemed to be a triumph of material things over human nature, of the logical and finite Understanding rather than the spiritual and infinite Reason. In fact, Emerson and other Transcendentalists frequently associated the market economy with the phenomenal world, with the half of the human experience dominated by Understanding and physical necessity. In his essay on Montaigne, for instance, Emerson described the "men of toil and trade and luxury" as part of the "animal world." The "trade in our streets," he wrote, "believes in no metaphysical causes."[98] Society itself seemed to be replacing its human leaders with mechanical ones. Industrialization set in motion processes that seemed to lack a human will but, dragging people along with them, set up factories here and railroads there, wages at this price and dividends at that. Emerson called this logic the "law for thing" and fretted that "it run wild, and doth the man unking."[99] When Marx complained that under capitalism, man was the "plaything of alien forces," he was making a similar point about the power-lessness of man's individual agency in the face of the impersonal and unwilled laws of the market. Following Carlyle, who had argued that Lockean philoso-phy implied that "the force of circumstance" determined one's fate, Transcen-dentalists associated this loss of human agency, this surrender to the prevailing and arbitrary conditions of the world, with the reigning British tradition of Lockean empiricism.

Thus, one of the central aspects of the Transcendentalist imagination that linked it with anticapitalism was the promethean will to dominate these "alien forces," to restore man's supremacy over the law of things by exerting rational and moral control over the world. At its broadest level, this sense that human rationality should have priority over the unwilled fatalism of materiality went back to Hegel and, before him, Kant. For Kant, individual human freedom was found in the victory over heteronomy, in the dominance of reason over material forces in the self. His followers, like Schiller, quickly spun out a political narra-tive in which man becomes free exactly when "he leaves the dominion of a blind necessity."[100] Just as morality involved a heroic process of exerting rational con-trol over the forces of the self, so did collective freedom involve an assertion of human authority over the inertia of physical desire, history, or the untamed marketplace, what Herbert Marcuse later called the "blind pressures and pro-cesses of the prevailing empirical order of life."[101]

Thoreau and Emerson saw the solution in both social and individual terms, in seizing control of the anarchic forces within and outside that tried to dictate to one's self the terms of life. In Emerson's *The Conservative*, an essential source for his political philosophy, he defined conservatism as a pessimism about human ability rooted in an unhealthy submission to the world as currently or-dered. Conservativism's "total legislation is for the present distress. . . . [it] takes as low a view of every part of human action and passion."[102] At its best, Emer-son's faith in what he called "an infinite hope for mankind" could spur a uto-pian reevaluation of society, an impatience with things as they were and a boundless optimism about mankind's ability to remake the world.[103] The cen-tral message of Thoreau's *Walden* is the possibility of individual revolution, of reclaiming one's inner life from the traditions and claustrophobic expectations of society—especially those created by the needs of the market. Thus, he ended his classic with the famous call to arms: "There is more day to dawn. The sun is but a morning star."[104] This faith in human potential (mankind's "infinite wor-thiness," as Emerson described it), in the remaking of the world or at least the self-as-the-world, was a far cry from the Burkean traditionalism that dominated the Unitarian New England elite or even the proto-libertarianism of Jacksonian Democrats.[105]

This Transcendentalist critique of property mirrored closely their hatred of slavery. Slaveholders demanded respect for their "property rights" with the same arrogance that Northern factory owners did, so it is no surprise that a critique of one would transfer to the other. But Transcendentalists had deeper theoretical reasons for connecting capitalism to slavery. They often described the slaveholder and his Northern allies with the same philosophical language of existential cowardice and moral betrayal as they did the capitalist. "The argument of the slaveholder," Emerson wrote, "is one & simple: he pleads Fate."[106] In other words, a slaveholder went with physical necessity and the momentum of past experience while denying the higher values of spirit, will, and Reason. This was the exact same philosophical critique that Emerson had made against the Northern rich, that they were examples of the dominance of the unwilled and unexamined parts of the psyche. Thus, it was no coincidence, he thought, that the "vulgarity of wealth" in the North voted to uphold slavery and against funding schools.[107] Thoreau and Fuller used similar language, associating both slaveholders and Northern capitalists with the moral degradation that comes with relying on wealth, with the surrender to the lower and unreasoning parts of the soul: greed, short-term interest, and narrow instrumental thought. Meanwhile, Emerson, more than many abolitionists themselves, realized that the fundamental logic of antislavery implied an attack on all forms of unearned wealth, on whether "dead" capital would dominate over "alive" labor, not just riches derived from enslavement. "Slavery & Antislavery is the question of property & no property, rent & antirent . . . every man must do his own work, or, at least, receive no interest for money . . . that is at last the upshot" of abolitionism, the Transcendentalists wrote in his journal.[108]

Black Transcendentalists shared this sense that the goal of philosophy was to impart moral order onto the unjust status quo. Two of the prominent black supporters of utopian socialism—Frederick Douglass and William C. Nell—shared this belief in a promethean philosophy, one that could imagine a new world and act to create it. In his comments on the Northampton Association, Frederick Douglass confirmed that the various "isms" of antebellum New England, including Transcendentalism, sought to "liberate mankind from the bondage of time-worn custom," implying the connection between the philosophical rejection of the given and the fight against slavery.[109] Nell, responding to the French Revolution of 1848, articulated clearly his political philosophy. Like Emerson, he split the political world up into "Conservative" and "Reformer," the first of whom was satisfied with the status quo, unable or unwilling to imagine a new society. The "Reformer," on the other hand, is marked by his dedication to abstract ideals, by the "freest investigation of all subjects connected with the progress of humanity." Unlike the Conservative, who is motivated by a fear for the currently existing institutions, the Reformer seeks to "make a practical application" of both his knowledge and his hopes.[110]

When talking about abolitionism and other reforms, black thinkers often evoked the "spirit of the age . . . the upward tendency of the oppressed throughout the world."[111] This optimistic faith in progress, shared by Nell and Douglass, is jarring to our postmodern ears, convinced as our age is that "grand narratives" of progress and emancipation are nothing but the delusions of the Whiggish middle class. But for black and abolitionist thought, the celebrations of progress were essential exactly because they contained an implicit criticism of the world as currently ordered. If antebellum America offered little beside the horrors of slavery and the degradations of racism, the black celebration of the progressive "spirit of the age" tied them to a fundamentally critical worldview, one contrasting the given present with the possibilities of an ideal future.

At its most basic, the Transcendentalist impulse expanded the set of possibilities open to New England reformers. They did not have to be content with accepting either slavery or capitalism as currently constituted but pushed themselves to imagine a world free of hierarchies. Narratives that presume market capitalism was the only possible alternative to slavery fail to see the rich sense of possibility and utopian desire that animated New England reformers, black and white. The Romantic critique of the market and the vision of a promethean man shaping his own self and social environment were powerful factors drawing the New England reform community to attack both capitalism and slavery. It would be the Transcendentalists surrounding George Ripley and the Boston Union of Associationists who played crucial roles realizing this vision in the antebellum labor reform movement.

The Socialist Challenge

Within this ideological mix of socialism, Transcendentalism, and abolitionism, a number of utopian socialist communities flourished. The most famous example of Transcendentalist economic experimentation was the utopian community at Brook Farm, home to George Ripley, Nathaniel Hawthorne (briefly), and Charles A. Dana, as well as a significant number of working-class New Englanders.

George Ripley, one of the leaders of the early Transcendentalists, had founded Brook Farm with the goal of uniting physical with mental labor and to serve as a model for future cooperative ventures. After some agonizing soul searching, Emerson declined Ripley's invitation to join, though he claimed to admire the effort and was a frequent visitor. Brook Farm has achieved almost legendary status, though it can appear a bit like a Rorschach test, one's interpretation of the community revealing as much about the observer's attitude toward Transcendentalism and socialism as about the experiment itself. To those such as Hawthorne, always skeptical of Transcendentalism's pretensions, Brook Farm could later be mocked as the daydream of privileged and ultimately self-centered idealists. His novel the *Blithedale Romance* is widely seen as criticism, occasionally humorous but always cutting, of his time at Brook Farm. To others, the commune's destruction in a fiery blaze is emblematic of the "dark side" of utopia, the inevitable failings of communalism.[112] Finally, optimists see in Brook Farm evidence of the commendable democratic experimentation of Transcendentalism, of an attempt to make real the promise of individual fulfillment through the communal reunion of manual and mental labor. Later followers of the Arts and Crafts movement would see Brook Farm as a precedent for their attempts to resist the dehumanizing mechanization endemic to Gilded Age capitalism.

Whatever one thinks about Brook Farm and antebellum socialism, its birth in a spirit of radical criticism of the marketplace is a stark reminder of the utopian politics of the era. At the end of his life, long after he had abandoned his socialist idealism, Charles A. Dana, an early member of Brook Farm, defined its social philosophy as the attempt to spread democratic relations into all spheres of life.[113] As we have seen, many utopian communities such as Hopedale and the Northampton Association invited black members and fugitive slaves to join their community. In 1844, after the convention attended by William C. Nell and Frederick Douglass, Brook Farm officially came under the spell of Charles Fourier's ideas, and they began following the French socialist into the formation of elaborate "Phalanxes," communal spaces where men and women would live and work together.[114] The *Liberator* ran positive articles on the association while it was operational.[115] Ever since Marx's fierce attacks against the idealistic communes of utopian socialism, which he derided as the "cookshops of the future," "duodecimo editions of New Jerusalem," and "castles in the air," many leftists have dismissed such schemes as unworkable fantasies, naive attempts to substitute class conflict with the chimera of interclass cooperation.[116] The pragmatism of Fourierism aside, it is clear that its adherents were motivated by a genuine dislike of the marketplace and a real sense of "the injustice of our common system of *Wages*, the tediousness, oppressiveness, and unhealthiness of our habits of *Labor*."[117]

Moreover, starting with Brook Farm itself (which had a significant working-class membership), Fourierism provided a real forum for Transcendentalist interaction with working-class New Englanders and their concerns.[118] The *Harbinger*, the newspaper put out by Brook Farm residents, is one of the best sources for sympathetic descriptions of New England working-class conventions and politics, like the 1845 New England Workingmen's Convention, to which Brook Farm sent delegates.[119] Recent histories of the New England labor movement have emphasized the degree to which idealist reformers such as the Brook Farmers were crucial, if "uneasy," allies with the more pragmatic bread-and-butter leaders of the trade unions.[120] A labor movement composed of pure wage laborers did not yet exist in New England; indeed, in the flux of a newly industrializing society, a clearly defined industrial working class was only barely visible. Instead, labor reform movements were "cross-class" institutions comprising manual laborers, reformers and intellectuals, farmers, and, until well into the postwar period, sympathetic small-scale employers, all united by a "producerist" ideology.

After Brook Farm's main building—its "Phalanstery"—burnt down in 1846 and the commune dissolved, many of its veterans formed the Boston Union of Associationists, the most prominent antebellum socialist organization in New England. The Union of Associationists had a number of goals, from the ideological task of spreading socialist doctrines (an undertaking they assigned to the unfortunately named "Group of Indoctrination") to the more pragmatic goal of signing workers up for social insurance policies ("guarantees"), of which they were a pioneer.[121] Along with their commitment to the New England labor reform movement, the Boston Union developed close ties to abolitionists, both ideologically and personally.[122] Its members drew heavily from the same brew of reform idealism and Transcendentalism that infused the greater abolition movement ("the relative bearing of the ideal with the actual was then briefly considered," ran the minutes of one typical meeting").[123] Fourier himself had strongly condemned chattel slavery as the worst kind of oppression, and the official line of the *Harbinger* was that cooperative principles would aid emancipation. "The first step" of Associationism with regard to slavery, the *Harbinger* declared, would be emancipation and reparations "for the past injustice . . . inflicted" upon slaves.[124] While the broader U.S. Fourierism movement contained many who wished to downplay the issue of slavery and opposed the

entry of black members into Phalanxes, the New England wing, as the Fourier-
ist William Henry Channing pointed out, was far more likely to oppose slavery
and embrace civil rights.[125]

At a personal level, networks of friendship and political allegiances within
Associationism introduced a significant number of socialists into abolitionism.
The Boston Union of Associationists was not a big organization (around eighty-
five people attended meetings over the course of about five years), but among its
members were future members of the abolitionist Boston Vigilance Committee
such as John Butome, Henry Bowditch, William Henry Channing, Charles
List, Henry Trask (who balanced his time protecting slaves with his day job as a
harness maker and his official duties as the president of the pro-labor New
England Industrial League), and Joseph Allyn.[126] Other members of the Associationists would join the even more radical Boston Anti-Man Hunting
League.[127] The records of ticket purchasers to Associationist lectures show an
even closer connection between the worlds of Fourierism and abolition, with
prominent antislavery activists such as Theodore Parker, Samuel Gridley Howe,
and Ellis Gray Loring paying to attend socialist lectures.[128] The related Religious Union of Associationists—a sort of socialist church led by William
Henry Channing—brought together a remarkable collection of Transcendentalists, traditional Protestants, "skeptics," and even Catholics and Jews to discuss social reform within a religious context.[129]

New England socialists, far more than their European comrades, paid close
attention to racial slavery. Some utopian socialist experiments occurred in rare
places in antebellum New England society in which black activists could enter
into meaningful domestic and social equality with white Northerners.[130] The
Northampton Association was the most egalitarian of the socialist communes.[131] Its Garrisonian founders actively sought out black members. Two of
its famous black members, David Ruggles, the controversial leader of the New
York Vigilance Committee who had shuttled Frederick Douglass to freedom,
and Sojourner Truth, spent years at Northampton, while Douglass was a prominent visitor. The Association's racial egalitarianism was obviously the main reason they felt comfortable joining, but black activists were also drawn to its
economic vision. Douglass fondly remembered how its members sought to
"curb and fix limits to individual selfishness; to diffuse wealth among the lowly;
to banish poverty."[132] According to Adin Ballou, "about half" of the Hopedale
Community, another communal association in Massachusetts, "zealously espoused the Temperance, Anti-Slavery, and Peace movements." In fact, as a fugitive slave, Douglass had often stayed with utopian communes. On April 3, 1842,

for instance, while on his first speaking tour, he spent the night at the Hopedale Community. Fugitive slaves, such as Rosetta Hall, who joined Hopedale in 1845, sometimes found safe homes in utopian communes.[133]

The "socialism" of this era, of course, had neither the ideological rigor nor the scientific pretensions of the socialism that would follow it. In fact, in the coming years, German immigrants—who were more likely to bring with them a Marxist rigor and an anticlerical bias—were often shocked at the fuzzy romanticism and softheaded idealism of the Yankee socialists.[134] In many ways, the self-styled "socialists" of antebellum New England are closer to the communitarian tradition than revolutionary socialism—as much an ill-focused spirit of protest against the market as a concrete program of action. A. Bronson Alcott and George Ripley were not Lenin or Trotsky. Today, though, the New England socialists' eclecticism looks good compared to the single-minded focus of some socialists who followed them. Thanks to what William Henry Channing called their "Idea of Unity in Variety," they were more able to take seriously slavery, women's rights, and peace issues alongside labor and economy.[135] And certainly, their open-minded idealism was preferable to the steely-eyed managerism of many later socialists. Interminable lectures about spiritualism—not the gulag—were the worst punishment Yankee socialists ever doled out. American reformers thus already had a rich philosophical and political tradition of socialist thought to build on when word of the bubbling socialist energy from Europe reached their shores.

Transatlantic Currents

By the late 1840s, the "Universal Reformers" had been drawn into a transnational discussion about slavery, labor, and freedom that brought them into direct collaboration with European revolutionaries. This had started as early as the beginning of the decade, when Garrison had begun a fruitful collaboration with British Chartists that had helped shape abolitionist support for labor. As early as 1842, for instance, he published a letter in the *Liberator* from a Chartist organizer that compared the "direct, and open and personal" slavery that existed in the American South with the "indirect" slavery of wages.[136] Wendell Phillips and Frederick Douglass, as well, encountered Chartist politics in their travels abroad and came to support the Charter.[137] But it was the Revolutions of 1848 that truly cemented this connection between European revolutionary politics and American abolitionism. Abolitionists celebrated and encouraged the

revolutions. Meanwhile, strong ideological and intellectual links connected antislavery and Transcendentalist ideas to what was occurring in Europe. It was
no coincidence that a Transcendentalist such as Margaret Fuller spent the last
years of her life in Rome, working (unsuccessfully) to create a democracy in
Italy while coming to realize the close affinities between European democrats
and American abolitionists.

In February 1848, banquets held by opposition parties in Paris erupted into
full-blown revolt, the National Guard began disobeying orders and siding with
the revolutionary crowds, and Louis Phillipe, the "bourgeois king," fled for
England. From a balcony of the Hôtel de Ville, the Romantic poet Alphonse
Lamartine declared France to be, once again, a republic. All of a sudden, decades of pent-up revolutionary fervor burst across the continent: in Germany,
Italy, Hungary, and elsewhere, coalitions of workers, idealistic students, and
shopkeepers overthrew monarchs and began the process of uniting their nations. Europe had seen cycles of revolution before—this was, after all, the third
major French revolt in sixty years—but these were something new. In Paris,
French workers, the "Red Republicans," marched under the slogan of "work and
wages," and under the leadership of the socialist Louis Blanc, the Provisional
Government created a series of national workshops that guaranteed work for
artisans and laborers. In Germany, Marx was publishing a revolutionary newspaper and circulating a manifesto calling for working-class revolution. Even in
that great bastion of bourgeois authority, London, the working-class Chartists
were threatening revolution as they planned a massive march on Parliament to
demand the vote. The word of the year, Emerson wrote, was "blouse" (the
French word for a working-class uniform) as, for the first time, representatives
of the working classes had shown the ability for mass political mobilization.[138]

Emerson himself happened to be in Paris during the Revolution and was a
(sometimes unwilling) link between the French revolutionaries and American
thought.[139] He even attended a French working-class meeting where, unbe-
knownst to the placid Transcendentalist, the revolutionary Louis Auguste Blanqui was planning one of his myriad uprisings.[140] Actual barricades in the street
made the cerebral Transcendentalist a bit nervous, and Emerson reacted to his
exposure to French radicals by developing an unfortunate admiration for the
slow liberal change of the British system. But despite this, there were actually
strong links between his ideas and the French revolutionaries. In the early
1840s, Emerson's writings had become immensely popular with French democrats, especially three professors at the Collège de France: Jules Michelet, Edgar
Quinet, and Adam Mickiewicz.[141] They used Emerson to advocate for a "demo-

cratic idealism," which they contrasted with the squalid materialism and repression of the era of the "bourgeois king." Quinet, the historian and philosopher, was particularly drawn to Emerson, declaring him to be, along with Vico, Condorcet, Herder, and Hegel, the greatest of modern thinkers. In one particularly Emersonian lecture, "L'idéal de la Democratie," Quinet argued that the presence of the divine spirit in every individual "creates a new code of rights and duties . . . repelling all that might diminish the interior dignity of mankind."[142] When Margaret Fuller found herself in Paris on the eve of the French Revolution of 1848, she found Mickiewicz, among others, lecturing on Emersonian Transcendentalism to the College de France.[143] Alphonse Lamartine, the Romantic poet and politician, who had the honor of declaring France to be a republic in 1848 and who helped lead the successful push for emancipation in the West Indies, was rumored to have said "the man on earth I most wish to see is Emerson."[144]

But, of the Transcendentalists, it was Margaret Fuller who most saw the relevance of the European revolutions for American slavery. The Transcendentalist editor toured Europe in the late 1840s, engaging with socialist and radical circles in Paris and Italy. While Emerson was feted and flattered by the British elite, Fuller received the opposite impression from bourgeois England. She was appalled by the "shocking inhumanity of exclusiveness" on the island.[145] The continent was hardly better. In Lyon, France, she met teenaged weavers, their fingers already worn thin from years of work, in crowded and filthy garrets.[146] In Paris, her friendships with George Sand, the French novelist, and Adam Mickiewicz, the Polish nationalist, pushed her further to the left, converting her to socialism, to which she gave the highest Transcendentalist complement, referring to the movement as the "idea," "thought," or "spirit" of the Old World revolutionaries.[147] She was in Italy when she heard about the revolution in Paris and became nearly intoxicated with enthusiasm, writing that the French could teach America "the needs of a True democracy . . . learn to reverence, learn to guard, the true aristocracy of a nation, the only really noble,—the LABORING CLASSES."[148] Befriending the Italian revolutionary Mazzini, she ended up covering the Roman republic for the *New York Tribune*, defending it from American accusations that Italians were too degraded and Catholic to sustain a successful democracy. As she spent more time with European leftists, Fuller grew to appreciate the antislavery activists from her home state. Declaring that she now found "something eternal in their desire and life," she increasingly compared abolitionists to European revolutionaries, pointing out, "I listen to the same arguments against the emancipation of Italy, that are used against the emancipation of our blacks."[149]

It is sometimes falsely assumed that all Americans welcomed these revolutions, at least until the violent "June Days" (street fighting between the new French Republic and even more radical working-class revolutionaries in Paris) disenchanted them. Yet many Americans, especially conservative politicians and white Southerners, distrusted the revolutions from the start.[150] John C. Calhoun condemned not just the revolutions but also the entire set of democratic aspirations that animated them.[151] Boston conservatives, though not as openly antidemocratic or antiliberal, were hardly less hostile. Daniel Webster, the chief enemy of Massachusetts abolitionists, scorned the revolutions for reasons rooted in a similar politics of anti-abstraction, privately dismissing the French Revolution as the product of "poets, editors, pretenders to literature, and idealists."[152] Meanwhile, the merchant-friendly press in Boston ran skeptical coverage of the revolutions even as they occurred.[153]

Along with whatever philosophical qualms they might have had, there was a very concrete reason the French Revolution made many Americans uncomfortable: slavery. One of the first acts of the French Provisional Government was to declare the immediate emancipation of all slaves in the French colonies. Before the decree had even reached Martinique, the slaves seized the moment and emancipated themselves. Southern planters were aghast, obviously, but so were many Northern conservatives. The *Boston Daily Advertiser*, the city's preeminent commercial journal, reported, in terror, on the news of freed slaves in Martinique, whom they accused of burning plantations under the revolutionary slogan "Liberté, Égalité, Fraternité."[154] The official organ of the national Whig Party, the *National Intelligencer*, fretted that the emancipation of the slaves in the West Indies would lead to "the bloodiest scenes" in the French colonies and, worse, inspire the "gravest disorders" in the American South.[155] The working-class specter that haunted Europe looked even more ghastly to many white Americans, twinned as it was with the unspeakable horror of slave rebellion.

Abolitionists meanwhile were thrilled. They especially celebrated the "consistency" of the revolution, proudly noting that the French working class had understood their own democratic uplift as connected with the emancipation of Caribbean slaves. "Consistency" quickly became a keyword that designated the possibility of an egalitarian politics that encompassed both white workers and black slaves. At a meeting of Garrisonians, their first resolution celebrated the "magnanimous consistency of the French people," who had freed themselves and "extended" freedom to the slaves. The fact that one of the first acts of the French Republic was to declare immediate emancipation was important because, as the *Liberator* wrote, it "frees the name of Republic from the odium which the inconsistency of America has heaped upon it, and blesses the world with the sight of a Republic without a slave."[156]

Boston abolitionists were first and foremost interested in the abolition of slavery in the French Republic, but they could not avoid the issues of class conflict that the French Revolution raised. Indeed, the Boston abolitionists overwhelmingly supported the nascent socialism of the Provisional Government. The Transcendentalist William Henry Channing declared that the revolution marked the final end of the conflict between the aristocracy and the middle classes, which was settled once and for all, and the welcome rise of class conflict between "the power of the combined capitalists, and the power of the cooperative producers."[157] Theodore Parker celebrated how the French were adding the "idea of fraternity" to the world stage, creating a "human brotherhood" by means of a "social revolution."[158]

A bigger meeting, held at Tremont Temple, demonstrated how the revolution had united abolitionists, such as Garrison and Francis Jackson, who served on the resolution committee, and socialists, such as Elizur Wright, Channing, Henry Trask, and John Cluer. The resolutions celebrated the French republicans' attempt to reconcile "the right of *property* with the still more sacred right to *live*." They even went so far as to resolve that "we cannot deny the right of those who will work, to the means of living."[159] While reporting on the meeting, the *Liberator* declared that the "cottonocracy of this city, and those who are controlled by it," refused to come to a meeting because it was "managed emphatically by THE PEOPLE."[160] On May 9, an even more radical group of "working men" met in Boston to celebrate the event. Addressed by Elizur Wright, among others, they celebrated the "noble efforts to give dignity and character to Labor" by France's new democratic institutions, acknowledged the danger posed by "the despotic attitude of the slave power at the South" to their own free institutions, and called for independent working-class political action. The *Liberator* showed its interest by publishing the minutes of the meeting.[161]

Abolitionist celebrations of the Revolutions of 1848 illustrated the rising tide of cosmopolitan working-class abolitionism. By the 1850s, one could hear Irish brogues and gruff German accents in abolitionist meetings alongside the nasally Yankee dialects. British immigrants, who continued to stream into the country, often brought with them the charged working-class ideas of the Chartist movement. John Cluer, for instance, a former mill worker, Chartist, and radical who moved to Boston in the 1840s, became a New England labor organizer and a member of the Boston Vigilance Committee and would be imprisoned during the unsuccessful attempt to free Anthony Burns.[162] The Scottish-born labor leader went on a lengthy tour of the New England countryside in 1851, raising money for the protection of fugitive slaves.[163] One of the more interesting characters in the Boston antislavery milieu was Henry Kemp, a Catholic Irish manual laborer who carried arms trying to rescue Anthony Burns in 1854.[164] When he first emigrated, Kemp had refused to be naturalized as it would imply swearing to return fugitive slaves.[165] He was a trusted associate of black radicals such as Lewis Hayden, as well as an outspoken defender of the Catholic Church, who believed that "the Catholic Church is thoroughly anti-slavery," confounding most narratives that describe Catholics, and the Irish in particular, as being all anti-abolitionist.[166] By the mid-1850s, Erskine Rose, a Jewish Polish immigrant, represented the small band of Eastern European immigrants in the abolitionist movement.

The biggest source of working-class immigrant support for the abolitionists, though, came from German refugees from their failed revolution. Throughout the country, the "48ers" played prominent roles in labor and free soil movements, helping to turn German communities into important constituencies for the Republican Party.[167] Theodore Parker, who had many contacts in German intellectual communities, was especially generous helping assist refugees, as he did when a penniless Adolf Douai ended up in Boston.[168] Boston's German Republican Association linked abolitionist and working-class politics, warning its members that the slave power would "gradually monopolize the real estate, cause proletarianism, and reduce the laborers to dependence and servitude."[169] In Boston, the most prominent German abolitionist was the fiery Karl Heinzen. Heinzen was an old drinking buddy of Karl Marx.[170] Like so many other German leftists, Heinzen eventually fell out with Marx, who accused him of preaching revolution to the rural peasants (rather than the urban proletariat) and, even more shockingly, a poor understanding of Hegel's dialectic.[171] Moving to New York, Heinzen started the newspaper *Die Pioneer*, which he transferred to Boston in 1860. *Die Pioneer* became the most important German-language abolitionist paper in New England. The *Liberator* often translated and reprinted its articles. Heinzen helped to lead the Boston *Sozialistischer Turnerbund*—the Socialist Gymnastic Union—and put the "turners" to work acting as bodyguards to Wendell Phillips when the patrician abolitionist was threatened by proslavery or pro-Union mobs.[172] Heinzen, who has recently gained notoriety as an early proponent of political terrorism, clashed with Garrisonians because of his repeated calls for the abolitionist movement to embrace political violence and reject religion.[173] But because of his leadership of the small community of

German radicals in the city, his advocacy of violence steadily bled into the rhetoric and ideologies of other abolitionists.[174]

Black Abolitionists and Transatlantic Radicals

Black northerners saw their struggles as related to fights for democracy and self-determination in Europe. Black Bostonian interest in European revolutionary movements went back to the earliest abolition societies. In the early days of Prince Saunders and the founding of the Smith School, Boston's blacks had celebrated the end of the slave trade, not on January 1, when the decree had gone into effect, but on the historically inaccurate, yet symbolically rich, day of July 14, when the Bastille had been stormed during the French Revolution.[175] David Walker, for instance, had been well aware of struggles in Europe for national independence and compared black plight to that of the Irish and Jews.[176] He also criticized the hypocrisy of white Americans who showed support for the Greeks (who were fighting a war for independence against the Ottoman Empire) and the Irish while ignoring the plight of African American slaves. In Walker's time and later, most black intellectuals viewed the European revolutions as largely national affairs. To compare their plight to the Greeks or Irish, as Walker did, was to make an argument about the national aspirations of black Northerners.

Perhaps the most interesting case of this black appropriation of left discourse occurred when a young Henry Highland Garnet—three years before his famous insurrectionary speech—repurposed the British Chartist Ebenezer Elliott's poem "The Jacobin's Prayer" to be about American slaves. For Garnett, Elliott's plea for the victims of Peterloo—"avenge thy plundered poor, oh lord"—lost none of its sense of righteous indignation when spoken for the victims of Virginia or Georgia.[177] Moreover, their long interest in Haitian affairs strengthened their international vision. Unsurprisingly, then, they warmly welcomed the 1848 revolutions. Frederick Douglass declared that when the king fled France, "a ray of hope penetrated the lowest confines of the American slave prisons, imparting firmness of faith to the whip-scarred slave, and fear and trembling to the guilty slaveholder."[178] Samuel Ringgold Ward agreed. Writing in the *Impartial Citizen*, a short-lived black newspaper, Ward evoked the imagery of European absolutism to condemn "the horrible Bastille of Slavery" while encouraging defiance of the Fugitive Slave Act.[179] Henry Highland Garnet, in England during the aftermath of the revolutions, was one of many black travelers to

favorably compare the French Republicans' decision to immediately free all slaves
with the American republic's odious decision to pass the Fugitive Slave Law.[180]

But until the Revolutions of 1848, one would be hard-pressed to find black
voices connecting their support for European revolutions to criticisms of the
marketplace. Even those such as Nell and Douglass, who had ties to utopian
socialism, generally avoided discussion of the plight of Northern workers so as
not to give ammunition to Southern propagandists, who, they worried, would
have jumped on the stories of ex-slaves disappointed with the free labor North.
In addition, black workers in Boston were largely excluded from the industrial
labor force. Well into the nineteenth century, most Boston blacks remained part
of the "picturesque proletariat," the Atlantic-orientated amalgamation of sailors,
dock workers, and casual manual laborers that could be found in port cities up
and down the coast. As James Freeman Clarke wrote, blacks were "not permitted
by social sentiments to engage in more than ten or twelve out of the three hundred and more occupations set down in the census for the white male population."[181] Outside of a small stratum of black professionals—such as the lawyer
Robert Morris Jr., the printer and author William C. Nell, and the doctor John
Rock—the vast majority of black men in Boston were sailors, manual laborers,
caterers, and waiters. A few, like Lewis Hayden and David Walker before him,
ran used clothing stores that catered to the transient sailing population. Black
women often worked as washerwomen or domestic servants. Studies have
shown that black Northerners gained no significant income advantage from literacy, unlike white workers, demonstrating their enforced lack of mobility.[182]

They were excluded from most industrial labor both by the choice of employers, who refused to hire even qualified black workers, and often by the opposition of white workers. Blacks thus were unlikely to have warm feelings for
the institutions of white working-class life, including the labor unions. Moreover, the 1830s had been the peak of the Jacksonian Democratic Party, and as
the raucous political party of the Northern working class cemented a political
alliance with the Southern planter elites, free blacks had good reason to be skeptical of overt displays of white class consciousness. At a cultural level, many
white workers were beginning to understand their own identities as defined
against black slaves, leading those white workers to steadfastly oppose any blur-
ring of the lines by the introduction of black coworkers.

The revolutions in Europe began to change this, as black observers saw
workers initiate revolutions that freed Caribbean slaves and proclaimed against
American slavery. William C. Nell was particularly inspired by the revolutions.
"The times are revolutionary," Nell declared triumphantly upon hearing of the

French Revolution, "society is progressing; the theme is freedom for all." The slaveholding United States, Nell argued, proved that simply having a republican form of government was no guarantee of universal justice or freedom. Thus, the preeminent political question of the era was "how shall Republics become truly free?" This emphasis on being "truly free" linked the causes of the slave with the European worker. The "consistent boon of liberty to her colonial subject," offered by the French republicans, augured "a hopeful tribute for the negro" because it provided a model that linked the fortunes of the great insurgent masses in Europe with the political emancipation of American slaves. "Let the bondmen of Republican America," Nell declared, hold the example of French revolutionaries in their mind.[183] Frederick Douglass, meanwhile, declared that the "revolution of France, like a bolt of living thunder, has aroused the world from its stupor . . . the despots of Europe—the Tories of England, and the slave-holders of America, are astonished, confused, and terrified; while the humble poor, the toil-worn laborer, the oppressed and plundered, the world around" were celebrating.[184]

Thanks in part to the European revolutionary energy, black intellectuals began embracing the economic and class concerns of the "48ers." William Powell, for instance, touring England, declared that "the peculiar institution of this country is the power of capital over labor," which he compared to U.S. slavery. "Whilst the systems of oppression in Europe and America, in their operation, are as far apart as poles," the black abolitionist noted, "still the effect is the same—the power of the strong over God's weak and defenceless poor."[185] Many black writers and intellectuals embraced the holy trinity of French revolutionary watchwords—Liberty, Equality, Fraternity—as Henry Johnson did when he celebrated the "impartial liberty" that was now enjoyed in France.[186] Black abolitionists were also particularly supportive of the British working-class movement, the Chartists. Frederick Douglass proudly called himself a Chartist, and Henry Highland Garnet pledged to unify the causes of slaves and white workers.[187] The Chartists, it should be pointed out, were divided between a radical "physical force" wing, which counted Karl Marx among its advocates, and a more moderate "moral force" wing, which tended to attract American abolitionists.[188]

As the example of Garnet and Douglass demonstrates, black abolitionists who traveled in Europe demonstrated a deep interest in democratic and left politics. William Wells Brown, the former fugitive slave, visited Paris as a delegate to the World Peace Conference in 1849 and noticed reminders of the recent revolution everywhere he went. As he entered the city, he noted that "a few months before was to be seen the flash from the cannon and the musket, and

the hearing of the cries and groans behind the barricades."[189] By the Church of
the Madeleine, he recalled "it was near this spot that some of the most interesting scenes occurred during the Revolution of 1848."[190] Brown met a number of
the members of the European left on his trip, including Victor Hugo, Pierre Be-
ranger, and, most interestingly, Louis Blanc, the socialist who had designed the
national workshops that had guaranteed work for the urban working classes.[191]
Brown was alternately fascinated by the revolutionary history of France—he
made a point of visiting Robespierre's home—and disgusted by its excesses. Part
of his unquiet clearly came from the fact that France, headed for the reactionary
dictatorship of Louis Napoleon, was currently invading Italy in order to "put
down the friends of political and religious freedom."[192] Nevertheless, from his
visits, it was clear that, for a touring abolitionist such as Brown, there was a
natural affinity between American abolitionists and European democrats.

For Brown, especially, the causes of the worker and the slave were closely
linked. In 1848, he had told the New England Anti-Slavery Association—
whom he referred to as "working men"—that "laboring people of the south,
whether black or white, were in a degraded condition" and that he hoped the
"working men of the north would calculate" this when making political decisions.[193] In England, Brown observed bitter strikes, including one that lasted
eighteen months, and interpreted them as evidence that the white working class
had more power and wealth than the American slaves.[194] On one occasion, he
was asked point-blank whether British abolitionism was derived from "the aristocratic part of the British subjects," a crude formulation of the idea that abolitionism was a privilege of the economically comfortable. Brown decisively
rejected the theory. Abolitionism in England, he declared, "proceeds, for the
most part, from that portion of the British people who admire republicanism,
and wish for its propagation."[195]

African American activists sought to capture some of the militancy of
European revolutionaries. Lewis Hayden, for instance, argued that African
Americans faced with the Fugitive Slave Law should emulate the French working
class. In 1850, as the black activist community debated the proper response to
the Fugitive Slave Law, Hayden offered the example of the recent revolution. At
a meeting of black Bostonians, Lewis Hayden referenced "the Blouses of Paris"
as an example "to the victims of Republican American despotism, to manfully
assert their independence, and to martyr-like DIE freemen, rather than LIVE
SLAVES."[196] Hayden's evocation of the French workers was particularly notable
since it came well after the "June Days" and their doomed uprisings to protect
the Revolution. Here the revolutionaries stood in for many of the characteris-

tics of the Romantic hero—principled, uncalculating, gleefully willing to throw away their lives for the freedom of the community. It was a remarkable statement of transnational solidarity with the avant-garde of the European left by an ex-slave from Boston.

In the aftermath of the revolutions, black Bostonians felt increasingly comfortable attacking the class power of the Boston elite. Samuel Ringgold Ward, for instance, started a newspaper called the *Impartial Citizen* that, for a brief time, provided a black alternative to the *Liberator*. In 1850, Ward ran a remarkable editorial that illustrated the growing tendency of black radicals to associate proslavery sentiment with the rich. There were, Ward argued, three pillars of elite power: cotton, money, and slavery. "The cottonocrats, cashocrats and slaveocrats in Boston," Ward wrote, singling out Whig congressman Samuel A. Eliot, "having control of this city, always see to it that their interests are represented in Washington." While these Whig politicians claimed to be motivated by devotion to the Union, it was clear to Ward that their primary allegiance was to "cotton, money, slavery, and all the monopolies combined therewith!"[197]

Socialist Abolitionism and Party Politics

Back in America, the Transcendentalist William Henry Channing, with the help of European left-wing thought, was cementing the relationship between Massachusetts labor and abolitionism. An early member of the Transcendentalist Club, Channing may be unfairly ignored in the historical literature because of confusion with his similarly named but more famous relatives: especially his uncle, the Unitarian theologian William Ellery Channing. In pictures, Channing appears thin, almost bird-like, but with a piercing intensity. He lacked the righteous fire of Parker or personal charisma of Fuller but had an understated earnestness that impressed nearly everyone he worked with. Serving as a minister at large to the poor in New York City, he had come face to face with the desperate poverty of the antebellum city, a poverty that seemed to grow in the shadows of idle wealth. In the early 1840s, he experienced a period of intense religious uncertainty, nearly falling into total disbelief when he came to believe that "Jesus Christ did not understand his own religion."[198] In this moment of religious doubt, he came under the influence of the writings of the French socialist and theologian Pierre Leroux, which restored Channing's sense of faith and purpose. Leroux was an eccentric theologian and political radical who mixed Eastern thought with a slightly vulgarized German idealism to develop a pantheistic

William Henry Channing

Figure 5. William Henry Channing was a prominent leader of the "socialist wing" of the Transcendentalist movement who was also deeply committed to antislavery agitation. Collection of the Massachusetts Historical Society.

and socialistic system. Leroux taught Channing to see the face of God in the progressive development of the human community, mankind's interrelated fate as an embodiment of the omnipresence of God. "This life we interchange with fellow-men," Channing told the religious wing of the Boston Union of Associationists, "and we live *well*, just in degree as we conspire with our age, our nation, our neighbors, to embody in Acts the Ideas through which God evermore flows in to re-animate mankind."[199]

Confronted with the spiritual promise of socialism, Channing was religiously and politically reborn. "So gigantic a Messiah may grow slowly," he acknowledged cautiously to John Sullivan Dwight in January 1846. By November, he was growing impatient: "We have a *Religion* to announce to our fellows. . . . We cannot fail."[200] The spiritual component of "associationism" renewed Channing's faith and devotion to the church, while channeling it into socialist and abolitionist politics. Among the worshipers at his Christian Union Church in New York City would be Horace Greeley himself, who, more than anyone, would popularize the socialist and antislavery principles of people such as Channing.[201] While largely ignored by scholars, especially in comparison to his uncle, Channing—of all the Unitarian theologians—has perhaps had the strangest popular afterlife when a brief quotation from a letter that he wrote to Margaret Fuller was discovered by an American newspaper in 1920—"To live content with small means; to seek elegance rather than luxury, and refinement rather than fashion; to be worthy, not respectable, and wealthy, not rich, to listen to stars and birds, babes and sages, with open heart . . . this is my symphony." Dubbed "My Symphony" and often miscredited to his uncle, William Ellery, Channing's letter is still today reprinted on inspirational posters, crocheted on religious pillows, and even recently turned into a popular children's book.

Along with Albert Brisbane, George Ripley, Charles A. Dana, and Horace Greeley, Channing was one of the most prominent advocates of utopian socialism in antebellum America. He contributed to Brook Farm and helped to lead the Boston Union of Associationists, founding its religious wing and encouraging the socialists to address women's issues. He collaborated with real working-class movements, as when he spoke alongside the famous Sarah Bagley, the radical labor organizer, at a meeting of the New England Workers' Association in 1845.[202] Far more than most of his colleagues, he familiarized himself with the haunts of the urban poor, including the prisons and poorhouses that housed the most unfortunate.[203] He edited a series of socialist journals, including the *Present*, the *Harbinger*, and, in 1849, the *Spirit of the Age*. These papers, especially the latter, combined a liberal and sometime eccentric religious vision with a surprisingly sophisticated understanding of European socialist politics. The *Spirit of the Age* ran antislavery pieces by Channing, Phillips, and others, along-side articles by or on the leading lights of the pre-Marxist European left, including Fourier, Proudhon, Victor Considerant, Leroux, Louis Blanc, and Étienne Cabet. It was as eclectic as it was utopian, drawing on German philosophy, Christian and Hindu religious texts, French socialism, and American abolitionists. Positioning himself between the violent left and reactionary right, he believed he was speaking in the middle classes' best interest that only if they voluntarily gave up some power and wealth to the poor could they prevent violence and anarchy. Part paternalist and part radical critic of economic inequality, Channing reported positively on the actions of local labor unions, including supporting the journeymen tailor strike of 1849.[204]

If his paternal hopes to "reorganize" society (and thereby head off a "revolution") seem naive, Channing's combination of economic and racial justice was admirable and forward looking. For Channing, both slavery and capitalism were manifestations of the oppression of labor, of the tendency of humans who, "by chains or cunning... by the whip or wages, man makes his brother a slave."[205] He was among the first of the Transcendentalist Club to become active in the antislavery struggle, speaking at abolitionist rallies and writing antislavery articles. By 1845, the *Liberator* could mention him in the same breath as William Lloyd Garrison and Wendell Philips, as a "practical martyr and apostle" of abolitionism.[206] He opened the *Spirit of the Age* to abolitionists such as Wendell Phillips and reprinted articles written by Frederick Douglass while sympathetically reporting on Proudhon and attacking "industrial feudalism."[207] The paper made a passionate plea that the "sacredness of labor" implied a concern for the rights of slaves, that even white workers would suffer if black civil rights were denied.[208] Even Frederick Douglass testified to Channing's dedication, writing, "One of the few it was my privilege to call upon, and to call upon often, was Rev. W.H. Channing. His congregation was small, and his salary was not large, but he gave like a prince."[209]

The ideological developments of abolitionists such as Channing and Nell, who all tried to combine working-class politics with abolitionist commitments in the 1840s, were reflected in changes in the political landscape. Throughout the 1840s, the Liberty Party had struggled to build alliances with working-class movements. Simultaneously, the Massachusetts Workingmen's Party, founded in 1845, was groping around for a base of support beyond the die-hard labor organizers. Soon both found a home in the new Free Soil Party. In 1849, after another disappointing showing by the Workingmen, labor leaders sought to unite with the new party that, in Massachusetts at least, had long been courting them by adopting their fiery populist appeal. As Channing reported, the interest of the Workingmen's Party in the Free Soil platform demonstrated that some were acknowledging that "social injury could result to the white race from the oppression and servitude of the black."[210] Throughout New England, in fact, the Free Soil Party brought together what one newspaper called "a formidable array of Loco Focos and Liberty men," helping to create a populist antislavery party.[211]

Meanwhile, the platform of the Free Soil Party took an anticorporate stance, declared itself prolabor, and sought to rewrite state election laws to remove the unfair distribution of legislative seats that advantaged mercantile Boston over the industrial and agricultural hinterland. The Free Soil Party's class consciousness gained its most famous slogan when aspiring politician and member of the Transcendentalist Town and Country Club, Charles Sumner, declared that their enemies, the Whig Party, had become dominated by an unholy alliance of the "Lords of the Lash and the Lords of the Loom." At the 1849 convention in Worcester that Channing lauded, Sumner took his class-conscious critique even further, bemoaning the influence of corporations on state politics and declaring that "the Money Power here has joined hands with the Slave Power."[212] The new alliance would gain political power after the election of 1850, when the state Democrats and Free Soil Party formed an unofficial coalition. With the Massachusetts General Assembly split between Cotton Whigs, Democrats, and Free Soilers, the latter two agreed to support each other's candidates: the Democrats got the governorship and the Free Soilers got the Senate position vacated by Daniel Webster. When outraged Whigs called the subsequent election of Charles Sumner to the Senate a "corrupt bargain," they were missing the real ideological links between the populist Democrats and antislavery Free Soilers.[213]

The labor movements and abolitionists did not always see entirely eye to eye, but, as Channing wrote, the fact that both found a home in the Free Soil Party was a valuable step toward the day when a "party of consistent progress and reform" would rise up.[214] Meanwhile, abolitionists increasingly reached out to workers and their supporters. Most notably, in 1849, the Massachusetts Anti-Slavery Society began a concerted effort to appeal to workers in class-conscious language, passing an official resolution that, with perhaps a bit of willed naïveté, declared that "the rights of the laborer at the North are identical with those of the Southern slave."[215]

Tensions still existed, but the significant difference from the 1830s was that abolitionists attempted, with some success, to address the concerns of workers. The anti-Sabbath campaign illustrated how abolitionists were increasingly sensitive to the plight of labor. A seamstress, claiming that she worked sixteen hours a day, six days a week, had written to Garrison pointing out that legal prescriptions against work on Sunday were her only protection from an even more exploitative work regime.[216] The anonymous worker revealed a potential problem with the abolitionist and Transcendentalist religious view—their enthusiasm for dismantling the irrational remnants of superstitious Christianity threatened to blind them to how the perfectly rational and disenchanted social order that might follow could be even worse for many Americans, stripped of the premodern protections for labor contained in traditional religion. But, rather than retreat to reactionary medievalism, as Carlyle did when confronted with this same problem, the abolitionists took pains to answer the seamstress' criticism with realistic secular legislation. The call for the meeting had bemoaned the long hours for workers and declared, in emphatic bold lettering, that workers *need more,* AND MUST HAVE MORE, *instead of less rest.*"[217] Responding directly to the seamstress, Garrison's solution was to call for state legislation guaranteeing workers at least one day of rest, demonstrable evidence of abolitionist willingness to intervene in the labor market. And, in order to ensure labor's support, abolitionist speakers outdid themselves in attacks on what Garrison called the "merciless employers and sordid monopolists, who are endeavoring to coin money out of the very life-blood of the people."[218]

This alliance was not restricted to formal politics. In the fall of 1849, many abolitionists lent their support to a major strike of the Association of Journeymen Tailors in Boston. Employers had cut journeymen tailors' wages by as much as 50 percent since 1843. In July, the union announced a new pay schedule and declared a strike at any employer who did not abide by it.[219] The strike gained steam throughout the summer, winning major shows of solidarity from other local unions.[220] Reporting on a meeting of the strikers, Frederick Douglass's *North Star* lamented that "England can no longer boast . . . of being the only country in the world that starves her workmen."[221] When, in September, forty wholesale cloth dealers agreed to a blacklist of any member of the union, Channing furiously denounced the "Industrial Feudalism" of the employers and ran the lengthy response of the workers.[222] Meanwhile, the Boston Associationists sent an address of support to the tailors declaring that by their strike, along with the "laboring men of Paris," the Boston tailors had "shown to the sons of toil every where, the inexpediency of their submission to the demands of Commerce which has heretofore required human labor as a mere subject of trade and speculation." Elizur Wright recommended the address, declaring the tailors to be fighting for "Labor's universal Emancipation."[223] The abolitionist poet George W. Putnam of Lynn published a poem celebrating "The Boston Tailors, and the men of Lynn, By UNION bringing out of darkness LIGHT."[224] In late 1849, the striking tailors began a worker-run cooperative; they called it an "Associative Union" in a clear nod to the ideological power of the Boston Union of Associationists. Assuming that abolitionists would be sympathetic costumers, they advertised in papers such as Douglass's *North Star.*[225] Channing himself lent them $20.[226]

But attention was soon diverted from the tailors' strike. In Washington, D.C., Southern politicians had begun pushing for a new Fugitive Slave Law to help them retrieve fugitives, too many of whom were finding homes in the urban North. And ironically, the very economic downturn that had led to the tailors' strike was convincing many New England politicians that they should trade a fugitive slave law for new protective tariffs. In the coming months, members of the new tailors' cooperative, especially Bernard Treanor, the secretary, would join Channing and other abolitionists in the new Boston Vigilance Committee that developed to resist the Fugitive Slave Law.

CHAPTER 4

Fugitive Slaves and the Many Origins
of Civil Disobedience Theory

The crowd around the courthouse was growing in the Boston night. For two days now, a thirty-year-old fugitive named Anthony Burns had lay imprisoned in the Boston courthouse under the aegis of the 1850 Fugitive Slave Act, awaiting rendition back to Virginia slavery. Now, on May 26, 1854, a group of militant abolitionists, comprising African Americans from Boston, led by Lewis Hayden, and a band of radical white abolitionists from Worcester, led by Thomas Wentworth Higginson, had brought axes to the courthouse door and were hacking at the entrance, determined to free Burns. Across town in Faneuil Hall, at a meeting of abolitionists called the Boston Vigilance Committee, temperatures were rising as Theodore Parker and Wendell Phillips were whipping up an overflow crowd. Phillips extended his finger in an accusing point: "I want to see that man set free in the streets of Boston," he demanded, as cries rose from the audience.[1] The plan, apparently, was that at the right moment, the crowd in Faneuil Hall would rush to reinforce Higginson and Hayden. But miscommunication and confusion had delayed the message. By the time the cries of "to the court house! To the Court House!" rang out in the crowded hall, the melee across town had already begun.[2]

In their ardor, the abolitionists at the courthouse had gotten impatient and, as soon as they had knocked a hole in the door, had rushed inside, without waiting for the Faneuil Hall crowd. Higginson remembered the first man to break down the door as a "stout negro" who "did not even look at me, but sprang in first, I following."[3] But the authorities were prepared. Waiting for them was a line of newly deputized U.S. marshals, many of them Irish immigrants—"of the rough, thief-catching order"—and eager for a fight with the preachy abolition-

NIGHT ATTACK ON THE COURT HOUSE.

Figure 6. A woodcut from Charles Emery Stevens's account of the attempt
to rescue Anthony Burns. Collection of the Massachusetts
Historical Society

ists.[4] The problem was that the small hole the abolitionists had torn in the door created a bottleneck, allowing only one in at a time. The police officers charged, swinging billy clubs. Higginson received a deep wound on his chin. As blows rained down on their heads, a shot rang out from the abolitionists' ranks and one of the marshal's deputies, a man named James Batchelder, dropped dead. The abolitionists wisely retreated, even as now-confused members of the Faneuil Hall audience began arriving outside. As a final act that seemed to symbolize both the brave idealism and, perhaps, the foolhardy otherworldliness of Transcendentalism, A. Bronson Alcott—his mind ever on the ideal—serenely walked up the steps to the courthouse, leaning on his cane, and asked, "Why are we not within?" before a bullet whizzed over his head. He then "turned and retreated, but without hastening a step."[5]

Burns would not be saved. A couple of days later, a small army marched the fugitive down the cobblestone streets to Boston Harbor and returned him to Virginia slavery. But his role in New England intellectual history had just begun. Nearly every writer and activist, it seemed, was horrified by the scene of Boston's authorities spending public money to return a man to slavery. To his Worcester congregation, Higginson gave a fiery and widely reprinted sermon defending his actions, promising not to retreat an inch. In Brooklyn, Walt Whitman wrote an uncharacteristically angry poem imagining the craven people of Boston re-crowning George III as king. John Greenleaf Whittier's poetic response also played with themes of shame and regional humiliation—"all love of home, all pride of place . . . sank smothering in that deep disgust."[6] A couple of weeks after the "riot," as Higginson and others waited in jail, Henry David Thoreau attended an antislavery meeting in Concord and was disgusted to find that his more mod-erate neighbors would not even refer to the attempted rescue. He went home and dashed out one of his most alienated and angry essays ever: *Slavery in Massachu-setts*. "My thoughts," Thoreau seethed, "are murder to the State, and involun-tarily go plotting against her."[7] It would be this essay that he would read at that year's Fourth of July celebration in Framingham, Massachusetts, right before William Lloyd Garrison notoriously burned the U.S. Constitution.

The problem, Thoreau thought, was not simply political cowardice—though that existed in spades. It was that men in Massachusetts had lost their ability to make a moral judgment on their own—they instead took their cues from newspapers, from their careers, from political parties . . . from anything but the voice of their own conscience. They no longer looked at a moral question such as slavery and asked what they as a human being thought about it. Instead, their social roles determined their thought—they asked what they as a Whig or a Democrat ought to think about it; what they ought to do in their jobs as judges, jurors, or police officers; or what the editor of the *Boston Post* or *Boston Mail* thought about it. They obeyed the laws of man and disobeyed the higher laws of conscience and morality. The result, for the men who had turned their bodies and mind over to the slavecatcher, was nothing less than a loss of their humanity—"they are just as much tools and as little men."[8] As was often true of Thoreau's writing, he perfectly expressed, in just a few economical para-graphs, a major theme in abolitionist thought: how the social roles Northerners inhabited—in their jobs, in their official duties, in their identities as political partisans—were distorting and limiting their moral reasoning.

Nowhere was the evidence of the influence of Transcendentalism on the abolitionist movement as clear as in the articulation of the civil disobedience tradition. Drawing on Transcendentalist ethics, abolitionists argued that no one could sign away his or her conscience and that an individual's relationship to what they called the "Higher Law" superseded laws, contracts, and roles made by men. As we will see, Transcendentalists such as Thoreau, Parker, Nell, and Higginson were intimately involved in campaigns of civil disobedience in the early 1850s and were the primary theoreticians defending the right to disobey unjust laws. Fidelity to what they began calling the Higher Law, they argued, entailed more than just a political commitment; to its followers, the Higher Law denoted an entirely different attitude toward morality, selfhood, and where one took one's goals in life from. To return fugitives and reject the Higher Law was to take your life's cues from instrumental logic, the sensuous demands of one's animal existence, or the suffocating pressure of social conformity. Normally this happened because you were loyal to your job or social role, where someone else had determined the ends for which you acted. Living by these Lower Laws was the first step toward losing basic humanity, to seeing yourself become nothing but the tool of another's will. The Higher Law ethos, on the other hand, demanded that you think about political questions yourself, setting moral goals that were in line with your own values, so you could bring one's political actions in line with the highest demands of your moral being. The Higher Law Ethos, then, was not just about following your conscience; it also contained a whole theory about how social roles distorted your thought and about what type of action could restore your moral reasoning.

The enactment of the 1850 Fugitive Slave Act engendered this intellectually fascinating public debate about laws, moral conscience, and obedience. As one Northern minister noted, the reaction to the law demonstrated that Americans were dividing up into dueling camps of ethical responsibility, warring "classes of consciences." There was the "LAW-ABIDING conscience" and the "HIGHER LAW" conscience," each of which was "repudiating and violently denouncing the other."[9] The question of fugitive slaves—long a smoldering point of dispute between regions—erupted as the South demanded a stringent new law guarding its constitutionally protected "property." In response, antislavery Northerners openly pledged to violate any such law, declaring their fidelity to a law "higher" than the Constitution. In Massachusetts, the other side was represented by Daniel Webster, his fellow Cotton Whigs, and Boston businessmen, who demanded that Northerners swallow their pride and follow the law. The North had made a sort of moral contract, they argued, implicitly agreeing to the Fugitive Slave Law in exchange for all the benefits that the Constitution brought. A few fugitives was the price Massachusetts had to pay to be part of the Union. The ensuing debate about civil disobedience riveted the North. As Ralph Waldo Emerson remarked, the new Fugitive Slave Act has "been like a university to the entire people. It has turned every dinner-table into a debating club, and made every citizen a student of natural law."[10]

But while Transcendentalism was crucial as an intellectual scaffolding to abolitionist rhetoric around resistance to the Fugitive Slave Act, it was the experiences and arguments of black activists that gave meaning to the Higher Law. After all, Higginson had *followed* a black man into the courthouse. Denied the protection of many American laws, black Northerners understood the value of disobeying them to keep their family and friends safe; defined legally as mere chattel, they were drawn to an ideological system that celebrated their ability to resist the political judgment of an immoral majority. As white thinkers sought to make sense of their new inclination to violate the law, they saw in the actions of black activists, as well as in the bravery of the fugitives they sought to protect, a model for principled disobedience. Out of this interaction between white and black intellectuals and activists arose a civil disobedience theory that would inspire generations to come.

The Politics of Fugitive Slaves

Throughout the antebellum period, fugitive slaves came north, to Philadelphia and New York, Detroit and Boston. In major Northern cities, they found anonymity in the crowded streets and protection and community in the associations of free blacks who protected and sheltered them.[11] Within just a few months in 1846 and 1847, John H. Lomax from Louisa County in Virginia, Littleton Barclay from Baltimore, James Morton from the Eastern Shore of Maryland, Joshua Holmes from Wilmington in North Carolina, and Elijah Conway of Newcastle County, Delaware, all found their way to Boston. They walked hundreds of miles on foot (as Mahlon Hopewell did), rode in buggies, or stowed away on steamboats; they survived boat wrecks and hid in swamps.[12]

The very ubiquity of fugitives (most Northern cities contained hundreds if not thousands of fugitives) and the centrality of the issue to antebellum politics blinded many observers to the most important fact about fugitive slaves: they were the direct product of slave resistance, the embodiment of a type of class conflict that was at the heart of slavery.[13] Every form of exploitation produces characteristic forms of resistance—if Northern wage labor was vulnerable to strikes, Southern slave labor was vulnerable to runaways and rebellions. This was the point that Charles Lenox Remond was making when he directly compared the act of running away to the resistance of white workers. When someone told an antislavery audience that only white workers went on strike, Remond interjected "except when they strike for Canada," highlighting the correspondence between slave escapes and labor conflict.[14] Had slaves been content with their condition, as antebellum (and many postwar) propagandists claimed, had they been too cowed by their enslavement to resist, then there would have been no fugitives, no William Wells Brown or Lewis Hayden, no dramatic memoirs by Frederick Douglass or Harriet Jacobs, no need for Fugitive Slave Acts and slavecatchers, no Vigilance Committees or slave rescues, no outraged speeches by Emerson or Parker about the need to protect fugitives, no personal liberty laws, no confrontations at Christiania or Syracuse, no Northern audiences weeping over Eliza's escape in *Uncle Tom's Cabin*, no furious Southerners demanding protection for their "property."

Escape on the part of the fugitive was one half of the act of black agency; the other was the creation of institutions by Northern free blacks, many of whom had been fugitives themselves, to protect runaways. Southern whites interpreted runaways as simple-minded innocents lured North by greedy and disingenuous abolitionists. This was a crude ideological self-deception, of course, but contained within it a kernel of truth: slaves were aware of abolitionist activity in the North, and the existence of free black communities acted as a "pull" that, along with the "push" of slavery, convinced some to escape. Northern free black communities, of course, were in constant danger, harassed by slavecatchers, denied most political rights, and harried by racism, underemployment, and the constant threat of everyday racist violence. Surrounded by a hostile nation, they resembled, in the words of one scholar, "maroon communities," essential sites of black political organizing within a proslavery nation.[15]

In Boston, as in other Northern cities, the protection of fugitives became one of the central tasks that constituted black community development.[16] The earliest evidence of voluntary organizations dedicated to protecting fugitive slaves came from black Bostonians well before the passage of the Fugitive Slave Act. Throughout urban centers in the North, blacks organized in the 1830s and 1840s in order to protect the streams of fugitives seeking freedom and anonymity in the streets of their cities. These black activists demonstrated what following the Higher Law looked like before white intellectuals even uttered the phrase. Practice, in this case, preceded theory. In Philadelphia and New York, Vigilance Committees, led by activists such as William Still and David Ruggles, were some of the most important institutions that protected runaways. Boston was no different, though at first Boston's blacks were relatively disorganized, responding to spur-of-the-moment crises with ad hoc solutions. In 1827, for instance, a couple, John and Sophia Robinson, were jailed for four months because they refused to hand over a five-year-old girl to her (white) guardians, whom they feared would sell the girl south. Although the Robinsons suffered jail time, the girl was successful protected.[17] Similarly, in 1836, a group of black women pulled off a daring rescue of two Maryland fugitives, Eliza Small and Polly Ann Bates. A black cleaning woman of "great size" restrained a court officer, while a throng of black women burst into the courthouse and whisked the two fugitives away to freedom.[18]

The first iteration of the Boston Vigilance Committee was a short-lived biracial organization of that name, founded in 1841 under the auspices of the black activist William C. Nell and the white minister Charles Torrey. They formed it in response to the recent rendition of John Torrence, a fugitive from North Carolina, by James Higgins, a Boston merchant. It pledged to pursue only legal and nonviolent means to aid fugitives coming north, attempting to set up networks with other Northern port cities.[19] The Committee immediately fell victim to sectarian infighting, with Garrison bemoaning the influence of Torrey, with whom he had tangled over issues of minister control, perfectionism, and feminism.[20] The organization appears to have sputtered out by the end of 1841. Torrey soon left Massachusetts, eventually dying as a martyr in a Maryland jail, attempting to aid runaways.[21] Black abolitionists, including Nell and Hilton, raised money for a Torrey monument in Mount Auburn, but the Vigilance Committee largely dissolved.[22]

In the wake of the Committee's dissolution, black activists, led by the indefatigable William C. Nell, formed the New England Freedom Association in 1842, creating a more formalized and permanent organization. According to Nell, the organization existed to "extend the helping hand to the 'chattel' who may have taken to itself 'wings,' and bid adieu to the 'peculiar southern institution.'"[23] Like later organizations, it served two purposes: to mobilize emergency responses to protect fugitives in immediate danger and to act as a welfare agency, linking new fugitives with shelter and employment and assisting their transition into free Northern life. The Freedom Association was almost entirely black led and black funded. Support came from black churches, which contributed what they could, but the lack of money was a constant source of woe.[24] As in later fugitive support organizations, the Freedom Association practiced a gendered division of labor. Men occupied the leadership while women assisted by raising money and helping to house refugees.[25]

That the Association was founded in 1842 is not coincidental. That same year, when George Latimer, a fugitive from Virginia, was arrested, a group of black activists was unsuccessful in its attempts to free him, though they roughed up a Boston constable in the process. White abolitionists, especially members of the Liberty Party, began mobilizing political support for the imprisoned Latimer. Henry I. Bowditch, a white Liberty Party activist, began a short-lived newspaper, the *Latimer Journal and North Star*, to draw attention to the plight of the fugitive, and a petition campaign that attracted 64,526 signatures eventually convinced the Massachusetts legislature to pass a personal liberty law, enhancing the rights of those accused of being fugitives and reducing the complicity of the Massachusetts state government in rendition.[26] The *Latimer Journal* highlighted both the threat that slavery posed to free Northerners as well as the plight of black slaves themselves. In this, its strategy foreshadowed the later Republican criticism of the "Slave Power." "We war not now with slavery at the South," the paper declared, "but with slavery here at the north."[27] They even went so far as to claim that Latimer was "WHITE in color," in an attempt to gain the support of white Northerners, who would presumably be more sympathetic to the plight of a light-skinned man.[28]

Throughout the early 1840s, Boston's blacks quietly operated the New England Freedom Association, successfully aiding numerous refugees. In 1845, it weathered a scandal when its secretary, Robert Wood, was forced to resign amid accusations of impropriety with funds.[29] Weakened, in 1846, the Association was unable to assist "Joe," a New Orleans fugitive who had hidden himself aboard the *Ottoman*, a Boston vessel. Upon Joe's discovery in Boston harbor, the shipowner, John H. Pearson, decided to have him sent back to slavery. Outraged abolitionists called a public meeting on September 24, 1846, which was addressed by the aging John Quincy Adams and which resolved to form a "committee of vigilance" tasked with taking "needed measures to secure the protection of the law."[30] The new Vigilance Committee was much larger than the 1841 version and also biracial. Black members such as Nell, Robert Morris, and Joshua Smith joined white members from the Liberty Party or the "Conscience" wing of the Whig Party and, increasingly, Garrisonians such as Samuel May, Ellis Gray Loring, and Samuel Sewall.[31]

The general agent of the committee, a Mr. Bourne, estimated that they assisted two fugitives per week.[32] Bourne was white, but important black activists such as William C. Nell, Joshua B. Smith, and Robert Morris were intimately involved, helping to find housing, employment, and other necessities for the fugitives.[33] Since the New England Freedom Association ceased operations, its energies appeared to have been folded into the new Vigilance Committee. Although Boston's blacks were arguably losing some control over their affairs, joining the white abolitionists also gave them access to a new base of money and legal power. For example, when John Lomax, a runaway slave from Louisa

County, Virginia, arrived in November 1846, having been defrauded of $600 by
a Baltimore lawyer, the patrician antislavery minister William Channing was
able to use contacts in the Baltimore legal community to discover the defrauder,
one E. G. Kilburne, and the Committee began legal proceedings against him.[34]

Passage of the Fugitive Slave Act

The increased boldness of black and white abolitionists came at a sensitive time
for centrist politicians. The fallout from the Mexican War had left the nation
more divided than at any time since the Missouri Compromise. The U.S. victory had added a tremendous amount of land to the nation, and with the discovery of gold in California, there was an urgent need to organize the territories
into states. This, of course, threatened the regional balance in the Senate. The
so-called Wilmot Proviso, which attempted to prevent the extension of slavery
into the Mexican Cession, failed to pass a divided Senate, as Southern Whigs
joined Southern Democrats in an increasingly common form of regional solidarity to defeat any antislavery measure. This left unanswered the question of
whether the new lands would be slave or free. Meanwhile, Southern "fire-eaters"
were meeting in Nashville, openly discussing secession. In the spring of 1850,
Henry Clay began putting together a set of compromises intended to ease tension. The Kentucky senator unveiled a compromise package that would allow
California admission as a free state; ban the slave trade within Washington,
D.C.; create the New Mexico Territory (which was assumed to be open to slavery); and, most important for our purposes, pass a law enhancing the ability of
the federal government to recapture fugitive slaves.

Abolitionists watched this maneuvering with a certain detached disdain.
Then, on March 7, 1850, Daniel Webster rose on the Senate floor to support
Clay's proposal. Massachusetts abolitionists had come to expect the worst of
slave-owning politicians like Clay, but the betrayal of Webster, Massachusetts's
most prominent politician, was a shock that even they did not expect. Cynics at
the time argued that Webster was simply attempting to mollify Southern opinion in preparation for a presidential run. Whatever the reason, in his speech, the
senator vehemently attacked Northerners who refused to return fugitive slaves
and framed his argument in terms of contractual necessity: "Every member of
every Northern legislature is bound by oath . . . to support the Constitution of
the United States; and the article of the Constitution which says to these States
that they shall deliver up fugitives."[35] The South, Webster acknowledged, had a

legitimate complaint that their constitutional rights were being trampled on by Northerners. Webster had long believed that government protection of property rights was paramount, and although he claimed to dislike slavery personally, he always acknowledged Southern whites' right to their "property."

Abolitionists erupted in an anger that, even for them, was unprecedented. The imperious Webster had never been solid on the cause of slavery, but the champion of "Liberty and Union" was widely regarded as Massachusetts's voice in national politics. Years later, abolitionists would continue to remember his endorsement of the Fugitive Slave Act as an especially execrable betrayal. To a convention of black activists, Webster's speech was a "humiliating renewal of his allegiance to the Slave power."[36] John Greenleaf Whittier wrote one of his most memorable poems, "Ichabod," portraying Webster as a fallen angel: "so lost! The light withdrawn . . . from those great eyes the soul has fled; when faith is lost, when honor dies, the man is dead."[37] Abolitionists saw a lesson in how Webster's unparalleled intelligence—no one doubted he had a brilliant legal mind—could not save him from moral ruin. The Whig politician became their foil, a symbol of the amorality of ambition, of brilliant intellect unmoored from any moral or religious conscience, of the tragic victory of Understanding over Reason.[38] "He wrote on Nature's grandest brow," Emerson mourned, "For Sale."[39] Decades later and continents away, another great theoretician of civil disobedience, Mahatma Gandhi, an avid reader of New England literature (and a fan of Wendell Phillips and Henry David Thoreau), would relate this portrayal of Webster as a cautionary parable for his audience of someone who "for all his great intellect . . . once sold his intellectual integrity for a price."[40]

On March 25, an overflowing crowd of abolitionists met at Faneuil Hall to register their disgust. Straining to see over the crowd, Alcott remembered the speeches as "eloquent for freedom and humanity."[41] Theodore Parker told the audience that the actions of Webster, Clay, and the others were "such as you might look for in the politicians of Austria and Russia"—the bastions of reactionary absolutism in the Revolutions of 1848. Parker's speech was learned and intricate but rather pedantic (the printed version contained long legal citations); he had not yet developed a strong philosophical critique of the law. On the other hand, Samuel Ringgold Ward, the black editor, was far more explicit. "I pledge you there is one, whose name is Sam Ward, who will never be taken alive," he thundered to "tremendous applause." Ward brought down the house by declaring that "crises as these leave us to the right of Revolution, and if need be, that right we will, at whatever cost, most sacredly maintain."[42] Two days later, black activists held an "anti-Webster" meeting, in which they cursed his "treachery to freedom," until the meeting dissolved into a "war of words" over whether to use violence in self-defense. The consensus, the *Liberator* reported, was that "in the struggle for Liberty or Death, each would act as in his judgment the emergency demanded."[43]

White and black abolitionists had both declared their willingness to disobey the law (though, characteristically, the black speakers did so more openly). On March 11, just days after Webster's speech, New York senator William Seward (a Whig but from the antislavery side) had criticized Webster's approach, declaring, in soon-to-be famous words, that there was a "higher law" above the Constitution. Meanwhile, Webster's natural allies, the Massachusetts Whigs, at first withheld their support from Webster.[44] In his journal, Massachusetts Whig legislator Charles Russell complained that, though he respected the senator, he did "not like the tone nor the sentiments of Mr. Webster."[45] Edward Everett, former secretary of state and a leading Whig, privately expressed "great despondence" at Webster's speech and doubted whether a fugitive slave law could be enforced in Massachusetts.[46]

Soon, however, the Boston Associates and their Cotton Whig allies began organizing a political and intellectual defense of Webster. Eight hundred prominent citizens—among them the Boston Associates and their trusted allies, men such as William Appleton, Rufus Choate, and Benjamin Curtis—signed an open letter in his defense in the conservative *Boston Daily Advertiser*.[47] The North, Webster and his allies began arguing, had years ago signed a sort of moral contract with the South. In return for the Constitution and the Union, which New England merchants benefited so much from, the North was obligated to return fugitive slaves. This was not an entirely novel argument. As early as 1843, for instance, George Ticknor had described the Constitution as "special bargain with the Southern States" in which the North had "promised to permit them to retake their slaves escaping into our States."[48] In the wake of the Fugitive Slave Act, these issues became even more salient, and the argument that the Constitution "contains an *explicit contract*, that . . . slaves, *shall be delivered up*" became more common.[49] A typical argument, made in 1850 by Boston's Cotton Whig congressman and compromise supporter, Samuel A. Eliot, emphasized that the roots of the Fugitive Slave Act were in the making of the Constitution. "Everybody saw and acknowledged that the union of these sovereign and independent States into one government was the remedy, and the only remedy for the existing evils . . . [therefore] it was agreed that persons escaping from labor to which they were bound in one Commonwealth, and found in another, should be returned to the State from which they have fled."[50]

If conservatives often spoke in the warm tones of moral obligations, it was not hard, in Wendell Phillips's words, to hear "the clink of the dollar" behind their high-minded praise of the Union.[51] When Eliot defended the Compromise of 1850, he reminded the audience of why they had needed the Constitution in the first place: the economic depression of the post-Revolution years, which had driven down commodity prices.[52] Restoring prosperity, according to Eliot, was the prime justification for the adoption of the Constitution and for its continued protection. Daniel Webster was even clearer. Thanking the "commercial classes" for their support of the Compromise of 1850, he reminded the audience that the original impetus for the American union had been "to create a government which should protect trade and commerce" and saw it as appropriate that merchants would now support the Union in its time of need. This was hardly a surprising statement coming from a man who believed that "the great object of government is the protection of property at home, and renown abroad," and considered merchants to be the best representatives for Boston.[53] Likewise, the *Boston Daily Post* (one of the papers of which Thoreau asked, "Is there any dust which their conduct does not lick, and make fouler still with its slime?") claimed that the abolitionists were "BREAKING FAITH with the compact that unites her with sister states" and were "doing substantial and growing injury to her great manufacturing, mechanical, commercial, and agricultural interests."[54] Conservative Boston newspapers nervously reported on every account of Southerners "excluding Northern goods from their purchases," with these sporadic boycotts providing a taste of what disunion could bring.[55]

Economic considerations contributed to conservative support of the Fugitive Slave Act because of another, even more sordid, compact. This was the implied deal with Southern Whigs over the tariff. New England businessmen had suffered from a classic crisis of overproduction since the mid-1840s, as new factories, including the heavily capitalized mills at Lawrence and Holyoke, produced more textiles than could be profitably absorbed by American consumers. Manufacturers reported "overproduction and consequent low price of cotton fabrics notwithstanding the high price of cotton."[56] Hoping that a new round of protection, replacing the 1846 free trade tariff, would keep out British imports and thereby relieve some of the stress, Cotton Whigs desperately pushed for new duties. Southern Whigs, however, "will not give a single vote for the Tariff until this slavery business is settled," Daniel Webster reported.[57] The *Boston Daily Advertiser* approvingly republished an article that asked "how can the Northern States hope for or expect protection for their labor, when unceasing war is waged upon a hundred millions of Southern property?"[58] For radicals, this intended payoff for the Fugitive Slave Act sullied it all the more. The *Commonwealth and Emancipator*, a Free Soil paper, charged Webster and his Whig allies with "prostrat[ing] themselves in the dirt before the Moloch of Slavery" in the "empty and idle hope of an increased tariff to help them out of the difficulties in which they have involved themselves by rash investments in new cotton factories which the demands of the market did not require."[59] That Webster was relying on financial support from Nathan Appleton and other textile industrialists to finance his personal life, even as he fought for the Fugitive Slave Act, only reinforced the suspicion that, as Phillips suggested, Webster was trading the lives of fugitives so that the mills of Lawrence could earn two million dollars in profits rather than one.[60]

Abolitionists Versus Contract Theory

Abolitionists' first step was to develop a theory that could respond to this idea that the supposed compact of the Constitution bound Northerners to return fugitives. Many antislavery politicians, in the newly founded Free Soil Party, of course, sought to demonstrate that one could protect fugitives and fight slavery using the tools of the Constitution. But the language of Article 4, Section 2 of the Constitution (the so-called Fugitive Slave Clause) and the 1842 Supreme Court decision of *Prigg v. Pennsylvania*, which had declared state personal liberty laws unconstitutional, forced many abolitionists to look for a moral justification outside of the Constitution. The black minister J. W. C. Pennington authored one of the first influential texts arguing that a moral contract did not obligate Northerners to return fugitives. A former slave from Maryland, Pennington had long and lasting connections to Boston's African American community. He helped William C. Nell organize conventions of black activists, and in 1849, he attended the World Peace Conference in Paris with William Wells Brown.[61] Pennington had long been concerned about the threat that slavecatchers posed to African American communities, writing as early as 1841 to the *Colored American* of the need for "more *vigilance* and watchfulness to keep our children and friends from falling into the vile hands of the slaveholder."[62] But it was his 1842 sermon, given to his Hartford, Connecticut, congregation, in response to the Latimer fugitive slave case that truly introduced a theoretical critique of constitutional contract theory. Printed into pamphlet form, his *Covenants Involving Moral Wrong Are Not Obligatory Upon Man* circulated among Boston's black and abolitionist communities during the years before the passage of the Fugitive Slave Act.

Pennington's sermon placed moral and divine laws over human ones. This meant that our "laws, oaths, promises, compacts, agreements, usages, and ordinances among men" could not be morally obligatory if they violated natural law.[63] Part moral philosophy and part evangelical jeremiad, Pennington's sermon argued that ethical behavior had to conform to the will of God. Arrangements made by men, society, or historical accident could not alter that moral imperative. After laying out this foundational ethical claim, he criticized the Constitution, specifically the exact lines on the return of fugitive slaves that conservatives such as Eliot and Webster invoked. As many abolitionists would, Pennington contrasted the absolute morality of the Declaration of Independence with the legalistic expediency found in the Constitution.

For Pennington, the logic of contracts encouraged individuals to displace their own moral compass, to act in bad faith by allowing, in a sense, the compact to do the thinking for them. Individuals gave up their moral sense to the Constitution, asking it to act as the umpire rather than make the difficult moral decisions themselves. As a result, morality was stripped from politics, since political debate was confined to interpretation of contractual clauses. The question of slavery, Pennington argued further, was a fundamentally ethical one, but people might try to ignore its moral dimensions. Echoing Garrison's claim about the primacy of man over constitutions, Pennington reminded his congregation that the Constitution was not "sovereign over the will and power of the people. . . . No, it is the creature of that will and power."[64] Americans had made the Constitution themselves, then set it up as a fetish to worship as if it were a power greater then themselves, greater than their consciences or individual wills. Not only did individuals not have the obligation to follow the clauses that demanded the return of fugitives, but, when necessary, they had the absolute duty to disobey the Constitution. Pennington quoted Isaiah that we are commanded to "hide the outcasts." Pennington did not use the phrase "higher law," which had not yet entered the movement's vocabulary, but he essentially meant the same thing when he described a moral law as that "which has its foundation in the nature of God, of man, and also of things," and which was superior to manmade laws.[65]

In the spring and summer of 1850, as the Fugitive Slave Act was being debated, abolitionists organized, hoping to stop the law. Though accustomed to hostile reactions, they were genuinely surprised at how fierce anti-abolitionist sentiment had become. In New York, Garrison, Frederick Douglass, and Samuel Ringgold Ward were mobbed at a meeting by Captain Rynder, the demagogic

Five Points leader, and his followers. All the victories that abolitionists had achieved to protect their free speech and assembly rights, the antislavery poet John Greenleaf Whittier worried, were threatened by the renewed nationalist fervor. "The signal has been given at Washington," he wrote to Garrison, "and commercial cupidity at the North is once more marshaling its mobs against us."[66] Despite the best efforts of Henry Clay and Daniel Webster, however, the compromise stalled, unable to pass the Senate with President Zachary Taylor clearly skeptical of the efforts. While the political scene remained murky, abolitionists continued to mobilize. Their strategy called for "a Hundred Conventions" throughout New England for the purpose of reminding all of "the duty of the people of the North to refuse assistance in the rendition of fugitive slaves." Stretched thin, Garrison increasingly invited Transcendentalists, including Parker, Caleb Stetson, and John Weiss, to address these conventions, helping to cement the alliance.[67]

On July 9, 1850, in one of the unexpected twists of American history, President Taylor, who had been threatening to veto any measure that was so friendly to slavery, suddenly died—the victim, supposedly, of a Fourth of July dessert of cherries and cream—and the more compromise-friendly Millard Fillmore took his place. Taylor's death shifted momentum away from free-labor Whigs and antislavery Democrats and toward nationalist Democrats, Cotton Whigs, and the South. The aging Henry Clay took a back seat while a new generation, led by Democrat Stephen Douglas, engineered the final compromise. Rather than try to pass an omnibus bill, Douglas split it into five separate bills, each of which passed with a different coalition of supporters. Unfortunately for Northern blacks, these maneuvers ended up stripping the provision that had protected the right to a jury trial for those accused of being fugitive slaves. Most of Massachusetts's delegation, including Webster in the Senate and Eliot in the House, still voted for the Fugitive Slave Act, which passed in September.

Civil Disobedience Theory

The Fugitive Slave Act was intended to salve sectional tensions. Instead, its passage set Massachusetts on fire. The New England Workingmen's Convention, meeting just days after the news of passage, resolved that the act was "an infamous usurpation, and a despotic enactment, not binding in law or conscience on the people, and ought to be resisted, if necessary, to death, by every friend to our country, to humanity and to justice."[68] Massachusetts's labor representatives were almost universally against the law, but it was black abolitionists who took the lead in mobilizing against it. Once again, it would be their initiative that would lead to a revival of the Vigilance Committee. On September 30, just weeks after the passage of the Fugitive Slave Act, Lewis Hayden organized an overflow meeting of free blacks calling themselves "friends of freedom." Attendees damned the "infernal slave-catchers" and agreed to defend one another even if it meant disobeying the law. The meeting's call for openly violent resistance to the law ran counter to the principles of William Lloyd Garrison, whose pleas for nonviolence were respectfully and politely ignored. Hayden's meeting ended with a call for all citizens, white and black, to meet at Faneuil Hall to organize around the issue.[69] At the ensuing meeting, on October 14, the crowd voted to reform the Boston Vigilance Committee. Timothy Gilbert, a prominent piano maker, was the official president, but the de facto leadership fell to an eight-person inner Executive Committee comprising Theodore Parker, Hayden, and a handful of trusted abolitionists. According to newspaper accounts, the galleries were "chiefly occupied by females, a majority of whom were colored."[70]

For the next ten years, the Boston Vigilance Committee was the organizational hub for the protection of fugitives in New England. The Committee would continue operations up until the Civil War, although it met less regularly after 1854, mostly because few slavecatchers dared set foot in Boston after that year. In total, 178 abolitionists eventually signed up—ranging from Harvard-educated ministers to a surprising number of working-class members, people such as Stephen Smith, a cabinetmaker; Uriah Ritchie, a mason; and William Holmes, a saddler. As with the previous organization, there was a semiautonomous black-led section, in which Lewis Hayden had risen to particular prominence, though old stalwarts such as Robert Morris and William C. Nell continued to play major roles. Morris, as a black lawyer, was in a unique position to assist fugitives who were caught up in a hostile legal system. Nell became a one-man employment agency, finding sympathetic employers willing to hire fugitives.[71] Protecting and housing new fugitives remained a central responsibility for the Committee. The Haydens' house soon became a popular resting spot for runaway slaves on their way to more permanent residence. In 1853, while researching a book, Harriet Beecher Stowe visited the Hayden home and discovered thirteen different fugitives, "of all colors and sizes," hiding out in the Haydens' basement.[72] Lewis Hayden was also clearly the liaison between black activists and white abolitionists during moments of crisis, when they needed to work together to protect or rescue a fugitive. While their participation in dramatic slave rescues has received the most attention, it was probably their day-to-day work on behalf of fugitive slaves that was most appreciated. Sallie Holley, for instance, while working as an antislavery agent in Boston, was told of a woman who had recently escaped from Southern slavery. Asking for a job at a drug store, the fugitive let slip her predicament. Luckily, the owner of the store was sympathetic. He immediately went to a member of the Vigilance Committee, who promptly found employment for her.[73] In this and other small cases, the Committee earned the trust of Boston's black population by working tirelessly to provide housing, employment, and legal help to fugitives at risk.

Almost every major Transcendentalist became involved in the Boston Vigilance Committee's activities. Emerson himself had significant contact with the Vigilance Committee.[74] When an earlier iteration of the Committee was created, at the meeting in 1846, he sent a letter of support that was printed along with the minutes. "I feel the irreparable shame to Boston of this abduction," he wrote, "If the merchants tolerate this crime,—as nothing will be too bad for their desert."[75] According to some accounts, he was at a crucial meeting in 1850 in which the Committee first pledged to violate the law in order to protect William and Ellen Craft.[76] He repeatedly spoke out against the Fugitive Slave Act after it had passed and called on "every lover of human rights" to assist by providing "substantial help and hospitality to the slave, and defending him against his hunters."[77] In November 1852, he donated money to the legal defense team of the Boston Vigilance Committee.[78] In 1854, when a Concord branch of the Vigilance Committee was created, Emerson was at the inaugural meeting, where he pledged to "aid and assist all in our power to help the fleeing bondman."[79] The Vigilance Committee even influenced his literary works. In an 1859 lecture on "Courage," Emerson spoke of the "leader and soul of Vigilance Committees . . . taken by honest, sincere men, who are really indignant and determined."[80] By this point, Emerson had gained the confidence of most radical abolitionists. When Wendell Phillips attended an Emerson lecture in 1855, he reported back to the annual convention of the Massachusetts Anti-Slavery Society that it was "one of the greatest and bravest ever made in the city of Boston" and that Emerson was "a man, whom literary fame had never tempted to a wrong."[81]

Emerson's support confirms his antislavery commitments, but his friend Thoreau went further, regularly performing illegal and clandestine services for the Vigilance Committee. The Committee often sent fugitives in trouble to the countryside, especially to strong antislavery towns such as Concord. As early as 1847, a fugitive had lodged with Thoreau at his cabin on Walden Pond. The fugitive eventually worked with A. Bronson Alcott, who described him in Transcendentalist terms as "self-relying."[82] On October 1, 1851, Thoreau wrote in his journal that Henry Williams, "an intelligent and very well-behaved man," had lodged with him the night before. He had escaped from Virginia and was running from Boston police officers. Williams, according to Thoreau, had letters from "Mr. Lovejoy from Cambridge," almost certainly the Reverend Lovejoy who was an active member of the Boston Vigilance Committee.[83] Indeed, the Committee's records make clear that Williams had been one of their wards: in November 1851, they reimbursed the black housekeeper Isabella Holmes for boarding Henry Williams for three weeks.[84] Later, in 1853, Thoreau reported that a free black woman who was attempting to raise money to buy her enslaved husband was lodging with him.[85] Thoreau was clearly and consciously violating the newly passed Fugitive Slave Act, which barred Northerners from knowingly assisting runaways.

Other Transcendentalists participated even more in the Vigilance Committee's work. Black intellectuals such as Nell and Hayden strengthened their preexisting ties to the personal and intellectual world of Transcendentalism through their work in the Committee. Among the white Transcendentalists who were official members of the Boston Vigilance Committee were Theodore Parker, the de facto leader and spokesman; A. Bronson Alcott, the pedagogue; Thomas Wentworth Higginson, the minister and writer; James Freeman Clarke; and William Henry Channing. After the Sims rendition, Alcott, normally too much the mystic dreamer to be particularly useful, joined the Vigilance Committee and began spending his nights on watch, looking out for slavecatchers. He described a typical day for a Committee member in his journal: "traversed the western portion of the city with John N. Spear, and visited the Watch House in Hanover Street. We met but a single watchman during our walk. Came home a little after midnight."[86] So connected would Transcendentalism become with opposition to the Fugitive Slave Act that none other than Daniel Webster blamed the resistance to the law on those who were carried away by "the puffs of the transcendental philosophy."[87]

The very act of bringing together such an unlikely biracial gathering of activists and intellectuals seems to have been intellectually stimulating. Members of the Vigilance Committee fought slavery at an ideological as well as practical level, producing pamphlets, speeches, books, poems, and even parodies of Bible verses.[88] William C. Nell, who was hired as one of the Vigilance Committee's agents, remarked that the Committee was "a school indeed for learning the Heart['s] perennial lessons."[89] Among the most important intellectual products of their activity were Theodore Parker's sermons that laid out clear arguments for the acceptability of civil disobedience; Henry David Thoreau's essay "Slavery in

Massachusetts," written in the aftermath of the Anthony Burns rendition; and
the pioneering histories of black Revolutionary War soldiers put together by
William C. Nell. The Committee's actions also left a mark on the classic literature of the American Renaissance.[90] Harriet Beecher Stowe visited Lewis
Hayden's house to research her *Key to Uncle Tom's Cabin*, and the rendition of
Anthony Burns inspired the bitter poem "A Boston Ballad," which appeared in
the first edition of Walt Whitman's *Leaves of Grass*.[91] The most mysterious connection that the Vigilance Committee had to American literature came in the
form of the ship it purchased in 1852 to rescue slaves held in Boston harbor. For
reasons that remain unclear, the Committee named it the "Moby Dick," just
months after Melville's novel was released in obscurity—an ironic fact, as
Melville's father-in-law, Lemuel Shaw, was the Boston judge who had overseen
the rendition of Thomas Sims, and Melville himself kept his distance from both
abolitionism and Transcendentalism.[92]

This intellectual production was crucial because it helped reluctant abolitionists to become willing to risk their lives and freedoms for the cause. After
attending a Vigilance Committee meeting in 1851, Thomas Wentworth Higginson complained in his journal about the lack of backbone among reformers.
To the brash young abolitionist, the meeting "left me with the strongest impressions of the great want of preparation, on our part, for this revolutionary work."
The respectable background of most reformers was the problem: "It takes the
whole experience of one such case to educate the mind to the attitude of revolution. It is so strange to find one's self outside of established institutions; to be
obliged to lower one's voice and conceal one's purpose; to see law and order,
police and military, on the wrong side, and find good citizenship a sin and bad
citizenship a duty."[93] Higginson's assumptions about the law-abiding upbringing of most reformers were not accurate, of course, for those activists such as his
comrade Lewis Hayden, whose illegal escape from slavery predated his abolitionism. But he did put his finger on a real problem: many abolitionists raised in
New England—including black activists born in the North such as William C.
Nell—needed a language and an ideology to understand the violations of the
law that the new Fugitive Slave Act demanded. It would be in Transcendentalism and the Higher Law Ethos that many abolitionists found a philosophical
language and set of justifications for their new illegal behavior.

Higginson himself had offered an example of what this language might
sound like. In 1850, he had taken the lead lobbying U.S. marshal and future
Union general Charles Devens, pleading with him to resign because the newly
passed Fugitive Slave Act would force him to return slaves to their masters. De-

vens had the obligation to disobey an immoral law whatever the demands of his career, Higginson wrote. "I ask you," he continued, "can you as a <u>man</u> with a reason, a conscience, and a heart become what the law calls on you to become— the paid tool of another's injustice and cruelty." (Devens did return a slave but, perhaps mitigating his sin, later anonymously offered to pay $1,800 to "buy" his victim's freedom.[94]) This language of "manhood," reason, and conscience, in opposition to being a "paid tool of another"—a language that was fraught with philosophical, gendered, and political meaning—would frame Boston radical opposition to the Fugitive Slave Law.

It was in their attack on the division of labor that we can first find the origins of this ideology. As early as his famous 1837 essay, "The American Scholar," Ralph Waldo Emerson had worried that people's tendency to overidentify with their professions threatened both their intellectual independence and their spiritual integrity. The process by which people became farmers, priests, or engineers, Emerson lamented, was too often one in which the logic and demands of that profession came to dominate the individual's inner life. In the modern division of labor, Emerson wrote, one ceases to be a "Man" but instead takes on a particular role, as farmer, merchant of cotton, or student of nineteenth-century U.S. history. In a "*divided* or social state," these roles limited one's ability to inhabit universal essences, what Emerson called the "One Man," those divine characteristics that unite all. A farmer "sees his bushel and his cart, and nothing beyond, and sinks into the farmer, instead of Man on the farm." This division of labor, Emerson thought, was particularly pernicious because of its consequences for how human minds work, how people interact with the world. These roles bounded your thinking, as someone else set the ends and goals for which you act. Too often, people confront situations by asking what a merchant would do in this situation rather than what a human should do. The particular skills, habits, and manners of thought that make for a good merchant, what Emerson called the "routine of his craft," have nothing to say about a moral question such as slavery, and the greed and materialism fostered in a market endeavor may make moral judgment even less likely.[95] Or, to use a relevant example, someone who was trained to *think* like a U.S. marshal might still need plenty of cleverness, even intelligence, to figure out how to capture a fugitive slave—but they would be acting based on goals that someone else had set for them. Worse, by refusing to call those goals into question, they were actually becoming used to forms of thinking that perverted who they were.

There was an almost proto-existentialist tone as Emerson asked his readers to resist being boxed into their professions and "social state." The division of labor was a classic example of alienation, of the specifically modern irony of how the tools and logics of industrial civilization—which we created to better our lives—now dominated us, leaving our lives shrunken and spiritually diminished. Perhaps this is not surprising as, via Nietzsche, many of Emerson's themes would be reflected in later European existential thought.[96] Like later existentialists, Emerson called on Americans to recognize the ultimate artificiality and narrowness of their social roles—that they had chosen to be a farmer or merchant—and did not therefore forfeit their moral freedom when they accepted those roles.[97] Still, Emerson's criticisms of what happened to individual psyches when boxed into narrow occupational roles contained an implicit criticism of the marketplace and foreshadowed later critiques of capitalism and bear comparison to Marx's notion of alienation. Just as Pennington had held that Americans were being held hostage to the Constitution—a document of their own creation—so Emerson worried that our creativity and moral authenticity were being drowned by our careers and the division of labor, things also of our creation.

Emerson's anxiety, of course, spoke to an economic truth experienced by thousands of New Englanders: changing employment patterns were upending the relationship between one's personality and the dictates of one's job. The transportation revolution had allowed for a tremendous economic specialization; the opening up of the fertile upper Mississippi River Valley forced rocky New England to diversify its economy, and industrialization had spurred growth in a wide array of secondary industries, from insurance and the law to railroads and real estate.[98] Cities such as Boston, Springfield, Worcester, and Lowell swelled with wage workers, professionals, artisans, retailers, and small manufacturers. By the eve of the Civil War, James Freeman Clarke noted "three hundred and more occupations" in Boston in which white men could find work (black workers, it should be noted, were largely left out of this economic development). For some New Englanders, this development meant that they would be working as a permanent employee of someone else—a clerk, secretary, journeyman, or simple wage worker. The goal for most remained economic self-ownership. But even for one who achieved it, what exactly did this economic independence mean when you were producing for the marketplace? Did not the dictates of the impersonal market control your actions, encouraging increasingly false self-presentations as much as a boss would? In the bustling antebellum cities and commercial fairways, both the midlevel clerk and the independent peddler wore a mask and played a role; worse, increasing numbers forgot that the mask was not their true face.

The old republican idea—that one's public and economic life was a transparent reflection of your true self—was increasingly difficult to attain. As early as the 1750s, moralists such as Rousseau had noticed how urbanization and the market economy encouraged vanity, hypocrisy, and acting; to *be* and to *appear* became more and more separate. Two of Herman Melville's great characters— Bartleby, who cannot be convinced to muster the energy to even exist, and the nameless Confidence Man, whose constant manipulation and dissembling seemed to undermine any sense of stable social reality—expressed well the disintegration of solid foundations for a self in the flux of market society. The long march toward the fragmentation and weightlessness of the modern alienated self had begun. Many Americans, especially in the new urban and industrial centers, experienced this as a disorientation, an anxious sense of lightness and pastlessness, and rushed to social clubs, new churches, benevolent associations, advice books, and political parties to try to fill this void.[99] Emerson's writings, then, were one of many responses to the need to construct new models for selfhood in an era when the old models would not do; his appeal to an artistic and democratic self was a reaction against the tendency of the marketplace to reduce one's inner life to the hollow dictates of commerce.[100]

But it was abolitionists who saw most clearly how the new demands to act and think through your social role—to let your job or social pressure dictate how you acted or thought—threatened New England's moral integrity. Henry C. Wright, for example, wrote in 1848 that when he had first met William Lloyd Garrison, "my conscience and reason said—'*he is right*,' my *position* as a minister was against him." Wright explained that "as a MAN, I felt that he was doing what all ought to do; but as a professional minster," he had to oppose Garrison. After a lengthy battle with his conscience, in which Wright worried that "in me, the *man*, was yet subservient to the *priest*," he finally quit the clergy and went fully into antislavery work.[101] Like Emerson, Wright saw hostility between the demands of society and his profession and the imperatives of moral integrity. The moral logic of being a good "man" and citizen stood in stark contrast to the roles that market society created for people. The anxiety about how the roles of employment limited Americans' selfhood was so deep that even at the graduation of a medical school, the abolitionist Henry I. Bowditch reminded the students not to identify *too* much with their new profession at the expense of morality: "Life is not given to us *chiefly* that we may become wonder-working mechanics, keen men of business, brilliant wits, deep scholars, wise philosophers, orthodox theologians, able jurists, or even learned and skillful doctors."[102]

After 1850, this language would become particularly common among those advocating disobedience of the Fugitive Slave Act. Theodore Parker told an audience that there were universal moral laws, common to all of humanity, in obedience to which one "attains moral manhood."[103] Individuals are not simply abstract men, Parker continued, and in real life have to take on particular roles in society. So be it, Parker declared, as long as "it be remembered that I am a man first of all, and all else that I am is but a modification of my manhood, which makes me a clergyman, a fisherman, or a statesman . . . valuable in so far as they serve my manhood, not as it serves them."[104] This, Parker argued, was the dilemma now facing all Massachusetts men as a result of the passage of the Fugitive Slave Act—whether their particular position as a federal marshal, police officer, judge, or juror would override their universal moral duty as human beings. Parker made clear that those who violated this rule, those who turned in a fugitive slave, risked their very manhood. Of a hypothetical man who followed his official duty, rather than his moral duty, Parker wrote, "His individual manhood is covered up and extinguished by his official duties; he is no longer a man but a mere president, general, governor, representative, sheriff, juror, or constable."[105]

This was not just rhetoric; a number of abolitionists used this philosophical language when justifying civil disobedience against the Fugitive Slave Act. Joseph Hayes, a captain of the Boston police, resigned his office during the Anthony Burns crisis because he did not wish to assist with the capture of a slave.[106] Charles Sumner, as he often did, translated the Transcendentalist impulse into concrete political action when he told a Free Soil convention that he could not assist the return of slaves because "I cannot forget that I am a *man*, although I am a *Commissioner*."[107] But the most important was Theodore Parker's campaign to convince jurors that, despite whatever oaths they had taken, they could still vote to free a fugitive slave. "The natural duty of a man," Parker wrote, "overrides all the special obligations which a man takes on himself as a magistrate by his official oath."[108] In a parable, Parker described a trial for a man (Mr. Greatheart) who has aided the escape of a slave. "If I have extinguished my manhood by my juror's oath, then I shall do my official business and find Greatheart guilty . . . but if I value my manhood, I shall answer after my natural duty to love a man and not hate him, to do him justice, not injustice, to allow him the natural rights he has not alienated, and shall say 'Not Guilty.'"[109] This campaign was so successful that it became difficult for known antislavery men to be accepted onto juries that dealt with slave renditions, so well known was their tendency to vote for freedom whatever the circumstances of the law.[110] Parker became obsessed with the topic, and when, in 1855, he was brought before a jury for his part in supposedly inciting the Anthony Burns riot (he humbly declared he was "on trial for my manly virtue"), Parker detailed the history of jury nullification. He argued that since judges used only narrow "technical inference" rather than the "intuition of conscience," jurors had the right to judge not simply by the facts of the case and of the law but also by their own individual moral sense—what he earlier called their "manhood as men"—as to whether the defendant deserved to be punished.[111] In 1855, his activism paid off and the Massachusetts legislature passed an act detailing the right of jurors to judge not only the facts of the case but also the law itself, giving juries significantly more power to free the accused.[112]

Obeying the logic of our jobs or official roles did not just make political cowardice more likely; it did this because it prevented people from accessing the higher parts of men's spiritual lives. Living wholly within one's social roles and letting the logic of these small systems of life dominate one's psyche cut people off, Emerson thought, from that "One Man," the universalism at the core of the world that gave access to the Higher Law. To Emerson, a good life entailed a reunion of the self with the larger forces of the universe, what he would call the "Oversoul." This "One Man" or "Oversoul" was the primal spiritual unity, the grand oceanic Godhead at the core of the universe that he saw as the singular fact of existence, closer to a pantheistic monism than most traditional Christian doctrines. There was an impersonality to these mystical experiences, a sense of self-abandonment to the great expanse, as when Margaret Fuller "saw there was no self; that selfishness was all folly . . . that I had only to live in the idea of the ALL."[113]

The romantic individuality of Transcendentalists, in other words, was miles away from the buffered, narrow, and self-contained individualism of modern liberalism. Many theologians and thinkers at the time, in fact, criticized Transcendentalism not for its individualism but for the opposite, for how it threatened to annihilate all that is distinct and particular about the self, dissolving our individuality into the infinite of the Absolute. William Adams, a conservative Presbyterian minister, declared in 1851 that social unrest was being caused by "the offspring of a Pantheistic philosophy, which overlooks and neglects our *individuality*."[114] Even James Freeman Clarke was disturbed by his colleagues' tendency to think "their personality disappears—they are united together in God. We do not think of ourselves as individuals in our spiritual movements." Underneath Clarke's discomfort was a horror at exactly what Fuller celebrated, the loss of self and the dissolution of individuality in moments of spiritual communion with the "All." "To be consistent," Clarke worried, Transcendentalism "must deny personal immortality in the future life, and assume that immortality consists in union or rather reabsorption of our spirits into God."[115] And it was this tendency of Transcendentalists to lose themselves in an impersonal mystic communion with the immanent spirit of the universe that Melville mocked in *Moby Dick*, with his fable of the "sunken-eyed young Platonist" tasked with looking for whales from the crow's nest but who "at last loses his identity; takes the mystic ocean at his feet for the visible image of that deep, blue, bottomless soul, pervading mankind and nature," loses his footing, falls into the ocean, and drowns.[116]

There was some truth to this charge. Individuals reached fulfillment, according to Emerson, not by seeking isolation but by allowing the Oversoul to flow through them as smoothly as possible. In a sense, then, Emerson's self was empty, simply a receptacle for "the inundation of the ethereal tides to roll & circulate through him. . . . he is caught into the life of the Universe."[117] Individuality needed connection with the infinite All. This communion with what he would call the Oversoul was threatened by petty and distracting social roles, which narrowed one's field of vision, putting up barriers to the flow of the Oversoul and encouraging materialism and compromise by channeling the spirit into ever more splintered compartments. The result seemed a paradox: the only way to participate in the universal soul of existence was to examine yourself, disallowing society to determine your thought. The quotidian community of manmade society threatened the more important spiritual community with the universe. Properly understood, then, only a man who stood above and before the corrupting influences of society, was able to connect with the Oversoul's moral energy and become an authentic social reformer. As Emerson wrote in *Culture*, "The saint and the poet seek privacy to ends the most public and universal."[118] An individual had the choice: to embrace the mean influences of society or the elevated influences of the universe's Oversoul. Yet in neither case was the individual self truly alone or self-contained. William James perceived this well and pointed out that there were "two tendencies in Emerson, one towards absolute Monism; the other towards radical individualism. They sound contradictory enough; but he held to each of them in its extremist form."[119]

If "manhood" stood in for authentic action, Transcendentalists described people who let themselves be cut off from the moral flow of the universe as becoming a "thing," a "tool," or some other lifeless material object. "Man is thus metamorphosed into a thing, into many things. . . . The priest becomes a form; the attorney, a statute-book; the mechanic, a machine; the sailor, a rope of a ship," Emerson had written.[120] Losing access to the Oversoul and to their humanity, people instead decline into the tools that they use, physical objects such as ropes and machines that lack autonomy and moral purpose, that become the symbols of their decline into someone else's means to an end. This contrast between humanness and being a "thing" evokes Marx's conception of reification and Martin Luther King Jr.'s later language about segregation "thingifying" its victims. But for abolitionists, though, this language about "things" brought to mind one of their favorite Coleridge quotations, a line from his essay on philosophical method that, among others, Douglass used as an epigram for *My Bondage and My Freedom*: "A *person* is eternally differed from a *thing*; so that the *Idea* of a Human Being necessarily excludes the Idea of property in that Being."[121]

Occasionally abolitionists contrasted being a "man" with being an animal, as Moncure Conway had and as Emerson did when he frequently described the Fugitive Slave Act as "quadruped law" rather than moral law.[122] Most notoriously, Charles Sumner shocked the Senate when he denied his obligation to assist with the rendition of slaves by quoting the Bible. "Is thy servant a dog," Sumner spit at Senator Butler of South Carolina, "that he should do this thing?"[123] Boston abolitionists almost never referred to their opponents as women, suggesting that (consciously at least) they intended the term "man" to refer to some sense of humanity or citizenship rather than gender. Far more commonly, abolitionists thought that when people ceased making moral decisions and lost their "manhood," they became "tools" or "machines," expressions that were often used to denigrate those who collaborated with slavery. Thoreau, for instance, condemned the trend whereby "men have become tools of their tools."[124] When, in 1849, black parents petitioned the school board to end the segregation of public schools in Boston, they condemned the board's efforts, which they saw as an attempt to buy them off, of putting a black man in charge of the segregated school. The petition declared that they "regard with suspicion and as unworthy as confidence, any individual who is identified with us, that will suffer himself to be a *tool* to suit the wishes of those who are opposed to the full enjoyment of our rights."[125]

A tool, of course, was not only something that lacked moral autonomy but was literally an instrument, the logic of instrumental reason personified. Bostonians who allowed themselves to participate in the rendition of a slave—to be, in the words of an antislavery preacher, "passive instruments, of slavery"—were abandoning their moral agency and thus moral personhood.[126] By collaborating with slavery, individuals were letting someone else direct their actions, decide for them what ends they would live for. As Moncure Conway wrote in an antislavery essay, "When you get a man who is a citizen, who feels that before he was a merchant or a mechanic he was a man, you can reason with him. . . . but when you get hold of one who thinks that the end and aim of creation was to fill his pocket . . . then you have got hold, not of a man, but of a piece of patent-leather or dry-goods."[127]

When one became a tool, Emerson thought, his mind was taken over by instrumental logic, Understanding in Transcendentalist terminology, capable of performing well his given tasks but never capable of transcending them. The tool of slavery did not literally lack thought, but he lacked the critical and ethical reflection that truly defined humanity: Reason. This person could be efficient but not good, logical but not truly rational, productive but not purposeful. The problem, Emerson suggested, was that Americans got so wrapped up in their employment (the means to one's life) that they ultimately forgot about the ends for which they lived. It was not just that thinking like a dry goods clerk, lawyer, or merchant might make it hard for you to achieve a good life; worse, you never stopped to even figure out what that good life might look like. A tool simply sought to achieve ends someone else gave them; a "man" thought about his or her own moral ends. Thomas Wentworth Higginson summed up the Transcendentalist criticism of instrumentalized ideas of employment. "Life is taken up in obtaining, by hook or crook, the means to support life," he wrote, "'to make a living' is the only object of labor—and what is the end of it;—only the body lives after all—and all the higher faculties of the soul, love, honor, integrity, courage—these sink, decay and only *make a dying*."[128] By considering only the best instrumental means to solve a problem given by someone else, mankind's conscience and thought had been reduced to nothing more than an elaborate machine whose levers were being pulled by another, "materialized intellect," Emerson called it.[129] The goal, instead, for the Transcendentalists was to offer an alternative mode of thought, one that was capable of self-reflection as well as self-interest, moral behavior as well as expediency.

Tools, factories, steam engines, and conveyor-belts—lifeless industrialization had come to symbolize the mechanical amorality of a Northern society incapable of reflecting on its complicity with slavery. In lectures, Emerson took to pairing these two seemingly incongruous things—"we are not safe with our fatal reliance on laws and machinery"—both symbols of a people incapable of moral judgment.[130] According to Thomas Wentworth Higginson, the problem was not simply that many officeholders in Massachusetts were weak compromising men but that the entire system—the machinery of a slaveholding society—produced such men. Higginson contrasted Northern tools (industrial machinery) with the tools Southerners used: "hoes, spades, axes, [Northern] politicians, and ministers." Imagining the mayor and governor chained by a Southern slaveowner,

Figure 7. This abolitionist woodcut suggests that, by preferring law over
justice, Daniel Webster is guilty of idolatry by worshiping the Constitution,
an instrument supposedly intended to produce freedom over
freedom itself. Courtesy of Houghton Library.

Higginson cried, "The Representative Men of Massachusetts—*These tools she
gives, Virginia, to thee!*"[131] It was not long before abolitionists began describing
Daniel Webster—that triumph of the amoral Understanding—as a "steam-
engine" whose "gigantic intellect" ran roughshod over any moral considerations
or sentiment for freedom.[132]

This specter of industrialization and moral mechanization owed much to
Thoreau's *Civil Disobedience*. Thoreau begins, like Higginson would do after
him, by associating government service with being a tool, writing about soldiers
that "the mass of men serve the state thus, not as men mainly, but as machines,
with their bodies," while acknowledging that very few "reformers in the great
sense, and *men*" serve the state with their consciences.[133] Thoreau's genius lay
in understanding that the systematic functioning of every individual act of

compromise and moral cowardice created a vast machine of injustice no longer dependent on the agency of any one individual. Thousands of individual tools created one vast factory of injustice. It is this background that makes sense of the famous imagery in *Civil Disobedience*: the "machine of government," injustice that takes on a rote mechanical aspect devoid of any necessary human agency. In such a system of bureaucratized evil—"the injustice has a spring, or a pulley, or a rope, or a crank, exclusively for itself"—the only solution is to "let your life be a counter friction to stop the machine."[134] Thus, in his journal, Thoreau would declare that slavery "is not the peculiar institution of the South" but rather that it existed "wherever a man allows himself to be made a mere thing or a tool."[135] Most men, he pessimistically thought, were little more than tools, going so far as to declare in his eulogy on John Brown that most men could not die because they had not truly lived but rather most "fairly ran down like a clock."[136]

Transcendentalists feared that, unable or unwilling to live by ultimate ends, people were letting their psyches be dominated by what Theodore Parker called "the world of matter." In Parker's world of matter, "all is mechanism, the brute involuntary, unconscious action of matter," and humans have no agency. This is the universe of Newtonian physics: cause and effect in the gray dull phenomenal world of impersonal material forces. It was the internalization of the "grim casual treadmill" that Romantics feared was the end result of science, industrialization, and soulless modernity.[137] Not only were one's interaction with the world disenchanted, with the elimination of magic, religion, and spirituality in everyday life, but even individuals' psychic agency was flattened, reduced to physical necessity and outside control. If one's life was determined simply by bodily desires or social norms—for comfort, sensual pleasure, or social approval—and if reason was, as Hume had taught, simply the slave of those passions, then free human agency and self-determination were impossible. All of one's inner self could be shown to be determined by physical forces, the thread of our lives measured and cut not by the caprices of distant Moirai but, much worse, by the relentless pounding of a thousand spinning jennys. In this vision of radical heteronomy, mankind's inner life was reduced to so many pistons firing and wheels turning. For Emerson, this was "Fate," the aspect of human existence determined by necessity, contingency, history, passivity, and the given.

Saving humanity from this fate, Parker claimed, was the possibility of a spiritual and moral sphere, what he revealingly called the "world of men," in contrast to the "world of matter." In that world, "man is an actor as well as a tool," capable of willpower, moral choice, and religious faith. The result was that one was a "man" insofar as he used his conscience and acted morally and a "tool" insofar as he let the material and social forces of the world determine his ends.[138] Only through active moral commitment did mankind transcend their passive bodies (bodies that were dependent on Newtonian laws of physics) and cease to be mere automata and become men, aware of their moral and spiritual freedom, each able to stand as an author of himself. There was a heroic element to this process, as becoming a man meant a near-Promethean expenditure of will, a godlike self-exertion over the necessity and dumb fatalism of nature. In Emerson's language, it was "Power," the always present possibility of rebellion, self-creation, control of one's existence, and moral agency.

Thus, adherence to the moral rules was possible only by cultivating a fierce independence that allowed individuals to ignore compromise and materialism. One might, Parker allowed, consult one's neighbors and authorities, but ultimately, he wrote, "I am to ask my own conscience, and follow its decision; not that of my next friend, the public, or the best of men."[139] If one lost this sense of right and wrong, Transcendentalist Charles Mayo Ellis argued, "he ceases to be a man."[140] Given this association of "manhood" with a strict morality, it should not be surprising that Transcendentalists often assumed that manhood was a rare, rather than a common, trait. Thoreau, for instance, asked, "How many *men* are there to a square thousand miles in his country?" answering, "Hardly one."[141]

The Higher Law theory sought to address the threat that intellectuals such as Alexis de Tocqueville and John Stuart Mill were diagnosing about democratic culture producing social conformity. As historians are now aware, the willingness of Northerners to do things such as return fugitive slaves seemed to confirm Tocqueville's concern that democratic equality could create conditions in which dissidents would be too scared to go against the overwhelming will of the majority. The rise of literacy, a free press, urbanization, and democratic politics—everything that we think of as civil society—all raised the possibility that public opinion would come to exercise a dictatorship over the inner self, a tyranny more fearsome because it was less obvious than an absolute monarch, one that operated on the soul rather than the body. Educated Northern men—with names such as Winthrop and Eliot, descended from the founders of Massachusetts—who happily sold away the best of New England's political legacy for the approval of newspapers and Southern politicians seemed the strongest evidence of such widespread conformity. As scholars have argued, abolitionists such as Wendell Phillip saw endless radical agitation as the only solution to this conformity.[142]

Transcendentalists added a philosophical critique. One of the Transcendentalists' concerns with Lockean empiricism had been that to the degree our values were created by our sensory experiences, those values would ultimately be held captive to the society that produced those experiences. How could someone know slavery was wrong if their only ideas were shaped by experiences in a society that thought it was right? What would happen to our moral values if they were rooted in physical sensation, in the demands of our roles, or the applause of social approval? The Higher Law theory sought to break that cycle by grounding antislavery ethics in values derived from nonmaterial experiences—"Reason," spiritual or religious commitments, or intuitive preferences for liberty.

Along with these elevated sources, the Higher Law could be found in some of the deepest parts of the unconscious self. In his distrust of relying solely on conscious reasoning, Emerson, in particular, went beyond Kantian rationalism and traditional idealism, seeing a certain mysterious depth at the heart of human existence, an unconscious energy, and source of will and power that cold logic could never fully grasp. Thus, "the soul is superior to its knowledge," our intuitions and unreflecting sparks of spontaneity more trustworthy than our labored thought.[143] One of Emerson's assumptions—and here he most clearly presaged Nietzsche—is that our surface consciousness, our immediate reflective faculty, what we might think of as the voice in our heads, is much more likely to be captured by social norms and the language and logic of others, while our unconscious intuitions remain our own. Emerson deemed as pedants and "bookworms" those people who let someone else's system imperialize the whole of their consciousness and mental horizon, creating a scholar "subdued by his instruments," dominated by the dazzle of "accepted dogmas."[144] It was a sort of metaphysics of social conformity, where instrumental reason ("Understanding") and our surface consciousness were the domains where social pressure ruled and our preconscious impulses the place for authentic moral action. In other words, if animalistic hedonism was one threat to just behavior, Emerson had little more faith in its antithesis, in soulless abstracting consciousness, the utter tragedy of the most sophisticated and educated people who, *exactly because of that education*, can speak to themselves, even in moments of intimate solitude, only in someone else's words. The result was that the Higher Law was more than simple universal political morality (as the old Natural Law might have been) but added to that a greater emphasis on the intuitions, willpower, aesthetic beauty, and vitality.

Most male Boston radicals, especially Garrison, Higginson, and Phillips, were sympathetic to the women's rights movement, but the centrality of the word "man" to their rhetoric raises profound questions about the relationship between their vision of the transcendent self and their ideas about gender. Radicals sometimes clearly used the language in a universal way, implying "all human beings" when they wrote "men." But not always, and their actions suggested that the rise of aggressive campaigns of civil disobedience that deployed this language of manhood coincided with a sidelining of many women activists.

The writings of Margaret Fuller, the Transcendentalist most associated with the women's rights movement, are especially illuminating in this regard and suggest the dangers that accompanied the abolitionist use of the word "man" to organize their politics. Fuller did occasionally capitalize the word "Man" and seemingly did endow it with the meaning of "self." At one point, she even went so far as to pointedly claim in her feminist manifesto, *Woman in the Nineteenth Century*, that "by Man I mean both man and woman: these are two halves of one thought."[145] But Fuller was also aware of the ways in which using the word "man" as a stand-in for admirable behavior served to demean women. "Let it not be said," she pleaded, "wherever there is energy or creative genius, 'She has a masculine mind.'"[146] Still, Fuller at least struggled with what gendered terminology meant, something that few male radicals did.

In fact, there is very concrete evidence about how Boston intellectuals understood the word "man," and it illustrates well the complexity of the issue. On May 2, 1849, in one of the early meetings of the Town and Country Club, members discussed whether women could join the group, even though their constitution used the word "men" when describing who was eligible. Although the membership voted down Higginson's amendment, which would have added the word "women" to the constitution, they ended up agreeing, in the words of Wright, that the "term men is generic, and includes women.'" By 22 to 16, the membership voted "that in the use of the word men in the first article of the Constitution, it shall be intended to signify all human beings; that there may be no limitation on account of sex or complexion."[147] Privately, Samuel May was shocked that the club would pretend that "'man' was generic and signified human beings!!"[148] Thus, it seemed that they believed the word "man" simply meant human.

The story was not over, though. Although the (male) Transcendentalist and abolitionist leadership had voted that the word "man" should be considered a universal indication for human being, the club never actually allowed a female member.[149] In a similar way, when abolitionists appealed to "manhood" to advocate disobedience, they probably considered themselves to be making universal arguments about personhood, even as they were simultaneously creating structures that excluded real women from their organizations. The Boston Vigilance Committee, for instance, was all male. A dedication to nominally universal values was concealing—perhaps to the speakers themselves—an informal process that created and often encouraged de facto exclusion. The seemingly abstract and de-racinated self who inhabited the Emersonian imagination—an invisible eyeball stripped of bodily differences yet still, paradoxically, coded as male—obscured women's positions and provided a language that allowed, even encouraged, sexual segregation of abolitionist politics under the guise of abstract universality.

The Boston Vigilance Committee in Action

The ink was barely dry on the Vigilance Committee's membership rolls when they gained national notoriety. Lewis Hayden's ability to mobilize black activists would be immediately tested with the appearance of slavecatchers searching for the Crafts, fugitives from Georgia. In October 1850, just weeks after the rebirth of the Vigilance Committee, William and Ellen Craft, who had sought safety in Boston after a daring escape in which Ellen posed as a white man and William her servant, sought their aid. It was Hayden who convinced the committee to take on the Crafts' case; in one abolitionist's recollection, Hayden's spontaneous plea to hide them convinced Charles Sumner and other white abolitionists to defy the law.[150] Theodore Parker married the couple, handing them a Bible and a sword as wedding presents, while abolitionist lawyers harassed the slavecatchers with a never-ending series of legal maneuvers, charging them in court with everything from kidnapping and slander to reckless carriage driving and failure to pay bridge tolls. Prominent Whig politicians derided the situation as "all a nigger affair," but in fact, the Crafts had aroused the deep support of both white and black Bostonians.[151] Fellow fugitives, such as James Williams, who "armed himself on that occasion and went out to fight for him," formed a sort of ad hoc militia to protect the Crafts.[152] Meanwhile, William hid at Lewis Hayden's home in Beacon Hill: when the slavecatchers arrived, they found a band of "brave colored men armed to the teeth" led by Hayden, who held a torch to a barrel of gunpowder and warned the agents that they would blow up the whole block rather than give up one fugitive.[153] The slavecatchers backed off and the Crafts fled to England, where they became popular antislavery lecturers.[154] To Nell, scenes such as this ragtag band of fugitives threatening self-immolation to hold the forces of American slavery at bay made Boston a "modern Thermopylae," a last brave stand for freedom.[155]

A couple of months later, in February 1851, the Vigilance Committee had its most dramatic victory with the rescue of Shadrach Minkins. A fugitive from Norfolk, Virginia, he had been working as a waiter before being identified by agents of his former master and arrested. Minkins was brought into the Boston courthouse, where a group of Committee lawyers, headed by Richard Dana and Robert Morris, met with him and began a series of legal delays to prevent the agents from taking him from Boston. Meanwhile, Hayden organized a group of twenty black men who, while the bewildered judge and guards looked on, burst into the courtroom, grabbed Minkins, and hurried him out. The abolitionist editor Elizur Wright, who happened to be in the courtroom on unrelated business, noted that "there was nobody to guard the prisoner" but Shadrach himself and joked that the fugitive "seemed sadly to lack the patriotism" to guard himself.[156] Conservatives were apoplectic: Daniel Webster sputtered that this was a "an act of clear treason," and Amos A. Lawrence, a prominent textile manufacturer, wrote to U.S. marshal Charles Devens, offering to "serve in any capacity" to help return slaves.[157]

The Vigilance Committee would not be so lucky two months later, when Thomas Sims was captured. This time, Boston authorities were ready—deploying hundreds of armed guards and encircling the courthouse with a heavy chain. The chain was an effective deterrent, but unintentionally, it was also a perfect symbol for the loss of Massachusetts sovereignty that the Fugitive Slave Act represented. The chains were an example of how, as Lydia Maria Child pointed out, the various security and military precautions needed for a slave rendition introduced into Boston the very customs and legal regime of slavery—such as the necessity of carrying a pass with you in order to enter government buildings.[158] William Henry Channing later declared that seeing the Boston courthouse surrounded by chains instantly converted him from nonresistance to the need for violent struggle against slavery.[159] Meeting in the office of the *Liberator*, the Vigilance Committee was unable to decide on a course of action. The main stumbling block seems to have been the unwillingness of Hayden to commit black activists. While publicly confident, he pulled Thomas Wentworth Higginson aside and admitted that "we do not wish any one to know how really weak we are. Practically there are no colored men in Boston; the Shadrach persecution has scattered them."[160] And so, as the Cotton Whig *Daily Advertiser* celebrated the end of the "troublesome affair," Sims was marched out of Boston, dressed in a new black suit and weeping, as three hundred Boston police officers escorted him back to slavery.[161] In Savannah, he was whipped in the public square thirty-nine times, "a living sacrifice," Frederick Douglass said, "to appease the slave god of the American Union."[162]

But the previous slave renditions would just be dress rehearsal for the capture of Anthony Burns. To William C. Nell, the tumult around Burns's

rendition—his arrest, the fiery mass meeting, the violent but unsuccessful rescue attempt—were "events unparalleled in the anti slavery history of the Nation."[163] Throughout the 1850s, the city government had been developing more
sophisticated methods to guard the captured slaves, and in response, the Vigilance Committee was deploying ever more confrontational and revolutionary
tactics to free them. When they collided in the Anthony Burns case, in
May 1854, Boston abolitionists would shed blood for the first time.

Tensions were high in the days after the failed attempt to free Burns. The
Boston Vigilance Committee, after all, had killed a U.S. marshal. Legal attempts to free Burns likewise failed. In a moment of morbid humor, Richard
Henry Dana, Burns's lawyer, noted in his journal the awkwardness of the pros-
ecuting lawyer, a Boston man unaccustomed to the logic of slavery, who was
unsure whether he could refer to the defendant as a "person," a small but revealing detail about the moral absurdity of the law.[164] Years later, Hayden admitted
that he had fired the shot that had killed Batchelder, making Hayden the first
Boston abolitionist to shed blood in the struggle against slavery.[165] Abolitionist
residences and stores throughout the city were draped in black, while proslavery
gangs roved the city attacking abolitionists. Dana was assaulted in the streets by
anti-abolitionist roughs, and as they did after the Sims rendition, many fugitives fled the city.[166] A group of abolitionist women presented Edward Greely
Loring, the U.S. commissioner who had returned Burns, with thirty pieces of
silver, Judas's reward (abolitionists had given the same poisoned gift to Daniel
Webster in 1851).[167] In a less dramatic gesture, Judge Loring found himself unable even to buy dinner, as his butcher refused an order of a roasting pig, telling
the commissioner that "I don't want any of that money you got for sending a
man back to slavery."[168] In Haverhill and Springfield, Stephen Douglas and
President Pierce were hung in effigy.[169] Hayden went into hiding while Higginson found safety in the reliably antislavery milieu of Worcester. When a different U.S. marshal sought to arrest him, a "stampede of negroes" stood in the
marshal's way, throwing rotten eggs and kicking at him; it was only with Higginson's intervention that the marshal left with his life.[170]

By 1854, the Vigilance Committee could boast of having assisted 230 fugitives.[171] It would remain in action nearly right up until the Civil War, assisting
at least twelve fugitives in 1858.[172] Their activity spread as far and wide as Bath,
Maine, where members boarded the *Franklin*, looking for an escaped slave
named Charles Mason, and Manchester, New Hampshire, where Boston members tracked a slavecatcher and warned his victim.[173] They had moved beyond
simply escorting slaves to Canada to begin actively securing their freedom. On

July 15, 1853, the Vigilance Committee got wind that a slave was aboard a ship in Boston harbor and a group of men, including "four or five colored men" (probably Hayden himself among them), took the *Moby Dick* into the harbor, found the guilty ship, demanded the slave under the threat of violence, and, as Nell wrote to a friend, "made a <u>freeman</u>."[174] Here, as in other actions, the Committee did more than simply house fugitives; they violently seized the slaves on the (not quite high) seas. Bearse, the *Moby Dick*'s captain, would be accused of "piracy" for another rescue in Boston harbor.[175] On one occasion, in 1855, Vigilance Committee members impersonated U.S. officers, seized a slave with a $500 bounty on his head, and neatly shuffled him off to Canada.[176] While there would not be any more public slave rescues, the Vigilance Committee continued to play important roles in aiding those who had freed themselves, often performing crucial work in private. In July 1856, for instance, the Vigilance Committee learned about Joseph Williams, a slave held on the *Growler*, a ship out of Mobile, Alabama, who had attempted to jump ship in Boston harbor and secured a writ of habeas corpus to have him freed.[177] And in 1859, the Vigilance Committee helped to secure the freedom of an escaped Mississippi slave, his back "covered with marks of the whip and branding-iron."[178]

Their civil disobedience, in other words, was increasingly veering into more violent and revolutionary activity, one that included "piracy," violent street protests, and breaking into jails. Soon on the plains of Kansas and in secretive societies throughout the North, men and women who adopted a similar sense of romantic political resistance were mobilizing against the slave power.

CHAPTER 5

Heroism, Violence, and Race

The anniversary of British emancipation in the West Indies had always been, since the 1830s, the most optimistic day in the antislavery calendar, a reminder that committed antislavery activists had once overturned one of the world's most profitable slave regimes. But by the late 1850s, a darker, more violent tone was seeping into these celebrations. Nowhere was this clearer than at the "Convention of Colored Citizens," held in New Bedford on July 24 and 25, 1858, to mark British emancipation. The Fugitive Slave Act was still the law of the land, Supreme Court Justice Taney had declared that black men were not citizens in the *Dred Scott* case, and racist demagogues such as Stephen Douglas were gaining popularity by proclaiming the United States a white man's government. The result, as the organizers of the convention noted, was a white "reign of terror" that hovered over the free black North.

The convention began on a militant note with a "handsome military display." An armed black militia, the New Bedford Blues, carrying twenty guns, marched to the New Bedford and Taunton depot to ceremoniously greet their Boston counterpart, the Liberty Guards, themselves holding twenty-five muskets.[1] Among the first speakers was Charles Lenox Remond. The Salem abolitionist had once been a pacifist and a loyal Garrisonian, and at the famous 1843 meeting in Buffalo where Henry Highland Garnet had first called for slave insurrection, Remond had rejected such calls for violence on moral and practical grounds. When, in 1847, Remond tentatively suggested that it would be moral for slaves to rise up against their masters, he was attacked in the pages of the *Liberator* by white abolitionists and promptly backed off.[2] After the passage of the Fugitive Slave Act, though, Remond began calling for federal troops to be withdrawn from Southern forts should there be a slave revolt.[3] In 1852, he joined Robert Morris before the Massachusetts legislature petitioning for a black militia.[4] Now, in 1858, he wanted black men to adopt a "defiant position towards every living man that stood against them . . . we must resist." Taking inspiration from Lucy Blackwell, who had refused to pay New Jersey taxes because, as a woman, she was denied the vote, Remond called for any form of resistance and defiance, both violent and nonviolent, to slavery and racism.[5] Black Northerners, he claimed, had to seize control of their own emancipation. They "must depend on our own self-reliance," and he defined the Emersonian value as rejecting white leadership in order to produce a "black William Wallace."

Remond's speeches on Monday, July 24, were only a warmup for the real conflict that took place on the next day. Remond clearly resented the presence of Josiah Henson, the black activist known as the model for Uncle Tom. Remond had made a series of not so subtle attacks on the Canadian abolitionist. He had suggested that a committee be appointed to craft a declaration to be smuggled south that would encourage revolt, acknowledging that "his resolution was in one sense revolutionary, and in another, treasonable." This finally provoked Henson, who responded by suggesting that it was easy for Remond to threaten violence since, unlike the slaves, he was unlikely to be hanged when the insurrection was put down. Remond, who was clearly frustrated by both the debate and the aggressive spread of slavery, ended the argument by sputtering in anger, "To the devil with the slaveholders!" It was, perhaps, because of encounters such as this that his admirer Alexander Crummell had compared the "fiery and impulsive" Remond to a warrior "with unsheathed sword, rushed into the thickest of a battle fray."[6] Although the group eventually voted down Remond's insurrectionary proposal, the debate was, according to the *Liberator*, "by far the most spirited discussion" of the meeting, evidence that more and more black thinkers were becoming interested in the possibility of violent, even treasonous, actions.[7]

It was not just Garrisonian pacifism that Remond was angrily rejecting but also the promise of white abolitionist benevolence itself. As he told the 1858 convention, he "was very sorry that so many colored people had suffered themselves to be led by white men—considerate white men, indeed, but white men, after all." Remond had been an early Garrisonian and, even during the schism between Frederick Douglass and Garrison, had refused to disavow the white pacifist. But as the 1850s progressed, he became increasingly pessimistic about the ability and willingness of white abolitionists to overcome racial prejudice. At an 1859 meeting of "Colored Citizens," Remond described abolitionists' "mean processes by which the colored people were excluded from participating in the deliberations of white assemblies."[8] "Few men," he told the Massachusetts Anti-Slavery Society in 1862, "could place themselves in the point of view of the black man."[9] If Remond experienced unexpected hostility from white abolitionists, he was equally angry at the seeming passivity of black comrades. Black men "smiled when they ought to frown," he told the convention of "Colored Citizens."[10]

As Remond's increasingly pessimist rhetoric suggests, the 1850s were a militant but fraught period for abolitionist politics. Tensions between white and black abolitionists boiled over into open conflict. Abolitionists, both black and white, began fantasizing about violent revolution at the same time they advised candidates for national office. Intellectuals embraced a politics of individual heroism and martyrdom while simultaneously mobilizing around a cultural politics rooted in New England's supposedly unique values. Abolitionists had always been suspicious of the political parties—even those who joined the Liberty or Free Soil Party worried about the affinity of antebellum politicians for compromise, horse trading, and corruption. But now, even as the Republican Party seemed to offer a popular antislavery vehicle, many abolitionists were convinced that their best hopes lay in secret and violent organizations. Just as the political mainstream opened up to them, they retreated to a world of conspiracies and secret societies. While earlier abolitionist anti-politics had been Garrisonian in origin and maintained a principled nonviolence, now abolitionists, led by black activists, tentatively at first, eagerly by the time the fighting in Kansas heated up, embraced violent means.

The moral enthusiasm of the Higher Law Ethos seemed to be splitting in two, producing, on the one hand, an arrogant moral elitism among some that could turn judgmental and racist, while at the same time, the frustrated desire for confrontation with slaveholders released impulses toward vitalism, physical power, and the lure of the irrational. Thus, the ethos took Transcendentalists in contradictory directions: they began to imagine New England as the brains of America, a physical manifestation of "ideas" and "spirit," those aspects of the self that Transcendentalist philosophy had long lauded. At the same time, reeling under a series of outrages—from Sumner's caning to the sack of Lawrence— they fantasized about violent redemption, the washing away of the nation's inequities in a final confrontation with slavery. They maintained a disdain for the bourgeois virtues of instrumental reason and calculated self-interest. But their Romantic and humanistic appreciation for the artistic and imaginative qualities of the self was shading into a celebration of the martial virtues: will, physical courage, and vital violent energy. This strange mix of violent fantasies and philosophical idealism provoked contradictory attitudes toward African Americans, whom they began to denigrate as lacking rational control and representing the sensuous side of life, even while simultaneously blaming them for not rising up in violent revolution.

And so Transcendentalist ideas contributed to a politics rooted in a set of exclusive regional and ethnic identities. This newfound pride in their New England and Anglo-Saxon heritage threatened to destroy the biracial alliance that had always given the world of abolitionism and Transcendentalism its intellectual and political vibrancy. Emerson and Theodore Parker, especially, began associating New England, as a region, with a set of abstract values, including a dedication to equality and liberty. New Englanders, they argued, had a greater tendency to think in abstractions and hence were more likely to be abolitionist "fanatics." This rhetorical celebration of New England's values dovetailed with a broader political project of mobilizing Yankee cultural identity in the fight against slavery. This strategy came at the expense of black abolitionists who felt increasingly marginalized. Positing both Southern whites and blacks as incapable of the same type of idealistic politics as antislavery Yankees, Parker and Emerson racialized the antislavery project, managing the unlikely achievement of simultaneously alienating both black Northerners and Irish immigrants, as well as legitimizing a nasty strand of abolitionist racism that blossomed in the late 1850s.

Secret Societies Versus Slavery

Old abolitionist dedication to pacifism was giving way to not just violent but often illegal and insurrectionary tactics. The tumult around Anthony Burns's rendition had convinced many of the need for secret and conspiratorial abolitionist organizations modeled on the revolutionary secret societies and Carbonari of Europe. One week after the "riot" of abolitionists had failed to free Burns, abolitionists at the New England Anti-Slavery Society met, discussing new, secretive organizations. J. J. Kelly, the black activist who had distinguished himself during the street fighting in front of the courthouse, called for an open rejection of nonresistant and pacifist principles. Meanwhile, white activists such as Stephen Foster demanded the "organization of secret clubs in every town in the State" that could protect fugitives. While still widely respected for his earlier leadership, William Lloyd Garrison was losing control of his own organization, and his feeble pleas that "secrecy and stealth are the methods of Slavery" were politely ignored.[11]

Black Bostonians already had been long forming organizations willing to use violence to protect their community. Even in Boston, black activists were increasingly discontent with Garrison's seemingly passive strategy of mobilizing public opinion and sought extrapolitical means to confront slavery and to protect themselves. Black Bostonians thus preceded their white colleagues in the formation of military-style abolitionist organizations. As early as 1853, black Bostonians were forming their own extralegal militia and were drilling in paramilitary style. Robert Morris, the black lawyer and Vigilance Committee member, played the biggest part in organizing what came to be called the "Massasoit Guards," named after the Indian sachem who had aided English colonists in the seventeenth century.[12] Eighty members eventually signed up.[13]

Morris had hoped for a legal charter from the state. Ever the lawyer, Morris noted that there was precedence: Rhode Island had granted a black militia official recognition. Starting in 1852, he led a series of petition drives and testified in front of the Massachusetts legislature along with William Watkins and Charles Lenox Remond in favor of such a charter and access to the state armory.[14] Throughout the 1850s, state officials stymied Morris's efforts on the grounds that the 1792 Federal Militia Act had explicitly used the word "white" in describing eligibility.[15] Although Morris's efforts to gain legal recognition were unsuccessful, the Guards kept meeting without official sanction, raising by subscription the money to buy weapons.[16] Eventually, a frustrated Morris gave up trying to achieve recognition, and the Guards ceased meeting. Nonetheless, the black laborer Lewis Gaul soon formed the Liberty Guards, which took its place (Morris disapproved because they did not have legal sanction). When, during the Civil War, black leaders began recruiting regiments such as the 54th and 55th Massachusetts, the legacies of the Massasoit and Liberty Guards would be fruitful sources of inspiration.

Publicly, leaders such as Morris and Watkins presented the Massasoit Guards as a simple matter of equal rights. Watkins testified to the Legislative Committee on the Militia of the Massachusetts General Assembly that "we base our petition upon the grand, fundamental, heaven-approving principle of *right: our absolute right to enjoy full civil privileges.*"[17] Certainly, the relatively innocuous desire for equal treatment was an important part of their motivation. But militia spokesmen such as Watkins and Morris knew that organizing the militia would be deeply challenging to many white Northerners' sense of political order. Watkins acknowledged that the existence of a black militia would scare "Southern bullyism" and Northern racists, "foreigners especially."[18] Morris and Watkins were savvy enough not to mention defiance of the Fugitive Slave Law when talking to the Massachusetts legislature, but they were certainly motivated by the desire to resist it, demonstrated by their repeated references to the revolutionary legacy of black soldiers and their willingness to, in the words of Watkins, "defend our lives, our fortunes and our sacred honors."[19]

Watkins, whose address in support of the militia was entitled "Our Rights as Men," defended militia service with the language of black masculinity. Watkins saw the ability to participate in the militia—which obviously implied an acceptance of violence—as central to the assertion of black manhood. Watkins hoped he and the other men asking for a charter were not viewed as "obsequious supplicants" but as "men, proud of, and conscious of the inherent dignity of manhood." Watkins identified the overlapping concepts of dignity and manhood with the ability of black men to participate equally in civil institutions and assert themselves politically and socially. He disdained the humility of those like the character of Uncle Tom from Stowe's recent novel, who submitted to injustice or discrimination with "Christian meekness and becoming resignation." Instead, Watkins praised the exploits of black veterans of the Revolutionary War and other conflicts.[20]

Meanwhile, white abolitionists also began forming military-style antislavery organizations. The Boston Vigilance Committee had already evolved, in some ways, into an insurrectionary organization. The short-lived Defensive League of Freedom, founded by John A. Andrew, James Freeman Clarke, and Ellis Gray Loring in the wake of Burns's rendition, raised money for the legal defense funds of fugitive slaves.[21] But it was the Boston Anti-Man Hunting League, which formed on July 19, 1854 (just months after the Burns case), that truly demonstrated the abolitionist turn toward violence and confrontation. Led by Henry Bodwitch, its members included a familiar cast of Transcendentalist stalwarts such as Parker, Higginson, Alcott, and William Henry Channing. Highly secretive, the members referred to the club publicly with the innocuous name of the "Pine Tree Reading Club" (until 1971, the flag of Massachusetts featured a pine tree on it) and developed a complicated system of passwords and doorkeepers at each meeting to ensure privacy. The black abolitionist George Downing, who was recruiting black volunteers, was told to come to the side door of a church right before 8 p.m. and "ask for the Pine Club" in order to come and bring any new members.[22] While many earlier abolitionist organizations had pledged to use "all legal means," the Anti-Man Hunting League declared they would use "all proper means" to stymie slave rendition, a one-word switch loaded with meaning.[23]

A fascinating training poster demonstrated exactly what the League considered those "proper means" to be.[24] Symbols for abolitionists surrounded a central slave hunter, visually choreographing the manner in which the

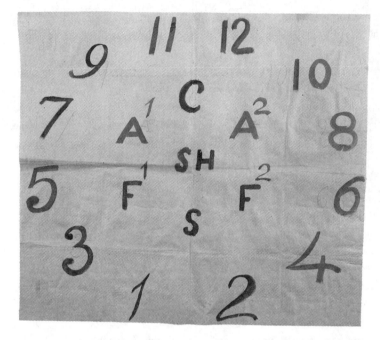

Figure 8. This poster—46 by 40 inches—demonstrates how the Anti-Man Hunting League proposed to capture a slaveholder (SH). Two men would grab his arms (A1 and A2) while another two would restrain his legs (F1 and F2) and a third would hold his head (C). The slave (S) would be shuttled to freedom by the circle of members (1–12) who surrounded them. Collection of the Massachusetts Historical Society.

Anti-Man Hunters would covertly encircle a man on the street and detain him, essentially kidnapping the kidnapper. As Bowditch described it, they hoped to "frighten him by taking him from his hotel and carrying him to confinement at our country lodges, and thus perhaps to persuade him to give up or sell the slave." The League drilled by subduing volunteers pretending to be slavecatchers and hoarded billy clubs that they would use during the attacks.[25] The affiliated League of Massachusetts Freemen set up branches in Marblehead, Worcester, West Roxbury, Cambridge, and Springfield.[26]

Cynics, it is true, snickered at the Harvard graduates in short-sleeves, play-acting as insurrectionists. Henry Wilson probably was not alone when he laughed at the League as "serio-comic" and wondered, reasonably enough, whether such antislavery warriors as the eighty-year-old Samuel May Sr. were really striking fear into the hearts of slaveowners.[27] There was no doubt that the abolitionists were mimicking, perhaps a bit clumsily, the dashing European revolutionaries such as Kossuth and Mazzini, whom they romanticized. In a letter to the British reformer Elizabeth Pease, Wendell Phillips admitted as much: "the long evening sessions—debates about secret escapes—plans to evade where we can't resist—the door watched that no spy may enter—the whispering consultations of the morning . . . All remind one of those foreign scenes which have hitherto been known to us, transatlantic republicans, only in books."[28] The elaborate theatrics of the Pine Tree Reading Club may have bordered on the absurd but were evidence of real political passion that was denied outlet in the normal political process. Blood, after all, had recently been shed, albeit not by a Harvard man but by the ex-slave Lewis Hayden.

The Pine Tree Club's embrace of violence, in theory if not in practice, fit the mood of the nation—especially after the caning of Charles Sumner.[29] Sumner was, in many ways, the political arm of the Transcendentalist radicals. His election to the U.S. Senate, just as Daniel Webster left, had symbolized a changing of the guard, as a new generation of radical antislavery politicians began replacing the timid Cotton Whigs. Even Garrisonians, who distrusted any politician who served under the U.S. Constitution, generally respected Sumner's antislavery credentials. So when Preston Brooks, a South Carolinian congressman, walked up behind Sumner and began viciously thrashing the seated senator, Massachusetts radicals felt the attack in personal, visceral terms. Lydia Maria Child became "literally ill for several days" after the attack and was only able to publicly protest when she got over her headaches and "painful suffocations about the heart."[30] The caning enflamed antislavery Northerners, still smarting from the Kansas-Nebraska betrayal, and helped strengthen support for the emerging Republican Party. But it was also freighted with cultural meaning, proving to abolitionists the violence and "barbarism" that marked the feudal South (as opposed to the supposedly intellectual and civilized North). Brooks's actions may have demonstrated the hotheaded violence that characterized the South, but Northern abolitionists saw no contradiction in responding with their own fantasies of violent revenge. Emerson wrote in his journal of the need to "cut down" the whole of the proslavery South and advocated that "we raise soldiers in Masstts" and flirted with the possibility of creating a "Northern Union."[31]

Inflammatory news was coming at a dizzying pace: the same issue of the *Liberator* that reported on the assault on Sumner also told of the sack of Lawrence, Kansas, by proslavery "border ruffians."[32] These two issues were obviously related, as Brooks had attacked Sumner because the Massachusetts senator had given a fiery speech accusing the South and Brooks's uncle Andrew Butler specifically of "raping" Kansas. As is well known, the fighting in Kansas helped radicalize the North.[33] As Theodore Parker wrote to a friend, the conflict in Kansas proved that "we <u>must fight</u> with iron tools to root slavery out."[34] Abolitionist militants moved seamlessly from the fight to protect fugitive slaves to the fight for Kansas.

Thomas Wentworth Higginson's experience demonstrates how participation in Higher Law radicalism in Massachusetts served as a gateway for entering the fighting in Kansas. Since Anthony Burns's rendition, Higginson had been looking for a community of abolitionists that could match his often-frustrated desire for violent confrontation with slavery. Massachusetts, with its ambitious antislavery politicians and pacifist Garrisonians, was a poor place for Higginson's style of politics. "All my life I had been a citizen of a Republic where I had seen my fellow-citizens shouting, and retreating, and retreating, before the Slave Power," he told the Massachusetts Anti-Slavery Society, "and I heard that away off, a thousand miles west, there was one town where men had made their stand, and said to Slavery, 'Thus far, but no farther.'"[35] His comparison of the Kansas settlers resisting slavery with Job's God delimiting the heavens and oceans gave a sense of the world-historical fight he saw himself in. Rushing to Kansas, he found it was far better suited to a self-expressive politics of grand romantic gestures and uncompromising abolitionism than was New England. He accepted leadership of a group of New England emigrants to Kansas in 1856, gleefully "expecting adventures."[36]

Riding from town to town on the prairie and talking to the grizzled Free Soil settlers, he found the "buoyant courage" he had been seeking. The Free Soil volunteers struck him as self-controlled, hardy, brash, jaunty, and indifferent to suffering or death, and he compared their leaders to a set of historical heroes, including the Spartan Leonidas, the Puritan John Hampden, Ethan Allen, Israel Putnam, and Oliver Cromwell.[37] In his journal, he commented that Kansas "seems like the English Civil Wars," a historical analogy on many people's mind at the time.[38] Higginson himself came too late to participate in the "battles" at Lawrence and Osawatomie, but he met veterans and helped introduce "Old Captain Brown" to the Northern public. The regular dispatches that he sent to the *New York Tribune* and later published as the book *A Ride Through Kanzas* helped to explain the conditions in Kansas to Northern audiences. While he was only in Kansas for a handful of weeks, his writings helped normalize the idea of violent confrontation with slaveholders, of private citizens arming themselves to fight against slavery, and of the coming of "a severer struggle" in the future.[39]

If Higginson was a brash romantic firebrand, Daniel Foster, another Boston radical who immigrated to the prairies of Kansas, cultivated the opposite demeanor. While Higginson wanted to be a Romantic hero, an American Garibaldi, Foster was one of many nearly forgotten people that the abolitionist movement churned up: quiet unambitious men who were willing to die doing their antislavery duty. Taciturn, earnest, and humorless, his rural upbringing always left him feeling awkward around the intellectual elite even after they welcomed him in. Foster had once been an Orthodox minster, and he never totally lost a certain taste for Jeremiad-style moralizing (as when he saw the "wickedness" of local gamblers as evidence of the moral corruption of the slave power).[40] He entered the abolitionist movement in the late 1840s, collaborating closely with black Bostonians on the issue of school integration, and helped arrange the publication of Thomas Jones's slave narrative. When the fugitive slave Thomas Sims was marched to the docks, Foster led a motley crew of abolitionists in public protest and prayer at the harbor. Many participants would long remember the dramatic moment as Foster prayed for God to "destroy the wicked power which rules us," while the sun rose over Boston harbor, and they watched Sims put on the boat that would return him to slavery.[41] By the 1850s, he had "consecrated myself wholly" to the abolition of slavery.[42] Along with working with the Boston Vigilance Committee, he published antislavery sermons and worked briefly for the Garrisonians but left in 1853 because he refused to stop distributing tracts by a political abolitionist.[43] As a minister in Concord, he was befriended by Emerson and Thoreau, who helped convince him to reject Orthodox Christianity. As with so many others, his transition toward Transcendentalist religious heresies, expressed in his essay "The Bible Not an Inspired Book," coincided with his increased abolitionist commitment.[44] Emerson "respected certain heroic traits which appeared in him," and Foster reported eating at his table (the easily scandalized abolitionist was shocked to find Emerson serving wine).[45] In 1854, he was one of the relatively few Americans to purchase a first edition copy of *Walden*, which he read to his family out loud.[46]

In 1856, his abolitionism brought him to Kansas, where he battled with the "Border Ruffians" and took to preaching with a pistol next to his Bible. At first, he was an itinerant preacher and claimed that he logged up to two thousand miles of travel and nearly bankrupted himself. He must have cut a strange figure: a grim threadbare preacher traveling the small prairie communities of Kansas, bringing not fire and brimstone orthodoxy but the gauzy Transcendentalism of Concord.[47] Later he declared that nothing but his own "fearlessness" had saved his life from pro-Southern gangs. Foster would go on to become a captain in the 37th Colored Volunteers during the Civil War. White officers in black regiments were conspicuous targets, and a Confederate sniper killed the abolitionist in 1864.[48]

The Heroic Style of Abolitionism

The abolitionist politics of the Fugitive Slave Act Era—clandestine, violent, and veering into the revolutionary—introduced new divisions into the movement. Garrisonian pacifists felt left out while women were often explicitly excluded from organizations that contemplated violence. But the new tactics spoke to a deep yearning among many New Englanders for a more expressive, morally rigorous, and heroic style of political activity. As the site of abolitionist activism shifted to the bleeding prairies of Kansas and the dimly lit hideouts of the secretive societies, Transcendentalists saw the possibility of making the antislavery movement an arena to cultivate the heroic virtues, to live out a vision of an expressive existence, where one's external political activity could seem to reflect something about one's internal sense of self. Transcendentalists would seek in the heroic acts of inspired individual resistance to the desperate timidity and enervating materialism of bourgeois modernity.

Transcendentalists had long worried that the abolitionist project (and political engagement more generally) might distract people from the supposedly more important project of personal self-development. Abolitionists, Emerson sometimes thought, started from a position of bad faith; compensating for the gnawing sickness of their internal self by trying to fix the outside world, antislavery radicals rushed to social reform because the voids in their soul were too daunting to reform. Phillips and Garrison, Emerson had worried, did not have time to develop an authentic self and "may wake up some morning & find that they have made a capital mistake & are not the persons they took themselves for."[49] And Thoreau likewise suspected that "what so saddens the reformer is not his sympathy with his fellows in distress but, though he be the holiest son of God, is his private ail."[50] But the heroic style of abolitionism, which came of age in the 1850s, seemed to answer their concerns, as it offered a vision of abolitionism that was as much about self-expression and the demonstration of personal valor as it was about dedication to an external political cause.

The Transcendentalists' self-overcoming heroism, their celebration of the individual who was able to resist the demands of material being and achieve moral freedom, was related to their rejection of Lockean materialism. Going back to the writings of Thomas Carlyle, they had associated Locke's theory of the mind with an abandonment of willpower, an acceptance of the world as it is. Carlyle accused Locke of denying free will: by basing individuals' knowledge only on what their senses told them, empiricists became passive receptacles of sensory experience, "mirrors" rather than "lamps."[51] "By arguing on the 'force of circumstance,'" the Scottish Romantic wrote, "we have argued away all force from ourselves."[52] Theodore Parker also linked Lockean philosophy to social conformity and political passivity, arguing that the "Sensationalism" of British empiricists taught that "all moral questions are to be decided by authority . . . not by reference to the facts of consciousness, but to the phenomena of history." Crucially, this meant that people would take their cues from "the most comfortable classes of society," those who were most able to create the conditions we experience.[53] An unheroic person was ultimately a conformist, someone whose idea of ethics was determined by his or her physical surrounding and history, what Parker called the "accidents of man."[54]

Rejecting the Lockeans' method of achieving truth purely through the senses, Emerson believed, was the first step toward self-reliance and heroism. But cold reason was barely preferable. There was something about our surface-level sensory experience and calculating consciousness—with its reliance on externally given phenomena, socially defined symbols and language, and inhuman mathematical logic—that was easily dominated by society, by "the voice of mankind."[55] Heroism, then, involved rooting action in "self-trust," in faith in the boundlessness of our thoughts and inner life, rather than in the superficial account our senses first give us. It was in the latent and unique quality of character and instinct, what Emerson called "deep force, the last fact behind which analysis cannot go," that political heroism was found.[56]

And so following the "higher" parts of the human self—its mind, spirit, latent character—was not a simple matter but instead required a heroic struggle against the lower mechanical and animalistic parts of the soul. Emerson, in particular, was interested in what he called "Power," the part of the human self that was capable of autonomous thought and moral action. "Power" alone, Emerson thought, was capable of transcending "Fate," the tyranny of material and historical facts. To act with power was heroic, self-transcending, and the sole path to spiritual and social freedom. The association of "Power" with liberation was abstract—Emerson blended a Kantian emphasis on moral autonomy with a proto-Nietzschean sense of self-overcoming—but also literal, exemplified in the actual liberation of enslaved people. In his essay *Character*, Emerson linked this transcendence of material conditions to emancipation, even slave rebellion.

Imagine a slave ship, Emerson asked his readers, "which should contain persons of the stamp of Toussaint L'Ouverture." Surely the qualities of their character, what he called their "higher nature," could "overmatch the tension of an inch or two of iron ring."[57] There is a certain willed naïveté here, as if the overwhelming horrors of the Middle Passage were no match for the willpower of one extraordinary individual. But Emerson chose it as a deliberately extreme example (though, of course, slave rebellions on ships did happen). Moreover, the citations of L'Ouverture by Emerson demonstrated the degree to which examples of black heroism and resistance framed canonical Transcendentalist understandings of moral autonomy.

At the level of both theory and attitude, Transcendentalists were drawn to a brash and haughty politics, moments of doomed but inspired heroism that displayed the actor's intrinsic moral worth. When Thoreau spoke of Lewis Hayden and Thomas Wentworth Higginson's failed attempt to free Anthony Burns, as he did in his essay "Slavery in Massachusetts," he referred to "the simple heroism of an action," unconcerned with its consequences.[58] In his essay on heroism, Emerson portrayed the hero as strong-willed, self-reliant, dedicated to an idea, laughing at death, and "scornful of petty calculations" of utility. The only contemporary American who illustrated these virtues was the abolitionist martyr Elijah Lovejoy, bravely facing a murderous mob to defend his beliefs, though he knew it to be suicide.[59] More than anyone in Emerson's world, though, it would be John Brown who would come to represent unpragmatic greatness, a man whose dedication to a moral principle trumped all calculation of personal safety, all expedient obedience to laws and social pressures.

Implicit in Transcendentalist celebration of heroism was a criticism of the bourgeois virtues—prudence, materialism, self-concern, and instrumental rationality. For Thoreau, nothing was as pathetic as the smallness of his neighbors, who asked what John Brown expected to "gain" from his raid, as if the principled courage of Brown could be reduced to calculations of profit.[60] The abolitionist leadership agreed: the National Anti-Slavery Society complained in 1854 that Northerners had given up the fugitive Anthony Burns because "material success" had left Northerners "weak, timid, selfish," and incapable of "heroism" and "self-sacrifice."[61] Thoreau, like many nineteenth-century intellectuals, was convinced that the dull industrial modernity of the Victorian era sapped the heroic virtues, leading America into an anesthetized future of comfortable numbness. Unlike Carlyle or Cobbett, though, Thoreau did not romanticize the chivalry of medieval Europe. He instead preferred the more republican ancient Greeks and Romans as models upon which, in his biographer's words, to build "a heroic life in the unheroic modern world."[62] For Thoreau, heroism meant "the autonomous, courageous, self-reliant, freestanding individual."[63] It was a criticism not so much of the material results of capitalist modernity as of the philosophy and spiritual values (or lack thereof) that seemed to result from it.

This self-expressive style of political radicalism sought to reunite the aesthetic with the ethical, the individual's redemption with the community's emancipation. A heroic abolitionism answered Emerson's earlier fear that political engagement would siphon off moral energy that would otherwise go into creating an authentic self. In the aftermath of the failed Burns rescue, Higginson recommitted himself, in a widely published sermon, to an abolitionist politics of self-expression. He started by declaring, melodramatically, that "existence looks worthless" under the rule of slavecatchers and that he could "only make life worth living for, by becoming a revolutionist." Higginson was convinced that Northerners would challenge the slave power only when they learned that "life is something more than dress and show. . . . there is some nobler aim in existence than a good bargain, and a fast horse, and an oyster supper."[64] In Higginson's vision, personal spiritual integrity was intricately bound up with radical political action. Moments of righteous, often violent, political acts, then, were the cure to the divisions of self and community that Transcendentalism had diagnosed.

As much as Transcendentalists had generally focused on the spirit rather than the body, a certain respect for physical courage and military prowess was reasserting itself. There had always been a vitalism, an embrace of unconscious energy, in some Transcendentalist thought. As early as 1841's *Self-Reliance*, Emerson had registered concerns about the falseness of an overintellectualized existence, of the ways a man can be "clapped into jail by his consciousness" if he loses his integral connection with the unconscious currents deep in his being.[65] And Romanticism had, since its early days, had elements that had been drawn to the gothic, the dark, and the macabre. Emerson himself had proved this in 1832 when he famously dug up the decomposing body of his first wife, in order to stare directly into the abyss of death's power. But it was not until the 1850s that this vitalism became an open celebration of physical power. Theodore Parker began acknowledging that there was some good in his great intellectual enemy—Locke. At least Locke's "sensational philosophy," the Transcendentalist wrote, "stood up for the body."[66] The most important result of this rediscovery of the body was Thomas Wentworth Higginson's 1858 essay "Saints and Their Bodies," which appeared in the new *Atlantic Monthly* and mocked the "moral and physical *anhaemia* . . . bloodlessness" of most Protestant divines and, by implication, the New England Transcendentalists. Like Thoreau, Higginson sought

inspiration from ancient Greece for "the union of saintly souls and strong bodies."[67] Where Thoreau and Alcott, as well as a number of food reformers such as
Sylvester Graham, had previously advocated some form of vegetarianism, the
red-blooded Higginson spoke "in defence of animal food" and physical exercise.[68] Higginson's essay predicted the "muscular Christianity" that would gain
popularity in the Gilded Age. The essay played a significant role in creating the
ideal of the athletic, "manly" college-educated gentleman that, once combined
with late nineteenth-century racial codes, would produce such square-jawed ex-
ponents of American imperialism and white supremacy as Teddy Roosevelt and
a thousand Tom Buchanans. Higginson's celebration of manliness came to border on the neurotic, and later in life, he would almost obsessively campaign
against Oscar Wilde's "unmanly manhood" and Walt Whitman's "nauseating"
poetry.[69]

The best parts of the newfound Transcendentalist interest in irrationalism
were Thoreau's writings on the moral value of wilderness. As Transcendentalists became obsessed with courage, heroism, and bodily
strength, they openly, even eagerly, embraced violence as both psychological
compensation and political tactic. They were moving beyond the legacy of earlier
Romanticism toward the darker celebration of vitality, the unconscious, will,
and violence that would mark late nineteenth-century antimodernism. Theodore Parker barely let a speech go by without some reference to his grandfather,
who had helped lead the Minutemen at Lexington. Toward the end of his life, he
even began rejecting the classic Christian virtues of humility and meekness, seeing them as limits to self-fulfillment. In a letter to James Freeman Clarke from
Rome, he contrasted the statues of Christian saints with those of ancient Roman
heroes. The saints lowered their eyes, were ashamed of their bodies, and passively
accepted the world. The classical Romans, on the other hand, were "strong able
bodied fellows who did their work manfully, eat their dinners, married their
wives and begat sons and daughters with thankfulness of heart."[70]

The best parts of the newfound Transcendentalist interest in irrationalism
were Thoreau's writings on the moral value of wilderness. Thoreau's friendship
with Emerson had been fraying throughout the 1850s, in part as Thoreau, happier on a solitary ramble through the woods, watched the older and wealthier
Emerson become increasingly comfortable in the gilded parlors of bourgeois
Boston. In *Walden*, "Walking," and other essays of the period, Thoreau turned
to a defense of the personal and existential value of access to untamed wilderness. He was unconcerned, of course, with simply stewarding natural resources
wisely (this would be only to exploit nature in a better and more long-term
manner). Instead, his defense of wilderness was decidedly nonutilitarian. He
wanted to preserve the truly noncivilized—"absolute freedom and wildness"—

so that humans could get in touch with the "primitive rank and savage" side of life.[71] His environmentalism, then, had a healthy dose of primitivism to it, as part of the value of wilderness was its ability to reacquaint mankind with the virtues that were threatened by the stifling politeness of civilized society: fidelity to instincts, roughness, a healthy "savagery," joyous aliveness, heroism, spontaneity, and self-respect.

Emerson sometimes dismissed black accomplishment, but he did acknowledge the possibility of black heroes, most notably Toussaint L'Ouverture, whom he referenced in a number of essays as evidence of black capability for genius, character, and intellect. He also, in this period, befriended Harriet Tubman, who stayed at Emerson's house and was another model for violent resistance that Emerson embraced. Black abolitionists, though, were using Transcendentalist language to craft their own pantheon of abolitionist heroism. James McCune Smith, in the introduction that he wrote to Douglass's 1855 autobiography, called Douglass an "American Representative man," a clear reference to Emerson's 1850 essay collection *Representative Men*.[72] For William C. Nell, though, there was a black Transcendentalist hero much closer to home: Crispus Attucks, the ex-slave who had helped to spark the American Revolution and had been martyred during the Boston Massacre. As early as 1841, Nell had become fascinated by the story of Attucks—then an obscure footnote in the story of the American Revolution—and in the 1850s began a campaign to garner public recognition for the hero.[73] In 1851, Nell, Hayden, and a group of black leaders petitioned the Massachusetts legislature to appropriate $1,500 to build a monument to Attucks.[74] The legislature demurred, citing a white boy who supposedly died before Attucks. In 1855, Nell was back at the State House testifying in favor of a monument.[75] Nell and other black abolitionists were particularly upset that the site of Attucks's death, which black activist Henry Johnson called a "sacred spot," was trampled when soldiers carried the fugitive slave Thomas Sims back into slavery.[76] By the late 1850s, Nell was organizing annual celebrations of Attucks's martyrdom on the day of the Boston Massacre, events that often featured calls for radical action.[77] Nell's celebration of black military participation was coached in patriotic terms, attempting to position their claims about civil rights in terms of their ancestors' military service. But his campaign always had not-so-subtle undertones of threat, implying that blacks could take up arms and bravely fight for freedom again if need be.

The image of Attucks served a number of ideological purposes for Nell. In the era of the *Dred Scott* decision, the celebration of a black hero of the American Revolution was an argument for black citizenship, a reminder that, contra

Chief Justice Taney, African Americans had participated in the creation of the American nation. In a time when many abolitionists looked back fondly at the fiery enthusiasm for liberty that marked the Revolutionary Era, Nell's story of Crispus Attucks served to integrate that Revolution, to prove black participation in the struggle for liberty.[78] Nell had many motives to celebrate Attucks, but it is interesting the degree to which his descriptions of the Revolutionary hero map onto the Transcendentalist image of the hero. In his description, in the *Colored Patriots*, of Attucks's martyrdom, he emphasizes Attucks's fearlessness and natural leadership. "He had been foremost in resisting, and was the first slain," Nell wrote, "as proof of a front engagement, he received two balls, one in each breast."[79]

Abolitionists, Transcendentalists, and Race

It was at one of Nell's Crispus Attucks's celebrations that the question of white racism within the Boston abolitionist movement finally came to a head. On March 5, 1858, a remarkable impromptu debate over the character of African Americans occurred between Theodore Parker and John Rock, a black lawyer and activist. That the debate about black character took place at the Attucks celebration was not coincidental. Nell and other Boston African Americans saw in Attucks's courage, militancy, and patriotism the types of heroic virtues that white Americans, such as Parker, were intent on denying to them.

Tension between white and black abolitionists had been building for some time. Black abolitionists, in Boston and elsewhere, had long grumbled that white activists—who led the abolitionist organizations, dictated the speakers at rallies, and controlled the purse strings—kept African American abolitionists in subordinate positions. And Theodore Parker was particularly controversial because his regular celebrations of Anglo-Saxon virtue had raised black criticisms as early as 1853, when a correspondent for *Frederick Douglass' Newspaper* had slammed a Parker lecture about "the Anglo-Saxons and their influence" as a "whining, canting, at-truth squinting piece of self-adulation."[80] The rivalry between the New York–based group of abolitionists, led by Gerrit Smith and Frederick Douglass, and the Boston abolitionists exacerbated racial tension within the abolitionist movement. In December 1854, James McCune Smith, a friend and close ally of Douglass, created a firestorm of controversy when he accused the "Old Organization," by which he meant the Garrisonian American Anti-Slavery Society, of refusing to permit black speakers on stage. The Boston abolitionists "do not, as organizations, treat black men as men, and therefore, do not regard them as such."[81] Some of the particulars of Smith's charge were unfounded—regarding the particular tour that Smith mentioned, the Society had reached out to J. Mercer Langston to be a speaker, but the black activist had not responded—and the continued loyalty of black radicals such as Nell, Remond, and William Wells Brown to the American Anti-Slavery Society demonstrated the complexity of the issue.[82] In the end, the spat dissolved into ugliness. Rather than take the possibility of their own racist practices seriously, the *National Anti-Slavery Standard* responded with a patronizing dismissal of Smith's charges. By January 1855, Smith was attacking those black activists who remained loyal to the "Old Organization," declaring that William Wells Brown, Charles Lenox Remond, and Robert Purvis did not count as authentic black supporters because they "are all *yellow* men. . . . Why do your folks thus 'cotton to' half white men."[83] No one came across well from the debacle, but Smith's overall message had resonated: black abolitionists played an important symbolic role in the movement but were expected to play second fiddle to the celebrity white abolitionists such as Garrison, Phillips, and Parker. Samuel Ringgold Ward, who was neither a Garrisonian nor a follower of Gerrit Smith, declared that "abolitionists differ and vary in their knowledge and estimate of the negro. Some think we are not to be encouraged to be anything more than a sort of half way set of equals."[84]

That New York abolitionists would attack Boston abolitionists was not particularly surprising, but by the late 1850s, Boston blacks were angry enough to question their own local allies. Most black Bostonians remained loyal to the person of William Lloyd Garrison but became increasingly willing to publicly disagree with his ideas. And they were even more critical of other Boston abolitionists. Even Nell, one of the black abolitionists most dedicated to interracial cooperation, complained in 1855 of white abolitionists who were "sometimes found deficient in a trying hour. . . . all who profess are not always fully imbued with the principle, thereby losing opportunities of squaring their practice with their preaching."[85] At the 1856 New England Anti-Slavery Convention, Charles Lenox Remond had taken the floor to object to Theodore Parker's constant evocation of racial stereotypes and declared that "he believed the Anglo-Saxon race was not the superior race often represented to be" since they seemed to lack "common humanity and decency."[86] In June 1858, Remond again took Parker to task, after Parker had given another ethnological speech. No one should use the platform of an antislavery society to talk about the "superiority of the Anglo-Saxon race," Remond argued, pointing out that, even if it was not Parker's intention, the "constant statements respecting those differences between the races of men . . . are put to a pro-slavery use by the mass of the community."[87] Charlotte Forten, too, wrote that she was disappointed by Parker's speeches, and though she declined to explain why, it is reasonable to assume that his attitude about race was part of the explanation.[88]

So when Rock confronted Parker at the 1858 Crispus Attucks rally, black frustration with the white Transcendentalist had been growing for some time. The proximate cause, though, of Rock's anger was a recent speech that Parker had given that was becoming a typical address for him, an exploration of how slavery was maintained by the unwillingness of blacks to rebel against their white masters. Parker was obsessed with the relationship between race and physical courage, repeatedly describing African Americans as cowardly and Anglo-Saxons as brave, even bloodthirsty. It is true that some black thinkers, such as Charlotte Forten, interpreted Parker's description of Anglo-Saxon aggressiveness as criticism of white character.[89] But given the increased Transcendentalist attraction to will and physical courage, Rock was correct to see Parker's descriptions of Anglo-Saxon bloodlust and vengeful violence as barely submerged fantasy and celebration. Abstract celebrations of white character were frustrating enough, but black thinkers such as Rock seethed when Parker scolded his African American allies on their supposedly natural timidity, as when the Transcendentalist had lectured that "the African is the most docile and pliant of all the races of men . . . the stroke of an axe would have settled the matter long ago. But the black man would not strike."[90]

Rock decided to use the Attucks celebration as an opportunity to refute Parker's arguments. The rebuttal to Parker was coordinated, clearly discussed with Nell, the organizer, beforehand. Long interested in the question of American racism—Rock had given a highly celebrated series of lectures on "The Races and Slavery" that argued that Africans were capable of "high mental and scientific cultivation"—he had a lawyer's ability to dissect the internal logic of an argument, to hang his opponents with their own words.[91] White Americans, he began by noting, had invested considerable time and energy into proving the cowardice of Africans, a fact that Attucks's memory should belie. Rock pointed to the central contradiction in the argument that slavery was sustained by black passivity: it had become an excuse for white inaction. "White men have no room to taunt us with tamely submitting," Rock told the audience, "if they were black men, they would work wonders; but as white men, they can do nothing."[92]

And so Rock turned the tables on Parker, attacking white character in the same language that Parker had used to denigrate the black one. Rock had a quality that was nearly unheard of among antebellum abolitionists: a sense of humor. Mocking Parker's obsession with his own whiteness, Rock claimed that "I know of no one who is more familiar with the true character of the Anglo-Saxon race than Mr. Parker." Of course, as Rock pointed out, there were thirty million white people in America arraigned against three million blacks. If Parker really thought that black people could easily win a war against those numbers, he implicitly must have assumed that it was white people who were cowardly, not black. Rock delighted in casting doubt on the supposed courage of white people. Even in the South, no Anglo-Saxons dared to advocate for the principles of their own Declaration of Independence—written by one of their own—for fear of the lynch mob. Cicero, Rock smilingly reminded the audience, had cautioned against buying slaves from the British Isles "on account of their stupidity." It was a popular line among black intellectuals, who were particularly eager to repeat this quotation as it served both to hoist whites—obsessed as they were with the genius of the classical Romans and Greeks—by their own petard and to suggest the degree to which racial stereotypes were a product of environment and history.[93] To Parker's Anglo-Saxon chauvinism, Rock responded with a full embrace of his own blackness, a love of his own heritage.

Standing up to respond, Parker replied that he had been speaking simply of the black past, not necessarily its future. He pleaded that he often had good things to say about Africans: they were kind, humble, religious, and forgiving. Sometimes, too, he seemed to be criticizing his beloved Anglo-Saxons for their love of violence. Of course, as Rock had pointed out, Parker's criticism of whites was always self-serving, his praise of Africans always double-edged. Both served to naturalize white power. Had he been born black, Parker continued, he would be as proud as Rock was of his blackness, but he simply could not agree that Africans had the same intrinsic courage and bloodlust as did the Anglo-Saxons.[94] The encounter left Parker chastened. To his credit, he perhaps was able to learn. Just days later, Parker wrote to historian George Bancroft to remind him to include stories of black courage during the American Revolution in his famous histories, citing the work of Nell, one small example of how the thought of black Bostonians helped to influence seminal works of American literature.[95]

Parker's ideas about white courage and black passivity had grown up in a climate where scientific racism was shaping many Americans' views of racial difference. The 1850s were important years for the development of international racial science, and the widely spread theories of Samuel Morton, Josiah Nott, and others formed the backdrop to Parker's ideas about race.[96] But ideas swirling around white Transcendentalist circles also played a role. Two white abolitionists in particular—Ralph Waldo Emerson and Parker himself—played important roles in legitimizing an abolitionist discourse that tied antislavery to a celebration of whiteness. So often did Emerson and, especially, Parker celebrate the supposed cultural and racial superiority of Anglo-Saxons that by 1858, *Frederick Douglass' Paper* could criticize an article for having "too much of that Teutonic Ethnological pride, peculiar to Boston writers and speakers of the transcendental school."[97] Their eventual embrace of racism was all the more notable because it seemed to contradict aspects of their thought: especially their earlier dismissal of the body as a category of analysis. Theodore Parker's transition to racial scientist illustrates the conflicted attitude toward race and toward the body that swirled among white Transcendentalist.

In his early writings, Parker had generally discounted racial differences. Central to Parker's early theology had been an idealism and epistemology that emphasized the mind and the divine spirit rather than the senses and the body. Theodore Parker at first saw the ability of all thinkers to access divine truth and open themselves up religiously as the central aspect of both his theology and his anthropology. In 1841, Parker grappled with and then rejected the racist doctrine of polygenesis, precisely because he believed that all humans possessed equal ability to access religious truth. In his major work on theology, Parker argued that all humans have both limited bodily needs and "sublime, permanent, and universal" spiritual wants and abilities. It was those spiritual facilities that underlay what Parker called the "religious element"—that from which is proven the "unity of the human race."[98] In 1841, still primarily interested in philosophy and religion, he had no trouble finding in the universality of the religious spirit proof that "human nature is the same in the men of all races, ages, and countries. Man remains always identical."[99]

One feature, in both Parker's theology and elsewhere in Transcendentalist writing, was a recurring image of the self as light, transparency, and elevation, "perpetual openness of the human mind to the new influx of light and power," as Emerson wrote.[100] William James thus described Transcendentalist philosophy as "a light shines through us on all things; *we* are nothing, but the light is all," and the description is apt for Parker as well.[101] They portrayed divine truth as light—flowing equally to all, past the limitations of the body, simply a vessel of divine inspiration. One's relationship to the truth was like that of an individual to the sun, orbiting from an equal distance and receiving its beneficial rays. It was only our own self-imposed limitations that prevented us from living in pure openness to the universe's flow. But while genius was simple "transparency," most men had what A. Bronson Alcott called "obstacles or biases within which reflect, refract or color the light," preventing "divine light to shine through."[102] Parker agreed, writing that religious sentiment, "like the heaven above, with its sun, and moon, and uncounted stars, is always over our head, though the cloud sometimes debars us of the needed light." He described Jesus as one whom "the light of God shone through."[103] The black Transcendentalist William C. Nell deployed this philosophical metaphor to understand the state of the abolitionist movement. Responding to growing black pessimism about the future of abolitionism, Nell wrote that "although the clouds do occasionally obscure the sun, no one in his sober senses doubts its existence." The "effulgent rays" of the abolitionist sun were always there, even if "there are continual obstacles in our pathway."[104]

This celebration of transparency and incorporeality allowed some thinkers to play down bodily difference—including racial difference—rejecting it as important to the human experience. It was Emerson, in his 1844 *Address on Emancipation in the West Indies*, who had best articulated the way this deracinated empty self could affect ideas about race. In a remarkable passage on "Toussaint, and the Haytian heroes," Emerson wrote, "here is man: and if you have man, black or white is an insignificance. The intellect,—that is miraculous! Who has it, has the talisman: his skin and bones, though they were of the color of night, are transparent, and the everlasting stars shine through, with attractive beams."[105] If the body was meaningless and preferable when transparent, one's color hardly mattered. Transcendentalist ideas contained a seeming paradox: the very return to nature and quest for truth that constituted the creation of a true self caused individuals to lose all the outer markings that characterized their physical self. One's position as brother, friend, or servant (or Anglo-Saxon or African) washed away in a sort of pantheistic communion of souls, not bodies, with nature. Hegel once quipped that in the "night of the Absolute," all cows looked black—in other words, certain absolutist philosophical commitments could overwhelm any appreciation for the differentiation that properly marked the human experience. Perhaps, the early Parker or Emerson might have responded, the advantage of this is that no cows look white either, that in the blinding sunshine of the Absolute, reduced to naught but a transparent eyeball, you cannot see whose ancestors went to Harvard and whose worked in cotton fields.

The result was that Transcendentalists rarely, if ever, based their opinions about race on the physical structure of black people or white people. In this they differed from most nineteenth-century racial scientists, such as Josiah Nott or Samuel Morton, and even from some black intellectuals, such as James McCune Smith, for whom the physical body was the domain upon which debates about black equality would be played out. Thoreau, for instance, who would remain haughtily uninterested in theories of racial inequality, was utterly dismissive of Morton's racial science. On Morton's attempt to measure the depth of one's humanity by the amount of mustard seeds you could cram into a skull, Thoreau simply wrote, "There is nothing out of which the spirit has more completely departed."[106]

Emerson and Parker's eventual acceptance of contemporary notions of racial science in the 1850s required them to violate the Romantic and idealist structures of their own philosophy. Still hints of their newfound appreciation for race could be found in their old ideas about the mind and the spirit. They increasingly described racially deficient peoples as those who were incapable of letting their mind and ideas dominate their bodies. They claimed that supposedly deficient people—African Americans, the Irish, and even Southern whites—were more shaped by fate and material reality than white New Englanders were.

Emerson had never fully embraced black equality.[107] In his earliest writings on the subject, as a nineteen-year-old scribbling in his journal, he had recorded negative impressions of "large lipped, lowbrowed black men in the streets" and questioned whether they had the same capacities for reason as white men.[108] Still, though, he held, even as a teenager in the conservative 1820s, that nothing could "ever reconcile the unperverted mind to the pardon of Slavery," which he called the "worst institution on earth."[109] Throughout his life, Emerson would question the ability and equality of black people (mostly, but not always, this was done in private) while never publicly wavering from a hatred of the institution of slavery. Long after Emerson died, Thomas Wentworth Higginson remembered that the Concord sage "always confessed to feeling a slight instinctive aversion to negroes."[110]

Still, for much of the 1830s and 1840s, when Emerson took public positions on race, he avoided overtly negative portrayals of African Americans or Indians. If anything, he was more likely to use them as examples of inspired heroism. The title of his 1843 lecture on the "Genius and National Character of the Anglo-Saxon Race" (part of a series on New England life and culture) may have hinted at his future chauvinism but was really a text on New England culture, with little language that was overtly ethnological and none that demeaned other groups of people.[111] In his 1844 lecture on West Indian emancipation, he celebrated the heroism and intellect of the Haitian revolutionaries and heralded the entry of Africans into the family of civilized mankind.[112] Frederick Douglass found nothing to complain about in his 1852 lecture on the "Anglo-Saxon" race, declaring "his lecture entirely free from bias or prejudice."[113] Even his private opinion seemed to thaw in the 1840s, as in his journals he famously emphasized the "life & promise" of African Americans and even praised America as a "smelting pot," an "asylum of all nations" that would combine Irish, German, Polish, African, and "Polynesian" immigrants into a "new race."[114] Despite his later turn toward racial science, he rarely expressed his newfound racial pessimism publicly—and, in contrast, often publicly mocked racism, as he did in his 1854 address on the Fugitive Slave Law—as if at some level he was always ashamed of his racist impulses.

But starting in the early 1850s, Emerson's views on race and African Americans in particular swung back toward his earlier elitism, and he became less optimistic and charitable. As early as 1851, Caroline Healey Dall was complaining that Emerson was becoming "a little too conservative—conservative of institution," and the *National Anti-Slavery Standard* was noticing how much less idealistic—"no more feeling in the skies, after the absolute"—the Emerson of 1855 was than the Emerson of 1845 had been.[115] Increasingly, he was arguing that Africans were a doomed race, destined to fall before white progress. There was both feigned humanitarian concern and a bit of fantasy in his prediction that "the black man will only be destined for museums like the Dodo."[116] There were a number of sources for Emerson's newfound racial conservativism. For one, the German idealism that he had drawn from had a long history of racism; both Kant and Hegel had publicly expressed reprehensible views of Africans. Another was his trip to England in 1848 that turned him into a bit of an anglophile. Receiving a warm embrace from the English aristocracy, Emerson increasingly viewed the Anglo-Saxon race as a meaningful category, one that superseded, in some ways, even his Americanism. His 1855 book *English Traits*, a largely celebratory travel narrative, often resorted to narratives about racial destiny to explain British history, as he described Anglo-Saxons as an energetic and domineering people.[117]

For Emerson, Africans became symbols of animality, of people whose material and sensual essences dominated their beings. Oddly enough, this was the exact same charge that he often threw at slaveholders—that they were people who let their animal greed dominate their moral sensibilities, their body master their mind. Emerson himself had often referred to slaveholders as "quadrupeds" and proslavery legislation as "quadruped law," emphasizing the animal-like nature of slaveholders. Emerson acknowledged, even reveled, in this correspondence, writing that "the negro & the negro-holder are really of one party. . . . the free negro is the type & exponent of that very animal law; standing as he does in nature below the series of thought."[118] Southerners, Emerson charged, suffered from the same lack of civilization, perhaps even the same inherent barbarism and animality that blacks and indigenous people did. "And as we cannot refuse to ride in the same planet with the New Zealander," Emerson told a New York audience, "so we cannot with the Southerner."[119] Both Southern whites and blacks, in Emerson's view, represented a triumph of the senses. Neither, according to the Transcendentalist, allowed Reason's rays of truth to reach them.

The metaphysics of Transcendentalism clearly contributed to racism. Emerson and Parker were projecting onto Africans those lower parts of the soul— the sensual, the sexual, the material, and the animal—in a clear attempt to distance themselves and their favored cultural group from these inherent parts of the human condition. As David Brion Davis has convincingly argued, this was a common way that nineteenth-century Northerners came to produce racism.[120] For instance, it is hard not to psychoanalyze Parker's understanding of black sexuality as fantasy, as a projection onto the African of parts of the human experience that his Victorian and Transcendentalist sensibilities tried to deny: "The African has the largest organs of generation in the world, the most erotic heat: he is the most poly-amorous of men," Parker wrote to a friend.[121] In this sense, it is not coincidental that Thoreau—by far the Transcendentalist most comfortable with wildness and the animal world—had the least psychological need to imagine and then disparage an image of a primal black man.

If Emerson was privately (and occasionally publicly) indulging in racist speculation, it was Theodore Parker who most prominently combined nineteenth-century racial science with radical abolitionism and New England Transcendentalism. The Anglo-Saxon people, he declared, were the most "progressive" in the world, with an "ethnological instinct for Freedom."[122] New Englanders were even more dedicated to liberty because they were more capable of abstract thought: there was "something in the blood of those Puritans who planted themselves on these shores, which gave their descendants a Power of Ideas and a Power of Action."[123] Parker was particularly eager to describe the genius of Anglo-Saxons (or Puritans, depending on the situation) as relating to their superior ability to have a "Power of Ideas" because of the importance of "ideas" to his thought. This crucially provided Parker with the ability to claim racial superiority that was based not on bodily difference but on mental and spiritual superiority. In addition, "ideas" played crucial roles in Parker's entire political philosophy, as "ideas" animated societies, provided the basis for social reform, and distinguished men from animals or tools.

The other side of Parker's New England chauvinism was his tendency to see in white Southern "blood" some sort of racial deficiency. Parker increasingly compared Southern planters to various supposedly racially inferior people, including the Spanish and Egyptians.[124] Part of this was due to their racial intermingling—demonstrating the depth of his commitment to racial science—but much of it was the product of the particular history of the South and its love of slavery. Parker described how the North had developed superior social institutions than the South, noting, "for though both the stems grow out from the same ethnologic root, one of them has caught such a mildew from the ground it hangs over, and the other trees it mixes its boughs among," that they were no longer the same people.[125] Differences with the white South were thus both climatic ("from the ground it hangs over") and based on the race mixing common in the South ("the other trees it mixes its boughs among"). In his sense that the South was becoming a different people, Parker was not alone, as it was related to the popular refrains about New England superiority. Emerson would interpret the secession crisis as a "a war of manners. The Southern climate and slavery generate a marked style of manners . . . we find the planters picturesque, but frivolous and brutal."[126]

Parker was also increasingly coming to believe in the inherent inferiority of other races, a belief that he was even more open and honest about in private than in public. In a letter to an organization called the Provident Association, which had solicited his opinion on charities in Boston, Parker asked that his name never be associated with what he wrote before launching into a crude racist diatribe. In charity, he declared, "you have to deal with exceeding bad material. The ethnology of pauperism is worth more than a hasty thought." He went on: Anglo-Saxon, "Scotch," and German pauperism was not an issue. Jewish poverty was not insignificant but would be taken care of by Jews themselves (since their distinctive trait was "thrift"). Black pauperism was slightly more complicated, since although "the negro is the least acquisitive of all men; his nature is tropical," charity associations would have no problem because "he is so pliant that we can do with him as we will." The biggest problem, he concluded, was the Irish. "The Irishman has three bad things," Parker wrote, "bad habits, bad religion, and, worst of all, a bad nature."[127]

His placement of the Irish on the bottom of the racial hierarchy was typical for Parker. "Lying, begging, stealing, are *instantial* of the genus 'Paddy from Corrrck,'" he sneered.[128] To Francis Jackson, Parker complained that the Irish were "the worst people in Europe to make colonists of; it is a bad nature which belongs to them—oppressive to the weak and servile to the strong."[129] Years later, Thomas Wentworth Higginson would recall Parker's frank "dislike of the Irish."[130] Unlike many race theorists, Parker was far more hostile to the Catholic

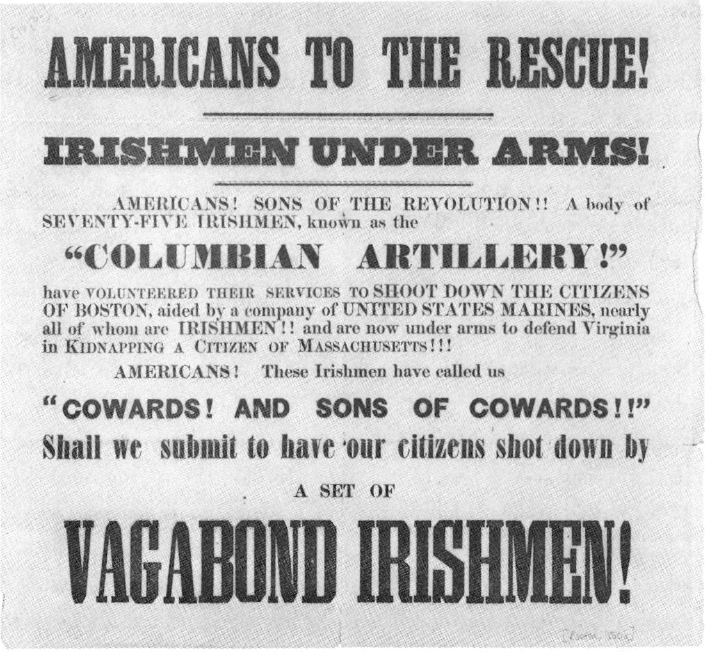
AMERICANS TO THE RESCUE!

IRISHMEN UNDER ARMS!

AMERICANS! SONS OF THE REVOLUTION!! A body of SEVENTY-FIVE IRISHMEN, known as the

"COLUMBIAN ARTILLERY!"

have VOLUNTEERED THEIR SERVICES TO SHOOT DOWN THE CITIZENS OF BOSTON, aided by a company of UNITED STATES MARINES, nearly all of whom are IRISHMEN!! and are now under arms to defend Virginia in KIDNAPPING A CITIZEN OF MASSACHUSETTS!!!

AMERICANS! These Irishmen have called us

"COWARDS! AND SONS OF COWARDS!!"

Shall we submit to have our citizens shot down by

A SET OF

VAGABOND IRISHMEN!

Figure 9. In the aftermath of the Anthony Burns rendition, abolitionists frequently resorted to crude anti-Irish rhetoric such as this handbill. Collection of the Massachusetts Historical Society.

Irish than he was to Africans or Native Americans, whom he regarded with some paternalism. The fact that Parker, like most other abolitionists, welcomed the "Teutonic" Germans while distrusting the "Celtic" Irish demonstrates that ethnicity rather than foreignness itself was the important factor.

Parker was speaking to the zeitgeist with his anti-Irish rhetoric. Following massive influxes of immigrants after the famine, a backlash had developed in New England against the Irish. Anti-Catholic zealots burned churches and mobbed Catholics, while even William Lloyd Garrison declared the Irish to be "the tools of priests and politicians."[131] In Boston, abolitionist anti-Catholicism was especially encouraged by the participation of Irish militias in the rendition of Anthony Burns. One representative broadside that appeared during that crisis asked, "Shall we submit to have our citizens shot down by a set of vagabond Irishmen," while calling for "Americans" to take up arms in resistance.[132] In the aftermath of the Burns crisis, Henry C. Wright had told the New England Anti-Slavery Convention that "every Catholic Irishman in the country" would die to defend slavery. When an Irish audience member complained, he was declared "pro-slavery" because he voted for Franklin Pierce.[133] That this anonymous Irish abolitionist was being forced to choose between a tepidly antislavery (but anti-immigrant) Whig Party and a pro-immigrant (but racist) Democratic Party was never acknowledged. Other Irish abolitionists, such as Henry Kemp and Patrick Toohey, were placed on the defensive, continually forced to defend their religion and nation in abolitionist meetings.[134]

But the most remarkable manifestation of this anti-Irish backlash was the shocking victories of the Know-Nothing Party in the 1854 state elections. Called "Sam" by local newspapers, the American Party in Massachusetts won an electoral sweep unlike any before it, gaining the entire state Senate, the governorship, and all but three seats in the state House.[135] The party's rise was due partly to the confusing and fluid nature of Northern politics, as the Whig Party was imploding in the wake of the Kansas-Nebraska Act. The law had made the Democratic Party toxic for antislavery voters, but the Republican Party had not yet put together a winning coalition. In this electoral chaos, the Know-Nothings spoke to a sense, especially strong in industrializing Massachusetts, that "Yankeedom" was under attack from both Irish immigrants and the Southern slave power. Rallying against what they called the "Cotton and Catholic Coalition" thus suggested a politics that would cleanse the Commonwealth of all outside influences.[136] In Massachusetts, the party, in the words of a Boston newspaper, was "decidedly anti-slavery," and a number of Massachusetts antislavery politicians, such as Anson Burlingame and Robert Hall, were elected as Know-Nothings.[137] In 1855, Know-Nothing votes helped elect Henry Wilson to the Senate, where he would eventually join Sumner as a Radical Republican.

In Massachusetts, the "American Party" reflected all the contradictions of New England reformism. Religiously bigoted, they passed some landmark legislation protecting black civil rights; virulent in their dislike of the Irish poor, they enacted pro-labor laws that restricted child labor.[138] Along with a literacy test intended to curtail the Irish vote, the Know-Nothing legislature passed a number of antislavery policies, including the integration of the Boston public school system, the strengthening of personal liberties laws, and the reincorporation of the New England Emigrant Aid Company.[139] The new governor, Know-Nothing Henry Gardner, even disbanded the Irish military companies that had contributed to Anthony Burns's rendition. Shutting down "all military companies composed of persons of foreign birth" was a potent symbol given the concurrent fight over black militias.[140] Although Theodore Parker declined to formally endorse the party, his ideas were so close to the vision of the Know-Nothings that in 1855, they came votes away from naming him as the chaplain of their legislature.[141]

There were noble exceptions to the anti-Irish trend among Massachusetts abolitionists. Even those who eagerly used the language of New England pride to appeal to the native-born were generally uncomfortable enshrining legal discrimination against the foreign born into law. Others reached out to the Irish. Robert Morris gained a reputation as the "Irish lawyer," a seemingly strange moniker for the first black lawyer in the state, because of his frequent advocacy of Irish clients. He even converted to Catholicism. Wendell Phillips never gave up on his admirable if quixotic hope to turn the Irish into antislavery voters, and privately, Thomas Wentworth Higginson tried to reason Theodore Parker out of his anti-Irish bigotry.[142] Lydia Maria Child maintained some of the old Romantic humanism, declaring that "human nature is essentially the same in all nations and ages; being modified only by laws that control and regulate it."[143] Charles Sumner, in language that both evoked New Englandism and sought to strip it of its exclusionary potential, asked the "descendants of the Pilgrims of another generation," not to reject the "Pilgrims of the present."[144] Sumner's friends in the group of antislavery politicians around Frank Bird largely avoided the Know-Nothing Party because they feared it would distract from the overall cause of antislavery. They rightly predicted that at the national level, the American Party would be forced to compromise with slaveholders in order to win elections in the South. The "Bird Club" would be rewarded for their fealty to pure antislavery principles when, after the collapse of the Know-Nothings, they became the de facto leaders of the Massachusetts Republican Party.

New England Nationalism

Twenty years earlier, abolitionists and Transcendentalists had been persecuted outsiders, but by the 1850s, they were threatening to become part of the establishment. It was a dual movement: many elite Northerners were moving to the left, after the traumas of the Kansas-Nebraska Act and Sumner's caning, and simultaneously, abolitionists, sensing the opportunity, were articulating their position in more mainstream language of New England traditionalism. As early as 1850, Alcott had noticed the strange popularity of ideas that had once been unspeakably radical. Theodore Parker and Emerson, he pointed out, had been "not only unpopular but obnoxious exceedingly," but they were now the most popular lyceum lecturers in the state. More surprisingly still, "even Phillips and Garrison and Pillsbury are now listened to with some respect."[145]

Shifting economic patterns were partly responsible. The late 1840s and early 1850s saw a massive boom in the construction of railroads, especially in the North and Northwest. These new lines tended to flow east to west, eliminating the Appalachian Mountains as effective barriers to commerce and communication. One effect of this was to partly shift the interests of Northern capital away from Southern cotton toward Western grain, iron, and lumber, causing a concurrent change in political commitments. Maria Weston Chapman made this point, in an 1857 letter to Samuel Sewall, explaining why the "terror of working with infidels has faded out of the minds" of moderates, writing that "the mercantile pillars of N. England churches are not now speculating in Alabama lands, as in 1835, but in Northwestern lands."[146] By 1858, Massachusetts senator Henry Wilson, in a reply to James Hammond's famous "Cotton is King" speech, could almost dare the Southern states to withdraw their cotton, boasting that textile manufacturing now only comprised 1/13 of Massachusetts's "productive industry."[147] Thus, the proslavery bias among the Northern bourgeoisie significantly lessened. Simultaneously, by knitting together the Old Northwest with the Northeast, the new railroads, canals, and telegraphs dramatically expanded the market for abolitionist and Transcendentalist activity. Celebrities such as Emerson and Wendell Phillips saw their audiences (and paychecks) rise notably as they spoke before lyceums and conventions in Chicago, Detroit, Cleveland, and elsewhere. Black intellectuals also were able to expand their reach out of the Eastern Seaboard, as William C. Nell did when he went on a tour of antislavery meetings in Michigan in 1858.[148] Especially eager to hear Transcendentalists and abolitionists were the millions of New England emigrants, farmers, small merchants, and artisans who had rushed into Ohio, Illinois, and even farther west.

One consequence of this revolution in communication and transportation was that Transcendentalist ideas spread far outside of their original home in New England. Jasper Douthit, for instance, was one of many people in the Old Northwest whose story illustrated the spread of New England ideas, as well as the mutual affinity of abolitionist politics and Transcendentalist theology. Douthit had grown up poor in the prairies of Shelby County in southern Illinois. He remembered intense "deep religious longings" that went unsatisfied in the traditional churches. Eventually, he became an itinerant phrenologist lecturer, and it was through a phrenology newspaper that he met his future wife, who was from Massachusetts and encouraged him to read Unitarian literature. Finally, interest in "the anti-slavery agitation caused me to read James Freeman Clarke's and Theodore Parker's sermons," he later remembered. He would walk 16 miles with the hopes of catching Parker in person. From there, he went on to Emerson—who would become a lifelong source of inspiration and a friend who even would lecture at his church in the 1860s. Spending most of his life in his home county, he became a rare voice of theological and political radicalism in an area dominated by pro-Southern Democrats. Eventually ordained as a Unitarian minister, he spent the Civil War barely surviving the threats of the Confederate-sympathizing "Knights of the Golden Circle" while reading Emerson and quoting Parker to his congregation.[149]

Middlebrow literary and political magazines, like those that drew Douthit to Emerson, exploded in popularity during this period and played a crucial role disseminating antislavery and Transcendentalist ideas. If the *Dial*, in all its numinous glory, was the representative journal of Transcendentalists during their early, rebellious phase, and the *Massachusetts Quarterly Review* the magazine that demonstrated their increasing political confidence and maturity in the late 1840s, it was the *Atlantic Monthly*, founded in 1857, that solidified their rapprochement with the literary and political establishment. The journal developed out of conversations held at a dinner party at the elite Parker House on May 5, between Moses Phillips, a publisher, and an uneasy coalition of abolitionist and mainstream literary figures, including Emerson and James Russell Lowell (who would become editor), and friends of the establishment such as Oliver Wendell Holmes Sr., Henry Longfellow, and Charles Eliot Norton, the son of Andrews Norton, the great anti-Transcendentalist polemicist. These were mostly members of Emerson's new Saturday Club, an elite social club founded in 1855.[150]

A reflection of the self-consciously literary class of New Englanders, the *Atlantic* was solidly antislavery—its second issue featured an article by the Garrisonian Edmund Quincy—but not utopian. Gone were the days when Transcendentalists' centrifugal energy urged them to gleefully question all aspects of state and society. Evidence of their new vision, the very first issue ran a lengthy article apologizing for British rule in India and hoping that the Sepoy Mutiny— the massive rebellion that British troops would soon bloodily suppress—would be quickly resolved in favor of the British.[151] It may have lacked the quirky independence of the *Dial* or the moral passion of the *Liberator*, but Southerners correctly perceived it as a form of antislavery cultural politics: the *Southern Literary Messenger* declared that the function of the *Atlantic Monthly* was "to wage war upon Southern society."[152]

Quincy's 1857 submission to the *Atlantic Monthly*, "Where Will It End?" demonstrated the regional vision that animated white abolitionists in the years before the Civil War. The oppression of black slaves, as well as their suffering and exploitation under a system of personal commodification, was almost absent from Quincy's narrative. Instead, his argument for a confrontation with slavery was based on two ideas: first, slaveholders' dismissal of the dignity of labor had created an oligarchy that threatened American democracy. Second, slavery threatened the culture and regional identity of New England. The patrician abolitionist seethed that "the intelligent, educated, and civilized portion of a race [Northerners] should consent to the sway of their ignorant, illiterate, and barbarian companions in the commonwealth, and this by reason of that uncouth barbarism, is an astonishment." Like Parker before him, Quincy seemed to be almost racializing Southerners, writing of their "reckless habits, and debasing customs, and barbarous manners."[153] Antislavery, in other words, was necessary to protect New England cultural superiority.

The New England pride that Quincy was appealing to was nothing new. But a militant and aggressive New Englandism, what Lewis Simpson once called "New England Nationalism," was becoming a particularly powerful draw in the 1850s.[154] The sense of regional pride had been best expressed in the 1853 festivities surrounding the Plymouth Monument Fund Drive. Originally, the plan was to create a nearly 150-foot statue of the "figure of faith," a sort of granite Statute of Liberty that would stand near the landing spot of the Pilgrims. Appropriately, this monument to Northern pride had to be scaled down, as funds failed to materialize during the "unstable economic climate" of the Civil War era.[155] The 1853 festival, though, was a monumental celebration that helped to cement the Pilgrims' special place in American mythology.[156] Meanwhile, Sarah Josepha Hale was lobbying, in the influential pages of *Godey's Lady's Book*, to turn the local story of the Pilgrims into the national holiday we know as Thanksgiving. When successful in 1863, Hale's campaign turned the origin story of Plymouth Rock (and *not* Jamestown), filtered through the domesticity of the Northern middle class, into a potent symbol of American identity.[157] As the celebration of the Pilgrims suggested, many conflated Massachusetts with New England as a whole, a point made clear by Charlotte Forten, who wrote that "my thoughts revert to New England—to Massachusetts, which I believe I am in the habit of considering as *all* New England."[158] Books such as Harriet Beecher Stowe's *Mayflower* were advertised for "the sons of New England . . . scattered to the remotest quarters of the Union," who missed the town greens, schoolhouses, and "Puritan Sabbaths" of their youth.[159] And of course, the so-called

Fireside Poets—John Greenleaf Whittier, James Russell Lowell, and others—all of whom were born in New England, took the stonewalls, small farms, and middle-class moralism of the region as the themes of their widely popular poems.

Radical abolitionists had a complicated relationship to this New England rhetoric. Slaveholders and their Northern allies had long accused abolitionism of being the product of New England cultural imperialism—one more lily-gilded Sunday school conspiracy to dictate the religion, drink, and morality of the Southern and Western people. To some Democrats such as Stephen Douglas—the not-so-proud son of Vermont—abolitionism seemed to symbolize all the hypocritical moral sanctimony that they had left New England to avoid.[160] One Pennsylvania newspaper, describing why New Englanders always voted for black suffrage, explained that common schools in New England taught from "Yankee text-school . . . with their driveling of abolitionism, transcendentalism, spiritualism, puritanism, and dawdling Christianity."[161]

And of course, on the other side, abolitionists had long railed against how slavery was maintained by the complicity of New Englanders. But as the abolitionists began tasting political popularity, they realized the potential in appealing to the pride and self-image of Yankees. To homesick emigrants in New York City or the Midwest and in front of "New England" and "Pilgrim" societies throughout the nation, they began selling antislavery as part of New England cultural identity. Abolitionism, they claimed, was part of the "idea" of New England, a manifestation of the cultural values that marked the region. Even if, in reality, most New Englanders still resisted the antislavery cause and happily supported the Union and cotton trade, there was, abolitionists claimed, a true "idea" of New England that persisted. Emerson, in his journal, commented that the "true Boston" was found in its lyceums, railroads, and "love of German literature," not the base "talks of Union, & fevers into proslavery" that constituted the transient surface-play of the city.[162] Theodore Parker identified the "idea" of New England with the spirit of liberty and equality that, supposedly, the Puritans had brought to Massachusetts.[163] Harriet Beecher Stowe linked "heroic" abolitionism to the inheritance of Puritan New Englandism, describing how "the heroic element was strong in me, having come down by ordinary generation from a long line of Puritan ancestry."[164]

Yankees, according to the abolitionist narrative, lived by abstract ideas and Reason, while Southerners simply followed their animal passions. As early as 1849, in a lecture on the "New England Intellect," Thomas Wentworth Higginson had attempted a "vindication of the New England development of the ideal side."[165] For Parker, this tendency toward idealism meant New Englanders were more open to social reform and more desirous of following abstract ideas (which Parker held to be the roots of the reform impulse). This explained why New Englanders were marked by their moral fanaticism: the same dedication to abstract ideas that led Puritans to follow Cromwell had led their descendants into the abolitionist crusade. "Our questioning brains," Wendell Phillips wrote, "impatient that their ideal perfection is not reached," forced New Englanders to agitate for political reform.[166] "There is an element even in the Yankee blood which obeys ideas," Phillips declared on a different occasion, "an impulsive, enthusiastic aspiration, something left to us from the old Puritan stock."[167] Once, in the Senate, Charles Sumner held it as an established fact of constitutional and moral reality that "Massachusetts cannot do an act of injustice." He did not understand why the entire Senate floor erupted in laughter.[168]

As Phillips's paean to New England's "impulsive, enthusiastic aspiration" highlights, abolitionists saw no contradiction in their belief in New England as a civilization of "ideas" and the new abolitionist politics of violence, courage, and will that they mobilized. They celebrated the North's libraries, lyceums, and self-control one minute and then fretted about over-civilization the next. Thoreau, in particular, was concerned that the comforts of civilization, the loss of "the primitive vigor of nature," had led to an enervation as physical as it was spiritual.[169] And Emerson, even as he considered Northerners more rational and educated than Southerners, had long cautioned against the dangers of a life lived only in the higher realms of reflective consciousness. This was not necessarily contradictory, as their hope for a North led by "ideas" sought to sublate the abolitionist politics of morality into a "fanatic" and violent devotion to liberty. "Ideas" would fire abolitionists with an enthusiasm that might reacquaint them with some of the self-abandonment and obedience to instinctual energies that the "savage" Southerner experienced regularly but inspired by abolitionist moralism rather than unthinking animality. Thoreau, sitting at Walden Pond, summed up the Transcendentalist hope: "is it impossible," he asked, "to combine the hardiness of these savages with the intellectualness of the civilized man?"[170] Combining a conscious act of moral control with the Dionysian release of violent impulses, it would be the enthusiasm of a principle rather than the passion of sensualism.

By the mid-1850s, this antislavery regionalism, this sense of New England's unique dedication to abstract liberty, had become central to Massachusetts abolitionist rhetoric. America, as one antislavery minister put it, was composed of two "radically distinct and even antagonistic stages of civilization."[171] This New England regionalism played an important role, bringing many skeptical white Yankees into the abolitionist fold. Lawrence Buell, for instance, has written that Ralph Waldo Emerson's "tribal ego," his firm sense of identification with New England "civilization" as opposed to Southern "barbarism," contributed to the famed writer's increasing dedication to antislavery.[172] For Emerson, New England "civilization" was marked by its middle-class culture: its schoolhouses, lyceums, technological improvements, and (supposedly) shared prosperity. But these were simply the outward manifestation of a broader moral superiority, the ability and willingness of New England culture to abide by abstract moral ideas. Anna Dickinson, the feminist orator, summed up the cultural politics of the slavery fight: "we had culture to put against their ignorance; schools against rum-shops; churches against race-courses; the brain of New England against the degradation of South Carolina."[173]

Abolitionists may have hoped that the "idea" of New England was about abstract dedication to equal rights and antislavery, but it was unclear, at a practical level, where black Northerners were supposed to fit into this vision of an idealized New England. If New England was marked by its "Puritan" legacy, what happed to the descendants of the slaves that the Puritans imported? Most New Englanders, even if they grudgingly conceded citizenship to free blacks, did not consider them within the affective embrace of New Englandism. And, as we have seen, even many radical white abolitionists contributed to narratives of racial exclusion. The central contradiction of New Englandism was, perhaps, best summed up in a small notice that would appear in the *National Anti-Slavery Standard* in 1864. The New York "New England Society"—an organization that mobilized and created both ethnic and class privileges—was intent on toasting black soldiers and making them "a subject of thought and discourse." The only problem? As the *Standard* admitted, the elite society made a point to reassure its anxious members that "the Negro did not actually dine with the New England Society."[174] Embraced as symbols of New England's moral enlightenment, actual living black people themselves were not always welcome in Yankee spaces.

For black intellectuals—especially William C. Nell and Charlotte Forten—this New Englandism was rent with contradictions and ambivalences. Although very aware of the limits of New England as a political and cultural space, both ended up contributing to the association of New England with revolutionary and abolitionist glory. Nell's *Colored Patriots of the American Revolution* played a significant role in a black reclamation of the American Revolution. Although it was written before the *Dred Scott* decision, it gave a different response from the one Taney would give to the question of whether African Americans had been citizens at the founding of the republic. By celebrating Crispus Attucks and other black military heroes of the Revolutionary

War—and by explicitly referring to anti-abolitionists as "Tories"—Nell was staking a claim that black New Englanders and their abolitionist allies were the true inheritors of the American Revolution. He continued this theme in his yearly celebrations of Crispus Attucks that he used as an opportunity to raise money, showcase the talent of young black writers and performers, and continue to make the case for black citizenship.[175]

Charlotte Forten, likewise, had long expressed ambivalence about New England's dedication to freedom. In an 1856 poem, she asked the graduating class of her normal school if "perfect freedom [is] here, in our own North?" "Too few," she answered, "who rightly know its worth."[176] But later in one of her first national publications, she had contributed a more positive 1858 essay on New England regionalism to the *National Anti-Slavery Standard*. Entitled "Glimpses of New England," the essay rambled through small towns in Massachusetts being left behind by industrialization, offering a charming view of historic buildings, crumbling colonial cemeteries, and eccentric locals. She was, in part, contributing to the construction of the fireside vision of New Englandism, as Winthrop's stern Calvinist city on a hill was transforming into Stowe's quaint white-clad home on a town green. However, Forten, unlike many other white writers, was acutely aware of how white racism survived in this new New England. The best part of New England, she claimed, was its "faithful little band of Abolitionists," and she told an amusing story of the "aristocrats" and "proslavery" citizens of Salem who were tricked into attending an antislavery lecture by Wendell Phillips. Moreover, she made a point of declaring that it was the abolitionists' courage "more than even those of the Pilgrim Fathers [that] hallow New England's rocky soil."[177]

Radicalism Triumphant

Even the Republican Party in Massachusetts had, in part, a Transcendentalist lineage. Among its predecessors was the short-lived "People's Party," founded in Concord in June 1854 at a meeting that Emerson (listed as an "Independent Democrat" and therefore probably a supporter of the recent *Appeal of the Independent Democrats*) had helped organize.[178] He served on the Committee of Correspondence, helping to write a series of resolutions dripping with imagery from the Revolution and New England Pride.[179] A small meeting, on July 7, followed in Boston that brought together former Whig, Democratic, and Free Soil politicians.[180] But the Concord-led push was quickly superseded by a call for a convention in Worcester spearheaded by more professional politicos such as Henry Wilson.[181] Although Emerson was no longer playing a leading role, the July 20 meeting in Worcester, which officially formed the Massachusetts Republican Party, was addressed by Theodore Parker.[182] The Republicans actively courted black voters, and Lewis Hayden became a prominent supporter, serving as a Boston delegate to the state convention in September and later becoming an important black politician.[183]

As in the rest of the nation, the Republican Party in Massachusetts was split between radical elements—represented by Sumner, John A. Andrew, and other Free Soil or Liberty Party members—and more moderate politicians who had been mainstream Whigs or Know-Nothings. Despite beginning in 1854, the Republican Party did not emerge as the sole and obvious vehicle for Massachusetts voters opposed to the Kansas-Nebraska Act until the 1855 gubernatorial election, which pitted Republican Julius Rockwell against Know-Nothing Henry Gardner. Gardner won, but the election would mark the beginning of the end for the nativist party. Many elected officials, including eventually Gardner himself, soon switched to the Republican Party, especially after the national Know-Nothing Party nominated Millard Fillmore, the uninspiring former president, at their 1856 presidential convention. The fighting in Kansas helped propel the presidential campaign of John Fremont, the Republican candidate for president, who carried Massachusetts and the rest of the upper North. American politics was now a contest between an entirely Northern party and an overwhelmingly Southern one, and the nation was one step closer to civil war.

The Radical wing of the Republican Party in Massachusetts was dominated by the Bird Club, an informal group surrounding the politico Frank Bird. Almost to a man, they were connected to Transcendentalist and abolitionist activity, albeit not generally of the Garrisonian stripe. There were Franklin Sanborn, friend of Emerson and Thoreau; Elizur Wright, former editor of the *Chronotype*, who had been a member of the Town and Country Club; Samuel Gridley Howe and John A. Andrew, members of the Boston Vigilance Committee; and, of course, Charles Sumner. Labor leaders were well represented as well. On top of Wright, who had long advocated labor reform in his papers the *Chronotype* and the *Commonwealth*, there were James Stone and William Robinson, leaders of the fight for the ten-hour day in Massachusetts.[184] The Bird Club, whose ideology had been crafted by two decades of Transcendentalist, abolitionist, and labor radicalism, would have an outsized effect on the Radical Republicans in the coming years.

Caring about electoral politics did not mean abandoning more radical approaches to antislavery politics. Three members of the Bird Club—Sanborn, Howe, and George Stearns—were plotting with John Brown at the same time that they were putting together the Massachusetts Republican coalition. The political impulse toward insurgent violent heroism was compatible, in some cases, with more traditional wheeling and dealing of electoral politics. As is well known, John Brown had close ties to New England Transcendentalists. When he had lived in Springfield, Brown had sought out Theodore Parker's preaching. Even though the stern Calvinist disagreed with the Transcendentalist's theology, he greatly respected his antislavery commitments. Once Brown began his antislavery crusade, he found Transcendentalists to be among his most loyal supporters. On visits to Concord, in March of that year, Brown dined at both Thoreau and Emerson's homes, who both donated to his cause.[185] A. Bronson Alcott, who attended Brown's speech in Concord, was struck by Brown's innate Transcendentalism: "he seemed superior to any legal traditions, able to do his own thinking, was an idealist, at least in matters of state, if not on all points of his religious faith."[186] Brown would return to Massachusetts two years later, only months before his raid, to raise money and to confer with the "Secret Six," his band of backers. They would come to include Higginson, Parker, and Franklin Sanborn.

In Brown's story, the heroism of the Secret Six—his abolitionist backers— has been told so many times that it has calcified into legend. But the celebration of the Secret Six obscures the roles of black supporters, who were probably more important than the famed white supporters. Frederick Douglass was one of the few Eastern abolitionists whom Brown truly respected and was one of the only people to be informed about the coming Harpers Ferry raid. Although Douglass declined to join or endorse the raid, because he rightly recognized that it would be suicidal, he did assist Brown with other aspects, including raising troops. J. Sella Martin, who lived in Buffalo before taking over a Boston ministry, attended "a secret meeting, called to secure the advice and cooperation of the colored people" of the North.[187] A lesser-known black contributor to Brown was the stalwart Lewis Hayden. Brown regularly stayed at Hayden's house while visiting Boston, and Hayden knew about Brown's plans. One day in October 1859, just before Brown's fateful raid, Hayden ran into Francis Merriam, the grandson of Vigilance Committee member E. S. Merriam, on the streets of Boston. "I want $500 and must have it," Hayden told the startled Merriam, and then divulged what he knew of Brown's campaign. Merriam gave him $600 in gold and left Boston to join Brown's force.[188] Merriam's eccentricity and poor

eyesight kept him from Harpers Ferry (and likely the gallows), but his story illustrates how connections forged in the biracial Boston Vigilance Committee
continued to play important roles in the revolutionary action that would lead to
the Civil War. Likely, the racist culture that denied the possibility of black
courage and resistance was, ironically, exactly the factor that obscured Hayden's
role, saving the black activist from persecution after Brown's raid failed.

As historians are coming to realize, it was Transcendentalists, especially
Thoreau and Emerson, who took the lead defending Brown in the immediate
aftermath of his capture. Most Northerners, even many abolitionists, sought to
distance themselves from Brown's actions, and for a few days, the captured insurgent seemingly had no friends. Thoreau and Emerson had been with A.
Bronson Alcott when they first heard news of Brown's raid, on October 19,
1859.[189] On October 30, even though the local Republican Party asked him not
to, Thoreau gave his speech "A Plea for Captain John Brown," one of the first
major defenses of Brown's actions. Thoreau's account of Brown drew on many
of the themes of heroic New Englandism. Brown was "like the best of those
who stood at Concord Bridge," Thoreau told the audience, implicitly contrasting the courage of the town's grandfathers with the meekness of the town's current residents. He was a "man of ideas and principles" who was misunderstood
by crass contemporaries, who could only ask "what will he gain by it?" failing to
understand that "heroes" do not judge actions by such self-interested instrumental criteria. Brown "did not value his bodily life in comparison with ideal
things," Thoreau told the Concord audience.[190]

Thoreau's lecture seems to have pulled Emerson out of his lethargy. In
November, Emerson gave two different speeches, each of which were widely
reprinted, that defended John Brown. Most important, in his speech on
November 8 (appropriately on "Courage"), he described Brown as "the new
saint awaiting his martyrdom, and who, if he shall suffer, will make the gallows
glorious like the cross." Emerson's phrase would capture the imagination both
of enemies, such as the *New York Herald*, who responded to Emerson that
Brown's "gallows will be the emblem of nigger redemption," and of Northern
abolitionists, who repeated Emerson's line.[191] Millions of Northerners who had
admired Brown's courage but were reluctant to support a man pilloried by every
major politician and newspaper now felt justified in airing their support, as they
had two of the most important American intellectuals on their side.

Not only did Thoreau play a crucial role in defending Brown and creating
his image as a Transcendentalist hero, but he even helped to protect some of
Brown's men, including the eccentric Francis Merriam, who Thoreau helped

shuttle to Canadian safety as authorities hunted the abolitionist.[192] Meanwhile, Emerson served, along with Higginson, Howe, and Samuel Sewall, on a committee raising money for Brown's legal defense.[193] On November 18, at a major fundraising rally in Boston, Emerson described Brown in language that evoked almost all of the major themes of heroic abolitionism: Brown was a "pure idealist" with a "perfect puritan faith." Emerson even described Brown as "transparent," a nod to the Transcendentalist idea of the transparent self.[194] Even after Brown's execution, Emerson continued working to raise money for the martyr's family, including speaking at a relief meeting in Salem, on January 6, 1860, where he described Brown as a "romantic character . . . living to ideal ends."[195] Emerson's close connection to the Brown family continued after the abolitionist's execution; in 1860, two of John Brown's daughters boarded with the Emersons while attending Franklin Sanborn's school.[196]

Black abolitionists, even those who rejected his methods, felt an immediate loyalty to Brown, a white man who seemed to truly understand the depths of their oppression. The black minister J. Sella Martin, for instance, eulogized Brown in language that clearly brought together the different strands of Transcendentalist ideas about heroism. Brown, Martin told a British audience, did not live according to "our idols of data, proof, conclusion," but rather was "acquainted with higher truths and breathing the atmosphere of a nobler conviction." He was able to reach these levels of heroism because he had a "spirit [that] caught the light and beauty of self-sacrifice while standing on the lofty summit of a mountainous faith."[197] Brown's heroism, then, came from his ability to transcend the petty calculations of his contingent existence, to open himself up to the flow of righteousness that pervaded the universe.

Transcendentalist support for Brown seems to confirm the connection between their politics of moral absolutism and the supposed irresponsibility of Brown's political violence. Behind the moral enthusiasm of every Emersonian idealist, some see a John Brown or an Ahab in waiting, a fanatic whose admirable commitment to moral principles threatens to become a crazed monomaniac crusade, their Robespierrian addiction to moral purity preventing them from engaging in healthy democratic compromise, blinding them to the innocents they have trampled in their quest for justice.[198] This stereotype, though, does a disservice to the motivation of Parker, Higginson, and the other Brown backers. It was to their credit, not their shame, that they understood that the normal rules of liberal discourse were inappropriate for such a crime as slavery, that they had to force a compromise-addicted society to take sides in a conflict between slavery and freedom. Writing to the mother of one of Brown's soldiers, who had died at Harpers Ferry, Parker quite presciently predicted that the raid "will strike terror into the Hearts of the Slaveholders and so weaken the bonds which now hold the slave."[199]

The politics of abolitionism in the 1850s offered few easy answers. On one hand, it appeared that the Northern public was moving to the left on the issue of slavery. Surprised at how many Northerners embraced John Brown, Thoreau offered a rare compliment to his neighbors: "The North is suddenly all Transcendental," he crowed in his journal.[200] As violent conflict between antislavery and proslavery forces became a normal part of the political landscape, and the Republican Party emerged as a solidly antislavery party, there were reasons for some hope in the eventual victory of the movement. From the perspective of older white abolitionists such as Garrison and Phillips, the transformation was remarkable. No longer shunned for their views, they saw significant sections of both mass and elite opinion shifting toward them. On the other hand, matters did not look as great for black intellectuals such as William Wells Brown or Charles Lenox Remond. Despite the rise of the Republican Party, national political trends remained grim in the era of *Dred Scott*. New England intellectual culture might have been embracing antislavery but was increasingly adopting racist language and assumptions to express that antislavery sentiment.

CHAPTER 6

A War of Ideas

In February 1863, Charlotte Forten was in the South Carolina Sea Islands helping to lead slaves in their transition to freedom. With help from her connections in the New England literary world—including her friendship with the antislavery poet John Greenleaf Whittier—Forten had landed one of the most interesting and consequential civilian jobs in the Civil War. The Sea Islands, one of the first parts of the Confederacy conquered by the Union, were now the site of a grand experiment in the transition to free labor, the recruitment of black soldiers, and the reconstruction of Southern life. Forten was working as a teacher to soldiers and acting as an assistant to the Union Army as it managed the upheavals of emancipation. As Forten watched, men and women once legally defined as chattel were overthrowing the world's most powerful slave regime, ending a forced labor system that had survived centuries.

On February 9, Forten mentioned a remarkable event in her diary: the company doctor, Seth Rogers, took time out to read to a group of black soldiers the poem "Boston Hymn," an antislavery piece by Ralph Waldo Emerson.[1] An uncharacteristically patriotic piece from Emerson, the poem begins with God telling the early Puritans, huddled in their ships, that "I am tired of kings." There follows a panoramic scene of American equality: "I will have never a noble, no lineage counted great; Fishers and choppers and ploughmen; Shall constitute a state." Something about the war had rekindled Emerson's romantic sense of equality, and sounding a bit like Whitman, he painted an image of an ideal democracy, of "the digger in the harvest-field, Hireling, and him that hires," creating a political community, the humblest ruling alongside the great. This ideal democracy, this utopian striving for political and social equality, was now tied to slaves' emancipation. The same God that announced the end of kings demanded the end of all bondage: "I break your bonds and masterships; And I unchain the slave." Intervening in a contemporary debate about compensation for the slaveo-wners, Emerson's God demands, "Pay ransom to the owner, and fill the bag to the brim; who is the owner? The slave is owner; And ever was. Pay him."

Emerson's poem had been written to read to the Boston elite as they cele-brated the Emancipation Proclamation from the safe confines of Tremont Temple. What did Forten's black soldiers, mustered in the South Carolina sun, think of the Transcendentalist poem? We have some evidence. A year later, Thomas Wentworth Higginson, the Transcendentalist firebrand and friend of Forten who was serving as a colonel of black troops, reported reading the exact same poem to soldiers, mostly ex-slaves, who served under his command. Hig-ginson remembered the "thrill" when he saw the soldiers respond to the line about slave-owners paying ransom to the slaves.[2] Black soldiers—ex-slaves re-cruited from the plantations of the very Fire-Eaters who had led the secession movement—were proof of the revolutionary nature of the American Civil War. Far away from the lush parlors of Brahmin Boston, men and women who needed no new reasons to hate slavery demonstrated the intersection between Transcendentalism, radical antislavery, and the imagination of those who fought for emancipation during the Civil War.

It can seem strange, almost inappropriate, to talk about the idealism of once-born Transcendentalism during an era best known for the unsentimental slaughter of thousands in the mud of Virginia and Tennessee. To many, the movement was itself over: Margaret Fuller had drowned in a shipwreck off Fire Island in 1850, and in 1862, Thoreau succumbed to tuberculous. The ending of Theodore Parker was both predictable and, in its own way, grislier. After dying in Florence of the same disease that would take Thoreau, rumors spread that his brain ended up hidden away in a box in a closet of the Perkins Institute, sent by an overeager Italian doctor to a nervous Samuel Gridley Howe, who did not know what to permanently do with his friend's pickled brain.[3] Emerson's most productive years were behind him, and a slow drift into early senility lay ahead of him. Where once Transcendentalism was a self-consciously identified "club of the like-minded" (albeit because "no two . . . thought alike"), by the 1860s, Transcendentalism was a diffuse philosophical spirit rather than a tight-knit group of people.[4] Those aspects of sunny Transcendentalism—it seemed—that time had spared could not survive the brutal reality of modern warfare. The tragic foreboding of a Melville or the pessimistic realism of Hawthorne might seem more apt to explain the mass death of modern trench warfare than the Panglossian optimism of an Emerson. Where was the Higher Law, we might ask, in the killing fields at Antietam or Cold Harbor?

Yet, it seemed like everywhere you looked in the Civil War North, one found Transcendentalists throwing themselves into political or military organizing, a politician quoting their words, or a journalist shaped by their ideas. To give a sense of how people who came out of the world of Transcendentalism led the Union war effort, consider the Town and Country Club, founded by Emerson in 1848. The Club had only lasted for a couple of years, dissolving in 1850. But now, during the Civil War, its veterans were a veritable who's who of the Radical war effort. The history books of William C. Nell, its "charge," played a crucial role in the debate over whether to arm black soldiers. Anson Burlingame had been an important Republican congressman during the late 1850s and was named ambassador to China during the Civil War. Samuel G. Howe helped to run the Sanitary Commission, arguably the most important civilian organization in the North aiding the war effort. Henry I. Bowditch spearheaded the formation of the Ambulance Corps after his own son died on the battlefield. William Henry Channing became the chaplain of the U.S. House of Representatives, where he met with Lincoln to advocate emancipation and later helped lead the Freedman's Relief Association, a privately operated forerunner to the Freedman's Bureau. Thomas Wentworth Higginson took command of a black regiment. John A. Andrew, governor of Massachusetts during the Civil War, was arguably the most important Northern state leader during the war, personally responsible for the creation of the famous 54th Massachusetts and a prominent voice for emancipation, black equality, and other radical war aims. Emerson himself wrote a series of influential articles in the *Atlantic Monthly* advocating emancipation. Even Thoreau, wasting away from consumption in his Concord home, would harangue every visitor with complaints about "what he calls the temporizing policy" of the Lincoln administration.[5] Most important, of course, was Charles Sumner, leader of the Radical Republicans in the U.S. Senate and one of the most consistent voices for black equality in Washington, D.C.[6] It was not a bad output for a club that Higginson had once described as a "flock of radical outcasts and 'jolly beggars.'"[7] So important were Transcendentalists to the war effort that the word "Transcendentalism" became in the mouths of Northern Democrats a synonym for fanatical abolitionists.

Accepted wisdom has too long held that the Civil War ushered in a retreat from the moral enthusiasms of the antebellum years. The absolutism, romanticism, and political idealism of the antebellum years, historians have claimed, crumbled in the face of the mass casualties and bureaucratic needs of the war era.[8] Pragmatism began to take shape in the crucible of war, taking the place of Transcendentalism in intellectual consciousness as a philosophy supposedly less morally rigid and better able to make sense of the horrors of war.[9] A recognizably modern worldview—complete with room for moral nuance, scientific formalism, and an appreciation for the social, rather than moral, roots of political struggle—was developing out of the exigencies of the war. This narrative has come uncomfortably close to denying the moral imperatives of the war, celebrating the supposed rejection of abolitionist moral absolutism as a sign of intellectual maturity. It runs the risk of being a sort of philosophical version of the political argument that the North was fighting for nothing broader than a restoration of constitutional authority and the protection of the Union.

But the Civil War was not the end of the Higher Law Ethos and Romantic Reform impulse. Instead, the war marked its triumph. The Higher Law Ethos had always sought not to luxuriate in abstract ideas but to deploy them to change and reform society, to make the doubleness of their philosophy productive by using inner Reason to change the outer world. Now the war was giving them, for the first time, the power to do what Emerson had called for back in 1836—"the introduction of ideas into life"—by remaking and reconstructing the nation according to what Lincoln called the "proposition" of equality and democracy.[10] In a way, the Southerners and Northern Democrats who accused Radical Republicans of being Jacobins and "fanatics" bent on remaking the Union were correct: New England intellectuals were committed to turning the conflict into a "war of ideas" that would realize a set of abstract political values—starting with emancipation, equality, and democracy. Their pamphlets were read around the campfires, their ideas debated by soldiers and ex-slaves. Pro-war intellectuals have a well-deserved bad reputation—like Hemingway's jaded narrator in *A Farewell to Arms* rolling his eyes at words such as "sacred" and "glorious," we are often rightfully skeptical of the well fed who speak in beautiful abstractions while other men kill and die in the mud. But the Civil War held the promise of revolutionary transformation. And making it a revolution required a revolutionary ideology. While the conservatives of the North spoke of the "Union as it was," it was the abolitionists and Transcendentalists who sung of America as it could be.

Their most important idea, obviously, was that the North should seize the opportunity to abolish slavery.[11] Abolitionists, though, did not stop there. The fact that, as historians have rightfully emphasized, the core of the Civil War was about slavery, should not blind us to the crucially important fact that Southern secession necessarily raised profound questions about American democracy, the nature of political equality, and the power of the federal government. In fact, it was remarkable how quickly abolitionists assumed that slavery was doomed and began addressing a wide range of other issues, from states' rights to a federal income tax. As early as May 1861, just one month into the war, William Lloyd Garrison was predicting that "the old Union is *non est inventus*, and its restoration, with its pro-slavery compromises, well-nigh impossible" and began looking forward to other questions that the war raised.[12] The meaning of democracy and the value of political equality became two of the most important. Before Lincoln made it official, abolitionists sought to turn the war into a rededication of political equality, to the proposition that all men are created equal. Many radical thinkers shared the president's apocalyptic sense that the war was a final fight over whether popular democracy or what Wendell Phillips called "aristocracy" and "class power" would rule America and the wider Atlantic world.[13]

Integral to how they thought about democracy and equality was their re-evaluation of the role of the federal government and the American nation. Their embrace of the federal government as an instrument of justice and emancipation was not a retreat from their earlier idealism but developed out of a theory that posited the central government and the U.S. nation-state as the most apt vehicle for Transcendentalist ideals of equality and democracy. In the crucible of war, they were developing new and influential ways to think about both the federal government as a legal entity and the American nation as a cultural and moral community. They had long ago rejected both the contractual nationalism based on a deification of the Constitution common among Democrats and the Burkean nationalism rooted in a historical traditionalism celebrated by their Whig opponents. While European nationalists generally celebrated their nation's authentic *volk* and tried to build commitments to the blood and soil of a mythical past, Transcendentalists and abolitionists instead began celebrating a Transcendentalist nationalism, one that valued the nation as both the bearer and fulfillment of ideals of equality and democracy. At its best, this vision of nationalism viewed America much as Transcendentalists viewed the individual self, a community capable of always being renewed, a hopeful vision of a nation held together by abstract ideals, not one bound by racial, legalistic, or historic confines. In the clash between the nation as it was and the ideals of equality and democracy—ideals that were simultaneously unrealized and yet also those that defined and held together the nation—they imagined America in a state of constant becoming, a never-finished experiment in equality and democracy.

But the embrace of the nation and the federal government came with risks, including a tendency to subordinate the demands of their African American allies to the broader national and patriotic project. Part of the reason for this is

that the tension between white and black abolitionists that had erupted in the
1850s continued to plague the antislavery movement. As white abolitionists increasingly spoke in nationalist language, they forgot the ways that black thinkers remained marginalized within that nation. Black intellectuals kept alive a
different vision of abolitionism, one more critical of the federal state and the
compromises of the Union effort, even while hopeful that it might protect their
rights. The abolitionist embrace of the nation was both a source of power for
many white abolitionists—allowing them access to unprecedented political influence and popular audiences—and a source of blindness, as they became increasingly unable to understand black discontent with the government.

The Beginning of Abolitionist Loyalty

Nearly everyone else realized immediately that the presidential election of 1860
was one of the most consequential in American history. Initially, though, Massachusetts abolitionists were more excited about their gubernatorial victory
than the presidential race. A close friend to Transcendentalists such as James
Freeman Clarke, the new governor, John A. Andrew, had worked with the
Boston Vigilance Committee and had joined Transcendentalist organizations,
such as the Town and Country Club. As a lawyer, he had made a name for himself representing men accused of assisting fugitives. He was one of the first major Massachusetts politicians to consult with African American leaders such as
Lewis Hayden, who rewarded him with loyal political support. Partly because
of his interest in black mobilization, he would become one of the most important war governors of the Civil War era, personally overseeing the raising of
black troops, defending their equal treatment, and extending patronage to
black leaders.

At first, though, black and white abolitionists had no such reasons to trust
the new president. While some were hopeful about Lincoln—as Wendell Phillips put it, "for the first time in our history the *slave* has chosen a President"—
abolitionists' wary skepticism of most politicians extended to this relatively
unknown man from Illinois. First, as Phillips himself acknowledged moments
after celebrating the Republican victory, Lincoln was "not an Abolitionist,
hardly an antislavery man," and had given a series of assurances that he would
not challenge slavery in the South or white supremacy in the North.[14] Lincoln
was full of surprises, though, and would, in fact, show a welcome backbone, refusing to compromise on his anti-extensionist platform before his inauguration.

The same steadfastness, though, could not be found in most other Northern politicians, who, as Garrison wrote privately to Oliver Johnson, were "shivering in the wind," unwilling to stand up to either Southern secessionists or Northern "ruffians in full sympathy with the Southern traitors."[15] Abolitionists were taken aback by the violence unleashed by Northern mobs as soon as Southerners even contemplated secession. Just a month before Lincoln's election, Garrison had boasted that "the struggle for freedom of speech and of the press has everywhere been fought, and the victory won."[16] But now, the black abolitionist George Downing noticed a "rowdy feeling, which now rules Boston."[17] In the same election that elevated Lincoln to the presidency and the abolitionist Andrew to the governorship, Boston, still a reliably conservative redoubt, elected Joseph Wightman as mayor. Wightman (John S. Rock had a field day with the new mayor's name, calling him Mayor "White Man") had run on both the Constitutional Union and Democratic tickets, and many abolitionists rightfully suspected that he would refuse to protect their free speech.[18]

The first major mob attack occurred on December 3, seventeen days before South Carolina seceded. A group of antislavery leaders—including Frederick Douglass, who had come down from his New York home—had called a meeting on the one-year anniversary of John Brown's execution. Just as in 1835, the abolitionists were interrupted by a riot of the privileged, as wealthy and respectable members of Boston's business community stormed the abolitionist meeting. A writer to the *Liberator* described the rioters as "the frequenters of State street, and of the avenues of wholesale trade in cotton goods."[19] It was an unpleasant reminder of the spirit of mob violence that abolitionists had hoped was dead. After abolitionists retreated, the mob of well-dressed "gentlemen," as Frederick Douglass called them, threw stones at black passersby and even attacked prominent black abolitionists with clubs.[20] Wary abolitionists took to arming themselves as they walked the streets of their hometown, and even his friends doubted that Wendell Phillips would survive the winter.[21]

Violence hung in the air of Boston for the next five months as national news trickled in. First South Carolina, then the rest of the Deep South seceded. Angry crowds in Syracuse, Ann Arbor, and elsewhere mobbed abolitionists in the street, blaming them—rather than Southern secessionists—for the crisis. Boston was a "dreadful time of mobs," as Sallie Holley remembered it.[22] An overwhelmed President Buchanan did nothing while Northern Democrats predictably bent over backward trying to appease the South, just as they had in 1850 and 1854. Less predictably, they were joined by a surprising number of Republicans, such as William Seward and Charles Francis Adams, all of whom endorsed conciliatory measures aimed at placating the secessionists. The most prominent such measure was the proposed Crittenden Compromise, which would have created an unrepealable constitutional amendment protecting slavery. On February 5, a "very large and respectable" meeting of Boston's "conservative citizens" at Faneuil Hall endorsed the proposed compromise.[23] Perhaps he was thinking of these conservatives when, in an April lecture, Emerson despaired of "the greed and hypocrisy of politics; from the fears of property . . . so vain and expense-loving" that marked the day.[24] Emerson, who generally hated such rough-and-tumble political confrontations, had himself stared down an angry mob who had invaded his speech before the Massachusetts Anti-Slavery Society on January 24 (the Transcendentalist cautioned against any concessions to the South).[25]

Throughout this time, black Bostonians attempted to shape the North's response to the secession crisis. On February 14, 1861, a massive meeting of "colored citizens of Massachusetts" was held at the Joy Street Church to respond to the Peace Conference and the Crittenden Compromises currently being discussed in Washington, D.C. To J. Sella Martin, these attempts to mollify the South constituted "one of the most atrocious onslaughts on human liberty" ever contemplated. Demonstrably rattled by the betrayal of those Republicans who had endorsed some compromise, Dr. J. B. Smith struck an Emersonian theme, arguing that "the colored man had placed too much confidence in the non-slaveholding States and placed too little reliance on themselves." Martin worried that the North was willing to "sacrifice those few colored men who have received a portion of the common liberty."[26] Amid the tense clamor of the Secession Winter, though, the black voices could barely be heard over the din of the respectable and educated Bostonians, frantically demanding ever more concessions to the South.

Then, on April 12, the first cannon shot arcing over Charleston Harbor ended, in one dramatic burst, the Northern temptation toward compromise. The phrase "saving the Union," one Transcendentalist pointed out, changed in a heartbeat from the "scarecrow of cowardice" to the "watchword of heroism."[27] When news of the bombardment of Fort Sumter reached the North, mass demonstrations spontaneously erupted from New York to Chicago calling for the raising of an army and the protection of federal property. Walt Whitman would long remember the "volcanic upheaval of the nation, after that firing on the flag at Charleston" as one of the most important "immortal proofs of democracy" in the war.[28] The sense of besieged gloom that had hung over abolitionists all winter long evaporated in an instant. Massachusetts troops, on their way down to

Washington, D.C., became some of the first causalities of the war when they were attacked by a pro-Southern mob in Baltimore on April 19, 1861. Not only were they some of the first volunteers to die, but they did so on the anniversary of the battles of Concord and Lexington, a potent symbol that stoked an already furious regional pride.

Boston's radical abolitionists were converted into flag-waving patriots overnight.[29] Wendell Phillips, hitherto probably the most prominent disunionist in the North, was closely watched. On April 21, when he appeared on a stage festooned with American flags to pledge his support to the Union war effort, he seemed to singlehandedly commit the entire abolitionist movement.[30] Black New Englanders wasted no time joining Phillips. On April 23, just two days after Phillips's speech, a meeting of black Bostonians, still legally prevented from serving in the militia or U.S. Army, met to sign up for a "Home Guard." When "a beautiful American flag" was brought onstage, the crowd erupted in "tumultuous enthusiasm."[31] A total of 125 black Bostonians would enroll in the Home Guard, a sort of precursor to the 54th Massachusetts. John Rock, who presided over the meeting, declared the black population "willing to fight in defense of Massachusetts."[32] A couple of months later, William P. Powell, a black abolitionist from New Bedford, summed up the transition that had occurred. "For one, I must confess that, heretofore, I have held in *utter contempt* the United States flag," Powell told a meeting of New Bedford African Americans. "But now the Stars and Stripes . . . never looked more beautiful, more hopeful. It represents, in this fearful crisis, the express will of the free States, the total annihilation of negro slavery."[33] Black churches and civic leaders would be conspicuous in raising money for the wounded soldiers of the Union Army, as they did to care for the wounded at the Second Battle of Bull Run.[34] For now, though, this black love of country was unrequited. In May, John T. Hilton and twenty-two other black Bostonians submitted a petition to the Massachusetts legislature repeating their old demand that the word "white" be removed from all militia laws in Massachusetts. By a vote of 139 to 56, the white legislators turned down their request.[35] And, earlier, when black Bostonians had tried to raise money for the Union war effort, a white police officer told them, "We want you d——d niggers to keep out of this; this is a white man's war."[36] For now, black volunteers would be barred from military service.

Black abolitionists such as Rock and Douglass may have been waving the flag, but they did so with wary eyes, always conscious of how tenuous the North's newfound interest in equality and liberty was. Theirs was a critical patriotism that balanced a support for the Union cause with a clear sense of the distance the North had to go in order to achieve its promises of democracy and equality. Most prominent was Frederick Douglass, who increasingly used the language of loyalty and patriotism during the war years, but with a hitch: for Douglass, as a biographer has noted, "*true* loyalty" was defined "narrowly by equating it with abolitionist sentiment."[37] Likewise, John Rock could, in the same speech, believe that the United States was "the most guilty of nations" and still celebrate "our nation . . . flying onward with the swiftness of Mercury."[38] These were heady days, and black abolitionists could be forgiven if there was a certain hesitation or indeterminacy to their public statements. One day, the news from the front—Fremont's emancipation proclamation, for instance—would give them a fleeting glimpse of a tomorrow of freedom and equality; the next day, they would hear of Lincoln's rescinding of the order and they would be harshly reminded of the bitter weight of the history they were combatting.

Still, for the first time in years, black abolitionists could imagine a positive future for the country and themselves in it. There was a forward momentum to their critical patriotism, even a sense of millennial hope that the nation might be remade. For William Wells Brown, the emancipation of slaves and the arming of black soldiers indicated the creation of a true American nationality for the first time: "We are now beginning to be a people," Brown told the New England Anti-Slavery Society, "we are to have a new Union and the black man is one of the forces which are to produce it."[39] Rock also used the language of national rebirth and renewal. "Our republic is not yet established," Rock explained, "the metal, such as it is, has been put in the crucible, and the refiner's fire is now working it."[40] Black abolitionists, in other words, were willing to embrace patriotism, but the America they celebrated did not yet exist; it was a latent and unfulfilled promise, a potentiality developing within the existing nation that required the "fire" of war and revolution to make real.

Creating an Abolitionist Nation

For years, abolitionists had denounced the U.S. government, condemned the Constitution, mocked unthinking patriotism, and demanded the peaceful disunion of the nation. Now, in a heartbeat, they seemed to reverse course, shifting to a wholehearted embrace of the Union, the flag, and the U.S. Army. Garrison, within days of secession, declared abolitionists' duty to stand with Lincoln and the Republican Party, as "they are the instruments in the hands of God to carry forward and help achieve the great object of emancipation."[41] Where before they sought to limit the power of the federal government (especially, but not only, to recapture fugitive slaves), now they demanded Washington take aggressive action against slavery, even if it violated the prerogatives of the individual states and, in some cases, the Constitution itself. "Neither do we care for legal or illegal technicalities, or constitutional prohibitions," William Powell told a group of "colored citizens" in 1861.[42] By 1862, Wendell Phillips could announce to a hall of abolitionists that "we are the Constitution and the patriots, everything else is treason," a marked change from two years earlier, when he would have happily reversed those designations.[43] The Civil War would mark a profound shift in how American reformers conceived of the emancipatory power of the federal government, and Boston radicals became some of the most vocal advocates of an activist federal government that could protect individuals from abuses committed by local authorities.

Many observers, both in antebellum times and today, have equated antebellum abolitionist distrust of the federal government to a similar distrust of federal power found among white Southerners. They thus detect a whiff of hypocrisy in the abolitionists' newfound embrace of Washington, D.C. At various times, it is true, both Garrison and Southern proslavery intellectuals wanted to abolish the Union or limit the power of the federal government, but that was where the similarities ended. Southern planters such as Calhoun hated the federal government because they thought it was insufficiently dedicated to the protection of slavery; Garrison wished to abolish it because any protection of slavery was too much. Calhoun feared the federal government might empower the democratic masses; abolitionists knew that by leaving out black and women voters, it did not. Slaveholders had to share power in Washington, D.C. with representatives from free states, some of whom had even been elected with black votes. Used to total mastery at home and in state politics, Southern planters always disliked the fact that there was a level of government that they did not wholly dominate. Calhoun's ideal of a decentralized system of power was intended to empower political (*not* racial) minorities and, by multiplying the choke-points in the democratic process, to stymie any expression of popular will. Confident in the ability of local elites (at least in the South) to maintain control, Calhoun and his allies wished to defend the particular, local, and specific power relations embedded within Southern society against the threat posed by the centralized, democratic, and "homogeneous" authority of the federal government.[44]

The fundamental difference came down to the question of democracy. Many abolitionists may have refrained from voting—a stance rooted in their

opposition to the Constitution as currently formulated—but, unlike slaveowners, they were some of the most dedicated democrats in America. Unlike the
self-proclaimed democrats in the Democratic Party, abolitionists wished to extend the franchise to women and African Americans while aiding democratic
radicals in Europe and elsewhere. Believing that true democracy was incompat-
ible with slavery, their disunionism, then, was intended to create a society (the
North) in which the wider Atlantic world would see a functioning and just democracy.[45] This was exactly how Wendell Phillips explained his newfound support of the Union after Fort Sumter. Wasn't he a hypocrite, critics kept asking
him, given that he had once encouraged Massachusetts to secede but was now
eager to wage a war to prevent South Carolina from doing the same? Massachusetts, Phillips replied, was a democracy in a way that a slaveholding state never
could be.[46] Until they granted the vote to slaves, Confederate secession could
not be an act of democratic resistance the way that abolitionist disunionism
would have been. Garrison agreed, writing that he had never considered secession a constitutional right but instead a revolutionary right, and revolutionary
rights could only be exercised in defense of just causes, to protect liberty and
democracy, not to further entrench slavery.[47]

For abolitionists, the problems with the federal government had never
been centralized authority as such but rather the uses to which that authority
was put. Admittedly, there was occasional awkwardness, as the abolitionists
who had burned the Constitution in public now advocated war to defend it.
But in reality, as soon as the slave power had removed itself from the nation,
Garrison and Phillips could turn to the federal government with little com-
punction. As Garrison joked, "When I said I would not sustain the Constitution because it was a covenant with death and an agreement with hell, I had no
idea that death and hell would secede."[48] As early as 1861, when Garrison published a short pamphlet on the war powers of the presidency, quoting John
Quincy Adams, among others, the abolitionist leader had embraced the idea
that federal power could be harnessed to end slavery.[49] One abolitionist paper
summarized the proper abolitionist attitude toward the federal government:
"What the slaveholder loves the Abolitionists must hate," it explained in 1863,
"and what the one endeavors to destroy the other must ... defend."[50] Another
way of saying this is that, in many ways, the Southern secessionists had realized
Garrison's goals for him; they had purged the nation of slavery. By their secession, the Southerners had created a Union that was (almost) free from the influence of slaveholders. The official position, thus, of the New England Anti-Slavery
Society was that the old pledge of "No Union with Slaveholders" remained in

effect throughout the war; its meaning simply changed from supporting disunion to opposing any compromise with the secessionist South.[51]

In fact, during the war, abolitionists were nationalists because they were
antislavery; the two concerns were deeply and intricately linked. Antislavery
ideology drew abolitionists toward supporting a source of democratic legiti-
macy that transcended the local particularistic authority of the slaveowners and
the states they controlled. Liberal nationalism implied an equality of male citizens—at least formally and legally—and thus abolitionists celebrated Attorney
General Edward Bates's 1862 decision confirming black citizenship in the nation. Throughout the Atlantic world, nation building went hand in hand with
the suppression of local and personalized authorities—the "secondary powers,"
as Alexis de Tocqueville termed them, of feudal lords, church authorities, slaveowners, and local estates.

And so abolitionists assaulted the doctrine of states' rights. Garrison had
always believed Calhoun's "state sovereignty" was nothing but "slave sovereignty."[52] But during the antebellum years, such critiques of states' rights had
coexisted awkwardly with a veneration of New England and Massachusetts as
well as a generalized assault on the moral compromises of the federal Constitution. Now, during the war, abolitionist texts resounded with arguments such as
those of the poet William Ross Wallace, whose poem "The Nation Supreme"
appeared in the *National Anti-Slavery Standard*. "State Law, State Rights, and
State Slavery? Yes, their demon-clouds too long . . . upon our Nation's temple."[53]
Instead, they advocated and proposed a series of sweeping increases in federal
power, including emancipation, civil rights protection, and even the imposition
of federal income taxes.[54]

Abolitionists were inventing new ways to think about the nation and the
federal government, distinct from older Whig and Federalist proponents of a
strong federal government. There was an old strand of Northern Whig nationalism that saw the federal government as a necessary counterbalance to the supposedly excessive individualism of democratic America. Abolitionists were
coming to similar support for a strong federal presence, but with the opposite
goal in mind, hoping that a strong national government would protect and encourage, rather than restrain, individual rights and freedoms. It would be the
national government that would emancipate slaves, protect the rights of freedmen, and ensure republican governance. The Transcendentalist C. A. Bartol,
for instance, was one of many who linked the new nationalism with the emancipation of slaves. "The abolition of the slavery" was the cause of the Civil War,
he declared in 1862, but "its direct object is the existence and authority of the

nation."[55] Moreover, as the war continued, they joined the chorus of Northerners redefining the meaning of American sovereignty. The common Radical Republican argument that the states themselves had seceded—not just the individual rebellious Southerners—raised the question of where federal authority derived. Increasingly, abolitionists would argue that American sovereignty owed nothing to the states but rather derived from the people themselves—a position that was consistent with both Romantic and cultural forms of nationalism, as well as the practical needs of Radical Republicans who sought to justify a strong national state. Rejecting earlier Democratic or Whig notions of American nationalism, abolitionists strove to define the nation as dedicated to a series of "ideas" about equality and freedom. No doubt this vision of the meaning of the American nation has been honored in the breach more than the observance, but its origins lie largely in abolitionist embrace of the nation during the Civil War.

As the federal government grew in importance, Washington, D.C. replaced Boston as the central site of abolitionist energy. The Washington, D.C. society lady who complained to Sallie Hollie about the "influx of snobs and free negroes into Washington" unwittingly captured the alliance of Transcendentalist intellectuals and black radicalism that was remaking the national capitol.[56] Few New England abolitionists had spent much time in the District of Columbia before the war began, both because of their disdain for the federal government and the hostility of its local population.[57] Moreover, before the war, black abolitionists could not safely travel through Washington, D.C. as it was in slave territory and a popular hunting grounds for kidnappers, such as those who had preyed on Solomon Northup in 1841. As late as January 1862, Charles Lenox Remond declared that "in Washington, he . . . would be no safer now than he was ten years ago."[58] Remond was not paranoid; a month later, Julia Blackwell, a free black woman from Washington, D.C., was mistaken for a fugitive, arrested, and nearly enslaved.[59] But even many white abolitionists would not have been safe traveling through Maryland and other slave states before the war. It was not until 1862, as Garrison marveled, that white abolitionists in Washington, D.C. were even able to "utter brave words of freedom; and nobody mobbed them."[60]

With the influx of the Union Army and the self-imposed exile of slaveholders, Washington, D.C. was becoming a friendly place for abolitionists to agitate. After a vicious debate in which proslavery border state senators linked abolition and racial mixing with "that sort of ethereal Christianity that is preached by Parker and by Emerson," Congress finally abolished slavery in the

District of Columbia in April 1862.[61] It was one of the first of a series of antislavery measures passed by the 37th Congress that would culminate in the Second Confiscation Act. Back in Boston, on the Sunday after news of the bill's passage reached New England, the emancipation of Washington, D.C. "was made the theme of discourse in the colored churches of Boston," as William C. Nell reported.[62]

For the first time, black abolitionists seriously turned their attention to the nation's capital. Frederick Douglass, soon to develop a friendly relationship with Lincoln, noticed this change as early as March 1862. "Washington," the abolitionist wrote, "has become to the nation . . . the grand centre for abolition meetings."[63] As if preparing black abolitionists for future activism, Nell arranged for Charles H. Brainard to give a lecture on the "men and manners" of Washington, D.C. at the black Joy Street Church in Boston in April 1862.[64] By the end of the war, black abolitionists would begin to fund lobbyists—George Downing was the first—as "a representative to go to Washington and plead for black interests."[65] Of course, Washington, D.C. remained a split city—home to not only Radical Republicans but also Southern sympathizers who did not accept the new order. Worse, remnants of the slave code still haunted black travelers. In June 1862, John S. Rock visited the capital and was shocked to discover that he would have to apply for a "pass," signed by a white sponsor, much like a slave would. If he could not receive one, he would have to set down a ludicrous $1,000 surety to guarantee he was not a fugitive slave.[66] "Is it not a shame," Rock wrote to Charles Sumner, "that even in Washington now when the district is free a man is still obliged to get some responsible person to vouch for his freedom."[67] And as in other U.S. cities, black men had to fear the random violence of the drunk or resentful white bully. William Henry Channing, the Transcendentalist activist, saved the life of a black bystander when he intervened to prevent a white soldier from attacking the man with paving stone.[68]

Still, it was no small victory that abolitionists could now speak freely in the District of Columbia. Two of the first to do so were the Transcendentalists James Freeman Clarke and William Henry Channing, who toured Washington, D.C. in November 1861 with Massachusetts governor John A. Andrew. Clarke visited hospitals and forts, preached before the Massachusetts 14th, and joined Channing to meet with Lincoln himself, who struck Clarke as "an honest, candid, modest, sagacious American citizen, who means to do his duty as well as he can."[69] He had not been to the District since 1851 and was struck by the changes to the national capital. The compromisers and "place-hunters" Clarke remembered from earlier had been replaced by politicians who "believe in IDEAS!"[70]

The next year, Frederick Douglass celebrated that Emerson was among those who may now "utter in safety their opinions on slavery in the national capital."[71] Douglass was not the only abolitionist who was thrilled when, in February 1862, the Concord Transcendentalist joined William Henry Channing and the antislavery congressman Owen Lovejoy to lecture in Washington as part of a course at the Smithsonian sponsored by the Washington Lecture Association. This was the first major series of abolitionist lectures in the District. The speech would be the source of his antislavery essay "American Civilization," later printed in the *Atlantic Monthly.* The cabinet members in attendance must have been impressed with the popularity of Emerson's abolitionism as he was invited to meet with a number of the members of the inner Cabinet, including Attorney General Edward Bates, Secretary of the Treasury Salmon Chase, and Secretary of the State William Seward.[72] On the same trip, Charles Sumner invited Emerson to the White House, where the Transcendentalist met Lincoln.[73] "The President impressed me more favorably than I had hoped," Emerson wrote, and he was flattered when Lincoln repeated back to the Transcendentalist a line from one of his lectures that the president had attended years earlier.[74]

It was William Henry Channing, the socialist activist, who took the lead among Washington, D.C. Transcendentalists. Channing had been living in England in the years before the Civil War but had been itching to return to the antislavery fight. He was so convinced of a looming war that, when he renewed his contract with a church in Liverpool, he demanded the right to leave on six months' notice if fighting broke out in the United States.[75] In June 1861, he published a short book attempting to rally British opinion against the Confederacy by describing the cause of the war to be "a conspiracy of the Slave Oligarchy to ruin, because they can no longer rule, the Republic."[76] In July 1861, he was back in Boston, arriving in time to receive news of the Union disaster at the First Battle of Bull Run. At a party with James Freeman Clarke, Wendell Phillips, and John Murray Forbes, Channing nearly broke down in tears at the news of the Union's rout until Wendell Phillips cheered him up by correctly insisting that Union defeat "was just what we wanted, and was perhaps the best thing that could have happened," because a longer war would make emancipation more likely.[77] Moving to the American capital in October 1861 to take control of a Unitarian church there, Channing immediately threw himself into the struggle. John Rock was only exaggerating a little when, in 1862, he declared that "there is but one loyal white church in Washington, and that is Rev. Mr. Channing's."[78] While serving as a Unitarian minister, Channing accepted the chaplaincy of the "Stanton Hospital" in Washington, D.C.[79] He worked for the Sanitary Commission, helped turn his church into an army hospital, and eventually served as a chaplain to the U.S. House of Representatives. Dedicated to turning the chaplaincy into a political tool—"the People's Church," he called it—Channing arranged to have Henry Highland Garnet give a sermon to the House of Representatives, the first black minister to do so.[80] Perhaps even more radical, violating both congressional traditions and the ancient proscriptions of St. Paul, he invited Mrs. Rachel Howland, a Quaker "prophetess," to preach before the House of Representatives. Finally, he helped to found the Freedman's Relief Union, rising to become its vice president.[81] Throughout 1861 and 1862, he tirelessly advocated for emancipation, becoming one of the first abolitionists to meet with Lincoln to do so. Future Speaker of the House Schuyler Colfax even credited him with helping to lay the groundwork of public opinion that made possible the Emancipation Proclamation.[82]

More dramatic than Emerson, whose literary fame protected him, or Channing, who was not as high-profile, was the hero's welcome afforded to Wendell Phillips when he visited in early 1862 to lecture in the same series as Emerson. Charles Sumner had helped to arrange both, writing to Phillips that "Washington is now as free to you & Garrison as Boston."[83] "A year ago Wendell Phillips would have been sacrificed to the devil of slavery anywhere on Pennsylvania avenue," the *National Anti-Slavery Standard* wrote, "To-day he was introduced by Mr. Sumner on to the floor of the Senate." Phillips's trip was a whirlwind. On March 14, he addressed the Senate, two days later he was hosted by the Speaker of the House at a private dinner attended by the vice president, and the next day, he addressed a Massachusetts regiment and "preached the Gospel of emancipation." Finally on March 18, he topped off his visit with an interview with Lincoln himself, certainly the first president to even pretend to respectfully consider the opinion of Wendell Phillips.[84] To abolitionists, stunned to see one of their own embraced by the most powerful people in America, it seemed like "a vast revolution in sentiment is going on."[85]

Active Ideas

For abolitionists such as William Henry Channing and Wendell Philips, Washington, D.C. was not just a place to hobnob with newly friendly Republican elites, but it was also where one found the biggest and most consequential concentration of potential abolitionist converts: the Union Army. Soldiers in their camps were more than just a captive audience for antislavery propaganda;

in the field, they would control the fates of the fugitives who crowded their lines. It was an urgent mission. As the black abolitionist Alfred M. Green wrote, the "Hunker Democracy, whose demagogues early sought for place and position in the army" dominated the Army leadership.[86] Reporters sent north anxious missives from the Union line reporting on the "conflict of opinion" among the troops, too many of whom, the abolitionists fretted, resisted "interfering in the least with the 'divine institution.'"[87] As Charles Sumner told the Senate, a number of Union generals, including Hooker, McCook, and Buell, had reputations of abusing fugitive slaves.[88] In January 1863, Daniel Foster, last seen as the armed Transcendentalist missionary to Kansas and now a chaplain in the Union Army, wrote to the *Liberator*, pleading for copies of the paper to distribute among the soldiers. They needed the antislavery paper to balance the Copperhead *New York Herald*, which a group of Democrats "floods" the army with, Foster reported, and which was all too popular around the campfires during the dark days after Fredericksburg.[89]

And so abolitionists inundated the Union Army with free antislavery tracts. The first major piece intended to make a Transcendentalist argument for emancipation was Moncure Conway's *The Rejected Stone*, published in late 1861 with Union soldiers in mind. Conway had been touring Ohio and saw an opportunity to convert the soldiers at Camp Dennison away from their "Hunkerish influences" and turn them into "a Holy Army of Crusaders." He wrote to a series of abolitionists, including Phillips, hoping that copies of the book he was writing would be sent to the front. He even offered to "visit the camps and see that the work gets into the soldiers' hands."[90] Conway gave up the royalties to allow the book to be distributed by abolitionists into the Union Army in cheap 20-cent editions.[91] The book was "eagerly read by the soldiers in their camps," according to one antislavery paper.[92] At least one soldier was profoundly affected: Conway met the mother of one who claimed that the book, packed in the inside pocket in his jacket, had stopped a bullet headed for his heart.[93]

Quoting Emerson and stealing imagery from Whitman, Conway introduced many of the themes that would mark Transcendentalist understandings of the war: the need for an idealistic antislavery general, the war as replicating on a national scale the conflict between Reason and sensuousness in the individual self, and the introduction of ideals of freedom, equality, and democracy into the meaning of the conflict. Responding to the recent defeat at the First Battle of Bull Run, he blamed the failure on careerist generals who had no "power of ideas" or dedication to "eternal Truth and Right."[94] The South had the advantage that the everyday violence of slavery had prepared them well for the barbarism of war; with less native ability to restrain themselves, the white Southerners easily and profitably surrendered to their animalistic violent impulses. If the North was to win, it would have to develop a passionate enthusiasm for freedom—some principle that could inspire an equally fierce fighting spirit among the fresh-faced farm boys manning the Union lines.[95] Conway's Transcendentalist war imagery hit a nerve; eager abolitionists sent Abraham Lincoln so many copies of the book that the president supposedly joked that "he had been fairly stoned with the Rejected Stone."[96]

Conway's sequel, 1862's *The Golden Hour*, has been read as evidence of growing abolitionist disenchantment with the Lincoln administration.[97] It is true that Conway, like many Americans, was shocked by the brutality of the war, as the death tolls from Shiloh, the Second Battle of Bull Run, and elsewhere filled the front pages back home. But Conway's later portrayal of the text as "against War" is mostly the product of his postwar disillusionment, not an accurate description of the text as written.[98] At the time, Conway emphasized the brutal, animal nature of the war not to advocate its end but because doing so illustrated how tragic it would be to sacrifice in vain, how useless the countless deaths would be if they only won the Union "as it was." Again, Conway argued that there was a natural affinity between violence and slaveholders (Phillips and Emerson would echo this point), and thus the Civil War was the inevitable extension of the violent "imposition of one will on another" that was the mark of the slaveholding aristocracy.[99] Because the North had no choice but to use the tools of war, it ran the risk of descending into the same animal sensualist brutality of the South if it did not have "an idea in this war."[100] If the isomorphism between the Transcendentalist heroic self and the war effort was unclear, Conway titled a chapter "Through Self-Conquest to Conquest."[101] For Conway, Emerson's overquoted advice to "Hitch your wagon to a star" was transformed into a call to turn the war into an ideological battle for emancipation, democracy, and equality.

Starting in 1862, Conway joined abolitionists, Transcendentalist, and labor supporters in the new radical paper the *Commonwealth*, intended to build support for Charles Sumner's reelection and, through it, emancipation and a thorough reconstruction of Southern society.[102] Conway, Franklin Sanborn, and James M. Stone (a former leader in the fight for the ten-hour day) served as its editors. Its main goal of supporting the Radical wing of the Massachusetts Republican Party did not stop it from playing a historic role in literary history.[103] Louisa May Alcott, raised among the elite of Massachusetts Transcendentalist and abolitionist thought, first published her "Hospital Sketches" in its pages.[104]

The *Commonwealth* also published black authors, such as William Wells Brown, whose book *The Black Man* was previewed in its pages. The paper even took time off from reporting on the death tolls of the war to print lengthy introductions to the philosophy of Hegel by William Torrey Harris (the future commissioner of education who would help lead the movement for public kindergarten).[105] We can be skeptical that too many Boston radicals were giving Harris's essays enough time to actually make much sense of the intricacies of *Geist's* self-development. But there was something appropriate about abolitionists reading Hegel after the battle of Gettysburg; if the antebellum years had been marked by Kantian moral idealism, Hegel's spirit of becoming, progression, and development through struggle and conflict fit well the temper of the war years.

The *Commonwealth* was an invaluable resource for understanding how Transcendentalism influenced public debate in the Civil War years. It published writings by the recently deceased Thoreau, memories of the original Transcendentalist Club, and printed notices of Emerson essays and speeches. In fact, it holds an unused version of an important Emerson essay on Lincoln's Emancipation Proclamation. This essay would be reprinted in the *Atlantic Monthly* as "The President's Proclamation," but a longer version appeared in the *Commonwealth*.[106] In this essay, Emerson celebrated the democratic enthusiasm that distinguished contemporary wartime politics, the momentous stakes of a war that was wresting the people out of the selfish lethargy that had marked antebellum political life. "Governments," he wrote, "usually administered in the interest of the governing class, in these happier seasons, share the thrill that electrifies the people, and act under the control of a sentiment." Lincoln's progress, Emerson thought, was simply the embodiment of an engaged public opinion, his actions the reflection of moral decisions made by millions of everyday Northerners. Interestingly, he made an argument about race that repeated a point that black abolitionists such as John Rock had long been making: that the history of even the English demonstrated that "no race has escaped the humiliation of a tyranny," since the English were once held as slaves. Although African Americans were not mentioned, the implication was that the former slaves had a glorious future ahead.[107]

By 1862, Boston abolitionists had settled on a slogan—the Union Army needed "a war of ideas"—that captured their desire that the Union effort seek to realize a political principle in its actions. The goal would be to reform and not just conserve the Union, to make ideas real, not simply let physical strength dominate. The influence of Transcendentalism was obvious and explicit. Lydia Maria Child wrote to a friend that "a soldier needs a great idea to fight for," and

James Freeman Clarke preached to his congregation that "an army is not as strong as a principle—*Ideas* lie back of armies, back of guns and cannon. Cannon and guns fight as the idea directs."[108] In an article whose title—"Want of Ideas in the Army"—gave away its message, the *Commonwealth* editorialized that "to make a General we want *ideas*."[109] Thus, ideas were expected to have a practical effect: they would inspire soldiers to the necessary frenzy to fight, but unlike in the South, it was a passion still guided by morality and reason, not raw animalistic violence. When the Woman's National Loyal League petitioned for what would become the Thirteenth Amendment, they wrote to Lincoln that "a lasting enthusiasm is ever based on a grand idea."[110] Emerson, in a lecture, looked forward to the day "when the cannon is aimed by ideas."[111] Whitman would later describe the purpose of the war as "the great Idea, the idea of perfect and free individuals."[112]

The word "idea" might seem trite, too common to shed meaningful light on something specific about Civil War era ideology. But the frequency with which abolitionists demanded an army inspired by "ideas," a general with "ideas" to conquer the South, and a policy informed by them suggests that there was something in the term that spoke to abolitionist hopes. "Ideas" denoted more than an appreciation for the abstract. They insisted on the role of moral judgment in the realm of politics even, maybe especially, in the face of wartime's burdens. A politics of ideas was one that retained an enthusiasm for principles, even a frenzied devotion for the abstract, the universal, and the moral amid the strict demands of wartime. More than anything, though, a celebration of ideas meant the desire to realize in the conflict ideological and intellectual goals, to instill a transcendent meaning to a war whose purpose was still undetermined. For Transcendentalists, "Ideas" spoke to the particularly human ability to use their Reason, conscience, and will to create mental life. The word had deep roots in their theory. Kant had considered "ideas" to be the concepts and questions that reason produces to order our abstract thought, notions such as the existence of the self. Kant did not believe reason was capable of solving most of these questions, but Coleridge, as was typical, took Kant's definition and added religious and moral dimensions that Transcendentalists then absorbed. For Coleridge, an "IDEA" was evidence of Reason's ability to contemplate "actual (or moral) truths."[113] In the maelstrom of a brutal war, then, abolitionists could see their embrace of values such as freedom, equality, and democracy as rooted in absolute unchanging Reason, not the arbitrary historical compromises that had created the antebellum Constitution. It is unlikely that every abolitionist propagandist was thinking in such metaphysical terms, but the more popular association of the antislavery cause with moral commitment as against the sensual slaveholders certainly influenced this rhetoric of "ideas."

It was not so much that intellectuals thought ideas could take the place of action, but, they hoped, that action might be informed by ideas. One of the earliest to make this clear was John Rock, who dismissed calls to focus only on action rather than critical thought in February 1862. "It is being continually thundered in our ears that the time for speech-making has ended," Rock began his speech. But, as long as "the *active* idea has found but little sympathy with either of our great military commanders," there would be a place for antislavery ideas. Those who were advocating unthinking action, Rock suggested, were unwittingly siding with the Democrats who wanted a nonideological war to preserve the Union as it was. Those who wanted to "fight without an object" he saw as expressing "the sentiment of the cotton brokers and secession sympathizers of Boston."[114] An "*active* idea" was one that, as Rock said later in the same speech, believed in both God *and* gunpowder—a principled struggle for eternal Right backed up by concrete force of arms.[115] This sense of the necessary mixture of the abstract and moral with the concrete and practical marked how Transcendentalists such as Emerson viewed the war as well. This Transcendentalist and abolitionist embrace of the value of the practical side of human affairs (as long as it is shaped by the ideal side) was not as great a change as it might seem. Most of the great Transcendentalist literature in fact had been shaped by exactly the struggle to realize one's ideals in the messy world, to find a way to bridge the seemingly impossible metaphysical task of uniting the ideal with the real.

As Rock had suggested, this push to invigorate the Army of the Potomac with "ideas" was a thinly veiled attack on those who resisted making the war ideological, especially the General George McClellan. The abolitionists detested "Little Mac," both because of his lackluster performance as a general and his steadfast refusal to use the Army of the Potomac as a tool of emancipation. In addition to McClellan, their main political opponent, though, was the Democratic Party, whose official position was that the war was being fought solely to restore the Union "as it was" and even many moderate Republicans who resisted developing an ideological meaning to the war. Lucy Larcom, who had moved on from her Lowell factory job and was now teaching school in Beverly, dismissed in her journal "all the frothy spoutings for 'Union' that we hear every day," instead longing for the day when "our battalions must be strengthened by *ideas*, by the *idea* of freedom."[116] In Massachusetts, the "People's Party" sought to break off from the Republican Party and elect a solidly conservative slate that would go "against Gov. Andrew, Senator Sumner, and the President's

I'M NOT TO BLAME FOR BEING WHITE, SIR!

Figure 10. Opponents resorted to crude race-baiting in an unsuccessful
attempt to deny Charles Sumner reelection in 1862. Courtesy of the
American Antiquarian Society.

Proclamation."[117] Little more than warmed over Cotton Whiggism, with an added dash of populist racism to appeal to Democrats, the People's Party failed to convince a skeptical Charles Francis Adams, their only potentially viable candidate, to challenge Sumner.[118] Worse for the nascent reactionaries, they failed to convince more than a handful of voters to support their party, as the Republicans nearly swept the 1862 elections in the Bay State, ensuring Sumner would be sent back to the Senate. Boston, of course, continued to vote conservative but was easily outvoted by a lopsided return for Republicans from the rest of the state.[119]

Transcendentalists were, perhaps, a bit anxious to celebrate "ideas" because they were relying on their opposite, brute material strength, to win the war. They needed a war of ideas to solve the great abolitionist paradox of the war years: in order to achieve their goals of equality and liberty, they were relying on forces and institutions that they had long defined as hostile to such values, most obviously the military power of the U.S. Army. Acutely aware that means had a way of dictating ends, Emerson was particularly concerned that the logic of war—not just its violence, but its any-means-to-an-end instrumentalism—might seep into the rest of American society. "Military strength," Emerson fretted, could "intrude on this sanctity and omnipotence of intellectual law."[120] Wendell Phillips was as active a supporter of the Union cause as existed, but even he worried that the tools used to prosecute the war—he focused on the "military spirit" and "money spirit," which were being empowered by the war—threatened the ideals for which they fought.[121] John Rock was likewise skeptical of the "traitors in the shape of Northern capitalists," who were congregating in Washington, D.C.[122] But, with a couple of idiosyncratic exceptions, such as the pacifist Ezra Heywood or the cranky Stephen Foster, Boston radicals did not reject the pull of military might; they just hoped to be able to control it with intellectual and moral power. Ideas had to be powerful enough to both conquer the South and resist the very logic of militarism and bureaucratic rationality being unleashed in their defense.

From the abolitionists' perspective, the "ideas" of equality and democracy would be the glue holding together the disparate states and peoples of the nation. Drawing on German Romanticism, they held that their nation was representative of a particular "idea," defined as democracy, liberty, or equality (or all three). "This new life needs that men should guide the nation's idea carefully in the new time and new crisis," Phillips told a New York audience.[123] Gerrit Smith delivered an important address on "The Sacredness of Nationality" that almost reduced the North's purpose in fighting to be entirely about the defense of its nationality.[124] The very articulation of a national idea—the belief that the nation was a place of transcendent cultural and political identity and not simply an alliance of convenience between distinct sovereign states—was a rebuke to the Democratic critics who embraced such a contractual vision of America's nationhood in order to reject any role for the federal revolution that the war was unleashing.

Across the Atlantic, this was the age of liberal nationalism, and it can be surprising to twenty-first-century readers the degree to which celebrating American nationalism did not mean retreating into parochial or xenophobic concerns. In fact, transnational voyages and solidarity often went hand in hand with the development of American nationalist identity. The black preacher J. Sella Martin's Civil War years demonstrate this well. Martin left Boston for the United Kingdom in late 1862, where he would remain for almost two years speaking before antislavery societies and trying to swing British public opinion toward the North. Like Phillips and other abolitionist nationalists, Martin based his sense that the United States was destined to remain one nation on a romantic sense of geographic destiny. "It was a physical impossibility for [Lincoln] to let the South go," Martin told the British workers, "unless he could dry up the Ohio, the Mississippi, and the other great rivers which, in their course to sea, bound all the States together in bonds indissoluble."[125] He especially reached out to the British working class. In 1863, he told a British audience that "he gave credit to the cotton operatives of this country for the patience" with which they had dealt with the cotton famine.[126] In fact, he would later conclude that, in Great Britain, sympathy with the American slave was directly related to whether one worked with one's own hands. "The lower classes," he told a Boston audience, "almost without exception, were friends to the Union," while the aristocrats and upper bourgeoisie all supported the South.[127] Martin saw no contradiction in celebrating American nationalism, even while making a plea for a transatlantic politics of solidarity between British workers and black slaves.

If the radical conception of the Civil War had echoes of the European Revolutions of 1848—in which demands for national unity, democracy, and working-class rights all mingled—it was partly because for some in Boston, the American Civil War was literally an extension of the European conflict. "The despotisms of the old world are rejoicing," John Rock told a New England crowd, in what they hoped would be the downfall of American "democratic institutions."[128] There was John Cluer, the Scottish-born labor leader who had cut his teeth with Chartists; he viewed the war as an extension of European class conflict: "the aristocracy of Europe were on the side of the South, the people sympathized with the

North," he told an antislavery meeting in January 1862.[129] Karl Heinzen, Marx's old drinking buddy, was hardly surprised at the unfriendly reception the Union cause received in Europe, as "North America is hated as a Republic." What the Union cause needed, the refugee from revolutionary Germany declared, was a revolution in France, which would win the American Civil War by eliminating the threat of European intervention in American affairs.[130] More broadly, German emigrants, many of whom had played a role in the revolution there, were crucial members of the Republican coalition, and a number of former revolutionaries played leadership roles in the Union cause. August Willich, the major general commanding the 32nd Indiana, who lectured his soldiers on Marxism, was only one of many such links between the European left and the Union's cause.[131] Marx himself threw in with the Union cause early, seeing the victory of the North as a prerequisite for that of socialism.

If in the 1850s, abolitionists had sought to relive the moral purity of the English Civil War, now it was the French Revolution's democratic idealism that provided the slogans and imagery for New England abolitionists. Phillips reached for this imagery when he celebrated the new spirit of the North, observing that "twenty millions of people are resolving that it shall mean 'Liberty, Equality, Fraternity.'"[132] By 1862, even William Lloyd Garrison defined the "inalienable rights of man" with the famous slogan of the French Revolution, while Elizabeth Cady Stanton and Susan B. Anthony wrote an open letter to Union soldiers claiming that the "traitors" were seeking to destroy "the eternal pillars of Justice, emblazoned with liberty, equality, fraternity."[133] The black abolitionist and emigrationist Lewis Putnam defined the war as partly about "political equality and fraternity."[134] Just as Marx observed of the French Revolutionaries of 1848, the American abolitionists were looking backward toward the last great successful revolution for the symbolism and slogans with which to understand their own (though their revolution would be neither tragedy nor farce). As symbols of liberation and modernity, the French Revolutionary slogans would come to be a target for the reactionary Confederate press. The *Richmond Examiner* was widely cited by abolitionists when it boasted that "for 'Liberty, Equality, Fraternity,' we have deliberately substituted Slavery, Subordination, and Government."[135]

The "idea" of the war, then, was not simply about the abolition of slavery but also about a rededication of the nation to democracy and equality. Just like Lincoln, abolitionists tended to talk about the meaning of the war in terms of a test of democracy. John Rock was acutely aware of the reality of American racism, but he still believed that "democracy is now undergoing a terrible trial . . . if this Government fails now, it will not be because we have reposed too much confidence in the people, but because we have relied too much on the few."[136] Wendell Phillips, in particular, understood the purpose of the war as being about a struggle between "two powers: Aristocracy and Democracy," an idea that united him with more moderates like Lincoln.[137]

Along with democracy, the idea of equality—as a legal, political, and spiritual value—came to dominate the Transcendentalist and abolitionist understanding of the war. Equality was not simply a guide for laws—as the war raged and the body count rose, it became something that could give spiritual purpose to the war, a sacred word that could redeem the cruel and senseless slaughter at the Wilderness and Cold Harbor. In 1862, John S. Rock declared that the Declaration of Independence's promise of equality was the "great charter" of their cause.[138] Abolitionist papers bolded the word "equality" and put it in italics, antislavery poets wrote hymns to it, and lecturers lauded it. Raising black troops in New Jersey, Charles W. Denison declared, "Equality before God and the Law! This is the motto for every banner of all colored troops, throughout the world."[139] The Impartial Suffrage League would describe it as "the gigantic form of EQUALITY, towering to heaven, stands before the nation, whichever way it may turn, and says in thunder tones, 'Accept me as a guide, and you shall be led to peace, prosperity, safety, and happiness.'"[140] As a rallying call, equality united both black and white: white because it connected the Union cause to democratic populism, black because it suggested the destruction of racism and Jim Crow laws in the North.

There was an analogy between Transcendentalist metaphysics and the radical vision of political equality. A central part of the appeal of Transcendentalism had been its hyper-Protestant belief that all people could experience inspiration without intervention or mediation. Thus, they attacked the power of religious authorities and narrow traditions that clouded the individual's horizons, interjecting themselves between the believer and God. Our natural state was in unadorned communion with the infinite, and all people had the ability to chase away those clouds that mediated our encounter with the Oversoul. The individual's background and characteristics should not matter to this encounter with Reason, simply the presence or (hopefully) nonpresence of "the mist, that stands 'twixt God and Thee."[141] Having committed themselves to this vision of spiritual equality, they were drawn to similar metaphors for political equality. As Theodore Parker had written, "All this is a Republic; it is a Democracy. There is no born priest to stand betwixt the nation and its God; no Pope to entail his 'nephews' on the Church; no bishop claiming divine right to rule over the people and stand betwixt them and the Infinite."[142] Just as the Transcendentalist subject stood naked before absolute Reason, so the citizen was to stand unadorned before a nation that cared not for their race, wealth, or background. This sense of the intermixture of the spiritual, religious, and political dimension of equality helps explains why someone such as the black abolitionist John Rock could declare that "slavery is treason against God, man, and the nation."[143]

This equality—as much a spiritual as a political value—was expressed spatially; the circle of a democratic society would replace the ladder of a hierarchical one. Imagery of circular orbits and constellations appeared in abolitionist discourse, representing the equitable nationalism that would replace the personal and racial hierarchies that marked Southern society. If Southern society was a ladder, a chain with planters on top and slaves on the bottom, abolitionists such as Phillips imagined Northern democracy to be a sphere, each person exercising an equal pull and power on every other, held together by a shared dedication to ideals of equality and democracy. Consider Charles Sumner's orbital rhetoric when arguing for the Fourteenth Amendment: "Hereafter the Equal Rights of All will take the place of Slavery, and the Republic will revolve on this glorious pivot, whose infinite, far-reaching radiations will be the happiness of the human family."[144] The only meaningful political authority derived not from some hierarchical power but the aggregate pull of every other member, the gravity of whose vote and influence kept all in equilibrium.

The world that Civil War–era Transcendentalism created helps to explain Lincoln's rhetoric at Gettysburg. Historians have long been struck by how the president used the 270-word address to elevate the meaning of the war, to sanctify an antislavery notion of American nationalism rooted in the unfulfilled promise of equality found in the Declaration of Independence. Garry Wills and others have seen the fingerprints of Transcendentalism in Lincoln's speech.[145] Certainly, Lincoln was thinking of Theodore Parker's ideas about democracy when he defined the war as a struggle for popular sovereignty. Parker had often defined democracy as the rule of all, by all, for all, a line that Lincoln adapted to end his speech. More than that, the address helped to popularize the idea that the war was not going to simply be about a restoration of the Union or simply the end of formal slavery but about a reconsecration of the nation to the "proposition" (Lincoln used a more elegant synonym for "idea") of equality. The powerful emotional appeal of Transcendentalist equality can even be seen in the design of the Gettysburg Cemetery, which spatialized the set of values of equality and nationalism that Transcendentalists had developed. A central monument of Liberty, representing the nation, is orbited by a semicircle of headstones, each of equal size, regardless of rank, state, or religion, evoking the orbital nationalism of Transcendentalist epistemology. This circular equality stood in stark contrast to the Confederate burial patterns that emphasized a vertical hierarchy led by generals or the state.

Transcendentalist ideas were on the mind of some of the black intellectuals who helped to shape Reconstruction, as well. Charlotte Forten's service in South Carolina has been read as one of the most notable instances of Northern culture coming face-to-face with Southern society during the heat of the war.[146] Forten's experience was indeed remarkable: as both an African American and an apostle of New England literary idealism, she was particularly able to bridge the world between Transcendentalist intellectualism and the experiences of the newly freed. Along with her friend Thomas Wentworth Higginson, who she often worked with in South Carolina, she helped to serve as a missionary for Transcendentalist and abolitionist nationalism. In 1862, she was a dissatisfied schoolteacher in Salem, Massachusetts. Close to both the Remond family and William C. Nell, as well as many of the leading white abolitionists, she nevertheless yearned to be of greater use to the antislavery cause. After being frustrated in her attempts to gain a position working with the freedpeople, she was "astonished, stupefied" in October 1862 to be finally granted a position but told she would have to leave the very next day for South Carolina.[147] Arriving in late October in Hilton Head, she became a teacher to the newly freed, sending back reports to the *Liberator* and the *Atlantic Monthly* that helped to shape Northern understanding of the conquered South.

She had certainly absorbed a great deal of the New England cultural superiority preached by Emerson and Phillips. Passing by Charleston, South Carolina, from the safe confines of her ship, she shuddered thinking that "we were even so near the barbarous place."[148] In an article for the *Atlantic Monthly*, she noted that "already Northern improvements had reached this Southern town [Hilton Head, South Carolina]."[149] She pointedly told her *Liberator* readers of celebrating Thanksgiving—a potent symbol of New England cultural nostalgia—almost as soon as she arrived in the South.[150] Writing back for the Northern audience of the *Liberator* or the *Atlantic Monthly*, she sometimes presented Southern black culture as exotic and even primitive, as when she described black musicians as "the shouting of the grown people . . . the barbarous expression of religion, handed down to them from their African ancestors."[151] If skeptical of Southern culture, she was far better positioned to understand how to impart a sense of pride in her black students than her white colleagues. When a white teacher told her black students the story of John Brown, Forten countered with that of

Toussaint L'Overture, "thinking it well they should know what one of their own color had done for his race."[152]

She had always appreciated Emerson, and the Transcendentalist remained an important figure for her, especially in South Carolina. As we have seen, she noted when the company doctor, Seth Rogers, read the "Boston Hymn" to a regiment of black soldiers collected on the South Carolina Sea Islands.[153] Forten clearly had Emerson on the mind while in South Carolina. Describing the newly freed slaves, she wrote, "They have what Emerson calls 'fine manners,'— that natural courtesy that comes from the heart."[154] In her aborted courtship with the company doctor, Seth Rogers, whom she knew from his participation in antislavery activities back in Massachusetts, the two read Emerson together.[155] Even on her sea travels down to the South, she seemed to evoke the Concord sage, describing the beauty of the sea as "infinite variety." The words are in quotation marks in her journal and possibly reference the essay *History*, in which Emerson mused on the tendency of history to have "at the surface, infinite variety of things, at the centre . . . simplicity of cause."[156]

In fact, by the middle of the war, Transcendentalism had become a symbol of the cultural conflict that the war had unleashed. To many Southern whites, Transcendentalism seemed to symbolize all the antinomian ills of a free society. The *Richmond Whig*, a prominent Virginian paper, in 1860 could write of the "transcendentalism" manifested in "rages, manias, fanaticisms, or whatever is the best expression for those delusions of mankind," all of which led to abolitionism.[157] In February 1861, one Virginian cited the popularity of Emerson's "radical opinions" and "blasphemies," alongside more familiar targets such as Garrison and Parker, to make the case for secession.[158] In April 1861, as armies were mobilizing, the *Southern Literary Messenger* reviewed a book by Emerson and declared that his thoughts "illustrate the utter worthlessness of the philosophy of free society" and lead to anarchism, and it called on Congress to arrest the author and suppress his writings.[159] In fact, as the war raged, many Southern explanations for the war located Emerson and other Transcendentalists as symbols of the cultural and political failings of the North. T. W. MacMahon, writing in 1862, included in his list of those who had alienated the South "Ralph Waldo Emerson, poet, fanatic, and metaphysician, [who] resolved upon not being outdone as a marvelous slanderer."[160] In Union prison, a bitter Confederate soldier named Daniel Hundley complained to his journal that "the transcendentalism of New-England has fast leavened the whole Yankee religion with a mystic creed not very dissimilar to the doctrine of the Buddhists of Hindostan; and Emerson and Beecher, as well as Grant and Sherman, and their followers, great and small, are sacrilegious enough to believe themselves a portion of the Deity."[161]

In the North, reactionary Democrats went further, claiming that Transcendentalism was linked to the Republican Party's supposed advocacy of race mixing. Samuel "Sunset" Cox, the race-baiting reactionary Democrat who helped to popularize the "miscegenation" slur (the claim that the Republican Party was encouraging interracial sex), often linked Transcendentalism to race mixing. On February 19, 1864, Cox took to the House floor to denounce the "new system, called by the transcendental abolitionists, 'Miscegenation.'"[162] Cox was veritably obsessed with Emerson and the Transcendentalists, convinced that "Parkers and Phillipses and the lesser spawn of transcendentalism" were modern versions of the fanatic Roundhead who "would reform men's morals by statute and make paradises by politics."[163] And in September 1864, just weeks before the election, the Central Campaign Committee of the New York Democratic Party released a pamphlet, "Miscegenation Indorsed by the Republican Party," which quoted, among other people, Emerson, drawing attention to lines in his poem "Voluntaries," which, supposedly, proved that the philosopher "thinks the negro is better than the white man."[164] Fear of the abolitionist project of federal restoration was tied up with both virulent racism against the newly freed and a disdain for the abstracting project of the Transcendentalists.

John S. Rock and Black Wartime Struggle for Equality

Black women played an underappreciated role in the war effort. In 1862, a group in Boston led by Sarah Martin formed the Fugitive Aid Society, an organization that linked earlier interests in intellectual clubs and elevation, sponsored lectures by black abolitionist leaders, and also raised money and supplies to meet the hardheaded demands of wartime. They invited important black orators such as Charles Reason and Frederick Douglass while also hiring Louise de Mortie (later celebrated by W. E. B. Du Bois as "a woman of feeling and intellect") to perform for the "suffering sick, aged, and infants among the contraband at Washington."[165] While in part an exercise in voluntary benevolence that was meant to signal a certain respectability—the organization was formed in part at the urging of Elizabeth Keckley (Mary Todd Lincoln's dress maker and founder of the Contraband Relief Association)—it spoke to the political and ideological aspirations on the black home front.[166] They both raised money

($25 and five barrels of goods in April 1862) and sponsored lectures on the brotherhood of man.[167]

It was a time of both millennial hope and frustrating contradictions; a nation willing to send its children to die to end slavery was unwilling to share a railroad car with a black lawyer. In 1862, Martin's husband, J. Sella, published a narrative poem that illustrated the ambivalence with which many black intellectuals continued to approach questions of nation and patriotism. The poem follows an unnamed white soldier from Massachusetts who fell wounded during the Baltimore Riot of 1861 (this occurred when the very first wave of Massachusetts troops had been attacked by an angry mob in Baltimore on their way to the front). The wounded white soldier returns as a hero to Boston, where he meets the escaped slave who had hid him from the fury of the Baltimore mob. Throughout the poem, Martin plays with the intense New England regionalism that animated so many abolitionists. The slave protagonist, we are told, instinctively welcomed the Yankee solders because he had heard, as a slave, that Massachusetts was a land of liberty. He arrives in Boston, though, to find nothing but accusing stares and hostile prejudice. Martin deploys the association of New England with liberty in order to shame Boston, as much as to celebrate it. When confronted by the slave who saved him, the white soldier is converted to abolitionism, but the broader population is not, suggesting both the possibility and difficulty of white conversion. The poem ends with a rousing defense of the unrealized emancipatory vision of abolitionist nationalism. "Henceforth freedom knows no order; Or peculiar scribes and priests."[168]

Martin's reaction to the war, a balance between caution and hope, was common among black intellectuals in Boston. As much as Emerson or Phillips, Martin was capable of imagining the utopian potential of the conflict. He imagined the nation as an edifice, torn down by rebels but rebuilt with "the stones of freedom . . . a noble structure . . . with the white man and the negro, standing one on either side."[169] But more than Phillips (and *far* more than Emerson), Martin saw New England's supposed dedication to equality and liberty as unfulfilled, a promise not yet realized. The slave, after revealing himself to the wounded white soldier, retreats into the Boston night, homeless and forgotten. "Love of masters—we have lost it," Martin warns, "love of slaves we too may lose." Martin's sense of the enduring reality of Northern discrimination, tempering his otherwise enthusiastic embrace of the Northern cause, marked the experiences of the war for many black intellectuals.

From the beginning, some black intellectuals withheld their total allegiance to the war effort. As soon as the war began, in the pages of the *Anglo-*

African, Alfred M. Green debated "R.H.V.," who was skeptical that black Northerners should join the war effort.[170] Of Boston's black leaders, Charles Lenox Remond was probably the most critical of the Lincoln administration. He described the Emancipation Proclamation as a "so-called Emancipation policy."[171] As late as August 1865, Remond would remain pessimistic about the wartime victories, declaring that the Union war effort had "failed" the slaves.[172] On the other hand, there were some black intellectuals, such as John S. Rock, who described the war with utopian language of creating a renewed "pure gold of the republic" that would have been at home in any Radical Republican meeting.[173] William C. Nell seems to have agreed with Rock, writing optimistically of the new state of affairs.

Nell used his historical sensibility to advocate for the enrollment of black soldiers. Nell, a historian at heart, had spent much of 1861 putting together memorial biographies of the black colleagues of John Brown who had died in Virginia. The articles, along with accompanying images drawn by Nell himself, appeared in the *Palm and Pine*, the Haitian-funded paper edited by James Redpath.[174] When Benjamin Butler famously redefined runaways as "contraband" and the debate about emancipation and black soldiers heated up, Nell wrote that black Americans "both as slave and nominally free" were performing the same acts of "prowess, sagacity, and patriotism" that they had in previous wars.[175] As soon as recruiting began for what would become the 54th Massachusetts, Nell linked his annual Crispus Attucks memorials to the cause. He helped to form the new Union Progressive Association, which replaced the defunct Adelphic Union as an agent of "mental and moral improvement."[176] In March 1863, a "detachment" from the black regiment sat on the stage of the Association as Nell exhorted the crowd that "this historic event is invested with special significance this day and hour, when the question is asked on every side, Is the colored man patriotic? Will he fight?"[177]

Starting in late 1862, the passage of the Second Confiscation Act and the Emancipation Proclamation opened the door to black soldiers, who soon began enrolling in a flood of men into the Union Army. Once again, Massachusetts was front and center in the debate. John A. Andrew, the Radical Republican governor, made recruitment of black soldiers a priority—as well as consciously officering the regiment with dedicated abolitionists. Black leaders such as Lewis Hayden and Douglass swung into action, recruiting soldiers from across New England and the North. Even Emerson joined in, speaking before fundraisers in March 1863, where he celebrated that the new black regiments would "elevate this hitherto oppressed race to a position where they may strike for their rights."[178] Emerson provided letters of introduction, helping to obtain officer-ships for men hoping to serve in black regiments.[179] On May 28, 1863, when the first full regiment—the famous 54th Massachusetts—proudly marched down the same street that fugitive slaves had once been dragooned down, abolitionists took it as a particularly providential sign.[180] "The patriotic history of Massachusetts," crowed the New England Anti-Slavery Society, "does not record a more honorable and meritorious act than that of being the first State in the Union to enroll a regiment of colored volunteers."[181] Black abolitionists tasked with re-cruiting soldiers traveled throughout the nation, venturing into occupied territory, as far south as Culpeper, Virginia, as George Downing did in 1864.[182] Perhaps more than anything, their participation in recruitment and other military efforts helped solidify links between individual black abolitionists and Republican Party patrons such as John A. Andrew, Charles Sumner, and George Julian (who wrote letters of recommendation for Downing and Charles Lenox Remond in 1864).[183]

John S. Rock was one of many who threw himself into organizing black troops. Few black people lived the contradictions of the Civil War era as much as Rock. As mentioned, he had been humiliated in Washington, D.C. by the still extant effects of the slave code. Coming home to Boston, he had barely been treated better. In October, he had been randomly and brutally attacked by a stranger on the streets. It was not clear whether the attacker was acting out of racist motivations, had lost his mind, or some combination.[184] "The position of the colored people in Massachusetts," he concluded, "is far from being enviable."[185] He coped with the racism he daily experienced partly through dark humor. One of his funnier stories involved a Southern slaveowner with a Frenchwoman on his arm—presumably a prostitute—that Rock had run into on the streets of Paris. Taking advantage of the fact that Rock, the African American, spoke far better French than the gallivanting Southerner, Rock de-cided to pull a prank, telling the increasingly horrified woman in French that "this gentleman has the intention to kidnap and sell you for a slave in the United States," ruining the amorous slaveowner's night.[186] Rock's story was humorous, of course, but the message of the story had layers, not only illustrating the moral and intellectual degradation of the slave-owning class but also demonstrating how the institution of slavery had ruined the reputation of Americans in the centers of European civilization. In his speeches, he consistently got laughs by reversing racial stereotypes—answering the charge that emancipation would mean sexual amalgamation, for instance, he mocked the assumption that black men were interested in such a union and bemoaned the fact that God had given

Africans "such a beautiful complexion" that white women would throw themselves at them.[187]

The war also brought new opportunities for Rock. He became a coveted
antislavery speaker. In September 1861, he was named justice of the peace, a relatively minor piece of responsibility but one that still recognized the possibility
of black citizenship and democratic leadership.[188] In 1862, he began raising
money for the National Freedman's Association.[189] And by 1863, he was a leader
in the campaign to raise troops for the 54th Massachusetts. He became a forceful advocate for the interests of black troops. Even before the formation of black
regiments, he publicized the possibility that black servants to white officers captured in battle might be sold into Southern slavery.[190] Later, he would be a
forceful advocate of black officers, lobbying the governor of Massachusetts to
ensure the promotion of a sergeant in the 54th Massachusetts.[191] In 1864, Rock
spearheaded a group of Massachusetts African Americans who donated a fresh
new flag to the 5th Colored Heavy Artillery, a regiment based in Natchez, Mississippi. Thanks to a rousing letter he sent along, we have a fascinating sense of
how one black abolitionist—and presumably a number of black soldiers—
conceived of the purpose of the war.

The cornerstone of Rock's message to the black soldiers revolved around the
same romantic appeal to equality and liberty that animated Lincoln, Phillips,
and other white abolitionists. He had told the 1864 Colored Convention that
"our brave men" were simply fighting for "equal opportunities and equal rights."[192]
Writing to the Mississippi soldiers, Rock expanded on this argument, telling the
black soldiers that the regiment's flag would represent "equal rights" and that "we
at the North are contending for, and shall not be satisfied, until we get equal
rights for all." While Rock made liberal use of the rhetoric of patriotism and loyalty (the soldiers were "loving sacrifices on the altar of your country"), he frankly
acknowledged that the country has "so long and so cruelly outraged and oppressed our people." This ambivalence that was inscribed in the black abolitionists' critical patriotism was a constant theme in Rock's public lectures and
speeches. Rock simultaneously believed that "there is a deep and cruel prejudice
lurking in the bosoms of the white people" of the North and that the problem
with American policy was that it was not democratic *enough*.[193] But if there was
an ambivalence to how Rock described the present condition, he saw in the struggle of black soldiers the possibility of breaking these bonds of the past, of what he
alternately called a "living future" and a "glorious future."[194] They were the embodiment of the "*active* idea" for which he had previously called: the possibility of
overcoming given injustice through a willed struggle toward abstract ideals.

But underneath the façade of the patriotic rhetoric, the treatment of the newly recruited black soldiers rankled the Boston black leadership. First there was the issue of black officers. At the meeting of the New England Anti-Slavery Convention, held just days after the 54th marched through Boston, tensions within the black leadership had erupted. Frederick Douglass, speaking first, surprised many by declaring that "I am not in favor of having the *first* black regiments commanded by colored men." Douglass went on to explain that "under oppression and calumny, the negro has lost confidence in himself, and may not do justice to his own powers"[195] (he hoped that later regiments would have black officers). Douglass, uncharacteristically, found himself nearly alone. Others, including George T. Downing, Charles Lenox Remond, and Robert Morris, vehemently disagreed. Morris went so far as to declare that, after learning about the denial of black officers, he was "determined not to lift a finger for that regiment and he had never asked and never would ask any man to enlist in it." Morris was not alone in this sentiment—William Wells Brown, who had been actively recruiting for the regiment, "testified to the difficulty he had found in some recruits, to be commanded wholly by white officers."[196]

The worse betrayal came to light when black soldiers opened their paychecks and realized they were receiving a lower pay than white soldiers. In June 1863, the solicitor of the War Department determined that black soldiers could be paid at the rate of laborers, rather than soldiers, and so were only "entitled to ten dollars per month and one ration; three dollars of which monthly pay may be in clothing."[197] In other words, black soldiers received lower pay than white soldiers *and* were expected to pay $3 a month for their uniforms. Not only was the second-class treatment insulting, but the low pay was especially outrageous because many recruiters had explicitly promised them equal pay.[198] One black soldier—Thomas D. Freeman—wrote to the black lawyer Robert Morris, asking, "Why is it we cannot receive the same rights as White Soldiers, the same Equality as they do." A veteran of Fort Wagner and one of the first black non-commissioned officers, Freeman had only received $50 for thirteen months of service.[199] Since black soldiers had to pay for their uniforms, some of the dead at Fort Wagner actually died in debt to the government.[200]

The War Department bureaucracy was largely to blame. According to one white officer of a black regiment, while "the rank and file were our warm friends," it seemed like "there was scarcely a bureau in Washington, New York, or New Orleans that did not . . . throw some impediment in its way; generally covertly, sometimes openly."[201] The Massachusetts legislature tried to make up the money, voting additional funds to cover the shortfall. The black troops, though, quickly rejected this overture, as that would symbolically acquiesce to their status as laborers rather than soldiers and, in the words of a letter of protest that the black troops sent, create the impression that they were "holding out for *money* and not from *principle*."[202] Even after Attorney General Bates ordered the Army to fix the matter in 1864, the War Department responded with a strange sophistical argument that only retroactively granted equal pay to those soldiers who were free before the start of the war, an omission that left out many soldiers.[203] There was a humorous angle to the whole matter; since their masters were not around to testify against them, this order, intended to prevent ex-slaves from receiving full pay, actually incentivized black soldiers to define "free" in a spiritual, rather than legal, sense. Many former slaves in the 54th Massachusetts could thus take the so-called Quaker Oath that they had "owed no man unrequited labor" in good conscience.[204] After all, in the sight of God, no one, whether enslaved by man's laws or not, owed unpaid labor to another.

After years of exclusion, African Americans were confronted with a series of questions about the nation in which they had finally received official citizenship. Almost as important as the Emancipation Proclamation was the 1862 declaration by Attorney General Edward Bates that African Americans were citizens under the terms of the Constitution, de facto overriding the part of the *Dred Scott* decision that had questioned black citizenship. Citizenship, in theory, implied an equal membership in the nation. "The phrase, 'a citizen of the United States,'" Bates claimed, "means neither more nor less than a member of the nation. And all such are politically and legally equal."[205] Some black intellectuals, such as Douglass, Nell, and Rock, saw a tremendous emancipatory potential in black entry into the American nation. In nineteenth-century thought, nationalism implied, among other things, a process by which local political hierarchies were replaced with a formally equitable political community—the ladder of society replaced with the circle of political equality. To some black activists, it seemed like this was beginning to occur.

At their core, the critique advanced by black skeptics such as Remond was that the two aspects that were supposed to come with citizenship—equality and membership in the nation—were unfulfilled, at least in any comprehensive sense. Unequal pay and unequal access to military promotions—in a war supposedly fought on their behalf—only highlighted the limitations of this new citizenship. Still, even if unfulfilled, the promise of equality and fair treatment was a vast improvement from years earlier, when inequality was openly preached. At a more practical level, the ascendance of the Republican Party brought previously impossible opportunities for some black political leaders. Lewis Hayden was named the messenger for the Secretary of the Commonwealth, a plum piece of patronage that by the 1870s would earn him $600 a year.[206] Hayden was becoming a political powerbroker—in 1862, he even hosted the governor of Massachusetts, John A. Andrew, for Thanksgiving dinner.[207] William C. Nell, more the scholar and less the powerbroker, was named as one of the first black employees of the Boston post office, a position available to the black writer after Charles Sumner's successful bill desegregating the post office.

*　*　*

In 1863, John Rock wrote to his friend Senator Charles Sumner with a strange request.[208] He wanted to be presented to practice before the U.S. Supreme Court.[209] Sumner appears to have demurred at first, skeptical that it could be done. It was not until the long-awaited death of Chief Justice Taney in October 1864 (the chief justice had "earned the gratitude of his country by dying at last," George Templeton Strong quipped) that Sumner thought Rock's request was possible.[210] In December, after the safely antislavery Salmon Chase was sworn in as the new chief justice, Rock had written to Sumner hoping that now "my color will not be a bar to my admission."[211] Sumner was now committed and began badgering the new chief justice to admit Rock. Finally, on January 23, Chase relented—dashing off a brief note in pencil to Sumner that "you can make your motion for Mr. Rock's admission at any time which suits your convenience."[212]

Rock's admission, of course, had symbolic importance because it would allow him to be the first African American lawyer able to argue in front of the Supreme Court. More important, though, was the fact that only citizens were allowed to be a lawyer in the Supreme Court. Admission, therefore, would be a frontal attack on the logic of *Dred Scott* at the site of its very origin, a "great personal favour as well as a great triumph," as Rock described it.[213] Rock's sponsor, Charles Sumner, was aware of the stakes. Writing to Salmon Chase to advocate for Rock, he admitted that "I know not how far the Dred Scott decision may stand in the way" but still believed that Rock's admission was necessary because it would strike a fatal blow against all of the accumulated American prejudice against African Americans. "Street cars would be open afterwards," Sumner declared, a bit optimistically.[214]

Three years earlier, Rock had needed to ask Sumner for a pass, as if he were a slave, to walk freely around Washington, D.C. Now, on February 1, 1865, he was presented to the chief justice of the Supreme Court and took an oath to be admitted to practice. The *New York Tribune* described the scene after Sumner

officially moved to admit Rock: "the grave to bury the Dred Scott decision was
in that one sentence dug. . . . the assenting nod of the great head of the Chief
Justice tumbled in the corse [*sic*] and filled up the pit, and the black counselor of
the Supreme Court got on to it and stamped it down."[215] It was the day after the
House of Representatives had passed the Thirteenth Amendment. The future
must have seemed open and bright. Soon afterward, Rock was invited by congressman John D. Baldwin to the House floor, where, as he reported back, "I
received the Congratulations of several members of that body."[216]

The war was coming to an end. In South Carolina, Union troops were
moving up the coast—in a couple of weeks, black troops led by William Lloyd
Garrison's son would march through Charleston, the heart of the secessionist
South. Lee's troops, stretched thin defending Petersburg, would soon be forced
to abandon Richmond. And in the Senate, Sumner and his allies were moving
on, beginning a furious debate about what the Reconstruction of the Union
would look like.

Slavery was forever abolished. The Fourteenth and Fifteenth Amendments
made strides toward the realization of, respectively, equality and democracy.
Reconstruction, even with all its compromises and inadequacies, would offer
tremendous opportunities to African Americans, both in the South and in the
North. But to a large degree, the fear of black intellectuals such as Rock and
Remond that the transcendent promises of the abolitionist Civil War would
remain unrealized would come true, especially in the dark days of Gilded Age
America. After the fall of Reconstruction, such talk of American dedication to
these abstract values of equality and democracy began to ring hollow, to sound
like mockery to later intellectuals, as a comforting illusion that Americans told
themselves in the era of industrial rapaciousness and Jim Crow cruelty. But the
dreams of John Rock and Wendell Phillips, of Ralph Waldo Emerson and
Charlotte Forten, would linger on, half submerged and forgotten, to accuse
later generations. The stories, of course, of how later generations would take up
the still incomplete project of democracy and equality of the Civil War generation are for other books.

Epilogue

In January 1872, John Mercer Langston was on his way to see Charles Sumner in Washington, D.C. and happened upon the Republican senator breakfasting with Ralph Waldo Emerson.[1] Few Americans had lived the monumental revolution of the Civil War years like Langston. Born a freedman in Virginia, he had attended Oberlin College, worked to protect fugitive slaves, and was now a professor and dean at Howard University, where he led the newly founded law school. Seizing the opportunity to gain a prestigious lecturer for his fledging school, Langston asked Emerson if he would be willing to attend as a "hearer and witness" of some exercises the coming Sunday. Emerson agreed—only to find himself standing the next day before an expectant audience of 150 ("faces all as dark as the night," the *New York Tribune* reporter described it) and giving an extemporaneous lecture to the Howard student body.[2] The Concord sage began slowly—he had not prepared anything and seemed unsure what the audience wanted of him. Emerson's mind was slowing—in a couple of years, he would sometimes forget even his own name. But if he did not have the fluency of previous years, he now had a sort of rough eloquence, as if reducing his philosophy to plain language gave it a rude dignity.

Langston asked him to recommend some books to the audience, and Emerson suggested Gibbon, Boswell, Confucius, Hindu religious texts, Goethe, Burke, and, above all, Shakespeare. But the main theme of his talk was the universality of human dignity and intellectual creativity. "Every mind that comes into the world," he told the audience, "has its own specialty . . . a disposition to attempt something of its own."[3] Emerson's by-now familiar demand that every individual search out their own path and defend themselves from the expectations of a society that would enforce conformity took on a different meaning in front of black students in the era of Reconstruction. All these years later, Emerson was still fascinated by the distinctly human capacity for intellectual rebirth, for eternal inspiration that "there is a thought waking every morning," if we are willing to listen.

Back in New England, black intellectuals continued to engage with Transcendentalism. In 1867, William C. Nell had visited Concord and spent an afternoon with many of the leading lights of Transcendentalism—the still quirky Alcott who was now dreaming of a permanent school of philosophy in Concord; Francis Sanborn, who in eight years' time had gone from plotting revolution to writing hagiographies of the early Transcendentalists; and, of course, Emerson himself. Nell continued to feel close to the Transcendentalists, writing to a friend that he had a "delightful time" at a "Fraternity Picnic" held in Walden Woods.[4] It was a reminder of the prewar years when the black historian had discussed philosophy and politics with famous white Transcendentalists.

But times were changing for Nell, the Transcendentalists, and even his old abolitionist movement. His one-time employer and mentor, William Lloyd Garrison, had retreated into a triumphant retirement, and a new generation of African American leaders was taking over the Boston black community's politics. Increasingly integrated into the Republican Party—which provided a valuable source of patronage and power for the black community but restrained the utopian imagination—Nell's old role as a mediator between white intellectuals and the black masses was decreasingly valuable. A job at the post office, arraigned by Charles Sumner, and a marriage had finally given Nell a taste of the bourgeois respectability his skin color had previously denied him.

The Higher Law did not die, but as Reconstruction gave way to the Gilded Age, it was increasingly submerged under new intellectual and political movements. Nowhere were the changes in white intellectual climate illustrated as well as the Radical Club, founded in 1867 by the triumphant white veterans of the Transcendentalist and abolitionist crusades. It was a veritable who's who of those antebellum radicals who survived the war—Higginson, Alcott, Julia Ward Howe, William I. Bowditch, Wendell Phillips, William Henry Channing, John Weiss, Emerson, and Garrison. White men with, increasingly, white hairs dominated. Discussions vacillated between hardheaded scientific inquiry—evolution was a particularly popular topic to discuss—and mystical self-contemplation. Younger intellectuals—drawn to Darwin and Mill—tended to snicker at the tone of doddering idealism that dominated the discussions of religion or ethics. A family friend of Emerson, a young medical student named William James, scoffed at what he called the weak "esthetic tea" of the Club. He was more drawn to a pretty woman in the audience named Alice Howe Gibbens—whom he would eventually marry—than the graying Transcendentalism of the lectures.[5]

It was not so much that scientific naturalism came to totally dominate the Boston intellectual worldview. Rather, the radical imagination was splitting into two separate and distinct realms: one tough-minded realm that studied society and nature and in which scientific formalism dominated, another tender-minded realm of religious and spiritual questioning where the Transcendentalist impulse held. The Transcendentalist political project, at its antebellum best, had united these realms, applying the numinous abstractions of their thought to concrete political projects. They had sought the face of the Oversoul in the solidarity of socialist utopias, demonstrated their antimaterial selfhood by disobeying the Fugitive Slave Act, and held up an ideal America in order to reveal the flaws in the existing one. But now, as intellectual and political culture shifted toward a celebration of the scientific, the tangible and the knowable, Transcendentalism appeared less and less able to bridge this gap. Correspondingly, it was becoming less relevant to the political climate of the late 1860s and 1870s, more a philosophy of personal reflection and religious obscurantism than a means to criticize the prevailing conditions of society. To Julia Ward Howe, thus, the fatal flaw of the Radical Club was the "intellectual bias" against religious belief and its obsession with ferreting out "superstition and intolerance" in the supernatural worldview.[6]

Ultimately, the same transcendental idealism that served Boston radicals well when they had been embattled outsiders now contributed to an elite self-righteousness and complacency once they were reintegrated into the establishment. Any political idealism has the possibility of sliding into hypocrisy, of becoming nothing but a shallow façade for political cynicism and self-willed ignorance. Ideals that were once aspirations, goals that we seek to enact, can become hypocritical delusions that conceal our interests or biases. The Emersonian spirit of individual becoming and self-development can inspire rebellion among the marginalized but also spiritual pride and self-righteousness among the rich. We can see one particularly depressing example of the irony of idealism in the moral decline of the Pierpont family. John Pierpont had been a radical abolitionist in Boston who wrote antislavery poetry and twice spoke in front of William C. Nell's Adelphic Union. But his grandson and namesake (the abolitionist's daughter married the Hartford banker Junius Morgan) used a similar moralistic attitude and spiritual self-regard not to further human emancipation but to conceal, perhaps even to himself, the Gilded Age inequalities and depredations for which he was, more than anyone, responsible. The Pierponts' descent into self-righteous moral depravity was extreme but not entirely unique. Philosophical idealism, as the erstwhile Radical Club attendee William James noted, can become decadent, self-serving, and egotistical—"sentimental and priggish," evoking little but a spoiled child in "a narrow, close, sick-room air" while pushing away action and practical result.[7]

An empyrean languor was developing, as if the former abolitionists could not be bothered to awake from the lavender-scented pillows of the Oversoul to think about the iron and soot problems of the Gilded Age city. It is notable that the strongest holdout to democratic idealism in Boston, Wendell Phillips, was the abolitionist who, while clearly influenced by Transcendentalist language and thought, had always maintained a more realistic, even pessimistic, sense of human frailty than his colleagues. For others, the healthy optimism that the world could and should conform with one's ideals—what Emerson had once called the "ideal Republic that you announce"—could turn into a world-weary *weltschmerz*, a resignation that humanity's messy realities would always disappoint.

Former abolitionists were slowly moderating their politics. Higginson maintained an optimistic faith in democratic improvement, but the young man who had been a fiery and uncompromising abolitionist was now a serene middle-aged man stroking his sideburns. Higginson's sense of above-the-fray detachment (as when he described Gilded Age politics as "the milder antagonisms of to-day") could sometimes edge into complacent cynicism.[8] By the 1880s, he had returned to the Democratic Party, a move that only shocked those friends of his who were blind enough to think the rival 1880s Republican Party was still a particularly progressive force. James Russell Lowell, now a diplomat for the federal government, gave a rousing and well-circulated defense of democratic idealism. But even the good-natured poet doubted the capacity of the urban immigrant masses for self-government.[9]

One unfortunate consequence of this shift in intellectual culture was that the first interpreters of Transcendentalism tended to depoliticize it. The official taming of Transcendentalism started early. In 1879, seemingly every newspaper in the North sent correspondents to A. Bronson Alcott's short-lived Concord School of Philosophy, nearly all of whom described Alcott, Emerson, and the other elderly Transcendentalists as quaint and harmless proponents of a dreamy idealism engaged in high-minded discussions of religion and the fine arts. The *New York Times* mocked them not as dangerous agitators but as ludicrous visionaries, engaged in inscrutable debates about pretentious nonsense.[10] Oliver Wendell Holmes Sr.'s extraordinarily influential 1884 biography of Emerson, which claimed that he "had never been identified with the abolitionists," stirred up significant opposition from still-living abolitionists (most conspicuously Thomas Wentworth Higginson) but set the tone for later understandings of Emerson and the movement more broadly.[11] Finally, George Santayana cemented the Transcendentalists' reputation as part of the "genteel tradition" in his famous 1911 essay, "The Genteel Tradition in American Philosophy."

But the Higher Law was not dead, even if many in Gilded Age America wished to deny it. Wendell Phillips and Lewis Hayden stayed true to their radical past. Phillips became the prominent link between the antebellum radical impulse and postwar politics. In his new career as a labor activist, he continued to savage the Boston elite (of which some of his abolitionist friends were now members in good standing and which he, having spent his inheritance on a lifetime of activism and charity, was now falling out of) even while maintaining his support for African American rights. When the Paris Commune shook the Atlantic world, Phillips was there to defend the workers. The aging abolitionist even committed the greatest of nineteenth-century heresies by questioning the gold standard. In 1872, he declared "God speed" to Marx's old First International.[12] Increasingly popular among workers and urban artisans, Phillips was tolerated and listened to at the Chestnut Street Radical Club, but the legendary abolitionist's proposals were increasingly answered with patronizing "good-natured laughter, which betrayed no sign of a new convert."[13] Joining Phillips as a prominent class-traitor was the stalwart William Henry Channing, who in 1869 was elected vice president of the Eight Hour League.

But Hayden, more than anyone, kept alive the vision of radical abolitionism in the years after the revolutionary energy of Reconstruction had faded. Like so many, the Civil War had claimed Hayden's son. Perhaps to fight off grief, he had doubled his already indefatigable energies, getting elected to the state General Assembly and leading campaigns to try to protect black Southerners. He poured energy into defending the rights of the black Masons in Boston, helping to spread black lodges throughout the nation.[14] Soon, "Lewis Hayden Lodges," named in honor of his activism, began springing up.[15] In Massachusetts politics, he was the leading voice trying to maintain support for Radical Reconstruction. On March 10, 1871, the veteran abolitionist submitted a petition to the state Senate asking that the representatives in Congress "take some measures to prevent the outrages committed upon loyal citizens in some of the Southern States."[16] Even after the end of Reconstruction, he stayed busy. In 1887, Hayden—his hair grayed after a lifetime of struggle and hardship— embarked on one last crusade. He was the lead signature on a petition campaign to finally achieve the goal that his friend William C. Nell had long fought for: an official recognition of the black revolutionary Crispus Attucks's role in the American Revolution.[17] The campaign was successful, and today—on Boston Commons near the intersection of Tremont and Avery Street—thousands of people walk by the 1889 monument to Attucks, a testimonial to the historical and political vision of a generation of Boston black radicals. Looking at the monument, Hayden declared that "they cannot take from us this record of history showing that . . . we participated in every great movement in the best interests of the country."[18] He died months later.

And so, underneath the tumult of Gilded Age and Progressive politics, even as academic intellectual life moved on to Pragmatism and other ideas, the Higher Law proved hard to kill. Radicals still passed along to each other worn books by Thoreau and speeches by Wendell Phillips. In 1878, the indefatigable Phillips took the train to Terre Haute, Indiana, at the invitation of a young labor organizer just getting started in socialist politics. Decades later, when that man, now the leader of the U.S. Socialist Party, was facing down the censor during World War I, Eugene Debs would look back to this meeting as an example of how the persecuted of one generation become the heroes of another.[19] Trying to Americanize the image of socialism, he would declare the workers' movement to be the logical conclusion of the thought of Emerson, Thoreau, Channing, and Horace Greeley.[20] Around the same time as this meeting between Debs and Phillips, one state over, in Illinois, the grandfatherly A. Bronson Alcott lectured to the Rockford Academy for Women, including a young woman, Jane Addams, who listened to the elderly Transcendentalist "in a state of ecstatic energy."[21] In Yosemite Valley, miles away from Concord, an aging Emerson met a young Scotsman named John Muir who wanted the Transcendentalist's blessing for his environmentalist crusade.[22] In her New York City newsletters, Emma Goldman took to quoting Thoreau and declaring Garrison, Phillips, and Emerson to be originators of her brand of anarchism.[23] Far away, in frozen Russia, Leo Tolstoy, defending his own version of Christian civil disobedience, asked, in bafflement, why Americans, in their mad Gilded Age dash for wealth, had forgotten the legacy of "Garrison, Parker, Emerson, Ballou, and Thoreau."[24] And in London, a young law student from India joined the London Emerson Club, where the future Mahatma gained a lifelong appreciation for the thought of Emerson and may have been introduced, for the first time, to the civil disobedience of Thoreau.

Perhaps our story can end where another begins. One hundred years after the abolitionists' triumph, in 1966, the Georgia legislature tried to prevent the black civil rights activist Julian Bond from taking the seat that he had won because of his opposition to the Vietnam War. Asked to respond, Martin Luther King Jr. gave a sermon on what it meant to be a "non-conformist." King had not yet come out against the Vietnam War himself, but he was clearly thinking about it. In language that Thoreau and Theodore Parker would have approved of, King defended Bond's right to "take a view against majority opinion." And when planning this speech, he found "consolation in the writings of

Emerson, whom he found 'eminently correct' in his defense of non-conformity."[25] It was not the only time that King and other leaders of the civil rights era found solace in the words of American Transcendentalists. In 1962, King wrote of his wonder at having read and reread Thoreau in college. "It goes without saying," King declared, "that the teaching of Thoreau are alive today . . . whether expressed in a sit-in at lunch counters, a freedom ride into Mississippi, a peaceful protests in Albany, Georgia, a bus boycott in Montgomery, Alabama, it is an outgrowth of Thoreau's insistence that evil must be resisted."[26]

It was not just Thoreau who was alive in those protests. Perhaps as the civil rights leader himself was aware, when King quoted Emerson or Thoreau, he was not simply putting to use a philosophy crafted by white intellectuals. Rather, as I hope this book has shown, he was reaching for a Higher Law philosophy that had been shaped and given meaning by thinkers and activists both black and white, famous and forgotten: Thomas Sidney and Alexander Crummell stalking the streets of Manhattan with a Coleridge book under their arms, William Henry Channing preaching solidarity at a socialist commune, William C. Nell organizing in a meeting of a black intellectual club, Theodore Parker thundering at his Boston congregation, Lewis Hayden finding space for yet another fugitive in his cramped house, Daniel Foster pulling his threadbare jacket up against the Kansas winds, Wendell Phillips staring down a hostile crowd to speak the abolition truth, and Charlotte Forten teaching newly freed children the biography of Toussaint L'Ouverture.

NOTES

INTRODUCTION

1. For Douglass's 1844 tour of Massachusetts, see "The Hundred Conventions in Massachusetts," *Liberator*, February 16, 1844. David Blight, *Frederick Douglass: Prophet of Freedom* (New York: Simon & Schuster, 2018), 136.

2. Christopher Clark, *The Communitarian Moment: The Radical Challenge of the Northampton Association* (Amherst: University of Massachusetts Press, 1995), 94. For more on Northampton radicals, see Bruce Laurie, *Rebels in Paradise: Sketches of Northampton Abolitionists* (Amherst: University of Massachusetts Press, 2015).

3. Frederick Douglass, "What I Found at the Northampton Association," in *The History of Florence, Massachusetts, Including a Complete Account of the Northampton Association of Education and Industry*, ed. Charles Sheffield (Florence, MA: Sheffield, 1895), 129–32.

4. Sojourner Truth, *Narrative of Sojourner Truth: A Northern Slave* (Boston: Yerrington and Son, 1850), 120.

5. "From the Clarksonian: Northampton Association of Education and Industry," *Liberator*, May 24, 1844.

6. Alice Eaton McBee, *From Utopia to Florence: The Story of a Transcendentalist Community in Northampton, Mass. 1830–1852* (Philadelphia: Porcupine Press, 1975), 20.

7. See William Adam to Wendell Phillips, June 29, 1841, Houghton Library, Harvard University.

8. Arthur Schlesinger Jr., *The Age of Jackson* (New York: Little, Brown, 1945), 382.

9. Anna Davis Hallowell, ed., *James and Lucretia Mott: Life and Letters* (Boston: Houghton, Mifflin, 1884), 385.

10. "New England Anti-Slavery Convention," *National Anti-Slavery Standard*, June 9, 1855.

11. For instance, Perry Miller's deeply influential 1950 anthology *The Transcendentalists*, which is still in print, contains selections from 107 pieces of writing, not a single one of which concerns slavery. George Hochfield's 1966 *Selected Writings of the American Transcendentalists* contains 49 entries, none of which discusses slavery. As late as 1995, Barbara Packer complained that "in its relentless pursuit of spiritual gain and its corresponding contempt for the world of the Understanding, Transcendentalism was of little immediate use to reformers who wanted to feed the hungry or free the slave." Perry Miller, ed., *The Transcendentalists: An Anthology* (Cambridge, MA: Harvard University Press, 1950); George Hochfield, *Selected Writings of the American Transcendentalists*, 2nd ed. (New Haven, CT: Yale University Press, 2004); Barbara Packer, *The Transcendentalists* (Athens: University of Georgia Press, 2007), 69. In the second edition, Hochfield added a Theodore Parker sermon against slavery, admitting that his earlier edition had been unfair

to leave out abolitionism. Only in 2007 did Philip Gura's excellent *American Transcendentalism* devote significant time to the abolitionism of Parker and others. Philip Gura, *American Transcendentalism: A History* (New York: Hill and Wang, 2007).

12. Thomas Wentworth Higginson, *Part of a Man's Life* (Boston: Houghton and Mifflin, 1906), 14.

13. Herman Melville, *Moby Dick; or, The Whale* (New York: Penguin, 1992), 172–73.

14. George Frederickson, *The Inner Civil War: Northern Intellectuals and the Crisis of the Union* (Urbana: University of Illinois Press, 1965).

15. "From the New England Christian Advocate: Errors of the Abolitionists," *Liberator*, August 27, 1841; "Rev. Nathaniel Colver," *Liberator*, January 29, 1841.

16. "The Transcendental Club and the Dial: A Conversation by A. Bronson Alcott, Boston, Monday Evening, March 23, 1863," *Commonwealth*, April 24, 1863.

17. Important texts on early black intellectual history include Patrick Rael, *Black Identity and Black Protest in the Antebellum North* (Chapel Hill: University of North Carolina Press, 2002); Erica Ball, *To Live an Antislavery Life: Personal Politics and the Antebellum Black Middle Class* (Athens: University of Georgia Press, 2012); Stephen Kantrowitz, *More Than Freedom: Fighting for Black Citizenship in a White Republic, 1829–1889* (New York: Penguin, 2012).

18. Walt Whitman, "Song of the Open Road," in *Leaves of Grass: The Complete 1855 and 1891–92 Editions* (New York: Penguin, 1992), 301.

19. Ralph Waldo Emerson, *Emerson: Essays and Poems* (New York: Library of America, 1996), 259.

20. James Marsh, *Preliminary Essay to* Aids to Reflection*, by Samuel Taylor Coleridge* (Burlington, VT: Chauncey Goodrich, 1840), xl.

21. William C. Nell to Amy Kirby Post, December 9, 1850, quoted in William Cooper Nell, *William Cooper Nell: Nineteenth Century African American Abolitionist, Historian, Integrationist: Selected Writings From 1832–1874*, ed. Dorothy Porter Wesley and Constance Porter Uzelac (Baltimore: Black Classic Press, 2002), 278.

22. James Freeman Clarke, *Nineteenth Century Questions* (New York: Houghton, Mifflin, 1898), 314–15.

23. "Slavery and the North," *National Anti-Slavery Standard*, September 23, 1854.

24. William James, *On Some of Life's Ideals* (New York: Henry Holt, 1899), 38.

25. Frederick Douglass to Ralph Waldo Emerson, February 5, 1850, Ralph Waldo Emerson Papers, Houghton Library, Harvard University.

26. Essential reading on New England abolitionism and the Boston black community includes Kantrowitz, *More Than Freedom*; Christopher Cameron, *To Plead Our Own Cause: African Americans in Massachusetts and the Making of the Antislavery Movement* (Kent, OH: Kent State University Press, 2014); Margot Minardi, *Making Slavery History: Abolitionism and the Politics of Memory in Massachusetts* (New York: Oxford University Press, 2010); Bruce Laurie, *Beyond Garrison: Antislavery and Social Reform* (New York: Cambridge University Press, 2005); James Horton and Lois Horton, *Black Bostonians: Family Life and Community Struggle in the Antebellum North* (New York: Holmes and Meier, 1999); Henry Mayer, *All on Fire: William Lloyd Garrison and the Abolition of Slavery* (New York: Norton, 1998). Recent important historical works on Transcendentalism include Robert Richardson, *Henry Thoreau: A Life of the Mind* (Berkeley: University of California Press, 1988); Robert Richardson, *Emerson: The Mind on Fire* (Berkeley: University of California Press, 1996); Charles Capper, *Margaret Fuller: An American Romantic*, vol. 1: *The Private Years* (New York: Oxford University Press, 1994); Charles Capper, *Margaret Fuller: An American Romantic*, vol. 2: *The Public Years* (New York: Oxford

University Press, 2007); Gura, *American Transcendentalism*; Dean Grodzins, *American Heretic: Theodore Parker and Transcendentalism* (Chapel Hill: University of North Carolina Press, 2002).

27. The best examples of treating the self as both real and a historical artifact are Jerrold Seigel, *The Idea of the Self: Thought and Experience in Western Europe Since the Seventeenth Century* (Cambridge: Cambridge University Press, 2005); Gerald Izenberg, *Impossible Individuality: Romanticism, Revolution, and the Origins of Modern Selfhood, 1787–1802* (Princeton, NJ: Princeton University Press, 1992).

28. Charles Taylor, *Sources of the Self: The Making of Modern Identity* (Cambridge, MA: Harvard University Press, 1989), 27.

29. For a fascinating discussion of how the Revolutionary-era demand that resistance to tyrants is obedience to God counterintuitively encouraged racism by blaming slaves for not rising up, see Francois Furstenberg, *In the Name of the Father: Washington's Legacy, Slavery, and the Making of the Nation* (New York: Penguin, 2006), 187–231.

30. Izenberg, *Impossible Individuality*, 8.

31. Thomas Wentworth Higginson, "The Clergy and Reform: An Essay for Visitation Day," July 16, 1847, Thomas Wentworth Higginson Papers, bMs Am 784 (237), Houghton Library, Harvard University.

32. William James, *Writings: 1878–1899* (New York: Library of America, 1992), 616.

33. Gura, *American Transcendentalism*, 5.

34. Ralph Waldo Emerson, *Selected Journals, 1841–1877* (New York: Library of America, 2010), 2:145.

35. Higginson expressed a similar sense that "it is perilous for a writer to constrict himself to a course of systematic thought, and better to fall back upon nature." Thomas Wentworth Higginson Journals 1849–1851, Thomas Wentworth Higginson Papers, bMS Am 784 (12), Houghton Library, Harvard University.

36. Irving Howe, *The American Newness: Culture and Politics in the Age of Emerson* (Cambridge, MA: Harvard University Press, 1986), 39. James Kloppenberg, for instance, while lauding the forward-looking feminism of Fuller, still doubts whether the Transcendentalist's "romantic longing" could make them efficient practitioners of "everyday political activity." James Kloppenberg, *Toward Democracy: The Struggle for Self-Rule in European and American Thought* (New York: Oxford University Press, 2016), 676.

37. Mary Elizabeth Sargent, ed., *Sketches and Reminiscences of the Radical Club of Chestnut Street* (Boston: Osgood, 1880), 6.

38. Richard Rorty, *Achieving Our Country: Leftist Thought in 20th-Century America* (Cambridge, MA: Harvard University Press, 1999), 35.

39. Emerson, *Essays and Poems*, 265.

40. It was John Hingham, of course, who famously described antebellum thought as marked by its boundlessness. He used the term to describe a culture of democratic expansion and optimism; I am referring more to a style of individual thought. There is a tradition of American political thought—Melville and particularly Reinhold Niebuhr—that has long rejected the ideal of boundless thought, seeing it as a source of demonic pride and arrogance rather than inspiration for social criticism. John Hingham, "From Boundlessness to Consolidation: The Transformation of American Culture, 1848–1860," in *Hanging Together: Unity and Diversity in American Culture*, ed. Carl J. Guarneri (New Haven, CT: Yale University Press, 2001), 149–66.

41. Elizabeth Cady Stanton to Rebecca R. Eyster, May 1, 1847, in Elizabeth Cady Stanton, *Elizabeth Cady Stanton as Revealed in Her Letters, Diary, and Reminiscences* (New York: Harper and Brothers, 1922), 2:15.

42. James Russell Lowell, *Democracy and Other Papers* (Boston: Houghton and Mifflin, 1898), 17.

43. Margaret Fuller, *Woman in the Nineteenth Century* (Mineola, NY: Dover, 1999), 9.

44. On the history of how Transcendentalism has been viewed, with special attention to its politics, see Charles Capper, "'A Little Beyond': The Problem of the Transcendentalist Movement in American History," *Journal of American History* 85, no. 2 (1998): 502–39.

45. Elkins, *Slavery*, 165.

46. Lionel Trilling, *The Liberal Imagination: Essays on Literature and Society* (New York: New York Review Books, 2008), 6–9.

47. Stanley Elkin connected abolitionism to Transcendentalism in a less-known chapter in his famous book *Slavery*. His position was challenged by both Aileen Kraditor and Anne Rose, both of whom disputed his connection between abolitionism and Transcendentalism. Bertram Wyatt-Brown, while acknowledging that abolitionism shared an ethical sensibility with Transcendentalism, still seems to agree with Rose that Transcendentalists themselves had no significant connection to abolitionist activity. Stanley Elkins, *Slavery: A Problem in American Institutional and Intellectual Life*, 2nd ed. (Chicago: University of Chicago Press, 1968), 140–206; Anne Rose, *Transcendentalism as a Social Movement, 1830–1850* (New Haven, CT: Yale University Press, 1981); Aileen Kraditor, *Means and Ends in American Abolitionism: Garrison and His Critics on Strategy and Tactics, 1834–1850* (New York: Pantheon, 1967), 23–26; Bertram Wyatt-Brown, *Yankee Saints and Southern Sinners* (Baton Rouge: Louisiana State University Press, 1985), 13–41.

48. Robert Penn Warren, *The Legacy of the Civil War* (Lincoln: University of Nebraska Press, 1998), 20.

49. The few exceptions tend to ask about Transcendentalism's relationship with the marketplace. See Richard Teichgraeber, *Sublime Thought/Penny Wisdom: Situating Emerson and Thoreau in the American Market* (Baltimore: Johns Hopkins University Press, 1995); Jeffrey Sklansky, *The Soul's Economy: Market Society and Selfhood in American Thought, 1820–1920* (Chapel Hill: University of North Carolina Press, 2002).

50. Len Gougeon, *Virtue's Hero: Emerson, Antislavery and Reform* (Athens: University of Georgia Press, 1990); Elise Lemire, *Black Walden: Slavery and Its Aftermath in Concord, Massachusetts* (Philadelphia: University of Pennsylvania Press, 2009); Sandra Petrulionis, *To Set This World Right: The Antislavery Movement in Thoreau's Concord* (Ithaca, NY: Cornell University Press, 2006). Ethan Kytle's excellent work on the importance of Romanticism addresses the influence of Transcendentalism on the activism of Theodore Parker and Thomas Wentworth Higginson. Ethan Kytle, *Romantic Reformers and the Antislavery Struggle in the Civil War Era* (New York: Cambridge University Press, 2014). Albert von Frank wrote an excellent study of the interaction between Transcendentalism and the attempted rescue of Anthony Burns. Albert von Frank, *The Trials of Anthony Burns: Freedom and Slavery in Emerson's Boston* (Cambridge, MA: Harvard University Press, 1998).

51. Andrew Delbanco, *The War Before the War: Fugitive Slaves and the Struggle for America's Soul from the Revolution to the Civil War* (New York: Penguin, 2018), 6.

52. Philip Gura bemoans the "bankruptcy of an American liberalism with which so many Americans met the nation's post-1837 crises," rooted in self-reliance and individualist moral perfectionism rather than institutional and social analysis. Philip Gura, *Man's Better Angels: Romantic Reformers and the Coming of the Civil War* (Cambridge, MA: Harvard University Press, 2017), 3.

53. John Burt, *Lincoln's Tragic Pragmatism: Lincoln, Douglas, and Moral Conflict* (Cambridge, MA: Belknap, 2013), 452.

54. In Louis Menand's widely popular *Metaphysical Club*, the abolitionists and Transcendentalists are largely portrayed as irresponsible and lacking the philosophical and moral maturity of the Pragmatists. Louis Menand, *The Metaphysical Club: A Story of Ideas in America* (New York: Farrar, Straus, and Giroux, 2001).

55. Wendell Phillips, *Speeches, Lectures, and Letters* (Boston: James Redpath, 1863), 100, 104, 106, 134.

56. Phillips, *Speeches, Lectures, and Letters*, 127.

57. Many historians agree with Phillips's argument that, in the words of Manisha Sinha, "Antislavery politics, or free soilism, grew out of abolition." See Manisha Sinha, *The Slave's Cause: A History of Abolition* (New Haven, CT: Yale University Press, 2016), 461. Other historians who make this case include James Brewer Stewart, *Abolitionist Politics and the Coming of the Civil War* (Amherst: University of Massachusetts Press, 2008); James Oakes, *The Radical and the Republican: Frederick Douglass, Abraham Lincoln, and the Triumph of Antislavery Politics* (New York: Norton, 2007); and Eric Foner, *The Fiery Trial: Abraham Lincoln and American Slavery* (Norton: New York, 2010).

58. "Speech of Wendell Phillips at the Cooper Institute, New York, on Tuesday Evening, December 22, 1863, On President Lincoln's Message and Proclamation," *Commonwealth*, January 1, 1864.

59. Max Weber, *Charisma and Disenchantment: The Vocation Lectures*, ed. Paul Reitter and Chad Wellmon (New York: New York Review of Books, 2020), 115.

CHAPTER 1

1. Alexander Crummell, *Africa and America: Addresses and Discourses* (Springfield, MA: Willey, 1891), 300.

2. W. E. B. Du Bois, *The Souls of Black Folk* (New York: Norton, 1999), 138.

3. Alexander Crummell, "The Necessities and Advantages of Education Considered in Relation to Colored Men," Alexander Crummell Papers, Schomburg Library, New York, NY.

4. Crummell, "Necessities and Advantages," 23.

5. Crummell, "Necessities and Advantages," 29.

6. Sinha, *The Slave's Cause*, 130.

7. Dorothy B. Porter, "The Organized Educational Activities of Negro Literary Societies, 1828–1846," *Journal of Negro Education* 5, no. 4 (October 1936): 555–76.

8. "Literary Societies," *Colored American*, October 5, 1839.

9. "The Phoenixonian Society," *Colored American*, July 13, 1839.

10. "San Francisco Literary Institute," *Pacific Appeal*, April 5, 1862.

11. Elizabeth McHenry, "'Dreaded Eloquence': The Origins and Rise of African American Literary Societies and Libraries," *Harvard Library Bulletin* 6, no. 2 (Summer 1995): 36.

12. Erica Dunbar, *A Fragile Freedom: African-American Women and Emancipation in the Antebellum City* (New Haven, CT: Yale University Press, 2008), 96–119.

13. "Boston Mutual Lyceum," *Liberator*, July 20, 1833; "Take Notice," *Liberator*, November 9, 1833.

14. "Caleb Stetson and John T. Sargent," *North Star*, March 17, 1848.

15. William C. Nell, *William Cooper Nell: Nineteenth-Century African American Abolitionist, Historian, Integrationist: Selected Writings from 1832–1874*, ed. Dorothy Porter Wesley and Constance Porter Uzelac (Baltimore: Black Classic Press, 2002), 221.

16. See Len Gougeon, "Emerson and the New Bedford Affair," *Studies in the American Renaissance* (1981): 257–64.

17. "Editorial Correspondence," *Provincial Freeman*, June 10, 1854.

18. Dorothy Porter, ed., *Early Negro Writing 1760–1837* (Boston: Beacon, 1971), 110.

19. On the Scottish Common Sense School in America, see Terrence Martin, *The Instructed Vision: Scottish Common Sense Philosophy and the Origins of American Fiction* (Bloomington: Indiana University Press, 1961); David Walker Howe, *The Unitarian Conscience: Harvard Moral Philosophy, 1805–1861* (Cambridge, MA: Harvard University Press, 1970).

20. Thomas Carlyle, *A Carlyle Reader*, ed. G. B. Tennyson (Acton, MA: Copley, 1999), 10.

21. James Kloppenberg, *Toward Democracy: The Struggle for Self-Rule in European and American Thought* (New York: Oxford University Press, 2016), 373. Daniel Walker Howe suggests that much of the Whig elite's support of the more moderate reform movements was rooted in Scottish faculty psychology. Daniel Walker Howe, *Making the American Self: Jonathan Edwards to Abraham Lincoln* (New York: Oxford University Press, 1997).

22. Gary Wills, *Inventing America: Jefferson's Declaration of Independence* (New York: Houghton Mifflin, 2002).

23. See Staughton Lynd, *Intellectual Origins of American Radicalism*, new ed. (New York: Cambridge University Press, 2009), 17–66.

24. Immanuel Kant, *Prolegomena to Any Future Metaphysics*, trans. James W. Ellington (Indianapolis, IN: Hackett, 2001), 4.

25. See Henry Steele Commager, "The Dilemma of Theodore Parker," *New England Quarterly* 6, no. 2 (June 1933): 257–77.

26. Theodore Parker, *The World of Matter and the Spirit of Man: Latest Discourses of Religion* (Boston: American Unitarian Association), 15–17.

27. See Frederick Henry Hedge, "Coleridge's Literary Character," *Christian Examiner* 14 (March 1833): 108–29.

28. The best recent histories of the rise of Transcendentalism are Packer, *The Transcendentalists* and Gura, *American Transcendentalism*.

29. Established by "the leading colored men in New York" in 1831. See Crummell, *Africa and America*, 278.

30. Crummell, *Africa and America*, 280.

31. This moment would be retold in Du Bois, *Souls of Black Folk*, 136.

32. Samuel Ringgold Ward, *Autobiography of A Fugitive Negro: His Anti-Slavery Labours in the United States, Canada, and England* (London: John Snow, 1855), 58.

33. Milton Sernett, *Abolition's Axe: Beriah Green, Oneida Institute, and the Black Freedom Struggle* (Syracuse, NY: Syracuse University Press, 1986), 69, 139.

34. Elizabeth McHenry, *Forgotten Readers: Recovering the Lost History of African-American Literary Societies* (Durham, NC: Duke University Press, 2002), 52–55.

35. See "Constitution of the Phoenix Society of New York," *New York Spectator*, August 8, 1833.

36. "To S.E. Sewall," *Liberator*, August 24, 1833.

37. "Gratifying Donation," *Liberator*, September 28, 1833.

38. "Phoenixonian Literary Society," *Colored American*, July 8, 1837; "Phoenixonian Society," *Colored American*, July 13, 1839; Crummell, *Africa and America*, 300.

39. Crummell, *Africa and America*, 300.

40. "For the Emancipator," *Emancipator*, September 26, 1839.

41. "To the Public," *Colored American*, September 23, 1837.

42. "Practical Anti-Slavery," *Liberator*, July 25, 1835.

43. "Right of Suffrage," *Colored American*, March 3, 1838.

44. "Mr. Editor," *Colored American*, April 12, 1838.

45. "New York Select Academy," *Colored American*, November 16, 1839; Crummell, *Africa and America*, 278.

46. Sernett, *Abolition's Axe*, 56.

47. Ward, *Autobiography of a Fugitive Negro*, 87–88.

48. Alexander Crummell, "Eulogium on the Life and Character of Thomas Sipkins Sidney," July 4, 1840, Black Abolitionist Papers, Reel 3, no. 478; Crummell, *Africa and America*, 278.

49. "Thomas Sipkins Sidney," *Colored American*, June 20, 1840. Of course, it is difficult to tell how much of Crummell's description of Sidney—the main source for Sidney's thought—was Crummell's projection and how much was real.

50. Crummell, "Eulogium on the Life and Character of Thomas Sipkins Sidney."

51. Crummell, "Eulogium on the Life and Character of Thomas Sipkins Sidney."

52. Some examples: "Epigram, by S.T. Coleridge," *Freedom's Journal*, February 7, 1829; "Extract from 'Religious Musings,'" *Colored American*, December 7, 1839; perhaps most interesting was an article entitled "Africa," which used a selection from the British Romantic to make the case for the civilized nature of Africans. "Africa," *Colored American*, June 9, 1838.

53. Frederick Douglass, *Autobiographies* (New York: Library of America, 1996), 103. On Douglass as a Romantic strongly shaped by American Transcendentalism, see Bill E. Lawson, "Douglass Among the Romantics," in *The Cambridge Companion to Frederick Douglas*, ed. Maurice S. Lee (New York: Cambridge University Press, 2009), 118–31.

54. According to Donald Yacovone, May was responsible for the first publication of Coleridge's poem, "Hymn Before Sunrise, in the Vale of Chamouni," in the United States. See Donald Yacovone, *Samuel Joseph May and the Dilemmas of the Liberal Persuasion, 1797–1871* (Philadelphia: Temple University Press, 1991), 28.

55. James Marsh, introduction to *Aids to Reflection*, by Samuel Taylor Coleridge (Burlington, VT: Chauncey Goodrich, 1840), xxxi.

56. There were at least five entries in this series. "The Reflector—No. 1," *Colored American*, September 28, 1839; "The Reflector—No. 2," *Colored American*, October 12, 1839; "The Reflector—No. 3," *Colored American*, November 2, 1839; "The Reflector—No. 4," *Colored American*, November 16, 1839; "The Reflector—No. V," *Colored American*, March 28, 1840.

57. "The Reflector—No. 1," *Colored American*, September 28, 1839.

58. "The Reflector—No. 1," *Colored American*, September 28, 1839.

59. "The Reflector—No. 4," *Colored American*, November 16, 1839.

60. "The Reflector—No. 5," *Colored American*, March 28, 1840.

61. Henry David Thoreau to Helen Louisa Thoreau, October 6, 1838, in Robert Hudspeth, ed., *The Correspondence of Henry David Thoreau*, vol. 1: *1834–1848* (Princeton, NJ: Princeton University Press, 2013), 49.

62. Emerson, *Emerson: Essays and Poems*, 198.

63. Lydia Maria Child, *The Letters of Lydia Maria Child* (Boston: Houghton and Mifflin, 1882), 169.

64. Julia Ward Howe, "The Results of Kantian Philosophy," *Journal of Speculative Philosophy* 15, no. 3 (July 1881): 274–92.

65. Franklin Sanborn, "The Kant Centennial at Concord," *Journal of Speculative Philosophy* 15, no. 3 (July 1881): 303.

66. Thomas Wentworth Higginson, *Cheerful Yesterdays* (Boston: Houghton, Mifflin 1898), 105.

67. Coleridge describes his mixture of Kantianism with Christianity in his memoirs, the famous *Biographia Literaria*. See Samuel Taylor Coleridge, *The Major Works Including Biographia Literaria* (New York: Oxford University Press, 2008), 231–33.

68. Eugene Lynch, *Address Delivered Before the Philomathean Society of Mount Saint Mary's College* (Baltimore: John Murphy, 1840), 6.

69. Francis Lieber, *Manual of Political Ethics: Designed Chiefly for the Use of Colleges and Students at Law* (Boston: Little, Brown, 1838).

70. "Personal Identity," *Liberia Herald*, May 1837.

71. Thomas Carlyle, *A Carlyle Reader*, ed. G. B. Tennyson (Acton, MA: Copley, 1999), 8.

72. Emerson, *Emerson: Essays and Poems*, 884.

73. Emerson, *Emerson: Essays and Poems*, 193.

74. Crummell, *Africa and America*, 284.

75. Alexander Crummell, *The Man; the Hero; the Christian! A Eulogium on the Life and Character of Thomas Clarkson: Delivered in New York, Dec. 1846* (London: Houlston and Stoneman, 1849), 59–60.

76. Quoted in Gregory U. Rigsby, *Alexander Crummell: Pioneer in Nineteenth-Century Pan-African Thought* (New York: Greenwood, 1987), 31.

77. Emerson, *Essays and Poems*, 262.

78. Ronald A. Bosco and Joel Myerson, eds., *The Later Lectures of Ralph Waldo Emerson, 1843–1871*, vol. 2: *1855–1871* (Athens: University of Georgia Press, 2001), 355.

79. Carlos Baker, *Emerson Among the Eccentrics: A Group Portrait* (New York: Viking, 1996), 33.

80. Emerson, *Essays and Poems*, 262; Crummell, *The Man; the Hero; the Christian*, 60.

81. Emerson, *Essays and Poems*, 196.

82. Jerrold Seigel, *The Idea of the Self: Thought and Experience in Western Europe Since the Seventeenth Century* (New York: Cambridge University Press, 2005), 444.

83. Seigel, *The Idea of the Self*, 452; Coleridge, *Major Works*, 283.

84. Henry David Thoreau, *A Week on the Concord and Merrimack Rivers* (Princeton, NJ: University of Princeton Press, 2004), 329.

85. Following Transcendentalist custom, I will capitalize these words when I use them to refer to the specific meaning given by Transcendentalist literature.

86. Immanuel Kant, *Groundwork for the Metaphysics of Morals*, trans. Mary Gregor (New York: Cambridge University Press, 1998), 57.

87. See, for instance, Herbert Marcuse, *Reason and Revolution: Hegel and the Rise of Social Theory* (Boston: Beacon, 1941), 43–45; see also Charles Taylor, *Hegel* (New York: Cambridge University Press, 1975), 116.

88. For a full description of Emerson's understanding of Reason and intuition, and for the influence that Coleridge and Wordsworth had over the Transcendentalist, see Patrick J. Keane, *Emerson, Romanticism, and Intuitive Reason: The Transatlantic "Light of All Our Day"* (Columbia: University of Missouri Press, 2005).

89. Quoted in Baker, *Emerson Among the Eccentrics*, 33.

90. Quoted in Baker, *Emerson Among the Eccentrics*, 33.

91. Baker, *Emerson Among the Eccentrics*, 33.

92. Ronald A. Bosco and Joel Myerson, eds., *The Later Lectures of Ralph Waldo Emerson, 1843–1871*, vol. 2: *1855–1871* (Athens: University of Georgia Press, 2001), 280.

93. Emerson, *Essays and Poems*, 80.

94. Paul Gilroy, *The Black Atlantic: Modernity and Double Consciousness* (Cambridge, MA: Harvard University Press, 1993), 97.

95. Caryn Cossé Bell, *Revolution, Romanticism, and the Afro-Creole Protest Tradition in Louisiana, 1718–1868* (Baton Rouge: Louisiana State University Press, 1997), 104.

96. "Mulatto Literature," *Pennsylvania Freeman*, September 15, 1853.

97. Patrick Bellegarde-Smith, "Haitian Social Thought in the Nineteenth Century: Class Formation and Westernization," *Caribbean Studies* 20, no. 1 (March 1980): 19–20.

98. Caryn Cossé Bell describes the New Orleans biracial journal *L'Album Littéraire* as containing "German historicism, the notion of the artist as a seer, the use of artistic media to evoke compassion for victims of injustice, and other aspects of literary Romanticism." Bell, *Revolution, Romanticism*, 105.

99. Wilson Jeremiah Moses, *Alexander Crummell: A Study of Civilization and Discontent* (New York: Oxford University Press, 1989), 30.

100. Alexander Crummell, *Jubilate: 1844–1894, The Shades and the Lights of a Fifty Years Ministry, A Sermon by Alex. Crummell, Rector* (Washington, DC: R. L. Pendleton, 1894), 14.

101. Rev. William Emerson was a member of the Sub-Committee on the African School that, in 1800, first created the African School in the first place. See William Crowell et al., *City Document-No.23: Report to the Primary School Committee, June 15, 1846 on the Petition of Sundry Colored Persons* (Boston: J. H. Eastburn, 1846), 16.

102. "Adelphic Union Lectures," *Liberator*, March 6, 1840.

103. "Formation of a Literary and Scientific Society," *Liberator*, January 2, 1837.

104. See "Notice," *Liberator*, April 30, 1836.

105. "Adelphic Union," *Liberator*, May 11, 1838; for instance, they sought donors by advertising in the pages of New York's *Colored American*. "Call to the Benevolent," *Colored American*, November 20, 1841.

106. "Notice," *Liberator*, January 2, 1837. Introductory lectures became traditional. Often, it seems, their topic was exhortatory and inspirational rather than specific to any topic or theme.

107. Edmund Quincy, *Introductory Lecture Delivered Before the Adelphic Union* (Boston: Isaac Knapp, 1839).

108. "Notice," *Liberator*, March 11, 1837; "Notice," *Liberator*, March 16, 1838. "Adelphic Union Lectures," *Liberator*, November 8, 1839.

109. "Adelphic Union," *Liberator*, January 12, 1844.

110. "Adelphic Union Library Association," *Liberator*, November 14, 1845.

111. "Adelphic Union Lectures," *Liberator*, March 30, 1838; this is likely the J. Joseph Fatal who appears in the 1850 census as a laborer living at 2 Southac Street.

112. William C. Nell to Robert Morris Jr., March 14, 1845, Charles Chapman Papers, Moorland-Spingarn Research Center, Howard University.

113. Theodore Parker, *The Life and Correspondence of Theodore Parker*, ed. John Weiss (New York: Appleton, 1864), 1:35.

114. See "Adelphic Union Library Association: List of Officers for the Ensuing Year," *Liberator*, October 11, 1844; "Adelphic Union Library Association," *Liberator*, November 1, 1844.

115. William C. Nell to Wendell Phillips, August 28, 1843, Wendell Phillips Papers, Houghton Library, Harvard University.

116. William C. Nell to Charles Sumner, December 29, 1845, Charles Sumner Papers, Houghton Library, Harvard University.

117. The right to petition was important because the lecture was given during the fight over the "Gag Rule." Charles Sumner, "On the Constitution Delivered Before the Adelphi [*sic*] Society of Colored People in the Winter of 1837," Charles Sumner Papers, Houghton Library, Harvard University.

118. *Liberator*, February 4, 1837, and January 28, 1837.

119. "Formation of a Literary and Scientific Society," *Liberator*, January 2, 1837.

120. "The Lecture of Wendell Phillips," *Liberator*, January 21, 1837.

121. "Adelphic Union," *Liberator*, November 14, 1845; "Adelphic Union Library Association," *Liberator*, January 24, 1845.

122. William C. Nell to Maria Weston Chapman, November 5, 1839, Black Abolitionist Papers, reel 2, no. 14, New York Public Library.

123. Quincy, *Introductory Lecture Delivered Before the Adelphic Union*, 3.

124. Quoted in Mia Bay, *The White Image in the Black Mind: African-American Ideas About White People* (New York: Oxford University Press, 2000), 43.

125. Henry David Thoreau, *The Journal: 1837–1861* (New York: New York Review Books, 2009), 259, 178.

126. Patrick Rael, "A Common Nature: African-American Responses to Racial Science from the Revolution to the Civil War," in *Prophets of Protest: Reconsidering the History of American Abolitionism*, ed. Timothy Patrick McCarthy and John Stauffer (New York: New Press, 2006), 184.

127. "Adelphic Union Lectures," *Liberator*, March 6, 1840.

128. William C. Nell, "A Means of Elevation," *North Star*, April 27, 1849.

129. Charles Follen, *Between Natives and Foreigners: Selected Writings of Karl/Charles Follen (1796–1840)*, ed. Frank Mehring (New York: Peter Lang, 2007), xxix–xxxix.

130. Mayer, *All on Fire*, 322.

131. See the chapter on "The Self" in James's *Principles of Psychology*. William James, *Writings: 1878–1899* (New York: Library of America, 1992), 174–209. Though it should be noted that James rejected the association of the Transcendental ego with free will.

132. Henry David Thoreau, *Walden* (Princeton, NJ: Princeton University Press, 2004), 134–35.

133. Alexander Crummell, "Sermon 79: Religion in the Life," Alexander Crummell Papers, Schomburg Library, New York.

134. For an analysis of the troubled relationship of self to soul in Whitman, see Wilfred McClay, *The Masterless: Self and Society in Modern America* (Chapel Hill: University of North Carolina Press, 1994), 63–69.

135. Emerson, *Essays and Poems*, 480.

136. Bell Gale Chevigny, ed., *The Woman and the Myth: Margaret Fuller's Life and Writings* (Boston: Northeastern University Press, 1994), 170.

137. This language, if not its philosophical content, was inspired by Hannah Arendt's description of the faculty of judgment. See Hannah Arendt, *The Life of the Mind* (New York: Harcourt, 1978).

138. Emerson, *Essays and Poems*, 385.

139. Thoreau, *The Journal*, 258–59.

140. Ryan Schneider, *The Public Intellectualism of Ralph Waldo Emerson and W. E. B. Du Bois: Emotional Dimensions of Race and Reform* (New York: Palgrave Macmillan, 2010); Bruce Dickson Jr., "W. E. B. Du Bois and the Idea of Double Consciousness," *American Literature* 64, no. 2 (June 1992): 299–309.

141. Chevigny, *The Woman and the Myth*, 184.

142. Emerson, *Essays and Poems*, 174.

143. "Consolation for Reformers," *North Star*, June 23, 1848.

144. "The Boston Massacre, March 5, 1770, Commemorative Festival in Faneuil Hall," *Liberator*, March 12, 1858.

145. See Dean Grodzins, "Theodore Parker and the 28th Congregational Society: The Reform Church and the Spirituality of Reformers in Boston, 1845–1859," in *Transient and Permanent: The Transcendentalist Movement and Its Contexts*, ed. Charles Capper and Conrad Wright (Boston: Massachusetts Historical Society, 2000), 73. In a typical scene, Nell reported to his friend the Quaker reformer Amy Post that "yesterday Lewis Hayden and my Sister Mrs. Gray with little Ira accompanied us to hear Theodore Parker." William C. Nell to Amy Kirby Post, July 15, 1850. See Nell, *William Cooper Nell*, 267.

146. Nell definitely attended on January 27, 1851, as his name was recorded in the books. He also may have attended on January 20, 1851, depending on interpretations of the January 29 letter. *A. Bronson Alcott, Notes on Conversations, 1848–1875*, ed. Karen English (Teaneck, NJ: Fairleigh Dickinson University Press, 2007), 142. Also see Nell, *William Cooper Nell*, 281.

147. "Letter from William C. Nell," *Liberator*, March 5, 1852.

148. William C. Nell, *The Colored Patriots of the American Revolution*, 2nd ed. (Boston: Robert Wallcut, 1855), 114.

149. "Heralds of Freedom," *Liberator*, January 9, 1857.

150. Kathryn Grover, *The Fugitive's Gibraltar: Escaping Slaves and Abolitionism in New Bedford, Massachusetts* (Amherst: University of Massachusetts Press, 2001), 170–74.

151. William Wells Brown, *The Black Man: His Antecedents, His Genius, and His Achievements* (Boston: James Redpath, 1863), 91.

152. "Communications," *North Star*, January 5, 1849; Sinha, *The Slave's Cause*, 327.

153. Peter Wirzbicki, "'The Light of Knowledge Follows the Impulse of Revolutions': The Haitian Influence on Antebellum Black Ideas of Elevation and Education," *Slavery and Abolition*, June 2015, 275–97.

154. Hilton is quoted in Louis Masur, *Rites of Execution: Capital Punishment and the Transformation of American Culture, 1776–1865* (New York: Oxford University Press, 1989), 17.

155. See, for instance, "Address: Delivered in the Colored Congregational Church. Hartford Conn., August 1, 1839, by Amos G. Beman, Pastor of the Colored Congregational Church in New Haven," *Emancipator*, November 7, 1839.

156. "The Self Elevator," *Self Elevator*, March 30, 1853.

157. "Your isolation must not be mechanical," Emerson wrote, "but spiritual, that is, must be elevation." Emerson, *Essays and Poems*, 273.

158. Henry Clapp Jr., *The Pioneer: or Leaves from an Editor's Portfolio* (Lynn, MA: J. B. Tolman, 1846), 82.

159. "What Are the Colored People Doing for Themselves," *North Star*, July 14, 1848.

160. "American Slavery," *Voice of the Fugitive*, August 13, 1851.

161. See Alexander Crummell, *The Future of Africa: Being Addresses, Sermons, Etc. Delivered in the Republic of Liberia*, 2nd ed. (New York: Scribner, 1862), 54, 96, 99, 134, 167.

162. "Rev. Sella Martin," *New Orleans Tribune*, July 9, 1865.

163. John Mercer Langston, *From the Virginia Plantation to the National Capitol or, the First and Only Negro Representative in Congress from the Old Dominion* (Hartford, CT: American Publishing Company, 1894).

164. "Equal School Rights," *Liberator*, February 8, 1850.

165. For more on Forten, see Lisa A. Long, "Charlotte Forten's Civil War Journals and the Quest for 'Genius, Beauty, and Deathless Fame,'" *Legacy* 16, no. 1 (1999): 37–48.

166. For a speakers' list of the Salem Lyceum, see *The Massachusetts Lyceum During the American Renaissance: Materials for the Study of the Oral Tradition in American Letters: Emerson, Thoreau, Hawthorne and Other New-England Lecturers*, ed. Kenneth Walter Cameron (Hartford, CT: Transcendental Books, 1969), 17–21.

167. Charlotte Forten Grimké, *The Journals of Charlotte Forten Grimké*, ed. Brenda Stevenson (New York: Oxford University Press, 1988), 188, 187, 274 (February 1, 1857; January 31, 1857; December 27, 1857).

168. Grimké, *Journals of Charlotte Forten Grimké*. She mentions lectures on pages 130, 147, 191, 278, and 353 and reading on pages 164, 266, 284, 447, 499, and 501 (March 14, 1855; December 25, 1855; February 11, 1857; January 20, 1858; January 28, 1859; September 7, 1856; November 15, 1857; February 4, 1858; February 8, 1863; July 26, 1863; August 1, 1863). For more on Forten's appreciation of Emerson, see Lawrence Buell, *Emerson* (Cambridge, MA: Belknap, 2003), 147–48.

169. Charlotte Forten Grimké to Wendell Phillips, October 2, 1867, Wendell Phillips Papers, Houghton Library, Harvard University.

170. Charlotte Forten, "Valedictory Poem," *Salem Register*, July 28, 1856.

171. Janet Carey Eldred and Peter Mortensen, *Imagining Rhetoric: Composing Women of the Early United States* (Pittsburgh, PA: University of Pittsburgh Press, 2002), 191.

172. Grimké, *Journals of Charlotte Forten Grimké*, 66 (June 4, 1854).

173. Charlotte Forten, "Interesting Letter from Miss Charlotte L. Forten," *Liberator*, December 19, 1862.

174. Leo Marx, *The Machine in the Garden: Technology and the Pastoral Ideal in America* (New York: Oxford University Press, 2000), 23.

175. Smith referred to "Bersekirs," meaning Germanic people, claiming that he "borrowed the name from Mr. Emerson." James McCune Smith, "Freedom and Slavery for Afric-Americans," *National Anti-Slavery Standard*, February 8, 1844. Smith was most likely reading *The American Scholar*, where Emerson writes, "but out of unhandselled savage nature, out of terrible Druids and Bersekirs, come at last Alfred and Shakespeare." For the original quote, see Emerson, *Essays and Poems*, 62.

176. H. Ford Douglass, "Speech of H. Ford Douglass, at the Celebration of the First of August at Abington," *Liberator*, August 17, 1860.

177. "Army Correspondence," *Weekly Anglo-African*, February 15, 1862.

178. For more on Douglass and Romanticism/Transcendentalism, see Ethan J. Kytle, *Romantic Reformers and the Antislavery Struggle in the Civil War Era* (New York: Cambridge University Press, 2014), 88.

179. Edward Wilmot Blyden, *Liberia's Offering: Being Addresses, Sermons, etc.* (New York: John Gray, 1862), 82.

180. Buell, *Emerson*, 255–60.

181. "Speech by R.W. Emerson," *Boston Courier*, July 29, 1845, in Robert Morris Papers, Boston Athenaeum.

182. Ednah Dow Cheney, "Reminiscences," in *Concord Lectures on Philosophy: Comprising Outlines of All the Lectures at the Concord Summer School of Philosophy in 1882*, ed. Raymond L. Bridgman (Cambridge, MA: Moses King, 1882), 73.

183. "The Boston Telegraph," *Frederick Douglass' Paper*, February 23, 1855.

184. "Nature," *North Star*, February 25, 1848.

185. Frederick Douglass to Ralph Waldo Emerson, February 5, 1850, Ralph Waldo Emerson Papers, Houghton Library, Harvard University.

186. See Hugh Egan, "'On Freedom'": Emerson, Douglass, and the Self-Reliant Slave," *ESQ: A Journal of the American Renaissance* 60, no. 2 (2014): 183.

187. "The Lecture of Ralph Waldo Emerson," *Frederick Douglass' Paper*, March 2, 1855. Some other occasions in which Douglass's paper—either the *North Star* or *Frederick Douglass' Paper*—reported on Emerson include January 21, 1848 (a description of an Emerson lecture in England); August 21, 1848 (reportage on Emerson's doings in England); February 16, 1849 (review of a lecture Emerson gave in Boston); April 6, 1849 (a brief quotation from Emerson's *The Young American*); February 16, 1855 (a brief selection from Emerson's lecture); and February 23, 1855 (brief defense of Emerson's abolitionist credentials). See "Emerson in England," *North Star*, January 21, 1848; "Mr. Emerson's Lectures," *North Star*, August 21, 1848; "Mr. Emerson on England," *North Star*, February 16, 1849; "The Influence of Trade," *North Star*, April 6, 1849; "Ralph Waldo Emerson on Parties and Trade," *Frederick Douglass' Paper*, February 16, 1855; "The Boston Telegraph," *Frederick Douglass' Paper*, February 23, 1855.

188. "Emerson on English Character," *New Orleans Daily Creole*, August 30, 1856.

189. "Battle of the Ants," *New Orleans Daily Creole*, August 6, 1856.

190. "Notice," *Liberator*, October 31, 1845.

191. "Equal Rights Meeting," *Liberator*, January 8, 1850.

CHAPTER 2

1. Harriet Beecher Stowe, *Key to Uncle Tom's Cabin* (Boston: John P. Jewett, 1853), 155.

2. Kantrowitz, *More Than Freedom*, 87–92. Clay, it is true, denied the mistreatment. See Sinha, *The Slave's Cause*, 405.

3. Moncure Daniel Conway, *Autobiography: Memories and Experiences* (New York: Negro University Press, 1964), 1:82.

4. Calvin Fairbank, *Rev Calvin Fairbank During Slavery Times: How He 'Fought the Good Fight' to Prepare 'The Way'* (Chicago: R. R. McCabe, 1890), 46.

5. James Freeman Clarke to Theodore Parker, December 4, 1845, James Freeman Clarke Papers, Houghton Library, Harvard University.

6. James Freeman Clarke to Lewis Hayden, February 9, 1887, Charles Chapman Papers, Moorland-Spingarn Research Center, Howard University.

7. See, for example, Lewis Hayden to James Freeman Clarke, March 20, 1887, James Freeman Clarke Papers, Houghton Library, Harvard University.

8. "First of August in Concord," *Liberator*, August 7, 1846.

9. See Randell Conrad, "Realizing Resistance: Thoreau and the First of August, 1846 at Walden," *Concord Saunterer* 12–13 (2004–5): 164–93.

10. "First of August in Concord," *Liberator*, August 7, 1846.

11. Thomas Wentworth Higginson, *Part of a Man's Life* (Boston: Houghton and Mifflin, 1906), 14.

12. Andrew Delbanco includes Emerson, though not Thoreau, on his list of white authors who were "amazingly adept at averting their eyes" from slavery. I, obviously, disagree with this. Delbanco, *War Before the War*, 158.

13. John Quincy Adams, *Memoirs of John Quincy Adams, Comprising Portions of His Diary from 1795 to 1848*, ed. Charles Francis Adams (Philadelphia: Lippincott, 1876), 10:344–45.

14. "Old American Anti-Slavery Society," *Liberator*, June 17, 1842.

15. "From the Providence Journals: The Anti-Slavery Convention," *Liberator*, May 6, 1859.

16. Stowe, *Key to Uncle Tom's Cabin*, 155.

17. Irving Howe, *The American Newness: Culture and Politics in the Age of Emerson* (Cambridge, MA: Harvard University Press, 1986), 19.

18. Emerson, *Essays and Poems*, 46–47.

19. Orestes A. Brownson, *New Views on Christianity, Society, and the Church* (Boston: James Munroe, 1836), 99.

20. Garrison et al., *Proceedings of the Anti-Slavery Meeting Held in Stacy Hall, Boston, on the Twentieth Anniversary of the Mob of October 21, 1835* (Boston: M. F. Wallcut, 1855), 43.

21. In December 1832, he took out Abbe Raynal's two-volume *Philosophical and Political History of the Settlements and Trade of the Europeans in the East and West Indies*. See Kenneth Walter Cameron, *Ralph Waldo Emerson's Reading* (Hartford, CT: Transcendental Books, 1962), 20.

22. Samuel May, one of Garrison's close associates, spoke before Emerson's church in May 1831. "Discourse on Slavery," *Liberator*, May 28, 1831.

23. James Freeman Clarke, *James Freeman Clarke: Autobiography, Diary and Correspondence,* ed. Edward Everett Hale (New York: Houghton, Mifflin, 1891), 219–20.

24. Octavius Brooks Frothingham, *Memoir of William Henry Channing* (Boston: Houghton, Mifflin, 1886), 81.

25. Frothingham, *Memoir of William Henry Channing*, 84.

26. Quoted in Len Gougen, *Virtue's Hero: Emerson, Anti-Slavery, and Reform* (Athens: University of Georgia Press, 1990), 63, 49.

27. Maria Weston Chapman, "Rough Draft of an Essay on Ralph Waldo Emerson," Anti-Slavery Collection, Boston Public Library.

28. Lydia Maria Child, "Letters from New York—No. 58," *National Anti-Slavery Standard*, May 4, 1843.

29. "Abolition Proceeding," in Orestes Brownson, *The Works of Orestes A. Brownson*, ed. Harry F. Brownson (New York: AMC Press, 1966), 15:64.

30. "Rev. O. A. Brownson," *Liberator*, August 31, 1838.

31. Chevigny, *The Woman and the Myth*, 438.

32. Julia Ward Howe, "Reminiscences," in *Concord Lectures on Philosophy: Comprising Outlines of All the Lectures at the Concord Summer School of Philosophy in 1882*, ed. Raymond L. Bridgman (Cambridge, MA: Moses King, 1882).

33. This was the son of the Secret Six Plotter, George L. Stearns. See Frank P. Stearns, "Charles Sumner," *Providence Journal*, May 22, 1906.

34. In her *Right and Wrong in Massachusetts*, Chapman refers to Ralph Emerson, of Andover, negatively. Maria Weston Chapman, *Right and Wrong in Massachusetts* (Boston: Dow and Jackson's Anti-Slavery Press, 1839), 86. Ralph Emerson, "Refuge of Oppression," *Liberator*, January 11, 1839. In another instance, Henry C. Wright asked a crowd, "Who is the God of humanity? . . . He is not the God of Moses Stuart or of Leonard Woods, or of Ralph Emerson" before catching himself and explaining, "I do not mean Ralph Waldo Emerson, but the Rev. Dr. Emerson." See Joseph Stiles, *Modern Reform Examined; or, The Union of North and South on the Subject of Slavery* (Philadelphia: Lippincott, 1857), 274.

35. "Words Fitly Spoken," *Liberator*, June 22, 1838.

36. Child, *Letters of Lydia Maria Child*, 169.

37. See, for instance, "Letters from New York, No. 47," *National Anti-Slavery Standard*, January 19, 1843; "Letters from New York, No. 50," *National Anti-Slavery Standard*, February 16, 1843.

38. See Yaconove, *Samuel Joseph May*, 73–75, quoted in Gura, *Transcendentalism*, xiii.

39. Ralph Waldo Emerson, *Emerson: Essays and Poems* (New York: Library of Congress, 1996), 262.

40. Karen English, ed., *A Bronson Alcott, Notes on Conversations, 1848–1875* (Teaneck, NJ: Fairleigh Dickinson University Press, 2007), 110.

41. Both Elkins and Wyatt-Brown believe that the abolitionists shared, in Elkins's words, an "overtone of guilt" with Transcendentalism. See Wyatt-Brown, *Yankee Saints and Southern Sinners*, 25.

42. Emerson, *Essays and Poems*, 262.

43. A. Bronson Alcott, Diary for 1848, 241, A. Bronson Alcott Papers, Houghton Library, Harvard University.

44. Emerson's letter to George Ripley is printed in Ralph Waldo Emerson, *The Selected Letters of Ralph Waldo Emerson*, ed. Joel Myerson (New York: Columbia University Press, 1997), 243–46.

45. Henry Steele Commager, "The Blasphemy of Abner Kneeland," *New England Quarterly* 8, no. 1 (March 1935): 29–41.

46. "Imprisonment of Abner Kneeland," *Liberator*, July 6, 1838.

47. Mayer, *All on Fire*, 102–3.

48. Robert Burkholder, "Emerson, Kneeland, and the Divinity School Address," *American Literature* 58, no. 1 (March 1986): 7–8.

49. William Lloyd Garrison, *The "Infidelity" of Abolitionism* (New York: American Anti-Slavery Society, 1860), 7.

50. Daniel Foster, *An Address on Slavery Delivered at Danvers, Mass.* (Boston: Bela Marsh and Cornhill, 1849), 39.

51. Nehemiah Adams, *A South-Side View of Slavery; or Three Months at the South in 1854* (Boston: T. R. Marvin, 1854); Moses Stuart, *Conscience and Constitution: With Remarks on the Recent Speech of the Honorable Daniel Webster in the Senate of the United States on the Subject of Slavery* (Boston: Crocker and Brewer, 1850).

52. "Ministers, as a Class," *Liberator*, July 22, 1864. Another time, Gannett was quoted as saying, "Silence . . . on this subject, is our duty. The evil is at a distance from us, and our interference can only make it worse." "How to Abolish Slavery," *Liberator*, July 4, 1845.

53. "A Call for Vigilance," *Liberator*, February 8, 1839.

54. "Anniversary of British West India Emancipation: Convention of the Colored Citizens of Massachusetts," *Liberator*, August 13, 1858.

55. "A South-Side View of Essex Street Pulpit," *Liberator*, April 15, 1859.

56. Garrison, *"Infidelity" of Abolitionism*, 6.

57. Garrison, *"Infidelity" of Abolitionism*, 7.

58. Garrison, *"Infidelity" of Abolitionism*, 10–11.

59. Quoted in Staughton Lynd, *Intellectual Origins of American Radicalism*, 2nd ed. (New York: Cambridge University Press, 2009), 109.

60. Lewis Perry, *Radical Abolitionism: Anarchy and the Government of God in Antislavery Thought* (Ithaca, NY: Cornell University Press, 1973), 122.

61. "New England Colored Citizens' Convention," *Liberator*, August 26, 1859.

62. "The Bible, if Opposed to Self-Evident Truth, Is Self-Evident Falsehood," *Liberator*, August 11, 1848.

63. Henry C. Wright, *The Errors of the Bible Demonstrated by the Truths of Nature; or, Man's only Infallible Rule of Faith and Practice* (Boston: Bela Marsh, 1858).

64. Charles Taylor, *Sources of the Self: The Making of Modern Identity* (Cambridge, MA: Harvard University Press, 1989), 401.

65. "Speech of Wendell Phillips, at Abington, Mass., August 1, 1855," *National Anti-Slavery Standard*, August 18, 1855.

66. Channing's ordination sermon was printed as William Henry Channing, *The Gospel Today: A Discourse Delivered at the Ordination of T. W. Higginson* (Boston: Wm. Crosby and H. P. Nichols, 1847).

67. Thomas Wentworth Higginson, *Man Shall Not Live by Bread Alone: A Thanksgiving Sermon: Preached in Newburyport, November 30, 1848* (Newburyport, MA: Charles Whipple, 1848), 10.

68. Howard Meyer, *Colonel of the Black Regiment: The Life of Thomas Wentworth Higginson* (New York: Norton, 1967), 57.

69. Tilden G. Edelstein, *Strange Enthusiasm: A Life of Thomas Wentworth Higginson* (New York: Atheneum, 1970), 90.

70. Thomas W. Higginson to his Mother, September 6, 1849, Thomas Wentworth Higginson Papers, Houghton Library, Harvard University.

71. J. G. Forman, *The Christian Martyrs; or, The Condition of Obedience to the Civil Government* (Boston: Wm. Crosby and H. P. Nichols, 1851), 39.

72. Richardson, *The Mind on Fire*, 124.

73. See Dean Grodzins, *American Heretic: Theodore Parker and Transcendentalism* (Chapel Hill: University of North Carolina Press, 2002), 238–333.

74. Chevigny, *The Woman and the Myth*, 171.

75. Emerson, *Essays and Poems*, 386

76. "Reverence (*Not for* God, *but*) for the Pulpit!" *Liberator*, September 21, 1838.

77. For the importance of Sabbatarianism to 1820s and 1830s evangelical antislavery, see Bertram Wyatt-Brown, "Prelude to Abolitionism: Sabbatarian Politics and the Rise of the Second Party System," *Journal of American History* 58, no. 2 (September 1971): 316–41; Kyle G. Volk, *Moral Minorities and the Making of American Democracy* (New York: Oxford University Press, 2014), 37–68.

78. "The Proposed Anti-Sabbath Convention," *Boston Recorder*, February 25, 1848.

79. "Anti-Sabbath Convention: To the Friends of Civil and Religious Liberty," *Liberator*, January 21, 1848.

80. Gougen, *Virtue's Hero*, 60.

81. Samuel May, "A Theological Common-Place Book," Samuel May Papers, Massachusetts Historical Society, p. 54.

82. "Entry for April 10, 1849," Diary: 1849–1852, Samuel May Papers, Massachusetts Historical Society.

83. "Second Annual Meeting" and "Church, Ministry, and Sabbath Convention," *Non-Resistant*, October 14, 1840.

84. Carlos Baker, *Emerson Among the Eccentrics: A Group Portrait* (New York: Viking, 1996), 190.

85. For accounts, see "Anti-Sabbath and Anti-Ministry Convention," *Liberator*, December 11, 1840.

86. "Bible Convention," *New Bedford Register*, April 6, 1842.

87. Ralph Waldo Emerson, "Chardon Street and Bible Conventions," *Dial* 3, no. 1 (July 1842): 102–4.

88. "Bible Convention," *Liberator*, January 7, 1842; "Is It Come to This," *New York Weekly Herald*, January 8, 1842.

89. See *Permanent Sabbath Documents of the American and Foreign Sabbath Union* (Boston: Perkins and Whipple, 1851).

90. "Anti-Sabbath Convention," *North Star*, February 11, 1848.

91. "Remarks of Rev. Theodore Parker," *Liberator*, May 12, 1848.

92. William Lloyd Garrison et al., *Proceedings of the Anti-Sabbath Convention, Held in the Melodeon, March 23d and 24th* (Boston: Published by the Order of the Convention, 1848), 91.

93. O. B. Frothingham, "Fellow-workers with God: A Sermon," *National Anti-Slavery Standard*, October 5, 1861.

94. Garrison et al., *Proceedings of the Anti-Sabbath Convention*, 87.

95. "Anti-Sabbath Convention," *Liberator*, January 21, 1848; Higginson agreed, writing that "it is much easier to give religion a divided seventh-part of every week, than to give it the due undivided proportion of every instant." Thomas Wentworth Higginson, *Things New and Old: An Installation Sermon* (Worcester, MA: Earle and Drew, 1852), 8.

96. Henry David Thoreau, *A Week on the Concord and Merrimack Rivers* (Princeton, NJ: Princeton University Press, 1980), 76.

97. "The Year's Record of Sadness and Gladness, a Sermon by Rev. O. B. Frothingham, Sunday, Dec. 29, 1861," *National Anti-Slavery Standard*, January 11, 1862.

98. Emerson, *Selected Journals*, 2:21.

99. William James, *The Varieties of Religious Experience* (New York: Penguin, 1902), 521.

100. Fredrick Douglass, *Autobiographies* (New York: Library of America, 1996), 53.

101. Stowe, *Key to Uncle Tom's Cabin*, 155.

102. Alexander Crummell, *Jubilate: 1844–1894, The Shades and the Lights of a Fifty Years Ministry, a Sermon by Alex. Crummell, Rector* (Washington, DC: R. L. Pendleton, 1894), 8.

103. Grimké, *The Journals of Charlotte Forten Grimké*, 61 (May 26, 1854).

104. Samuel Ringgold Ward, *Autobiography of a Fugitive Negro; His Anti-Slavery Labours in the United States, Canada, and England* (London: John Snow, 1855), 67.

105. Nell, *William Cooper Nell*, 109–10.

106. Nell, *William Cooper Nell*, 115.

107. "From the New York Sun," *National Anti-Slavery Standard*, May 18, 1848.

108. "Address, from the Council of the Philadelphia Association, for the Moral and Mental Improvement of the People of Color," *Pennsylvania Freeman*, August 3, 1837.

109. William C. Nell, "Colored Ministers," *North Star*, April 7, 1848.

110. Charles Capper, *Margaret Fuller: An American Romantic Life; The Private Years* (New York: Oxford University Press, 1992), 291–97.

111. Francis E. Kearns, "Margaret Fuller and the Abolition Movement," *Journal of the History of Ideas* 25, no. 1 (January 1964): 124.

112. Margaret Fuller to Maria Weston Chapman, December 26, 1840, quoted in Chevigny, *The Woman and the Myth*, 238.

113. Nancy Craig Simmons, "Margaret Fuller's Boston Conversations: The 1839–1840 Series," *Studies in the American Renaissance* (1994): 215.

114. Ednah Dow Cheney, *Reminiscences of Ednah Dow Cheney* (Boston: Lee and Shepard, 1902), 205.

115. Quoted in Albert von Frank, "Margaret Fuller and Antislavery" A Cause Identical," in *Margaret Fuller and Her Circles*, ed. Brigitte Bailey, Katheryn P. Viens, and Conrad Edick Wright (Lebanon: University of New Hampshire Press, 2013), 144.

116. Maria Stewart, *Maria Stewart: America's First Black Woman Political Writer, Essays and Speeches*, ed. Marilyn Richardson (Bloomington: Indiana University Press, 1987), 38.

117. Stewart, *Maria Stewart*, 30.

118. Stewart, *Maria Stewart*, 47.

119. Howe, *American Newness*, 31.

120. Nell, *William Cooper Nell*, 25.

121. Fuller, *Woman in the Nineteenth Century*, 11.

122. Chevigny, *The Woman and the Myth*, 248.

123. Chevigny, *The Woman and the Myth*, 168, 169.

124. Caroline Healey Dall, *Selected Journals of Caroline Healey Dall*, vol. 1: *1838–1855*, ed. Helen Deese (Boston: Massachusetts Historical Society, 2006), 203.

125. Dall, *Selected Journals of Caroline Healey Dall*, 1:345.

126. Quoted in Anna M. Speicher, *The Religious World of Antislavery Women: Spirituality in the Lives of Five Abolitionist Lecturers* (Syracuse, NY: Syracuse University Press, 2000), 80.

127. John White Chadwick, ed., *A Life for Liberty: Antislavery and Other Letters of Sallie Holley* (New York: Putnam, 1899), 68, 113, 121, 160, 149.

128. "Letter from Miss Putnam," *National Anti-Slavery Standard*, February 17, 1866.

129. Emerson, *Emerson: Essays and Poems*, 984.

130. Baker, *Emerson Among the Eccentrics*, 266–67.

131. "Meeting of Colored Citizens," *Liberator*, February 7, 1845.

132. See Rufus Choate to J. I. Bowditch, September 9, 1842, Jonathan Ingersoll Bowditch Papers II, Massachusetts Historical Society.

133. Gougen, *Virtue's Hero*, 93.

134. Charles Capper, *Margaret Fuller: An American Romantic; The Public Years* (New York: Oxford University Press, 2007), 263.

135. "Editor's Address," *Massachusetts Quarterly Review* 1, no. 1 (December 1847): 4.

136. Kinley J. Brauer, *Cotton Versus Conscience: Massachusetts Whig Politics and Southwestern Expansion, 1843–1848* (Lexington: University of Kentucky Press, 1967), 75.

137. Emerson, *Selected Journals*, 2:246.

138. John G. Palfrey, *Papers on the Slave Power, First Published in the "Boston Whig," in July, August, and September, 1846* (Boston: Merrill, Cobb, 1846), 26.

139. Henry David Thoreau, *Collected Essays and Poems* (New York: Library of America, 2001), 203.

140. "Imprisonment for Conscience Sake," *Non-Resistant*, February 26, 1840; Charles Lane, "State Slavery—Imprisonment of A. Bronson Alcott—Dawn of Liberty," *Liberator*, January 27, 1843.

141. Henry David Thoreau, *Collected Essays and Poems* (New York: Library of America, 2001), 155–61.

142. Perry, *Radical Abolitionism*, 117–28.

143. Emerson, *Essays and Poems*, 137.

144. Jack Turner, "Emerson, Slavery, and Citizenship," *Raritan* 28, no. 2 (Fall 2008): 129.

145. Emerson, *Selected Journals*, 2:552.

146. See "Constitution of the New-England Non-Resistance Society," *Non-Resistant*, January 1, 1839; "The Life-Taking Principle," *Non-Resistant*, October 28, 1840.

147. "Declaration of the Sentiments Adopted by the Peace Convention, Held in Boston, September 18, 19, and 20, 1838," *Non-Resistant*, January 1, 1839; "Remarks on the Bunker-Hill Monument," *Non-Resistant*, September 23, 1840.

148. "Great Meeting of the Colored Citizens," *Liberator*, October 25, 1839.

149. Nell, *William Cooper Nell*, 93.

150. Quoted in Perry, *Radical Abolitionism*, 83.

151. "First Annual Meeting of the New England Non-Resistance Society," *Non-Resistant*, November 2, 1839.

152. Emerson, *Selected Journals*, 1:711.

153. "Second Annual Meeting of the New England Non-Resistance Society," *Non-Resistant*, October 14, 1840.

154. Theodore Parker, *The Life and Correspondence of Theodore Parker*, ed. John Weiss (New York: D. Appleton, 1864), 1:157.

155. Edmund Quincy, "No Governmentalism," *Non-Resistant*, September 9, 1840.

156. Thoreau, *Collected Essays and Poems*, 342.

157. "Political Transcendentalism," *Boston Daily Evening Transcript*, March 17, 1848.

158. Lydia Maria Child to Abigail Williams May, March 15, 1874, May/Goddard Family Papers, Schlesinger Library.

159. Ednah Dow Cheney, *Reminiscences of Ednah Dow Cheney* (Boston: Lee and Shepard, 1902), 114–15.

160. "American Anti-Slavery Society," *National Anti-Slavery Standard*, May 18, 1848.

161. "New England Anti-Slavery Convention," *National Anti-Slavery Standard*, June 9, 1855.

162. "New England Anti-Slavery Convention," *New York Times*, June 1, 1855.

163. "Transcendentalism," *National Anti-Slavery Standard*, November 25, 1841.

164. "Man the Reformer," *National Anti-Slavery Standard*, June 10, 1841.

165. "Letter from Laura Hosmer," *National Anti-Slavery Standard*, August 15, 1844.

166. "Correspondence of the Concord Convention," *Emancipator and Republican*, October 1, 1845.

167. Robert Richardson Jr., *Henry Thoreau: A Life of the Mind* (Berkeley: University of California Press, 1986), 150–51.

168. "West India Emancipation," *Spirit of the Age*, August 18, 1849.

169. Charles Sumner to Ralph Waldo Emerson, May 7, 1851, in Beverly Wilson Palmer, ed., *The Selected Letters of Charles Sumner* (Boston: Northeastern University Press, 1990), 1:333.

170. "Mr. Ralph Waldo Emerson," *Boston Semi-Weekly Advertiser*, May 23, 1851.

171. See Hugh Egan, "'On Freedom': Emerson, Douglass, and the Self-Reliant Slave," *ESQ: A Journal of the American Renaissance* 60, no. 2 (2014): 183–208.

172. Margaret Fuller, "The Liberty Bell," *Liberty Bell* (1846), 80.

173. Samuel May to Mary Carpenter, May 29, 1847, in Wendell Phillips Garrison and Francis Jackson Garrison, *William Lloyd Garrison: The Story of His Life Told by His Children* (Boston: Houghton, Mifflin, 1885), 3:188.

174. Ralph Waldo Emerson, "Editor's Address," *Massachusetts Quarterly Review* 1, no. 1 (1847): 6.

175. Parker, *Life and Correspondence of Theodore Parker*, 1:268.

176. Thomas Wentworth Higginson to his Mother, April 13, 1847, Thomas Wentworth Higginson Papers, Houghton Library, Harvard University.

177. For a full list of authors, see Clarence L. F. Gohdes, *The Periodicals of American Transcendentalism* (Durham, NC: Duke University Press, 1931), 167–69.

178. Emerson, *Selected Journals*, 2:347.

179. William C. Nell to Amy Kirby Post, December 12, 1849, in Nell, *William Cooper Nell*, 250. The minutes of the Town and Country Club read as follows: the "committee have satisfied themselves that the man who has, at present, charge of the Room, should be retained—as a point of economy—he having shewed himself faithful &prudent& his wages being less than one half

the price asked by several other applicants for the situation—There was a great loss of the property of the club stationary, periodicals &c., when the room was in charge of a boy & all sorts of irregularities were suffered from the fact that no reliance could be placed on the boys who under took the charge of the Room. These difficulties were entirely removed on the 'accession of the present incumbent' (to borrow an elegant phrase) & the Committee therefore confidently recommend that he be retained in service—at least until the end of this financial year." See Kenneth Cameron, "Emerson, Thoreau, and the Town and Country Club," *Emerson Society Quarterly*, no. 8 (1957): 12.

180. Cameron, "Emerson, Thoreau, and the Town and Country Club," 5.

181. See Nell, *William Cooper Nell*, 250.

182. See Nell, *William Cooper Nell*, 250.

183. "William C. Nell," *Liberator*, February 24, 1854.

184. English, *A Bronson Alcott*, 142.

185. "Medley," *North Star*, December 5, 1850.

186. Nell, *William Cooper Nell*, 320.

187. "Abby Kelley's Letter," *National Anti-Slavery Standard*, December 23, 1841.

188. "The Abolition Movement," *New York Herald*, August 12, 1845.

189. Rev. James Porter, *Three Lectures Delivered in the First Methodist Church, in Lynn Mass.* (Boston: Reid and Rand, 1844), 22.

190. "France," *Boston Recorder*, April 16, 1841.

191. Chancellor Harper, James Henry Hammond, William Gilmore Simms, and Thomas Dew, *The Pro-Slavery Argument, as Maintained by the Most Distinguished Writers of the Southern States* (Philadelphia: Lippincott, Grambo, 1853), 149, 172.

192. "Letter from the Editor," *North Star*, May 16, 1850.

193. "From the New England Christian Advocate: Errors of the Abolitionists," *Liberator*, August 27, 1841; "Rev. Nathaniel Colver," *Liberator*, January 29, 1841.

194. Robert Knox, *The Races of Men: A Fragment* (Philadelphia: Lea and Blanchard, 1850), 240.

195. "Impertinence of the Abolitionists. Slavery Forever!" *Liberator*, December 11, 1857.

196. A. Bronson Alcott Diary for 1848, 287, A. Bronson Alcott Papers, Houghton Library, Harvard University.

CHAPTER 3

1. "Signs of the Times: A Call to the Friends of Social Reform in New England," *Present* 1, no. 5-6 (December 15, 1843): 207-8. Nell's name is listed in the call in this issue of the *Present* but misspelled as "Wm C. Kell." See also "A Call to the Friends of Social Reform in New England," *Liberator*, December 8, 1843.

2. Nell's support is listed in Adin Ballou, *History of the Hopedale Community: From Its Inception to Its Virtual Submergence in the Hopedale Parish* (Lowell, MA: Thompson & Hill, 1897), 119.

3. Emerson, *Selected Journals*, 2:208.

4. "Social Reorganization—Convention at Boston," *New York Daily Tribune*, January 1, 1844.

5. Waldo Martin, *The Mind of Frederick Douglass* (Chapel Hill: University of North Carolina Press, 1984), 28.

6. "Social Reorganization—Convention at Boston," *New York Daily Tribune*, January 1, 1844.

7. "Signs of the Time: Social Reform Convention at Boston," *Present* 1, nos. 7, 8 (January 15, 1844), 278.

8. Frederick Douglass, "What I Found at the Northampton Association," in Charles Arthur Sheffield, ed., *The History of Florence, Massachusetts. Including a Complete Account of the Northampton Association of Education and Industry* (Florence, MA: Charles Sheffield, 1895), 129–30.

9. Nell, *William Cooper Nell*, 437.

10. "Adelphic Union Library Association," *Liberator*, January 26, 1844.

11. George Fitzhugh and A. Hogeboom, *A Controversy on Slavery Between George Fitzhugh, ESQ., of Virginia, Author of "Sociology for the South," and A. Hogeboom, ESQ., of New York* (Oneida, NY: Oneida Sachem Office, 1857), 8.

12. Douglass, "What I Found at the Northampton Association," 130.

13. For analyses of abolition that tie it to capitalism or the ideological needs of marketplace, see Eric Williams, *Capitalism and Slavery* (Chapel Hill: University of North Carolina Press, 1994); David Brion Davis, *The Problem of Slavery in the Age of Revolution, 1770–1823* (Ithaca, NY: Cornell University Press, 1975); Thomas Bender, ed., *The Anti-Slavery Debate: Capitalism and Abolitionism as a Problem of Historical Interpretation* (Berkeley: University of California Press, 1992); John Ashworth, *Slavery, Capitalism, and Politics in the Antebellum Republic*, vol. 1: *Commerce and Compromise, 1820–1850* (New York: Cambridge University Press, 1996).

14. "The Disunion Question," *Liberator*, February 5, 1848.

15. Ralph Waldo Emerson, *Selected Journals, 1841–1877* (New York: Library of America, 2010), 2:324.

16. "Universal Reform," *Liberator*, August 22, 1845.

17. See, for instance, Seth Rockman, *Scraping By: Wage Labor, Slavery, and Survival in Early Baltimore* (Baltimore: Johns Hopkins University Press, 2009); Walter Johnson, *River of Dark Dreams: Slavery and Empire in the Cotton Kingdom* (Cambridge, MA: Belknap, 2013); Sven Beckert, *Empire of Cotton: A Global History* (New York: Knopf, 2014).

18. "Wendell Phillips on the Political Situation," *New York Times*, December 20, 1863.

19. Karl Marx, *The Revolutions of 1848: Political Writings*, ed. David Fernbach (New York: Verso, 2010), 296.

20. Karl Marx, *Capital: A Critique of Political Economy*, vol. 1, trans. Ben Fowkes (New York: Penguin, 1990), 925.

21. George Combe, *Notes on the United States of America During a Phrenological Visit in 1838–9–40* (Edinburgh: MacLachlan, Steward, 1841), 1:92.

22. Boston numbers come from an 1851 letter to R. J. Ward by Abbott Lawrence; national numbers come from *One Hundred Years of American Commerce*. According to R. H. Edmonds, there were 613,498 bales of cotton consumed in the United States itself from 1849 to 1850. If Lawrence was correct, then in 1849, Boston consumed 270,693 bales of cotton, roughly 44 percent of the total consumed by Americans. Lawrence provided five years' worth of data for Boston, and they all hover around this percentage. A total of 239,953 of 642,485 bales came through Boston (37 percent) in 1848 and 193,549 out of a national load of 428,000 (45 percent) in 1846. In the late 1840s, Boston consistently consumed around 40 percent to 45 percent of the national total of cotton. Amos Adams Lawrence to R. J. Ward, February 10, 1851, Amos A. Lawrence Papers Box 43, Massachusetts Historical Society; R. H. Edmonds, "American Cotton," in *One Hundred Years of American Commerce: Consisting of One Hundred Original Articles on Commercial Topics Describing the Practical Development of the Various Branches of Trade in the United States with the Past Century and Showing the Present Magnitude of Our Financial and Commercial Institutions*, ed. Chauncey Depew (New York: D. O. Haynes, 1895), 1:233.

23. "Branches of Industries in Massachusetts," *Voice of Industry*, March 20, 1846.

24. "Northern Agitation—Is It to Stop?" *Boston Post*, December 3, 1860; "A New Way to Settle the Cotton Question," *Boston Post*, December 3, 1860.

25. Rufus Choate to Dr. Andrew Nichols, January 14, 1832, in *The Works of Rufus Choate with a Memoir of his Life*, ed. Samuel Gilman Brown (Boston: Little, Brown, 1862), 1:35–36.

26. Harriet Beecher Stowe, *A Key to Uncle Tom's Cabin; Presenting the Original Facts and Documents upon Which the Story Is Founded* (Boston: John P. Jewett, 1853), 154–55.

27. On the Cotton Whigs, see Thomas O'Conner, *Lords of the Loom: The Cotton Whigs and the Coming of the Civil War* (New York: Scribner, 1968); William Hartford, *Money, Morals, and Politics: Massachusetts in the Age of the Boston Associates* (Boston: Northeastern University, 2001); Kinley Brauer, *Cotton Versus Conscience: Massachusetts Whig Politics and Southwestern Expansion, 1843–1848* (Louisville: University of Kentucky Press, 1967).

28. *Address of the Committee Appointed by a Public Meeting, Held at Faneuil Hall, September 24, 1846* (Boston: White & Potter, 1846), 15.

29. Henry Adams, *History of the United States of America During the Second Administration of James Madison* (Cambridge, MA: Scribner, 1890), 9:104.

30. Ralph H. Orth and Alfred Riggs Ferguson, eds., *The Journals and Miscellaneous Notebooks of Ralph Waldo Emerson, 1843–1847* (Cambridge, MA: Harvard University Press, 1971), 418.

31. Amos Adams Lawrence to R. J. Ward, February 10, 1851, Amos A. Lawrence Papers Box 43, Massachusetts Historical Society; Edmonds, "American Cotton," 1:233.

32. Elihu Burritt, *A Plan for Brotherly Copartnership of the North and South, for the Peaceful Extinction of Slavery* (New York: Dayton and Burdick, 1856), 21–22.

33. Bell Gale Chevigny, ed., *The Woman and the Myth: Margaret Fuller's Life and Writings* (Boston: Northeastern University Press, 1994), 182.

34. Sinha, *The Slave's Cause*, 348–49.

35. Theodore Parker, *Saint Bernard and Other Papers* (Boston: American Unitarian Association), 297. Historical studies have confirmed Parker's impressions that the abolitionist rank and file came primarily from the working and middling classes. Leonard Richards, *"Gentlemen of Property and Standing": Anti-Abolition Mobs in Jacksonian America* (New York: Oxford University Press, 1970). On the background of the antislavery rank and file, see Bruce Laurie, *Beyond Garrison: Antislavery and Social Reform* (New York: Cambridge University Press, 2005), 7.

36. "Reorganization of Society," *Liberator*, September 6, 1844.

37. "To the Workingmen of New England," *Liberator*, July 4, 1845.

38. "Workingmen's Meeting," *Liberator*, September 6, 1844.

39. "Mass Meeting," *Liberator*, June 20, 1845.

40. "New England Fourier Society," *Liberator*, January 3, 1845.

41. "First Annual Meeting of the New England Workingman's Association," *Voice of Industry*, June 12, 1845.

42. See, for instance, "Robert Owen on Universal Reform," *Liberator*, October 18, 1844, or the 1845 article condemning Longfellow for not writing "oftener in aid of Universal Reform." "H. W. Longfellow," *Liberator*, December 26, 1845.

43. "The Hopedale Community," *Liberator*, December 12, 1851; "Letter from Mr. Garrison," September 25, 1846.

44. Marx, *The Revolutions of 1848*, 80.

45. Thomas Wentworth Higginson, *The Magnificent Activist: The Writings of Thomas Wentworth Higginson*, ed. Henry Mayer (New York: Da Capo Press, 2000), 7; Theodore Parker to Dr. Francis, March 13, 1844, in *Life and Correspondence of Theodore Parker*, ed. John Weiss (New York: Appleton, 1864), 1:229.

46. Thomas Wentworth Higginson to Waldo Higginson, November 30, 1847, Thomas Wentworth Higginson Papers, Houghton Library, Harvard University.

47. Lydia Maria Child, *Letters of Lydia Maria Child* (Boston: Houghton and Mifflin, 1882), 199.

48. "Meeting of Colored Citizens of New Bedford," *National Anti-Slavery Standard*, October 26, 1861.

49. "Report of the West Bloomfield A.S. Convention," *North Star*, April 26, 1850.

50. Samuel Ringgold Ward, *Autobiography of a Fugitive Negro* (London: John Snow, 1855), 40.

51. Ward, *Autobiography of a Fugitive Negro*, 201, 239.

52. "Speech of John S. Rock, ESQ," *Liberator*, February 14, 1862.

53. Len Gougeon and Joel Myerson, eds., *Emerson's Antislavery Writings* (New Haven, CT: Yale University, 1995), 35.

54. Parker, *Saint Bernard and Other Papers*, 297.

55. "Negro Emancipation," *Patriot*, September 24, 1863.

56. Josiah Quincy, *Whig Policy Analyzed and Illustrated* (Boston: Phillips, Sampson, and Co., 1856), 7–8.

57. James Freeman Clarke, *The Rendition of Anthony Burns: Its Causes and Consequences* (Boston: Crosby, Nichols, 1854), 20.

58. Amos A. Lawrence to Robert C. Winthrop, August 20, 1850, Amos A. Lawrence Papers Box 43, Massachusetts Historical Society.

59. Herbert Aptheker, *Abolitionism: A Revolutionary Movement* (Boston: Twayne, 1989), 44.

60. See Kathryn Grover, *The Fugitive's Gibraltar: Escaping Slaves and Abolitionism in New Bedford, Massachusetts* (Amherst: University of Massachusetts Press, 2001), 281.

61. Higginson, *Cheerful Yesterdays*, 115.

62. "Final Statement of Both Petitions," *Latimer Journal*, May 10, 1843. Population from Jesse Chickering, *A Statistical View of Massachusetts from 1765–1840* (Boston: Little, Brown, 1846).

63. "Twenty-Ninth Annual Meeting of the Massachusetts Anti-Slavery Society," *National Anti-Slavery Standard*, February 1, 1862.

64. "British and Foreign Anti-Slavery Society," *Anti-Slavery Reporter*, August 1, 1851.

65. William Wells Brown, *The Works of William Wells Brown, Using His "Strong, Manly Voice,"* ed. Paula Garrett and Hollis Robbins (New York: Oxford University Press, 2006), 26.

66. On Wright, see Laurie, *Beyond Garrison*, 17–19, 67–70; Lawrence Goodheart, *Abolitionist, Actuary, Atheist: Elizur Wright and the Reform Impulse* (Kent, OH: Kent State University Press, 1990).

67. Gougen, *Virtue's Hero*, 151.

68. Sterling F. Delano, "The Boston Union of Associationists (1846–1851): 'Association is to me the Great Hope of the World,'" *Studies in the American Renaissance* (1996): 26.

69. "Socialism and Abolitionism," *Daily Chronotype*, January 8, 1850.

70. "City Intelligence," *Boston Courier*, April 16, 1849.

71. "The Regulation of Wages," *Commonwealth and Emancipator*, February 22, 1851.

72. Lucy Larcom, *A New England Girlhood: Outlined from Memory* (Boston: Houghton, Mifflin and Co., 1889), 154.

73. Daniel Dulany Addison, ed., *Lucy Larcom: Life, Letters and Diary* (Boston: Houghton and Mifflin, 1895), 9, 54, 125, 12.

74. Lucy Larcom, *The Poetical Works of Lucy Larcom* (Boston: Houghton and Mifflin, 1884), 253.

75. Lucy Larcom, *An Idyl of Work* (Boston: Osgood and Company, 1875), 135–36.

76. O'Conner, *Lords of the Loom*, 46.

77. "A Mile of Girls," *Voice of Industry*, December 26, 1845.

78. Larcom, *New England Girlhood*, 204, 255.

79. Harriet H. Robinson, *Loom and Spindle or Life Among the Early Mill Girls with a Sketch of "The Lowell Offering" and Some of Its Contributors* (New York: Thomas Crowell, 1898), 83.

80. Robinson, *Loom and Spindle*, 92–93.

81. Robinson, *Loom and Spindle*, 174.

82. Ralph Waldo Emerson, *Ralph Waldo Emerson: The Selected Journals: 1841–1877*, ed. Lawrence Rosenwald (New York: Library of America, 2010), 42.

83. Adam Smith, *The Theory of Moral Sentiments* (Indianapolis, IN: Liberty Fund, 1982), 232–33.

84. See Richard Teichgraeber III, *Sublime Thoughts/Penny Wisdom: Situating Emerson and Thoreau in the American Market* (Baltimore: Johns Hopkins University Press, 1995) for a discussion of Emerson and Thoreau and the marketplace.

85. "Theodore Parker on Nebraska," *New York Times*, February 23, 1854.

86. For the relationship between German idealism and revolutionary movements, see Herbert Marcuse, *Reason and Revolution: Hegel and the Rise of Social Theory* (New York: Routledge, 1986).

87. Friedrich Engels, "Social Reform on the Continent," in Karl Marx and Frederick Engels, *Collected Works* (New York: International Publishers, 1975), 3:404.

88. Thomas Carlyle, *A Carlyle Reader*, ed. G. B. Tennyson (Acton, MA: Copley, 1999), 3–24.

89. Ralph Waldo Emerson, *Emerson: Essays and Poems* (New York: Library of America, 1996), 281.

90. Emerson, *Essays and Poems*, 1113.

91. Emerson, *Essays and Poems*, 745.

92. Emerson, *Essays and Poems*, 727.

93. Emerson, *Essays and Poems*, 270.

94. Marx, *The Revolutions of 1848*, 81.

95. Henry David Thoreau, *The Journal: 1837–1861* (New York: New York Review Books, 2009), 516. My analysis of Thoreau, along with more in this book than I can probably recount, was shaped by Staughton Lynd's classic *Intellectual Origins of American Radicalism*, 2nd ed. (New York: Cambridge University Press, 2009).

96. Thoreau, *Collected Essays and Poems*, 362.

97. Thoreau, *Collected Essays and Poems*, 350.

98. Emerson, *Essays and Poems*, 691.

99. Emerson, *Essays and Poems*, 1113.

100. Friedrich Schiller, *On the Aesthetic Education of Man*, trans. Reginald Snell (New Haven, CT: Yale University Press, 1954), 28.

101. Herbert Marcuse, *Reason and Revolution: Hegel and the Rise of Social Theory* (Boston: Beacon, 1960), 18.

102. Emerson, *Essays and Poems*, 185–86.

103. Quoted in Mary Elizabeth Sargent, ed., *Sketches and Reminiscences of the Radical Club of Chestnut Street* (Boston: Osgood, 1880), 6.

104. Henry David Thoreau, *Walden* (Princeton, NJ: Princeton University Press, 2004), 333.

105. Emerson, *Essays and Poems*, 146.

106. Emerson, *Selected Journals*, 2:603.

107. Emerson, *Selected Journals*, 2:592.

108. Emerson, *Selected Journals*, 2:326.

109. Douglass, "What I Found at the Northampton Association," 130.

110. William C. Nell, "The Morning Dawns," *North Star*, May 5, 1848.

111. Mitch Kachun, "'Our Platform Is as Broad as Humanity': Transatlantic Freedom Movements and the Idea of Progress in Nineteenth-Century African American Thought and Activism," *Slavery and Abolition* 24, no. 3 (2003): 12.

112. Sterling Delano, *Brook Farm: The Dark Side of Utopia* (Cambridge, MA: Belknap, 2004); Philip Gura, *Man's Better Angels: Romantic Reformers and the Coming of the Civil War* (Cambridge, MA: Belknap, 2017).

113. Richard Francis, *Transcendental Utopias: Individual and Community at Brook Farm, Fruitlands, and Walden* (Ithaca, NY: Cornell University Press, 2007), 46–49.

114. On the history of Fourierism in America, see Carl Guarneri, *The Utopian Alternative: Fourierism in Nineteenth-Century America* (Ithaca, NY: Cornell University Press, 1994).

115. See "The Brook Farm Association at West-Roxbury," *Liberator*, November 7, 1845.

116. Karl Marx, *Capital*, vol. 1 (New York: Penguin, 1976), 99; Marx, *The Revolutions of 1848*, 96.

117. "Social Reorganization—Convention at Boston," *New York Daily Tribune*, January 1, 1844.

118. In their records, Brook Farm kept track of the previous employment of its members, a significant amount of which were cordwainers, carpenters, bakers, pewterers, farmers, and other workers. See "Members of Brook Farm," Brook Farm Papers Reel 1, Massachusetts Historical Society.

119. "New England Workingmen's Convention," *Harbinger*, September 27, 1845.

120. See David A. Zonderman, *Uneasy Allies: Working for Labor Reform in Nineteenth-Century Boston* (Amherst: University of Massachusetts Press, 2011), 2.

121. "Item 5," Boston Union of Associationists Records, Houghton Library, Harvard University.

122. For more on the Boston Union, see Sterling F. Delano, "The Boston Union of Associationists (1846–1851): 'Association Is to Me the Great Hope of the World,'" *Studies in the American Renaissance* (1996): 5–40.

123. January 10, 1849, Boston Union of Associationists Records, Houghton Library, Harvard University.

124. "The Question of Slavery," *Harbinger*, June 21, 1845; "Our Policy—Slavery—Letter from Mr. MacDaniel," *Harbinger*, July 17, 1847.

125. Guarneri, *The Utopian Alternative*, 258.

126. "Roll of Boston Union of Associationists," Item 8, Boston Union of Associationists Records, Houghton Library, Harvard University; Membership of the Boston Vigilance Committee comes from two sources: the membership list in the Boston Public Library records and Austin Bearse, *Reminiscences of Fugitive Slave Law Days in Boston* (Boston: Warren Richardson, 1880), 3–6. On Trask, see Zonderman, *Uneasy Allies*, 68.

127. Membership Book, Book 5, Boston Anti-Man Hunting League Records, Massachusetts Historical Society.

128. Untitled List of Ticket Sales, Records of the Boston Union of Associationists, Item 4, Harvard University.

129. Frothingham, *Memoir of William Henry Channing*, 236.

130. Sinha, *The Slave's Cause*, 355–58.

131. Christopher Clark *The Communitarian Moment: The Radical Challenge of the Northampton Association* (Amherst: University of Massachusetts Press, 2003).

132. Douglass, "What I Found at the Northampton Association," 129.

133. Ballou, *History of the Hopedale Community*, 3, 77, 143.

134. Timothy Messer-Kruse, *The Yankee International: Marxism and the American Reform Tradition* (Chapel Hill: University of North Carolina Press, 1998).

135. Channing, quoted in Zoltan Haraszti, *The Idyll of Brook Farm: As Revealed by Unpublished Letters in the Boston Public Library* (Boston: Massachusetts, Trustees of the Public Library, 1937), 35.

136. "Interesting Letter from England," *Liberator*, July 15, 1842.

137. Peter Wirzbicki, "Wendell Phillips and Transatlantic Radicalism: Democracy, Capitalism, and the American Labor Movement," in *Wendell Phillips, Social Justice, and the Power of the Past*, ed. A. J. Aiséirithe and Donald Yacovone (Baton Rouge: Louisiana University Press, 2016); Betty Fladeland, "'Our Cause Being One and the Same': Abolitionists and Chartism," in *Slavery and British Society, 1776–1846*, ed. James Walvin (Baton Rouge: Louisiana State University Press, 1982), 69–99.

138. Emerson, *Selected Journals*, 2:418.

139. See Daniel Koch, *Ralph Waldo Emerson in Europe: Class, Race, and Revolution in the Making of an American Thinker* (New York: Palgrave Macmillan, 2012).

140. Reynolds, *European Revolutions*, 34.

141. Reynolds, *European Revolutions*, 4.

142. Quoted in Maurice Chazin, "Quinet an Early Discoverer of Emerson," *PMLA* 48, no. 1 (March 1933): 152.

143. Megan Marshall, *Margaret Fuller: A New American Life* (Boston: Houghton Mifflin, 2013), 286.

144. Quoted in Lawrence Buell, *Emerson* (Cambridge, MA: Belknap, 2003), 48.

145. Reynolds, *European Revolutions*, 59.

146. Bell Gale Chevigny, ed., *The Woman and the Myth: Margaret Fuller's Life and Writings* (Boston: Northeastern University Press, 1994), 359.

147. Larry Reynolds, *European Revolutions and the American Literary Renaissance* (New Haven, CT: Yale University Press, 1998), 64.

148. Chevigny, *The Woman and the Myth*, 446.

149. Reynolds, *European Revolutions*, 64; Margaret Fuller, "Margaret Fuller on the Italian Revolutions," in *The American Transcendentalists: Essential Writings*, ed. Lawrence Buell (New York: Modern Library, 2006), 253.

150. Edward Berenson, "American Perspectives on the French Republic," in *The French Republic: History, Values, Debates*, ed. Edward Berenson, Vincent Duclert, and Christophe Prochasson (Ithaca, NY: Cornell University Press, 2011), 359.

151. Charles Wiltse, "A Critical Southerner: John C. Calhoun on the Revolutions of 1848," *Journal of Southern History* 15, no. 3 (August 1949): 299–310.

152. Webster, quoted in Reynolds, *European Revolutions and the American Literary Renaissance*, 18.

153. "The Prospects of the French Revolution," *Boston Daily Advertiser*, April 5, 1848.

154. "Martinique—Murder!—Incendiarism!—Abolition of Slavery!" *Boston Daily Advertiser*, June 24, 1848.

155. Berenson, "American Perspectives on the French Republic," 359.

156. "Abolition of Slavery in the French Colonies," *Liberator*, April 14, 1848.

157. "Sketch of W. H. Channing's Speech," *Liberator*, April 14, 1848.

158. Theodore Parker, *The Collected Works of Theodore Parker*, ed. Frances Power Cobbe (London: Trübner, 1863), 5:89.

159. "Boston Meeting of Sympathy for the French," *Harbinger*, April 22, 1848.

160. "Sympathy for the French," *Liberator*, April 21, 1848.

161. "Working Men's Revolution Meeting," *Liberator*, May 26, 1848.

162. Albert von Frank, *The Trials of Anthony Burns: Freedom and Slavery in Emerson's Boston* (Cambridge, MA: Harvard University Press, 1998), 137.

163. "Extracts from a Letter from Upton," *Commonwealth and Emancipator*, March 15, 1851.

164. von Frank, *The Trials of Anthony Burns*, 64; George Adams, *The Boston Directory for the Year 1852, Embracing the City Record, a General Directory of the Citizens, and Business Directory, with an Almanac* (Boston: George Adams, 1852), 145.

165. "The Cause of Freedom in the Old World," *Liberator*, May 12, 1848.

166. Thomas Wentworth Higginson called Kemp an "energetic Irishman"; see Higginson, *Cheerful Yesterdays*, 148; "Annual Meeting of the Massachusetts A.S. Society," *Liberator*, February 2, 1855.

167. Bruce Levine, *The Spirit of 1848: German Immigrants, Labor Conflict, and the Coming of the Civil War* (Champaign: University of Illinois Press, 1992).

168. See Theodore Parker to James Freeman Clarke, April 24, 1857, Houghton Library, Harvard University.

169. "Spirit of the German Press in the United States," *European*, December 6, 1856.

170. Francis Wheen, *Karl Marx: A Life* (New York: Norton, 2001), 40–43.

171. Oscar Hammen, *The Red 48'ers: Karl Marx and Friedrich Engels* (New York: Charles Scribner's Sons, 1969), 156–57.

172. On Turners, see Bruce Levine, *The Spirit of 1848: German Immigrants, Labor Conflict, and the Coming of the Civil War* (Champaign: University of Illinois Press, 1992), 91; Carl Wittke, *Against the Current: The Life of Karl Heinzen* (Chicago: University of Chicago Press, 1945); James Stewart, *Wendell Phillips: Liberty's Hero* (Baton Rouge: Louisiana State University Press, 1998), 214.

173. See David Rapoport, ed., *Terrorism: Critical Concepts in Political Science* (New York: Routledge, 2006), 1:97–114.

174. Mischa Honeck, *We Are the Revolutionists: German-Speaking Immigrants and American Abolitionists After 1848* (Athens: University of Georgia Press, 2011), 137–71.

175. Prince Saunders to Paul Cuffee, June 25, 1812, Black Abolitionist Papers.

176. David Walker, *Walker's Appeal to the Coloured Citizens of the World*, ed. Peter P. Hinks (University Park: Pennsylvania State University Press, 2000), 9.

177. "Speech of Henry H. Garnet," *National Anti-Slavery Standard*, June 11, 1840.

178. Frederick Douglass, "France," *North Star*, April 28, 1848; see also "Frederick Douglass' Address," *North Star*, August 4, 1848.

179. Samuel R. Ward, "Editorial Correspondence," *Impartial Citizen*, September 14, 1850.

180. "British and Foreign Anti-Slavery Society," *Anti-Slavery Reporter*, August 1, 1851.

181. James Freeman Clarke, *The Present Condition of the Free Colored People of the United States* (New York: American Anti-Slavery Society, 1859), 3.

182. James Oliver Horton, *Free People of Color: Inside the African-American Community* (Washington, DC: Smithsonian Institution Press, 1993), 185–97.

183. "William C. Nell, "The Morning Dawns," *North Star*, May 5, 1848.

184. "France," *North Star*, April 28, 1848.

185. William Powell, "Letter from William Powell," *Liberator*, February 7, 1851.

186. Henry Johnson, "Address of H. W. Johnson Delivered at the First of August Celebration," *North Star*, August 21, 1848.

187. See Richard Bradbury, "Frederick Douglass and the Chartists," in *Liberating Sojourn: Frederick Douglass and Transatlantic Reform*, ed. Alan Rice and Martin Crawford (Athens: University of Georgia Press, 1999), 169–86; Betty Fladeland "'Our Cause Being One and the Same': Abolitionists and Chartism," in *Slavery and British Society, 1776–1846*, ed. James Walvin (Baton Rouge: Louisiana State University Press, 1982), 97.

188. For Marx's view of Chartism, see Karl Marx, *Surveys from Exile: Political Writings*, vol. 2 (New York: Verso, 2010), 262–71.

189. William Wells Browns, *Three Years in Europe; or, Places I Have Seen and People I Have Met* (London: Charles Gilpin, 1852), 29–30.

190. Brown, *Three Years in Europe*, 31.

191. Brown, *Three Years in Europe*, 35, 81, 118–19.

192. Brown, *Three Years in Europe*, 48.

193. "New England Anti-Slavery Convention," *North Star*, June 16, 1848.

194. "Semi-Annual Meeting of the American-Anti-Slavery Society," *National Anti-Slavery Standard*, October 7, 1854.

195. "Sketch of W. W. Brown's Lecture," *National Anti-Slavery Standard*, December 30, 1854.

196. See Bruce Laurie, *Beyond Garrison: Antislavery and Social Reform* (New York: Cambridge University Press, 2005), 236.

197. "The Fugitive Slave Bill," *Impartial Citizen*, October 5, 1850.

198. Lindsay Swift, *Brook Farm: Its Members, Scholars, and Visitors* (New York: Macmillan, 1900), 218.

199. William Henry Channing, *The Christian Church and Social Reform. A Discourse Delivered Before the Religious Union of Associationists* (Boston: Crosby and Nichols, 1848), 3.

200. Frothingham, *Memoir of William Henry Channing*, 213.

201. Gura, *Man's Better Angels*, 88.

202. "Workingmen's Association at Boston," *National Aegis*, June 4, 1845.

203. Charles Capper, *Margaret Fuller: An American Romantic Life, The Public Years* (New York: Oxford University Press, 2010), 206.

204. "Social Revolution," *Spirit of the Age*, October 20, 1849.

205. "Social Reorganization," *Present*, October 15, 1843.

206. "Universal Reform," *Liberator*, August 22, 1845.

207. "Mrs. Eliza Garnaut," *Spirit of the Age*, October 20, 1849; "Gov. Briggs and Frederick Douglass," *Spirit of the Age*, July 7, 1849; "European Socialism: Proudhon," *Spirit of the Age*, October 6, 1849; "Revolution-Reaction-Reorganization," *Spirit of the Age*, August 4, 1849.

208. "The Free Democratic Party," *Spirit of the Age*, September 29, 1849.

209. Octavius Brooks Frothingham, *Memoir of William Henry Channing* (Boston: Houghton, Mifflin, 1886), 258.

210. "The Free Democratic Party," *Spirit of the Age*, September 29, 1849.

211. "Free Soil Convention in Vermont," *Boston Semi-Weekly Advertiser*, August 23, 1848.

212. Charles Sumner, *Orations and Speeches in Two Volumes* (Boston: Ticknor, Reed, and Field, 1850), 2:328.

213. For a Whig take on Sumner's election, see Nathan Appleton to Fanny Longfellow, May 23, 1851, Nathan Appleton Papers, Massachusetts Historical Society.

214. "The Free Democratic Party," *Spirit of the Age*, September 29, 1849.

215. Quoted in Aptheker, *Abolitionism: A Revolutionary Movement*, 44.

216. Garrison et al., *Proceedings of the Anti-Sabbath Convention*, 34.

217. Garrison et al., *Proceedings of the Anti-Sabbath Convention*, 7.

218. Garrison et al., *Proceedings of the Anti-Sabbath Convention*, 38.

219. "Journeymen Tailors," *Boston Evening Transcript*, July 20, 1849. For a statement of the strikers' grievances, see "Tailors' Strike in Boston, Mass," *New York Daily Tribune*, August 21, 1849.

220. "Mechanic's Meeting in Faneuil Hall," *Boston Daily Transcript*, August 22, 1849.

221. "Strike for Wages," *North Star*, August 31, 1849.

222. "Social Revolution," *Spirit of the Age*, October 20, 1849.

223. "New Year's Greeting to the Tailors and All Workers," *Daily Chronotype*, January 1, 1850.

224. "The Associations of Workingmen," *National Era*, January 17, 1850.

225. "The Journeymen Tailor's Clothing Store," *North Star*, November 30, 1849.

226. See Treanor's preface to the new Tailor's Association in John R. Commons et al., *A Documentary History of American Industrial Society* (Cleveland, OH: Arthur H. Clark, 1910), 8:282.

CHAPTER 4

1. "Another Interesting Letter on the Anthony Burns Meeting," *Boston Transcript*, June 3, 1911.

2. Richard Henry Dana, "A Recollected Journal of the Anthony Burns Case," Dana Family Papers, Box 40, Massachusetts Historical Society.

3. Higginson, *Cheerful Yesterdays*, 153–54.

4. Richard Henry Dana, "A Recollected Journal of the Anthony Burns Case," Dana Family Papers, Box 40, Massachusetts Historical Society.

5. Higginson, *Cheerful Yesterdays*, 158.

6. John Greenleaf Whittier, *The Complete Poetical Works of John Greenleaf Whittier* (Boston: Houghton and Mifflin, 1892), 316.

7. Thoreau, *Collected Essay and Poems*, 346.

8. Thoreau, *Collected Essay and Poems*, 342.

9. Rev. Samuel T. Spear, *The Law Abiding Conscience and the Higher Law Conscience with Remarks on the Fugitive Slave Question* (New York: Lambert and Lane, 1850), 6.

10. Quoted in Barbara Packer, *The Transcendentalists* (Athens: University of Georgia Press, 2007), 223.

11. The best works on the protection of fugitives are Eric Foner, *Gateway to Freedom: The Hidden History of the Underground Railroad* (New York: Norton, 2015); David Blight, ed., *Passages to Freedom: The Underground Railroad in History and Memory* (Washington, DC: Smithsonian Institution Press, 2004).

12. Committee of Vigilance Records, Agent's Records, Phillips Papers, Houghton Library, Harvard University.

13. See Foner, *Gateway to Freedom*, 22; I am influenced here by John Ashworth's interpretation of Southern class relations, if not all the conclusions that he draws from his interpretations. John Ashworth, *Slavery, Capitalism, and Politics in the Antebellum Republic*, vol. 1: *Commerce and Compromise, 1820–1850* (New York: Cambridge University Press, 1996); John Ashworth, *Slavery, Capitalism, and Politics in the Antebellum Republic*, vol. 2: *The Coming of the Civil War, 1850–1861* (New York: Cambridge University Press, 2007).

14. "Semi-Annual Meeting of the American Anti-Slavery Society," *National Anti-Slavery Standard*, October 7, 1854.

15. Steven Hahn, *The Political Worlds of Slavery and Freedom* (Cambridge, MA: Harvard University Press, 2009), 1–53.

16. Kantrowitz, *More Than Freedom*.

17. See James Oliver Horton, *Free People of Color: Inside the African-American Community* (Washington, DC: Smithsonian Institution Press, 1993), 36.

18. James Oliver Horton and Lois Horton, *Black Bostonians: Family Life and Community Struggle in the Antebellum North*, rev. ed. (New York: Holmes and Meier, 2000), 107.

19. "Communications: Boston Vigilance Committee," *Liberator*, June 11, 1841.

20. "Boston Vigilance Committee," *Liberator*, June 18, 1841.

21. On Torrey, see Stanley Harrold, "On the Borders of Slavery and Race: Charles T. Torrey and the Underground Railroad," *Journal of the Early Republic* 20, no. 2 (Summer 2000): 273–92.

22. "Meeting in Aid of the Torrey Monument," *Emancipator and Republican*, July 8, 1846.

23. "Aid the Fugitive," *Liberator*, April 7, 1843.

24. See, for instance, "The Fugitive," *Liberator*, August 28, 1846.

25. "Aid for the Outcasts," *Liberator*, May 30, 1845.

26. Horton and Horton, *Black Bostonians*, 108.

27. "Our Prospects," *Latimer Journal and North Star*, November 16, 1842.

28. "The Latimer Journal," *Latimer Journal and North Star*, November 11, 1842.

29. "New England Freedom Association," *Liberator*, December 12, 1845.

30. "The Meeting in Faneuil Hall," *Boston Daily Evening Transcript*, September 25, 1846.

31. Samuel G. Howe et al., *Address of the Committee Appointed by a Public Meeting, Held at Faneuil Hall, September 24, 1846* (Boston: White and Potter, 1846), 39.

32. Entry for April 21, 1847, Records of the Vigilance Committee, Boston Anti-Man Hunting League Records, Massachusetts Historical Society.

33. See Howe et al., *Address of the Committee*, 8.

34. Committee of Vigilance, 1846, Agent's Records, Folder 1573, Wendell Phillips Papers, Houghton Library, Harvard University.

35. Daniel Webster, *The Great Speeches and Orations of Daniel Webster* (Boston: Little and Brown, 1879), 617.

36. "Report of the West Bloomfield A.S. Convention," *North Star*, April 26, 1850.

37. John Greenleaf Whittier, *The Poetical Works of John Greenleaf Whittier* (Boston: Ticknor and Fields, 1857), 2:99–100.

38. Thomas Wentworth Higginson, *Elegy Without Fiction: A Sermon Preached October 31, 1852*, Broadside, American Antiquarian Society.

39. Emerson, *Political Writing*, 153.

40. Mahatma Gandhi, "What is Moral Action?" *Indian Opinion*, January 19, 1907.

41. A. Bronson Alcott, *The Journals of Bronson Alcott*, ed. Odell Shepard (Boston: Little, Brown, 1938), 230.

42. "Speech of Rev. Samuel R. Ward," *Liberator*, April 5, 1850.

43. William C. Nell, *William Cooper Nell: Nineteenth Century African American Abolitionist, Historian, Integrationist: Selected Writings from 1832–1874*, ed. Dorothy Porter Wesley and Constance Porter Uzelac (Baltimore: Black Classic Press, 2002), 258–59.

44. William Hartford, *Money, Moral, and Politics: Massachusetts in the Age of the Boston Associates* (Boston: Northeastern University, 2001), 152.

45. Entry for March 24, 1850, Diary of Charles T. Russell, vol. 1, Bostonian Society.

46. Edward Everett to Robert L. Winthrop, March 14, 1850, Edward Everett Papers, Massachusetts Historical Society.

47. "Approval of the Speech!" *Liberator*, April 12, 1850.

48. George Ticknor, *The Life, Letters, and Journals of George Ticknor* (Boston: James Osgood, 1877), 2:217.

49. "Act for the Extradition of Slaves," *Boston Semi-Weekly Courier*, October 14, 1850.

50. "Samuel A. Eliot's Letter," *Daily Chronotype*, October 31, 1850.

51. Phillips, *Speeches, Lectures, and Letters*, 215.

52. "Samuel A. Eliot's Letter," *Daily Chronotype*, October 31, 1850.

53. "Daniel Webster's Speech to the New York Deputation," *Daily Chronotype*, November 21, 1850.

54. Thoreau, *Collected Essays and Poems*, 341; "Redemption of Massachusetts," *Boston Daily Post*, October 11, 1855.

55. "President Fillmore's Letter," *Boston Semi-Weekly Courier*, November 24, 1850.

56. "The Eastern Cotton Mills," *Commonwealth and Emancipator*, May 17, 1851.

57. Quoted in Hartford, *Money, Moral, and Politics*, 159.

58. "Protection to Northern and Southern Labor," *Boston Weekly Messenger*, October 16, 1850.

59. "Madness of the Webster Whigs," *Commonwealth and Emancipator*, January 18, 1851.

60. Robert Remini, *Daniel Webster: The Man and His Times* (New York: Norton, 1997), 200; "Mr. Webster's Subsidy," *Commonwealth and Emancipator*, July 5, 1851.

61. For more on Pennington, see Christopher L. Webber, *American to the Backbone: The Life of James Pennington, the Fugitive Slave Who Became One of the First Black Abolitionists* (New York: Pegasus, 2011).

62. "Freedom's Son and Daughter," *Colored American*, June 26, 1841.

63. J. W. C. Pennington, *Covenants Involving Moral Wrong Are Not Obligatory upon Man* (Hartford, CT: John C. Wells, 1842), 4.

64. Pennington, *Covenants Involving Moral Wrong*, 11.

65. Pennington, *Covenants Involving Moral Wrong*, 10, 5.

66. John Greenleaf Whittier, *The Letters of John Greenleaf Whittier*, ed. John Pickard (Cambridge, MA: Belknap, 1975), 2:155.

67. For a list of speakers, see William Lloyd Garrison to Samuel May, July 16, 1850, in *The Letters of William Lloyd Garrison: 1850–1860: From Disunionism to the Brink of War*, ed. William Merrill and Louis Ruchames (Cambridge, MA: Belknap, 1975), 4:30–33.

68. "Workingmen's Convention," *Daily Chronotype*, October 11, 1850; "The Fugitive Slave Law," *Liberator*, October 25, 1850.

69. "Meeting of the Colored Citizens of Boston," *Liberator*, October 4, 1850; Gary Collison, *Shadrach Minkins: From Fugitive Slave to Citizen* (Cambridge, MA: Harvard University Press, 1997), 82.

70. "Meeting to Consider the Condition of Fugitive Slaves in Boston," *Boston Weekly Messenger*, October 16, 1850.

71. "Help the Fugitive," *Daily Chronotype*, December 4, 1850; "Notice of Meetings, &c.," *Liberator*, March 24, 1854.

72. Austin Bearse, *Reminiscences of Fugitive Slave Law Days in Boston* (Boston: Warren Richardson, 1880), 8.

73. John White Chadwick, ed., *A Life for Liberty: Antislavery and Other Letters of Sallie Holley* (New York: G. P. Putnam's Sons, 1899), 109.

74. "Ralph Waldo Emerson," *Commonwealth and Emancipator*, April 26, 1851.

75. Howe et al., *Address of the Committee*, 31.

76. Chaplin and Chaplin, *Life of Charles Sumner*, 157. This story is repeated in Calvin Fairbank, *Rev. Calvin Fairbank During the Slavery Times, Edited from His Manuscript* (Chicago: R. R. McCabe, 1890), 79.

77. "Letter from Mr. Emerson," *Boston Daily Evening Transcript*, April 23, 1851.

78. *Account Book of Francis Jackson, Treasurer of the Vigilance Committee of Boston*, Facsimile (Boston: Bostonian Society, 1979), 69.

79. Theodore Parker, *Life and Correspondence of Theodore Parker*, ed. John Weiss (New York: Appleton, 1864), 2:143.

80. "Emerson on Courage," *Liberator*, November 18, 1859.

81. Various, *Proceedings of the Massachusetts Anti-Slavery Society at the Annual Meetings Held in 1854, 1855, and 1856* (Boston: Massachusetts Anti-Slavery Society, 1856), 38.

82. A. Bronson Alcott, *The Journals of Bronson Alcott*, ed. Odell Shepard (Boston: Little, Brown, 1938), 190.

83. Henry David Thoreau, *The Journal: 1837–1861* (New York: New York Review Books, 2009), 85.

84. *Account Book of Francis Jackson*, 8.

85. Thoreau, *The Journal*, 234.

86. Alcott, *The Journals of Bronson Alcott*, 243.

87. "Fugitive Slaves—Letter of Daniel Webster," *National Era*, June 6, 1850.

88. "Another Chapter in the Book of Daniel," *Liberator*, March 14, 1851.

89. Nell, *William Cooper Nell*, 278.

90. Theodore Parker, *The Collected Works of Theodore Parker*, vol. 5: *Discourses of Slavery*, ed. Francis Power Cobbe (London: Trübner, 1863), 134–63, 225–44; Nell, *Colored Patriots*; Thoreau, *Collected Essays and Poems*, 333–47.

91. Austin Bearse recounted Stowe and Hayden meeting in Bearse, *Reminiscences*, 8; on Whitman, see von Frank, *Trials of Anthony Burns*, 253–57.

92. Sidney Kaplan, "The *Moby Dick* in the Service of the Underground Railroad," *Phylon* 12, no. 2 (1951): 173–76.

93. Higginson, *Cheerful Yesterdays*, 144–45.

94. Thomas Wentworth Higginson to Charles Devens, September 29, 1850, Thomas Wentworth Higginson Papers, Houghton Library, Harvard University. For the story of Devens, see Child, *Letters of Lydia Maria Child*, 189.

95. Emerson, *Essays and Poems*, 54.

96. For the relationship between Emerson and Nietzsche, see George Stack, *Nietzsche and Emerson: An Elective Affinity* (Athens: University of Ohio Press, 1992); Lawrence Buell, *Emerson* (Cambridge, MA: Belknap, 2003), 218–20. Lewis Perry also explicitly links Emerson's ethics to Sartre's. See Lewis Perry, *Boats Against the Current: American Culture Between Revolution and Modernity, 1820–1860* (New York: Rowman and Littlefield, 1993), 206, 308.

97. Emerson's ethics bear close comparison to Simone de Beauvoir's piercing mockery of the "serious man," who seeks to get "rid of his freedom by claiming to subordinate it to values which would be unconditioned," pretending that "he is no longer a man, but a father, a boss, a member of the Christian Church or the Communist Party." Simone de Beauvoir, *The Ethics of Ambiguity*, (New York: Philosophical Library, 1948), 49, 52.

98. Daniel Walker Howe, *What Hath God Wrought: The Transformation of America, 1815–1848* (New York: Oxford University Press, 2009), 566.

99. Lewis Perry, *Boats Against the Current: American Culture Between Revolution and Modernity, 1820–1860* (New York: Oxford University Press, 1993), 71–78.

100. See Jeffrey Sklansky, *The Soul's Economy: Market Society and Selfhood in American Thought, 1820–1920* (Chapel Hill: University of North Carolina Press, 2002), 40.

101. Henry Wright, "My First Acquaintance with Garrison and Anti-Slavery," *Liberty Bell*, 1848, 149, 152.

102. Henry I. Bowditch, *An Apology for the Medical Profession* (Boston: Ticknor and Fields, 1863), 7.

103. Parker, *Collected Works*, 5:136.

104. Parker, *Collected Works*, 5:140.

105. Parker, *Collected Works*, 5:152–53.

106. Charles Emery Stevens, *Anthony Burns: A History* (Boston: John P. Jewett, 1856), 277–79.

107. "Charles Sumner on the Fugitive Slave Law," *Daily Chronotype*, November 14, 1850.

108. Parker, *Collected Works*, 5:150–51.

109. Parker, *Collected Works*, 5:155.

110. See "Trial by Jury," *Commonwealth and Emancipator*, July 5, 1851.

111. Theodore Parker, *The Trial of Theodore Parker* (Boston: Published for the Author, 1855), 2, 70; Parker, *Collected Works*, 5:156.

112. *Acts and Resolves Passed by the General Court of Massachusetts in the Year 1855: Together with the Messages* (Boston: William White, 1855), 590.

113. Quoted in Megan Marshall, *Margaret Fuller: A New American Life* (New York: Houghton Mifflin, 2013), 65. See also Sharon Cameron, "The Way of Life by Abandonment: Impersonal Emerson," in *The Other Emerson*, ed. Branka Arsic and Cary Wolfe (Minneapolis: University of Minnesota Press, 2010), 3–40.

114. William Adams, *Christianity and Civil Government* (New York: Scribner, 1851), 25.

115. James Freeman Clarke, "What Is Man," November 12, 1843, Box 30, Perry-Clarke Papers, Massachusetts Historical Society.

116. Melville, *Moby Dick*, 172–73.

117. Emerson, *Selected Journals*, 2:169.

118. Emerson, *Essays and Poems*, 855. For more on the connection between the private self and the public political life, see Nancy Rosenblum, *Another Liberalism: Romanticism and the Reconstruction of Liberal Thought* (Cambridge, MA: Harvard University Press, 1987).

119. William James, *Manuscript Essays and Notes* (Cambridge, MA: Harvard University Press, 1988), 318.

120. Emerson, *Essays and Poems*, 54.

121. Samuel Taylor Coleridge, *A Dissertation on the Science of Method; or, the Laws and Regulative Principles of Education* (London: Richard Griffin, 1854), 56–57.

122. Len Gougeon and Joel Myerson, eds., *Emerson's Antislavery Writings* (New Haven, CT: Yale University Press, 1995), 79.

123. "Debate in Congress on the Boston Petition," *Liberator*, July 7, 1854.

124. Thoreau, *Walden*, 37.

125. Emphasis in original. *Report of a Special Committee of the Grammar School Board, Presented August 29, 1849, on the Petition of Sundry Colored Persons, Praying for the Abolition of the Smith School: With an Appendix* (Boston: J. H. Eastburn, 1849), 5.

126. Samuel Willard, *The Grand Issue: An Ethico-Political Tract* (Boston: John Jewett, 1851), 3.

127. Moncure Conway, "The Citizen and the Drama," *Dial* 1, no. 12 (December 1860): 763.

128. Thomas W. Higginson, *Merchants: A Sunday Evening Lecture* (Newburyport, MA: A. A. Call), 28.

129. Emerson, *Selected Journals*, 2:552.

130. Ronald A. Bosco and Joel Myerson, eds., *The Later Lectures of Ralph Waldo Emerson, 1843–1871*, vol. 2: *1855–1871* (Athens: University of Georgia Press, 2001), 2:140.

131. Thomas Wentworth Higginson, *Massachusetts in Mourning: A Sermon Preached in Worchester, on Sunday June 4th, 1854* (Boston: James Munroe, 1854), 5–7.

132. George Talbot, "Nulla Vestigia Retrosum," *Liberty Bell*, 1852, 178.

133. Thoreau, *Collected Essays and Poems*, 205.

134. Thoreau, *Collected Essays and Poems*, 211.

135. Thoreau, *Journal: 1837–1861*, 651.

136. Thoreau, *Collected Essays and Poems*, 414.

137. Isaiah Berlin, *The Roots of Romanticism* (Princeton, NJ: Princeton University Press, 1999), 87.

138. Parker, *Collected Works*, 5:226–27.

139. Parker, *Collected Works*, 5:138.

140. Charles Mayo Ellis, *An Essay on Transcendentalism* (Boston: Crocker and Ruggles, 1842), 73.

141. Thoreau, *Collected Essays and Poems*, 209.

142. McDaniel, *The Problem of Democracy in the Age of Slavery*.

143. Emerson, *Essays and Poems*, 396.

144. Emerson, *Essays and Poems*, 277.

145. Margaret Fuller, *The Essential Margaret Fuller*, ed. Jeffrey Steele (New Brunswick, NJ: Rutgers University Press, 1992), 245.

146. Fuller, *Essential Margaret Fuller*, 264.

147. Minutes of Meeting, May 2, 1849, Records and Papers of the Town and Country Club, A. Bronson Alcott Papers, Houghton Library, Harvard University.

148. "Entry for May 2, 1849," Diary: 1849–1852, Samuel May Papers, Massachusetts Historical Society.

149. Ralph Waldo Emerson, *The Selected Letters of Ralph Waldo Emerson*, ed. Joel Myerson (New York: Columbia University Press, 1997), 351.

150. Jeremiah Chaplin and J. D. Chaplin, *Life of Charles Sumner* (Boston: D. Lothrop, 1874), 157.

151. "Hon. David A. Simmons," *Daily Chronotype*, October 27, 1850.

152. See James Williams, *Life and Adventures of James Williams, a Fugitive Slave* (San Francisco: Women's Union Print, 1873), 22.

153. Quoted in Collison, *Shadrach Minkins*, 98–99.

154. For more on the Crafts, see "Great Excitement in Boston," *National Era*, November 7, 1850.

155. Nell, *William C. Nell*, 278.

156. "Massachusetts Safe Yet!!" *Commonwealth and Emancipator*, February 22, 1851.

157. See Jeffrey Amestoy, *Slavish Shores: The Odyssey of Richard Henry Dana, Jr.* (Cambridge, MA: Harvard University Press, 2015), 148; February 17, 1851, A. A. Lawrence to Charles Devins, Amos A. Lawrence Papers, Massachusetts Historical Society.

158. Child, *The Letters of Lydia Maria Child*, 72.

159. Mary Elizabeth Sargent, ed., *Sketches and Reminiscences of the Radical Club of Chestnut Street* (Boston: Osgood, 1880), 74.

160. Thomas Wentworth Higginson, *The Magnificent Activist: The Writings of Thomas Wentworth Higginson*, ed. Howard Meyer (New York: Da Capo, 2000), 62.

161. "The Hunker Joy," *Commonwealth and Emancipator*, April 19, 1851.

162. Henry Mayer, *All on Fire: William Lloyd Garrison and the Abolition of Slavery* (New York: Norton, 1998), 411–12.

163. William C. Nell to Amy Kirby Post, June 13, 1854, in Nell, *William C. Nell*, 384.

164. Richard Henry Dana Jr., Note on A. Burns Case, Dana Family Papers, Box 40, Massachusetts Historical Society.

165. See William F. Channing to T. W. Higginson, February 6, 1898, T. W. Higginson to unknown, April 6, 1874, Thomas W. Higginson Papers, Houghton Library, Harvard University. For a contemporary account of the Burns rendition, see William Spencer, *The Boston Slave Riot and Trial of Anthony Burns* (Boston: J. S. Potter, 1854). For Thomas W. Higginson's memories, see Higginson, *Cheerful Yesterdays*, 147–58. The best modern account is von Frank, *The Trials of Anthony Burns*.

166. "Subsequent Events," *National Anti-Slavery Standard*, June 10, 1854.

167. George Putnam to Charles Chapman, February 8, 1885, Charles Chapman Papers, Moorland-Spingarn Research Center, Howard University.

168. George Putnam to Charles Chapman, February 8, 1885, Charles Chapman Papers, Moorland-Spingarn Research Center, Howard University.

169. "The Boston Slave Case," *National Anti-Slavery Standard*, June 17, 1854.

170. "Great Excitement in Worcester," *Boston Daily Atlas*, October 31, 1854.

171. Francis Jackson to Theodore Parker, June 11, 1854, Boston Public Library, Anti-Slavery Collection.

172. "Fugitive Slaves Aided by the Vigilance Committee Since the Passage of the Fugitive Slave Bill, 1850," Papers of the Massachusetts Anti-Slavery Society, New York Historical Society.

173. "A Fugitive Slave," *Frederick Douglass' Paper*, September 29, 1854; "Theodore Parker's Thanksgiving Sermon," *Frederick Douglass' Paper*, December 22, 1854; "The Fugitive Slave Case in Manchester, N.H.," *Frederick Douglass' Paper*, June 30, 1854.

174. Bearse, *Reminiscences*, 34–35; see William C. Nell to Amy Kirby Post, July 21, 1853; Nell, *William C. Nell*, 342.

175. Bearse, *Reminiscences*, 37.

176. "From Our Boston Correspondent," *Frederick Douglass' Paper*, May 25, 1855.

177. "Fugitive Slave Case at Boston," *National Era*, July 24, 1856.

178. Recent Events in Boston," *Liberator*, October 7, 1859.

CHAPTER 5

1. "Anniversary of British West India Emancipation: Convention of the Colored Citizen of Massachusetts," *Liberator*, August 13, 1858.

2. "Our Pledge," *Liberator*, July 9, 1847.

3. Horton, *Free People of Color*, 89, 91.

4. William C. Nell, *The Colored Patriots of the American Revolution*, 2nd ed. (Boston: Robert Wallcut, 1855), 101.

5. For more on the role of violence in black abolitionist thought, see Kellie Jackson Carter, *Force and Freedom: Black Abolitionists and the Politics of Violence* (Philadelphia: University of Pennsylvania Press, 2019).

6. Alexander Crummell, *Africa and America: Addresses and Discourses* (Springfield, MA: Willey, 1891), 291.

7. "Anniversary of British West India Emancipation: Convention of the Colored Citizen of Massachusetts," *Liberator*, August 13, 1858.

8. "New England Colored Citizens' Convention," *Liberator*, August 19, 1859.

9. "Twenty-Ninth Annual Meeting of the Massachusetts Anti-Slavery Society," *National Anti-Slavery Standard*, February 1, 1862.

10. "New England Colored Citizens' Convention," *Liberator*, August 19, 1859.

11. "New England Anti-Slavery Convention," *National Anti-Slavery Standard*, June 10, 1854.

12. For more on the Massasoit Guards, see Stephen Kantrowitz, "Fighting Like Men: Civil War Dilemmas of Abolitionist Manhood," in *Battle Scars: Gender and Sexuality in the American Civil War*, ed. Nina Silber and Catherine Clinton (New York: Oxford University Press, 2006), 20–21.

13. "The New Coloured Military Company," *National Anti-Slavery Standard*, August 25, 1855.

14. Nell, *The Colored Patriots of the American Revolution*, 101–7.

15. See, for example, "Manuscript Regarding a Petition," Robert Morris Papers, Boston Athenaeum.

16. "The Massasoit Guards," *Liberator*, September 14, 1855.

17. William Watkins, *Our Rights as Men: An Address Delivered in Boston* (Boston: Benjamin Roberts, 1853), 18.

18. Watkins, *Our Rights as Men*, 18–19.

19. Watkins, *Our Rights as Men*, 3.

20. Watkins, *Our Rights as Men*, 6.

21. See Ellis Gray Loring et al., *The Defensive League of Freedom* (Boston: s.n., 1854).

22. James Freeman Clarke to George Downing, February 1, No Year, George T. Downing Papers, Howard University.

23. "Constitution," Book 1, Boston Anti-Man Hunting League Records, Massachusetts Historical Society.

24. "Diagram to Show the Drill the Anti-Man-Hunting League Had for the Running Off of a Slave or Man-Hunter," Boston Anti-Man Hunting League Records, Massachusetts Historical Society.

25. Henry Ingersoll Bowditch, *Life and Correspondence of Henry Ingersoll Bowditch*, ed. Vincent Bowditch (Boston: Houghton, Mifflin, 1902), 1:274

26. Book 2, Boston Anti-Man Hunting League Records, Massachusetts Historical Society.

27. Henry Wilson, *History of the Rise and Fall of the Slave Power in America* (Boston: Houghton and Osgood, 1874), 2:442

28. Quoted in Wendell Phillips Garrison and Francis Jackson Garrison, *William Lloyd Garrison, 1805–1879: The Story of His Life Told by His Children* (Boston: Houghton Mifflin, 1894), 3:324.

29. Manisha Sinha, "The Caning of Charles Sumner: Slavery, Race, and Ideology in the Age of the Civil War," *Journal of the Early Republic* 23, no. 2 (Summer 2003): 233–62.

30. Child, *The Letters of Lydia Maria Child*, 78.

31. Emerson, *Selected Journals*, 2:669.

32. "Important News from Kansas—Destruction of Lawrence," *Liberator*, May 30, 1856.

33. Good histories of the Kansas fighting include Nichole Etcheson, *Bleeding Kansas: Contested Liberty in the Civil War Era* (Lawrence: University of Kansas Press, 2004); Kristen Tegtmeier Oertel, *Bleeding Borders: Race, Gender, and Violence in Pre–Civil War Kansas* (Baton Rouge: Louisiana State University Press, 2009).

34. Theodore Parker to F. W. May, Esq., October 26, 1856, May/Goddard Family Papers, Schlesinger Library.

35. "Anti-Slavery Festival," *Liberator*, January 16, 1857.

36. Thomas Wentworth Higginson, *The Magnificent Activist: The Writings of Thomas Wentworth Higginson, 1823–1911*, ed. Howard Meyer (New York: Da Capo, 2000), 83.

37. "Anti-Slavery Festival," *Liberator*, January 16, 1857.

38. "Notebook on Trip Through Kansas," Thomas Wentworth Higginson Papers, Houghton Library, Harvard University.

39. Higginson, *The Magnificent Activist*, 97.

40. Daniel Foster, *An Address on Slavery Delivered at Danvers, Mass.* (Boston: Bela Marsh and Cornhill, 1849), 15.

41. "Slavery in Boston," *Commonwealth and Emancipator*, May 17, 1851; Journal Entry for April 14, 1851, Daniel Foster Papers, Box 1, Massachusetts Historical Society.

42. Daniel Foster, *The Constitution of the United States* (Springfield, MA: Samuel Bowles and Company, 1855), 36.

43. Daniel Foster, *Our Nation's Sins and the Christian's Duty: A Fast Day Discourse* (Boston: White and Potter, 1851); "We Learn from the Lowell American," *Frederick Douglass' Paper*, July 22, 1853; "Reply of Mr. May," *Frederick Douglass' Paper*, August 12, 1853.

44. Daniel Foster, "The Bible Not an Inspired Book," *Liberator*, November 14, 1851.

45. See Ralph Waldo Emerson to Henry Whitney Bellows, February 23, 1858, in *The Letters of Ralph Waldo Emerson*, vol. 9: *1860–1869*, ed. Eleanor Marguerite Tilton (New York: Columbia University Press, 1994), 552; see journal entry for May 11, 1851, Daniel Foster Papers, Box 1, Massachusetts Historical Society.

46. Laura Dassow Wallis, *Henry David Thoreau: A Life* (Chicago: University of Chicago Press, 2017), 365.

47. Daniel Foster to E. E. Hale, December 14, 1857, New England Emigrant Aid Company Papers (Microfilm Edition).

48. Biographical Matter, Daniel Foster Papers, Box 1, Massachusetts Historical Society.

49. Emerson, *Selected Journals*, 2:625.

50. Thoreau, *Walden*, 78.

51. M. H. Abrams, *The Mirror and the Lamp: Romantic Theory and the Critical Tradition* (New York: Oxford University Press, 1953).

52. Quoted in Leo Marx, *The Machine in the Garden: Technology and the Pastoral Ideal in America* (New York: Oxford University Press, 2000), 173.

53. Theodore Parker, *The World of Matter and the Spirit of Man: Latest Discourses of Religion* (Boston: American Unitarian Association, 1907), 16.

54. Parker, *Collected Works*, 5:129.

55. Emerson, *Essays and Poems*, 374.

56. Emerson, *Essays and Poems*, 269.

57. Emerson, *Essays and Poems*, 498.

58. Thoreau, *Collected Essays and Poems*, 343.

59. Emerson, *Essays and Poems*, 375, 380.

60. Thoreau, *Collected Essays and Poems*, 402.

61. "Twenty-First National Anti-Slavery Bazaar," *National Anti-Slavery Standard*, July 1, 1854.

62. Robert Richardson Jr., *Henry Thoreau: A Life of the Mind* (Berkeley: University of California Press, 1986), 26, 69.

63. Richardson, *Henry Thoreau*, 84. On Thoreau's conception of heroism, see also Nancy Rosenblum, *Another Liberalism: Romanticism and the Reconstruction of Liberal Thought* (Cambridge, MA: Harvard University Press, 1987), 115–18.

64. Higginson, *Massachusetts in Mourning*, 15.

65. Emerson, *Essays and Poems*, 261.

66. Parker, *The World of Matter and the Spirit of Man*, 36.

67. Thomas Wentworth Higginson, *Outdoor Papers* (Boston: Ticknor and Fields, 1863), 7, 5.

68. Higginson, *Outdoor Papers*, 12.

69. Christopher Looby, ed., *The Complete Civil War Journal and Selected Letters of Thomas Wentworth Higginson* (Chicago: University of Chicago Press, 2000), 377.

70. Theodore Parker to James Freeman Clarke, November 9, 1859, James Freeman Clarke Papers, Houghton Library, Harvard University. William James comments on these letters in his famous *Varieties of Religious Experiences*, seeing them as evidence of the healthy-minded, once-born, religious type. William James, *The Varieties of Religious Experiences: A Study in Human Nature* (New York: Penguin, 1982), 81–83.

71. Thoreau, *Collected Essays and Poems*, 225; Thoreau, *Walden*, 210.

72. James McCune Smith, introduction to Frederick Douglass, *My Bondage and Freedom* (New York: Miller, Orton, Mulligan, 1855), xxv.

73. On Nell as a historian, see Margot Minardi, *Making Slavery History: Abolitionism and the Politics of Memory in Massachusetts* (New York: Oxford University Press, 2010), 95.

74. Nell, *The Colored Patriots of the American Revolution*, 13–14.

75. Dorothy Porter Wesley and Constance Porter Uzelac, eds., *William Cooper Nell: Nineteenth Century African American Abolitionist, Historian, Integrationist: Selected Writings from 1832–1874* (Baltimore: Black Classic Press, 2002), 410.

76. Quoted in Mitch Kachun, "From Forgotten Founder to Indispensable Icon: Crispus Attucks, Black Citizenship, and Collective Memory, 1770–1865," *Journal of the Early Republic* 29 (Summer 2009): 270.

77. Stephen Kantrowitz, "A Place for 'Colored Patriots': Crispus Attucks Among the Abolitionists, 1842–1863," *Massachusetts Historical Review* 11 (2009): 97–118.

78. Tavia Nyong'o, *The Amalgamation Waltz: Race, Performance, and the Ruses of Memory* (Minneapolis: University of Minnesota, 2009), 67.

79. Nell, *The Colored Patriots of the American Revolution*, 16.

80. "For Frederick Douglass' Paper, Der Hagel," *Frederick Douglass' Paper*, March 25, 1853.

81. "Jas. McCune Smith vs. the Standard," *National Anti-Slavery Standard*, January 13, 1855; "A Mendacious Blunderer," *National Anti-Slavery Standard*, December 23, 1854.

82. "Frederick Douglass' Paper," *Liberator*, August 26, 1853.

83. "Reply to Anti-Slavery Standard," *National Anti-Slavery Standard*, February 3, 1855.

84. *The Provincial Freeman*, June 10, 1854.

85. Nell, *The Colored Patriots of the American Revolution*, 116.

86. "New England Anti-Slavery Convention," *Liberator*, June 6, 1856.

87. "New England Anti-Slavery Convention," *Liberator*, June 4, 1858.

88. Grimké, *Journals of Charlotte Forten Grimké*, 135.

89. Forten, it is worth pointing out, thought very highly of Parker, who invited her to his study and lent her books. She wrote in her journal that she had a "very pleasant interview" with Parker, a "genial hearted" man. Grimké, *Journals of Charlotte Forten Grimké*, 125, 187 (January 30, 1855; January 31, 1857).

90. Parker, *Collected Works*, 6:289, 290.

91. "The Races and Slavery," *National Anti-Slavery Standard*, May 12, 1855.

92. "The Boston Massacre, March 5, 1775: Commemorative Festival in Faneuil Hall," *Liberator*, March 12, 1858.

93. William Wells Brown, *The Black Man: His Antecedents, His Genius, and His Achievements* (Boston: R. F. Wallcut, 1863), 34.

94. "The Boston Massacre, March 5, 1775: Commemorative Festival in Faneuil Hall," *Liberator*, March 12, 1858.

95. Theodore Parker to George Bancroft, March 16, 1858, Theodore Parker Papers, vol. 3, 286, Massachusetts Historical Society.

96. The best works on racial science are Bruce Dain, *A Hideous Monster of the Mind: American Race Theory in the Early Republic* (Cambridge, MA: Harvard University Press, 2003); George Frederickson, *The Black Image in the White Mind: The Debate on Afro-American Character and Destiny, 1817–1914* (Middleton, CT: Wesleyan University Press, 1987).

97. "The Atlantic Monthly," *Frederick Douglass' Paper*, December 31, 1858.

98. Grodzins, *American Heretic*, 290.

99. Parker, *Collected Works of Theodore Parker*, 1:14.

100. Emerson, *Essays and Poems*, 196.

101. William James, *Manuscript Essays and Notes* (Cambridge, MA: Harvard University Press, 1988), 319.

102. Amos Bronson Alcott, *Notes on Conversations, 1848–1875*, ed. Karen English (Teaneck, NJ: Fairleigh Dickinson University Press, 2007), 148.

103. Parker, *Critical and Miscellaneous Writings*, 163.

104. "Recent Meetings Among the Colored Citizens of Boston," *Liberator*, July 15, 1859.

105. Emerson, *Essays and Poems*, 991.

106. Henry David Thoreau, *I to Myself: An Annotated Selection from the Journal of Henry D. Thoreau*, ed. Jeffrey Cramer (New Haven, CT: Yale University Press, 2007), 148–49.

107. The literature on Ralph Waldo Emerson and race is massive. See Gougen, *Virtue's Hero;* Cornel West, *The American Evasion of Philosophy* (Madison: University of Wisconsin Press, 2001); Peter Field, "The Strange Career of Emerson and Race," *American Nineteenth Century History* 2, no. 1 (Spring 2001): 1–32; Nell Irvin Painter, *The History of White People* (New York: Norton, 2010), 151–89; Eduardo Cadava, "The Guano of History," in *The Other Emerson*, ed. Branka Arsic and Cary Wolfe (Minneapolis: University of Minnesota Press, 2010), 101–29.

108. Emerson, *Selected Journals*, 1:58.

109. Emerson, *Selected Journals*, 1:60.

110. Thomas Wentworth Higginson, *Contemporaries* (Boston: Houghton Mifflin, 1899), 270–71.

111. In fact, the title may have been chosen to attract listeners when he gave the lecture outside of New England. Ralph Waldo Emerson, *The Later Lectures of Ralph Waldo Emerson, 1843–1871*, ed. Ronald A. Bosco and Joel Myerson (Athens: University of Georgia Press, 2001), 1:7–18.

112. Emerson, *Essays and Poems*, 990.

113. "Emerson's Lecture Before the Rochester Athenaeum," *Frederick Douglass' Paper*, December 3, 1852.

114. Emerson, *Selected Journals*, 2:35, 2:291.

115. Helen Deese, ed., *The Selected Journals of Caroline Healey Dall*, vol. 1: *1838–1855* (Boston: Massachusetts Historical Society, 2006), 333; "Emerson," *National Anti-Slavery Standard*, February 17, 1855.

116. Emerson, *Selected Journals*, 2:627.

117. For an analysis of how Emerson's celebration of English national traits contributed to nineteenth-century racism, see Nell Irvin Painter, *The History of White People* (New York: Norton, 2010), 151–89.

118. Emerson, *Selected Journals* 2:586.

119. "Ralph Waldo Emerson's Lecture," *National Anti-Slavery Standard*, February 17, 1855.

120. David Brion Davis, *The Problem of Slavery in the Age of Emancipation* (New York: Knopf, 2014), 15–44.

121. Theodore Parker to David Wasson, December 12, 1857, Theodore Parker Correspondence 4:182, Massachusetts Historical Society.

122. "Address of Theodore Parker," *Liberator*, May 23, 1856.

123. Theodore Parker, *The Relation of Slavery to a Republican Form of Government* (Boston: William L. Kent & Co., 1858), 20.

124. Michael Fellman, "Theodore Parker and the Abolitionist Role in the 1850s," *Journal of American History* 61, no. 3 (1974): 678.

125. Parker, *Collected Works*, 6:252.

126. Ralph Waldo Emerson to Herman Grimm, June 27, 1861, in Frederick William Hollis, ed., *Correspondence Between Ralph Waldo Emerson and Herman Grimm* (Boston: Houghton and Mifflin, 1903), 61.

127. Parker, *Life and Correspondence*, 1:397.

128. Parker, *Life and Correspondence*, 1:397.

129. Theodore Parker to Francis Jackson, August 21, 1859, Theodore Parker Papers, vol. 3, 67, Massachusetts Historical Society.

130. Thomas Wentworth Higginson, *Contemporaries* (Boston: Houghton Mifflin, 1899), 271.

131. "The New England Anti-Slavery Convention," *National Anti-Slavery Standard*, June 13, 1863.

132. Broadside, "Americans to the Rescue," Anti-Slavery Collection, Boston Public Library.

133. "New England Anti-Slavery Convention," *National Anti-Slavery Standard*, June 10, 1854.

134. Patrick Toohey, for instance, told the New England Anti-Slavery Convention that he "wished to suggest to the Abolitionists the propriety of refraining from unjust reflection on the Irish race" in 1863. See "The New England Anti-Slavery Convention," *National Anti-Slavery Standard*, June 13, 1863.

135. Laurie, *Beyond Garrison*, 274–79.

136. Dale Baum, *The Civil War Party System: The Case of Massachusetts, 1848–1876* (Chapel Hill: University of North Carolina Press, 1984), 29.

137. "Know-Nothing State Council," *Boston Semi-Weekly Courier*, May 3, 1855. See Tyler Anbinder, *Nativism and Slavery: The Northern Know Nothings and the Politics of the 1850* (New York: Oxford University Press, 1994); John Ashworth, *Slavery, Capitalism, and Politics in the Antebellum Republic*, vol. 2: *The Coming of the Civil War, 1850–1861* (New York: Cambridge University Press, 2007), 515–44.

138. Baum, *The Civil War Party System*, 28.

139. *Acts and Resolves Passed by the General Court of Massachusetts in the Year 1855: Together with the Messages* (Boston: William White, 1855), 815, 674, 924, 506.

140. Susannah Ural Bruce, *The Harp and the Eagle: Irish-American Volunteers and the Union Army, 1861–1865* (New York: New York University Press, 2006), 46.

141. "Legislative," *Boston Courier*, January 8, 1855.

142. Parker, *Life and Correspondence*, 1:395.

143. Lydia Maria Child, *The Patriarchal Institution, as Described by Members of Its Own Family* (New York: American Anti-Slavery Society, 1860), 49.

144. Quoted in Baum, *The Civil War Party System*, 32.

145. Alcott, *The Journals of Bronson Alcott*, 227.

146. Maria Weston Chapman to Samuel Sewall, August 9, 1857, Robie-Sewall Papers, Massachusetts Historical Society.

147. Henry Wilson, *Are the Working-Men "Slaves?" Speech of Hon. Henry Wilson, of Mass.* (Washington, DC: Buell and Blanchard, 1858), 4.

148. "Sketch of a Tour to the West," *Liberator*, November 12, 1858.

149. Jasper Douthit, *Jasper Douthit's Story: The Autobiography of a Pioneer* (Boston: American Unitarian Association, 1909), 52, 53, 81. Thanks to Douthit's descendant, Andrew Fagal, for this citation.

150. For the history of the Saturday Club, see Edward Waldo Emerson, *The Early Years of the Saturday Club, 1855–1870* (Boston: Houghton, Mifflin, 1918).

151. "British India," *Atlantic Monthly* 1, no. 1 (November 1857): 85–93.

152. Quoted in Randall Fuller, *From Battlefields Rising: How the Civil War Transformed American Literature* (New York: Oxford University, 2011), 20.

153. Edmund Quincy, "Where Will It End?" *Atlantic Monthly* 1, no. 2 (December 1857): 242.

154. See Lewis Simpson, *Mind and the American Civil War: A Mediation on Lost Causes* (Baton Rouge: Louisiana State University Press, 1989), 35. On regionalism in canonical New England literature, see Thomas Constantinesco and Cécile Roudeau, "Limning New Regions of Thought: Emerson's Abstract Regionalism," *ESQ* 60, no. 2 (2014): 293–326; Lawrence Buell, "The New England Renaissance and American Literary Ethnocentrism," *Prospects* 10:409–22.

155. Peter Gomes, ed., *The Pilgrim Society, 1820–1970: An Informal Commemorative Essay* (Boston: Nimrod, 1971), 17.

156. *An Account of the Pilgrim Celebration at Plymouth, August 1, 1853* (Boston: Crosby, Nichols, 1853).

157. See Amy Kaplan, "Manifest Domesticity," in *The Futures of American Studies*, ed. Donald Pease and Robyn Wiegman (Durham, NC: Duke University Press, 2002), 111–34.

158. Charlotte Forten, "Interesting Letter of Charlotte L. Forten," *Liberator*, December 19, 1862.

159. "Advertisements: The Sons of New England," *National Anti-Slavery Standard*, April 21, 1855.

160. John Burt, *Lincoln's Tragic Pragmatism: Lincoln, Douglas, and Moral Conflict* (Cambridge, MA: Belknap, 2013), 277.

161. "The Party of Grand Moral Ideas," *Harrisburg Weekly Patriot and Union*, June 8, 1865.

162. Emerson, *Selected Journals*, 2:554–55.

163. See Parker, *Collected Works*, 4:253–4:257.

164. Quoted in Sacvan Bercovitch, *The Puritan Origins of the American Self* (New Haven, CT: Yale University Press, 2011), 87.

165. Thomas Wentworth Higginson, "The New England Intellect," Papers of Thomas Wentworth Higginson, Houghton Library, Harvard University.

166. "Address of Wendell Phillips, Delivered Before the Twenty-Eighth Congregational Society, at Music Hall, Boston, July 6, 1862," *National Anti-Slavery Standard*, July 12, 1862.

167. Phillips, *Speeches, Lectures, and Letters*, 281.

168. Charles Sumner, *His Complete Works* (Boston: Lee and Shepard, 1890), 12:184.

169. Thoreau, *Journal*, 407.

170. Thoreau, *Walden*, 13.

171. Joseph Henry Allen, *The Great Controversy of States and People* (Boston: Crosby and Nichols, 1851), 8.

172. Lawrence Buell, *Emerson* (Cambridge, MA: Belknap, 2003), 266.

173. William Kelley et al., *Addresses of Hon. W. D. Kelley, Miss Anna Dickinson, and Mr. Frederick Douglass* (Philadelphia: s.n., 1863), 3.

174. "The Negro at the New England Dinner," *National Anti-Slavery Standard*, January 2, 1864.

175. For Nell on Attucks, see Stephen Kantrowitz, "A Place for 'Colored Patriots': Crispus Attucks among the Abolitionists, 1842–1863," *Massachusetts Historical Review* 11 (2009): 97–117.

176. "Valedictory Poem," *Salem Register*, July 28, 1856.

177. Charlotte Forten, "Glimpses of New England," *National Anti-Slavery Standard*, June 19, 1858.

178. "The People's Party in Massachusetts," *National Era*, July 6, 1854; "Anti-Nebraska Meeting in Concord," *Daily Atlas*, June 27, 1854.

179. "The People Moving," *Liberator*, June 30, 1854.

180. "The Fusion Convention of the 20th," *National Aegis*, July 12, 1854.

181. Francis Curtis, *The Republican Party: A History of Its Fifty Years' Existence and a Record of its Measures and Leaders* (New York: Knickerbocker Press, 1904), 1:194–95.

182. "The Meeting on the Common," *National Aegis*, July 26, 1854; Stephen M. Allen, *Origin and Early Progress of the Republican Party in the United States, Together with the History of Its Formation in Massachusetts* (Boston: Getchell Brothers, 1879), 17.

183. "Meeting of the 'Republicans,'" *Boston Courier*, August 31, 1854.

184. Bruce Laurie, "The 'Fair Field' of the 'Middle Ground': Abolitionism, Labor Reform, and the Making of an Antislavery Bloc in Antebellum Massachusetts," in *Labor Histories: Class, Politics, and the Working-Class Experience*, ed. E. Arnesen, J. Greene, and B. Laurie (Urbana: University of Illinois Press, 1998), 56–57.

185. Jeffrey Rossbach, *Ambivalent Conspirators: John Brown, The Secret Six, and a Theory of Slave Violence* (Philadelphia: University of Pennsylvania Press, 1982), 104–5.

186. A. Bronson Alcott, "New England Reformers: Brown, the Hero," *Commonwealth*, May 29, 1863.

187. Moncure Conway et al., *The Martyrdom of John Brown: The Proceedings of a Public Meeting Held in London on the 2nd December, 1863* (London: Published by the Emancipation Society, 1864), 19.

188. Anita Robboy and Stanley Robboy, "Lewis Hayden: From Fugitive Slave to Statesman," *New England Quarterly* 46, no. 4 (December, 1973): 608.

189. David S. Reynolds, *John Brown, Abolitionist: The Man Who Killed Slavery, Sparked the Civil War, and Seeded Civil Rights* (New York: Knopf, 2005), 344.

190. Thoreau, *Collected Essays and Poems*, 397, 399, 407.

191. Reynolds, *John Brown, Abolitionist*, 367.

192. Rossbach, *Ambivalent Conspirators*, 239.

193. Edward J. Renehan Jr., *The Secret Six: The True Tale of the Men Who Conspired with John Brown* (New York: Crown, 1995), 214.

194. Ralph Waldo Emerson, *The Collected Works of Ralph Waldo Emerson*, vol. 10: *Uncollected Prose Writings, Addresses, Essays, and Reviews*, ed. Ronald A. Bosco and Joel Myerson (Cambridge, MA: Belknap, 2013), 387.

195. Emerson, *The Collected Works of Ralph Waldo Emerson*, 10:392.

196. Gougeon, *Virtue's Hero*, 252.

197. Conway et al., *The Martyrdom of John Brown*, 18–19.

198. See, for instance, Gura, *Man's Better Angels*, 241–66.

199. Theodore Parker to Eliza Eddy, November 19, 1859, Theodore Parker Correspondence, Massachusetts Historical Society.

200. Quoted in Laura Dassow Wallis, *Henry David Thoreau: A Life* (Chicago: University of Chicago Press, 2017), 457.

CHAPTER 6

1. Grimké, *Journals of Charlotte Forten Grimké*, 447 (February 8, 1863).

2. Gougeon, *Virtue's Hero*, 306.

3. Van Wyck Brooks recounts this story, which one can, and should be, as skeptical of as one likes, in *New England Indian Summer*.

4. Gura, *American Transcendentalism*, 5.

5. A. Bronson Alcott, Journal for 1862, Entry for January 1, A. Bronson Alcott Papers, Houghton Library, Harvard University.

6. Membership list in "Notes on Town and Country Club," A. Bronson Alcott Papers, Houghton Library, Harvard University.

7. Thomas Wentworth Higginson to James Russell Lowell, July 5, 1849, James Russell Lowell Papers, Houghton Library, Harvard University.

8. George Frederickson, *The Inner Civil War: Northern Intellectuals and the Crisis of the Union* (Urbana: University of Illinois Press, 1965).

9. Louis Menand, *The Metaphysical Club: A Story of Ideas in America* (New York: Farrar, Straus, and Giroux, 2001).

10. Emerson, *Essays and Poems*, 38.

11. James Oakes has convincingly argued that the Republican Party was eager to abolish slavery as quickly as constitutionally possible. They were not reluctant emancipationists as many historical narratives have argued. James Oakes, *Freedom National: The Destruction of Slavery in the United States, 1861–1865* (New York: Norton, 2013). Recent studies have demonstrated an early commitment of Union soldiers to abolishing slavery. Chandra Manning, *What This Cruel War Was Over: Soldiers, Slavery, and the Civil War* (New York: Knopf, 2007).

12. William Lloyd Garrison, "The Relation of the Anti-Slavery Cause to the War," *National Anti-Slavery Standard*, May 18, 1861.

13. Quoted in Peter Wirzbicki, "Wendell Phillips and Transatlantic Radicalism: Democracy, Capitalism, and the American Labor Movement," in *Wendell Phillips: Social Justice and the Power of the Past*, ed. A. J. Aiseirithe and Donald Yacovone (Baton Rouge: Louisiana State University Press, 2016), 170.

14. Phillips, *Speeches, Lectures, and Letters*, 294.

15. William Lloyd Garrison, *The Letters of William Lloyd Garrison*, vol. 5: *Let the Oppressed Go Free: 1861–1867*, ed. William Merrill and Louis Ruchames (Cambridge, MA: Belknap, 1975), 6.

16. "Letter from William Lloyd Garrison," *Liberator*, November 9, 1860.

17. "Affairs About Boston," *Weekly Anglo-African*, March 2, 1861.

18. Garrison, *Letters*, 5:5; "Speech of John S. Rock," *Liberator*, July 18, 1862.

19. "Notes on the Tremont Temple Mob," *Liberator*, December 14, 1860.

20. "Mobocratic Assault upon an Anti-Slavery Meeting in Boston," *Liberator*, December 7, 1860; "Frederick Douglass at Music Hall," *Liberator*, December 14, 1860.

21. Carl Wittke, *Against the Current: The Life of Karl Heinzen* (Chicago: University of Chicago Press, 1945); James Stewart, *Wendell Phillips: Liberty's Hero* (Baton Rouge: Louisiana State University Press, 1998), 214.

22. John White Chadwick, ed., *A Life for Liberty: Antislavery and Other Letters of Sallie Holley* (New York: G. P. Putnam's Sons, 1899), 177.

23. William Schouler, *A History of Massachusetts in the Civil War* (Boston: E. P. Dutton, 1868), 1:43.

24. Ronald A. Bosco and Joel Myerson, eds., *The Later Lectures of Ralph Waldo Emerson, 1843–1871*, vol. 2: *1855–1871* (Athens: University of Georgia Press, 2001), 201.

25. "Speech of Ralph Waldo Emerson," *Liberator*, February 1, 1861.

26. "Affairs About Boston," *Weekly Anglo-African*, March 2, 1861.

27. Moncure Conway, *The Rejected Stone: or Insurrection vs. Resurrection in America* (Boston: Walker and Wise, 1861), 30.

28. Walt Whitman, *Poetry and Prose* (New York: Library of America, 1982), 706–7.

29. "Our Boston Correspondence," *National Anti-Slavery Standard*, April 27, 1861.

30. Phillips, *Speeches, Lectures, and Letters*, 406.

31. "Meeting in Boston," *Weekly Anglo-African*, May 4, 1861; "Sentiments of the Colored People of Boston upon the War," *Liberator*, April 26, 1861.

32. "Meeting of Colored Citizens," *Boston Traveler*, April 30, 1861.

33. "Meeting of Colored Citizens of New Bedford," *National Anti-Slavery Standard*, October 26, 1861.

34. See "From the Boston Correspondent . . . ," *Pacific Appeal*, October 11, 1862.

35. William Schouler, *A History of Massachusetts in the Civil War* (Boston: E. P. Dutton, 1868), 1:177–78.

36. Quoted in Kantrowitz, *More Than Freedom*, 263.

37. David Blight, *Frederick Douglass' Civil War: Keeping Faith in Jubilee* (Baton Rouge: Louisiana State University Press, 1989), 155.

38. "Speech of John S. Rock, ESQ," *Liberator*, June 12, 1863.

39. "New England Anti-Slavery Convention," *Liberator*, June 5, 1863.

40. "Speech of John S. Rock, ESQ," *Liberator*, June 12, 1863.

41. Garrison, *Letters*, 5:17.

42. "Meeting of Colored Citizens of New Bedford," *National Anti-Slavery Standard*, October 26, 1861.

43. "Public Educators: Address of Wendell Phillips," *National Anti-Slavery Standard*, November 22, 1862.

44. Through the Civil War, abolitionists such as Wendell Phillips called for making "our institutions homogeneous," by which he meant a more nationalized legal and political regime. Phillips, *Speeches, Lectures, and Letters*, 429.

45. See Caleb McDaniel, *The Problem of Democracy in the Age of Slavery: Garrisonian Abolitionists and Transatlantic Reform* (Baton Rouge: Louisiana State University Press, 2013).

46. Phillips, *Speeches, Lectures, and Letters*, 406.

47. "Southern Disunionists and Northern Disunionists," *Liberator*, April 19, 1861.

48. Quoted in Chadwick, *A Life for Liberty*, 188.

49. William Lloyd Garrison, *The Abolition of Slavery: The Right of the Government Under the War Power* (Boston: R. F. Wallcut, 1861).

50. "Anti-Slavery Patriotism," *National Anti-Slavery Standard*, March 14, 1863.

51. "The Old Pledge," *National Anti-Slavery Standard*, June 14, 1862.

52. Quoted in Mayer, *All on Fire*, 522.

53. "The Nation Supreme," *National Anti-Slavery Standard*, November 29, 1862.

54. "Taxation," *Commonwealth*, April 22, 1864.

55. C. A. Bartol, *The Nation's Hour: A Tribute to Major Sidney Willard* (Boston: Walker and Wise, 1862), 12.

56. Chadwick, *A Life for Liberty*, 189.

57. The exceptions are chronicled in Stanley Harrold, *Subversives: Antislavery Community in Washington, D.C., 1828–1865* (Baton Rouge: Louisiana State University Press, 2002).

58. "Twenty-Ninth Annual Meeting of the Massachusetts Anti-Slavery Society," *National Anti-Slavery Standard*, February 1, 1862.

59. "Slave Catching in Washington," *Weekly Anglo-African*, March 8, 1862.

60. "Mr. Garrison's Speech at New York," *Liberator*, January 24, 1862.

61. Henry Wilson, *History of the Antislavery Measures of the Thirty-Seventh and Thirty-Eighth United-States Congresses, 1861–1864* (Boston: Walker and Wise, 1864), 48.

62. William C. Nell, "Emancipation in the District of Columbia," *Liberator*, May 2, 1862.

63. John Blassingame, ed., *The Frederick Douglass Papers: Series One, Speeches, Debates, and Interviews* (New Haven, CT: Yale University Press, 1985), 3:517.

64. "Life Pictures at Washington," *Liberator*, April 4, 1862.

65. "Convention of Colored Citizens of Boston," *National Anti-Slavery Standard*, December 9, 1865.

66. "Hail Columbia," *Lowell Daily Citizen and News*, June 3, 1862.

67. John S. Rock to Charles Sumner, June 5, 1862, Charles Sumner Papers, Harvard University.

68. "Speech of Rev. M. D. Conway," *National Anti-Slavery Standard*, August 9, 1862.

69. Edward Everett Hale, ed., *James Freeman Clarke: Autobiography, Diary and Correspondence* (Boston: Houghton, Mifflin, 1891), 280–81.

70. Hale, *James Freeman Clarke*, 275–77.

71. Blassingame, *The Frederick Douglass Papers*, 3:517.

72. Gougeon, *Virtue's Hero*, 276; Conway, *Autobiography*, 1:310.

73. Robert Richardson, *Emerson: The Mind on Fire* (Berkeley: University of California Press, 1996), 548.

74. Emerson, *Journals*, 2:780. For more on this meeting, see Stephen Cushman, "When Lincoln Met Emerson," *Journal of the Civil War Era* 3, no. 2 (Summer 2013): 163–83.

75. Octavius Brooks Frothingham, *Memoir of William Henry Channing* (Boston: Houghton, Mifflin, and Co., 1886), 303.

76. William Henry Channing, *The Civil War in America; or, The Slaveholders' Conspiracy; An Address* (Liverpool: W. Vaughn, 1861), 7.

77. Sarah Forbes Hughes, ed., *Letters and Recollections of John Murray Forbes* (Boston: Houghton and Mifflin, 1899), 1:227.

78. "Speech of John S. Rock ESQ," *Liberator*, July 18, 1862.

79. "Personal," *National Anti-Slavery Standard*, December 6, 1862.

80. Frothingham, *Memoir of William Henry Channing*, 316.

81. Channing's war years are described in Frothingham, *Memoir of William Henry Channing*, 308–18.

82. Frothingham, *Memoir of William Henry Channing*, 332.

83. Charles Sumner to Wendell Phillips, December 8, 1861, in Beverly Wilson Palmer, ed., *The Selected Letters of Charles Sumner* (Boston: Northeastern University Press, 1990), 2:85; for more on Phillips during Civil War, see Melinda Lawson, *Patriot Fires: Forging a New American Nationalism in the Civil War North* (Lawrence: University of Kansas Press, 2002), 129–59.

84. "Wendell Phillips in Washington," *National Anti-Slavery Standard*, March 22, 1862.

85. "Our Washington Correspondence," *National Anti-Slavery Standard*, March 22, 1862.

86. Alfred M. Green, *Letters and Discussions on the Formation of Colored Regiments and the Duty of Colored People in Regard to the Great Slaveholders' Rebellion in the United States* (Philadelphia: Ringwalt and Brown, 1862), 8.

87. "Anti-Slavery at Washington," *Liberator*, February 28, 1862.

88. See the speech "The Conduct of Our Generals Towards Fugitive Slaves," in Charles Sumner, *The Works of Charles Sumner* (Boston: Lee and Shepard, 1880), 6:489–98.

89. "Letter from Rev. Daniel Foster," *Liberator*, January 23, 1863.

90. Moncure Conway to Wendell Phillips, December 9, 1861, in Wendell Phillips Papers, Houghton Library, Harvard University.

91. Conway, *Autobiography*, 1:305; "The Rejected Stone," *Liberator*, March 28, 1862.

92. "Mr. Conway Going to England," *National Anti-Slavery Standard*, April 11, 1863.

93. Conway, *Autobiography*, 1:305.

94. Conway, *The Rejected Stone*, 68–69.

95. Conway, *Rejected Stone*, 69–71.

96. "Mr. Conway Going to England," *National Anti-Slavery Standard*, April 11, 1863.

97. Frederickson, *Inner Civil War*, 123.

98. Conway, *Autobiography*, 1:312.

99. Moncure D. Conway, *The Golden Hour* (Boston: Ticknor and Fields, 1862), 28.

100. Conway, *Golden Hour*, 44.

101. Conway, *Golden Hour*, 65.

102. See David Donald, *Charles Sumner and the Rights of Man* (New York: Knopf, 1970), 74.

103. Conway, *Autobiography*, 1:328.

104. Conway, *Autobiography*, 1:328.

105. "Philosophy of the Absolute," *Commonwealth*, September 18, 1863.

106. As far as I know, this longer version seems not to have been noticed by scholars. It does not appear in the various versions of his complete works or in the edited volumes of his political writings. The *Commonwealth* version contains about 1,000 words that have not been replicated elsewhere.

107. Ralph Waldo Emerson, "The President's Proclamation," *Commonwealth*, November 15, 1862.

108. James Freeman Clarke, "The Plagues of Egypt and America: A Sermon, Preached in Boston, Sept, 26th, 1862, Being the Sunday Following the President's Proclamation," *Commonwealth*, October 11, 1862.

109. "Want of Ideas in the Army," *Commonwealth*, November 15, 1862; Child, *Letters of Lydia Maria Child*, 154.

110. "The Woman's National Loyal League: Address to the President," *National Anti-Slavery Standard*, May 30, 1863.

111. Bosco and Myerson, *The Later Lectures of Ralph Waldo Emerson*, 325

112. Walt Whitman, *Poetry and Prose* (New York: Library of America, 1982), 475.

113. Coleridge, *Aids to Reflection*, 143.

114. "Speech of John S. Rock, ESQ," *Liberator*, July 18, 1862.

115. "Speech of John S. Rock," *Christian Recorder*, February 22, 1862.

116. Daniel Dulany Addison, ed., *Lucy Larcom: Life, Letters, and Diary* (Boston: Houghton Mifflin, 1895), 109.

117. "The People's Party Held a State Convention," *Salem Register*, October 11, 1862.

118. "Matters and Things," *Liberator*, December 5, 1862.

119. "State Elections," *National Anti-Slavery Standard*, November 8, 1862.

120. Bosco and Myerson, *The Later Lectures of Ralph Waldo Emerson*, 2:240.

121. "Speech of Wendell Phillips," *National Anti-Slavery Standard*, February 13, 1864.

122. "Speech of John S. Rock, ESQ," *Liberator*, July 18, 1862.

123. "Wendell Phillips, ESQ, at the New York City Anti-Slavery Society, Cooper Institute, May 7th, 1862," *Liberator*, May 23, 1862.

124. "The Sacredness of Nationality," *National Anti-Slavery Standard*, January 16, 1864.

125. "The Rev. Sella Martin," *Patriot*, September 24, 1863.

126. "The Rev. Sella Martin," *Patriot*, September 24, 1863.

127. "Reception of J. Sella Martin," *National Anti-Slavery Standard*, June 18, 1864.

128. "Speech of John S. Rock, ESQ," *Liberator*, June 12, 1863.

129. "Twenty-Ninth Annual Meeting of the Massachusetts Anti-Slavery Society," *National Anti-Slavery Standard*, February 1, 1862.

130. "Our Perils from Abroad," *Liberator*, January 3, 1862.

131. See Andrew Zimmerman, "From the Rhine to the Mississippi: Property, Democracy, and Socialism in the American Civil War," *Journal of the Civil War Era* 5, no. 1 (March 2015): 3–37.

132. "Lecture by Wendell Phillips, ESQ.," *National Anti-Slavery Standard*, December 7, 1861.

133. "Mr. Garrison's Speech at New York," *Liberator*, January 24, 1862; "Address to the Soldiers of the Second Revolution," *National Anti-Slavery Standard*, May 30, 1863.

134. Lewis H. Putnam, *The Review of the Revolutionary Elements of the Rebellion and of the Aspect of Reconstruction; with a Plan to Restore Harmony Between the Two Races in the Southern States* (Brooklyn, 1868), 13.

135. "The Apostles of Slavery," *New York Times*, June 2, 1863.

136. "Speech of John S Rock, ESQ," *Liberator*, August 15, 1862.

137. Quoted in Wirzbicki, "Wendell Phillips and Transatlantic Radicalism," 170.

138. "Speech of John S. Rock," *Liberator*, July 18, 1862.

139. Charles W. Denison to Robert Morris, September 11, 1863, Robert Morris Papers, Boston Athenaeum.

140. "The Impartial Suffrage League," *Right Way*, September 22, 1866.

141. Coleridge, *On the Constitution of Church and State*, 227.

142. Parker, *Collected Works*, 5:298–99.

143. "Speech of John S. Rock, ESQ," *Liberator*, February 14, 1862.

144. Quoted in Garrett Epps, *Democracy Reborn: The Fourteenth Amendment and the Fight for Equal Rights in Post-Civil War America* (New York: Henry Holt, 2006), 115.

145. Garry Wills, *Lincoln at Gettysburg: The Words That Remade America* (New York: Simon and Schuster, 1993).

146. Edmund Wilson, *Patriotic Gore: Studies in the Literature of the American Civil War* (New York: Norton, 1994), 239–57.

147. Grimké, *Journals of Charlotte Forten Grimké*, 382.

148. Grimké, *Journals of Charlotte Forten Grimké*, 387.

149. Charlotte Forten, "Life on the Sea Islands," *Atlantic Monthly*, May 1864, 587.

150. Charlotte Forten, "Interesting Letter from Miss Charlotte L Forten," *Liberator*, December 19, 1862.

151. Forten, "Life on the Sea Islands," 593–94.

152. Forten, "Life on the Sea Islands," 591.

153. Grimké, *Journals of Charlotte Forten Grimké*, 447 (February 8, 1863).

154. Charlotte Forten, "October 27th, 1862, at Sea," Black Abolitionist Papers, Howard University Library, Moorland Spingarn Research Center, Grimke Papers.

155. Wilson, *Patriotic Gore*, 225.

156. Emerson, *Essays and Poems*, 242.

157. "White and Black Slavery—Philanthropy That Sees Far Off," *Richmond Whig*, January 24, 1860.

158. William H. Holcombe, "The Alternative: A Separate Nationality, or the Africanization of the South," *Southern Literary Messenger*, February 1861, 81, 87.

159. George William Bagby, "Notices of New Works," *Southern Literary Messenger*, April 1861, 326.

160. T. W. MacMahon, *Cause and Contrast: An Essay on the American Crisis* (Richmond, VA: West and Johnston, 1862), 122.

161. Daniel Robinson Hundley, *Prison Echoes of the Great Rebellion* (New York: S. W. Green, 1874), 109.

162. Congressional Globe, 38th Congress, 1st Session, p. 709 (February 19, 1864).

163. Samuel Cox, *Eight Years in Congress, from 1857–1865. Memoir and Speeches* (New York: Appleton, 1865), 286, 297–99.

164. Kaplan, "The Miscegenation Issue in the Election of 1864," 319; *Miscegenation: Indorsed by the Republican Party, Campaign Document, No. 11* (New York: 13 Park Row, 1864), 5–6.

165. "Fugitive Aid Society," *Liberator*, December 5, 1862; "The Fugitive Aid Society," *National Anti-Slavery Standard*, November 22, 1862. For Du Bois on Louise de Mortie, see W. E. B. Du Bois, *Darkwater: Voices from Within the Veil* (Mineola, NY: Dover, 1999), 103–4.

166. Judith Harper, *Women During the Civil War: An Encyclopedia* (New York: Routledge, 2007), 77–78.

167. "Fugitive Aid Society," *Liberator*, November 21, 1862; "A Benevolent Object," *Liberator*, April 4, 1862.

168. J. Sella Martin, *The Hero and the Slave: Founded on Fact* (Boston: W. F. Brown, 1862), 8.

169. Martin, *Hero and Slave*, 11.

170. This debate was printed in Alfred M. Green, *Letters and Discussions on the Formation of Colored Regiments and the Duty of Colored People in Regard to the Great Slaveholders' Rebellion in the United States* (Philadelphia: Ringwalt and Brown, 1862).

171. "Annual Meeting of the Massachusetts Anti-Slavery Society," *National Anti-Slavery Standard*, February 7, 1863.

172. "Speech of C. L. Remond," *National Anti-Slavery Standard*, August 19, 1865.

173. "The New England Anti-Slavery Convention," *National Anti-Slavery Standard*, June 13, 1863.

174. Nell, *William Cooper Nell*, 606.

175. "The War, and Colored American Auxiliaries," *Liberator*, September 6, 1861.

176. "An Appeal to the Friends of Education," *Liberator*, January 16, 1863.

177. "Crispus Attucks Celebration," *Liberator*, March 20, 1863.

178. "Levee in Aid of the Colored Regiments," *Douglass' Monthly*, April 1863.

179. See Ralph Waldo Emerson to George Luther Stearns, December 20, 1863, in Eleanor Tilton, ed., *The Letters of Ralph Waldo Emerson*, vol. 9: *1860–1869* (New York: Columbia University Press, 1994), 123.

180. See "Our Boston Correspondence," *National Anti-Slavery Standard*, June 6, 1863.

181. "The New England Anti-Slavery Convention," *National Anti-Slavery Standard*, June 13, 1863.

182. See "Civil War Pass," George Downing Papers, Moorland-Spingard Research Center, Howard University.

183. "George Julian January 19, 1864," George Downing Papers, Moorland-Spingard Research Center, Howard University.

184. "Brutal Outrage," *Boston Herald*, October 30, 1862.

185. "Speech of John S. Rock, ESQ," *Liberator*, August 15, 1862.

186. "A Carolinian in Paris," *Cincinnati Daily Commercial*, January 6, 1860.

187. "Speech of John S. Rock, ESQ," *Liberator*, June 12, 1863.

188. "Mr. John S. Rock," *Pine and Palm*, October 12, 1861.

189. "Association for the Relief of Destitute Contrabands," *Boston Traveler*, September 30, 1862.

190. "Selling the Servants of Union Officers into Slavery!" *Liberator*, August 15, 1862.

191. Various, *Proceedings of the National Convention of Colored Men, Held in the City of Syracuse* (Boston: J. S. Rock and Geo L. Ruffin, 1864), 23.

192. Various, *Proceedings of the National Convention of Colored Men*, 23.

193. "Speech of John S. Rock, ESQ," *Liberator*, February 14, 1862.

194. John S. Rock to Soldiers of 5th Regiment, U.S. Heavy Artillery, Natchez, Mississippi, May 30, 1864, Ruffin Papers, Moorland-Spingarn Research Center, Howard University.

195. "The New England Anti-Slavery Convention," *National Anti-Slavery Standard*, June 6, 1863.

196. "The New England Anti-Slavery Convention," *National Anti-Slavery Standard*, June 13, 1863.

197. Henry Pearson, *The Life of John A. Andrew: Governor of Massachusetts* (Boston: Houghton and Mifflin, 1904), 2:96.

198. "Payment of Colored Soldiers," *Commonwealth*, April 29, 1864.

199. Corporal Thomas D. Freeman to Robert Morris, April 25, 1864, in Robert Morris Papers, Boston Athenaeum.

200. "Pay of Colored Troops," *National Anti-Slavery Standard*, January 30, 1864.

201. Daniel Ullman, *Address by Daniel Ullman, L.L.D. Before the Soldier's and Sailor's Union of the State of New York on the Organization of Colored Troops and the Regeneration of the South* (Washington, DC: Great Republic Office, 1868), 3.

202. Quoted in Pearson, *Life of John A. Andrew*, 104; "The Massachusetts Colored Troops," *National Anti-Slavery Standard*, April 30, 1864.

203. Edward Bates, *Opinion of the Attorney General on the Pay, etc., of Colored Soldiers* (Washington, DC, no publisher, 1864); "Col. Higginson on the Payment of Colored Troops," *National Anti-Slavery Standard*, August 20, 1864.

204. Joseph Glatthaar, *Forged in Battle: The Civil War Alliance of Black Soldiers and White Officers* (New York: Free Press, 1990), 174.

205. "Can Colored Men be Citizens of the United States," *National Anti-Slavery Standard*, January 10, 1863.

206. Edgar Brown, *Annual Register of the Executive and Legislative Departments of the Government of Massachusetts* (Boston: Wright and Potter, 1861), 3; for records of his wages, see Charles Endicott, *Report of the Auditor of Accounts of the Commonwealth of Massachusetts for the Year Ending December 31, 1872* (Boston: Wright and Potter, 1873), 109.

207. "Personal," *National Anti-Slavery Standard*, January 17, 1863.

208. For more of Rock's entry into the Supreme Court, see George A. Levesque, "Boston's Black Brahmin: Dr. John S. Rock," *Civil War History* 26, no. 4 (December 1980): 333–36.

209. John S. Rock to Charles Sumner, December 30, 1863, in Charles Sumner, *The Papers of Charles Sumner*, ed. Beverly Wilson Palmer (Alexandria, VA: Chadwyck-Healey, 1988), 30:127.

210. Allan Nevins and Milton Halsey Thomas, eds., *The Diary of George Templeton Strong* (Seattle: University of Washington Press, 1988), 250.

211. John S. Rock to Charles Sumner, December 17, 1864, in Sumner, *The Papers of Charles Sumner*, 32:130.

212. Salmon Chase to Charles Sumner, January 23, 1865, in Charles Sumner, *His Complete Works* (Boston: Lee and Shepard, 1890), 12:98.

213. John S. Rock to Charles Sumner, December 24, 1864, in Sumner, *The Papers of Charles Sumner*, 32:171.

214. Charles Sumner to Salmon Chase, December 21, 1864, in Sumner, *Complete Works*, 12:98.

215. "The Dred Scott Decision Buried in the Supreme Court—A Negro Lawyer Admitted by Chief Justice Chase," *New York Tribune*, February 7, 1865.

216. John S. Rock to Charles Sumner, February 1, 1865, *The Papers of Charles Sumner*, 32:463.

EPILOGUE

1. Langston recounts this in his autobiography, *John Mercer Langston, From the Virginia Plantation to the National Capitol or, the First and Only Negro Representative in Congress from the Old Dominion* (Hartford, CT: American Publishing Company, 1894), 301–2; see also John Mercer Langston, *Freedom and Citizenship: Selected Lectures and Addresses* (Washington, DC: R. H. Darby, 1883), 27.

2. "What Books to Read: An Address Delivered Before the Law Students of Howard University," *New York Tribune*, January 11, 1872.

3. "What Books to Read: An Address Delivered Before the Law Students of Howard University."

4. Nell, *William Cooper Nell*, 671.

5. Quoted in Amy Kittelstorm, *The Religion of Democracy: Seven Liberals and the American Moral Tradition* (New York: Penguin Books, 2015),174.

6. Julia Ward Howe, *Reminiscences: 1819–1899* (Boston: Houghton, Mifflin, and Co., 1900), 286, 282.

7. William James, "The Sentiment of Rationality," in William James, *Writings: 1878–1899* (New York: Library of America, 1992), 523.

8. Steven Kantrowitz's description of postwar Higginson as a "bitter reactionary" is unfair to the abolitionist. As Leslie Butler shows, he remained dedicated to democracy and liberal reform throughout the period, even if he no longer had the revolutionary fire he once had. Leslie Butler, *Critical Americans: Victorian Intellectuals and Transatlantic Reform* (Chapel Hill: University of North Carolina Press, 2007); Kantrowitz, *More Than Freedom*, 429.

9. James Russell Lowell, *The Writing of James Russell Lowell in Prose and Poetry: Literary and Political Addresses* (Boston: Houghton and Mifflin, 1886), 6:7–37.

10. "The Concord School," *New York Times*, August 26, 1879.

11. See Gougeon, *Virtue's Hero*, 8.

12. Phillips, *Speeches, Lectures, and Letters*, 169.

13. Sargent, *Sketches and Reminiscences of the Radical Club*, 165.

14. Stephen Kantrowitz, *More Than Freedom*, 378–89.

15. Stanley J. Robboy and Anita Robboy, "Lewis Hayden: From Fugitive Slave to Statesman," *New England Quarterly* 46, no. 4 (December 1973): 610.

16. *The Journal of the Senate for the Year 1871* (Boston: Wright and Potter, 1871), 191.

17. *A Memorial of Crispus Attucks, Samuel Maverick, James Caldwell, Samuel Gray, and Patrick Carr* (Boston: Printed by Order of the City Council, 1889), 11.

18. Robboy and Robboy, "Lewis Hayden," 612.

19. Eugene Debs, *Pearson's Magazine* 37, no. 5 (May 1917): 397–402.

20. Nick Salvatore, *Eugene V. Debs: Citizen and Socialist* (Chicago: University of Illinois Press, 1982), 186.

21. Jane Addams, *20 Years at Hull House: With Autobiographical Notes* (New York: Macmillan, 1911), 50.

22. For an analysis of this moment and the complex way Transcendentalist ideas shaped environmentalist thought, see Jedediah Purdy, *After Nature: A Politics for the Anthropocene* (Cambridge, MA: Harvard University Press, 2015), 116–37.

23. See Chris Dodge, "Emma Goldman, Thoreau, and Anarchists," *Thoreau Society Bulletin* no. 248 (Summer 2004): 4.

24. Leo Tolstoy, "A Message to the American People," *North American Review* 172, no. 533 (April 1901): 503.

25. http://www.thekingcenter.org/archive/document/transformed-nonconformist-0, accessed July 3, 2017.

26. Martin Luther King Jr., "A Legacy of Creative Protest," *Massachusetts Review*, Autumn 1962.

INDEX

Adams, Charles Francis, 225, 242
Adams, Henry, 107
Adams, John Quincy, 65, 66, 149, 230
Adams, Nehemiah, 73, 74
Addams, Jane, 263
Adelphic Union Library Association, 27, 31,
    45–49, 55, 56, 61, 77, 103, 251, 260
Afric-American Female Intelligence Society, 85
African Americans: in abolitionist move-
    ment, 3, 4, 19; American Civil War effort
    and, 250–51; citizenship of, 255, 256; critical
    patriotism of, 227–28; embracing violence,
    181–83; European revolutionary move-
    ments and, 131–35; heroism and, 193–94;
    Higher Law Ethos and, 146; New England
    nationalist pride and, 212–13; non-
    resistance ideology and, 92; as sailors,
    88–89; secession and, 226; as soldiers,
    219–20, 251–55; support of John Brown,
    217
Alcott, A. Bronson, 2, 4, 31, 45, 48, 55, 70, 72,
    78, 80, 88, 91–93, 99, 101, 102, 104, 125, 143,
    151, 158, 159, 183, 198, 206, 215, 216, 259, 261,
    263
Alcott, Louisa May, 70, 237
American Anti-Slavery Society, 88, 94, 100,
    194, 195
American Civil War, 219–23, 226–28, 240;
    European perceptions of, 243–44;
    Transcendentalist ideas in, 236–40, 242,
    245, 246–49; Union Army in, 235–36, 238,
    240
Amistad, 23, 32
Andrew, John A., 183, 214, 221, 224, 225, 233,
    240, 251, 252, 256
Anthony, Susan B., 244
Anti-Sabbatarianism, 78–79, 80–81, 139–40
Appleton, Nathan, 154
Arendt, Hannah, 274 n.137

Aristotle, 29
Atlantic Monthly, 191, 208–9, 221, 234, 238,
    247

Bagley, Sarah, 137
Ballou, Adin, 124, 263, 284 n.2
Bancroft, George, 197
Bates, Edward, black citizenship order of
    (1862), 231, 255
de Beauvoir, Simone, 296 n.97
Benson, George, 103
"Bible Convention," 79–80
"Bird Club," 206, 214–15
Blanc, Louis, 126, 134, 138
Blanqui, Louis Auguste, 126
Blyden, Edward, 14, 60
Blackwell, Lucy, 179
Bond, Julian, 263
Boston, 53–55, 106–8, 111–12, 142–44, 242;
    anti-abolitionist violence in, 225; cotton
    consumption in, 106, 285 n.22. *See also*
    New England, economy of
Boston Anti-Man Hunting League (Pine
    Tree Reading Club), 124, 183–85
Boston Union of Associationists, 113, 121,
    123–24, 137, 141
Boston Vigilance Committee, 7, 63, 124, 129,
    141, 142, 148–50, 157–60, 173, 174–77, 183,
    187, 214, 216, 224; Transcendentalists on,
    159
Bowditch, Henry I., 98, 124, 149, 163, 184, 221
Brainard, Charles, 233
Brisbane, Albert, 137
British emancipation, 178
Brook Farm, 2, 72, 94, 102, 121–23, 137, 289
    n.118
Brown, John, 15, 112, 215–18, 225, 247, 251
Brown, William Wells, 113, 133–34, 147, 154,
    195, 218, 228, 238, 254

Brownson, Orestes, 31, 45, 65, 67, 68–69
Buell, Lawrence, 211
Burlingame, Anson, 205, 221
Burns, Anthony, 59, 129, 130, 142–44, 160,
    165, 175–76, 181, 183, 190, 205
Burritt, Elihu, 108

Calhoun, John C., 128, 229, 231
Carlyle, Thomas, 29, 31, 38, 71, 116, 119, 140,
    189–90
Cavell, Stanley, 14
Channing, William Ellery, 67, 68, 73, 135, 137
Channing, William Henry, 11, 48, 55, 68, 75,
    88, 93, 97, 99, 102–4, 124, 135–41, 159, 175,
    221, 233–35, 259, 262, 264
Chapman, Maria Weston, 47, 48, 69–70, 79,
    80, 84, 92, 97, 207, 278 n.34
Chartist movement, 125–26, 129, 133
Chase, Salmon, 15, 234, 256
Cheney, Ednah Dow, 60, 84
Child, Lydia Maria, 36, 68, 69, 70, 83, 94, 95,
    110, 175, 185, 206, 238
Choate, Rufus, 89, 106, 152
Clapp, Henry, Jr., 57, 103
Clarke, James Freeman, 7, 11, 30, 45, 48, 59, 63,
    68, 79, 87, 97, 112, 132, 159, 162, 165, 183, 192,
    208, 224, 233, 234, 239
Clarkson, Thomas, 39, 43, 67
Clay, Henry, 62, 106, 150, 156
Cluer, John, 129, 243
Cole, Thomas, 45, 46, 47
Coleridge, Samuel Taylor, 6, 19, 26, 30, 32–35,
    37, 38, 41–42, 50, 113, 167, 239
Colored American, 33, 34–35, 48
Commonwealth, 237–38, 239, 310 n.106
Congregationalism, 72
Conway, Moncure, 9, 167–68, 237; Golden
    Hour (1862), 237; Rejected Stone (1861),
    236–37
Cotton Whigs, 108, 115, 139, 152–53, 156, 185
Cousin, Victor, 30, 49
Cox, Samuel "Sunset," 249
Craft, William and Ellen, 158, 174
Crittenden Compromise, 226
Crummell, Alexander, 23–25, 31–34, 38,
    39–45, 48, 82, 271 n.49

Dall, Caroline Healey, 59, 87–88, 201
Dana, Charles A., 121–22, 137
Dana, Richard Henry, 175, 176
Debs, Eugene, 263

Defensive League of Freedom, 183
Denison, Charles, 245
Devens, Charles, 160–61, 175
Dewey, John, 6, 13
Dial, 2, 15, 91, 98, 114, 208
Dickinson, Anna, 212
Douai, Adolf, 130
double consciousness, 49–53
Douglas, Stephen, 156, 176, 178, 210
Douglass, Frederick, 1–3, 8, 28, 35, 46, 53, 56, 58,
    61, 81, 82, 97, 99, 102–3, 120, 122, 124–25, 131,
    133, 138, 141, 155, 167, 175, 179, 193, 194, 200,
    215, 225, 227–28, 233, 234, 249, 255; African
    American troops and, 251, 254; Ralph
    Waldo Emerson and, 53, 60–61, 277 n.187
Douglass, H. Ford, 60
Douthit, Jasper, 207–8
Downing, George, 183, 225, 233, 252, 254
Dred Scott case (1857), 178, 193, 212, 218, 255,
    256–57
Du Bois, W. E. B., 5, 23–24, 44, 52, 249
Dumas, Alexandre, 44

Elkins, Stanley, 16, 269 n.47, 279 n.41
Ellison, Ralph Waldo, 14
Eliot, Samuel A., 135, 152–53, 155, 156, 171
Emancipation Proclamation (1863), 220, 235,
    238, 251, 255
Emancipation, 222–23, 244, 257
Emerson, Ralph Waldo, 2–6, 25, 43, 70–71,
    93, 219–20, 226, 258, 296 n.97; abolitionism
    and, 67–73, 91, 95–97, 111, 120, 151, 158, 167,
    185, 188; American Civil War and, 234, 238,
    239, 242, 248, 251–52; black thinkers and,
    55–58, 63, 86, 99, 193, 264; John Brown and,
    216–17; The Conservative, 119; Emancipa-
    tion in the British West Indies, 25, 95, 199;
    epistemology and, 36, 41, 42, 43; European
    revolutions of 1848 and, 126–27; Frederick
    Douglass and, 8, 61, 98, 277 n.187; heroism
    and, 189–91; influence on future social
    movements, 263–64; New England pride
    and, 210, 212; quoted, 3, 6, 12, 13, 14, 17,
    38–39, 89, 90, 104, 145, 222, 261, 263; racism
    of, 198–203; religious ideas of, 76, 77–79,
    81, 165; Republican Party and, 213–14;
    selfhood and, 39–42, 50–53, 161–63, 166,
    168, 172; Self-Reliance, 39, 56–58, 116–17,
    191; socialism and, 102, 113, 115, 116–20
European revolutions of 1848, 125–31
Everett, Edward, 152

Fairbank, Calvin, 62–63
federal government, 223–24, 228–32
Fichte, Johann Gottlieb, 31, 49, 100
Fillmore, Millard, 156, 214
Follen, Karl, 31, 48–49
Forten, Charlotte, 4, 26, 58–60, 82, 196, 209, 212–13, 219–20, 247–48, 257, 264, 302 n.89
Foster, Daniel, 73, 187–88, 236, 264
Foster, Stephen, 94, 181, 242
Fourier, Charles, 102–4, 122–24, 138
Fox, George, 37
France: abolition of slavery (1848) in, 128–29; American Civil War and, 244
Freedom's Journal, 28
Free Soil Party, 75, 95, 113, 138–39, 154, 164, 180
Fremont, John, 214, 228
Frothingham, Octavius, 81
Fugitive Aid Society, 249–50
Fugitive Slave Act (1850), 142, 145, 150–56, 178; resistance to, 155–59
fugitive slaves, 146–50. *See also* slavery
Fuller, Margaret, 2, 8, 13, 15, 50, 51, 53, 69, 70, 77–79, 83–90, 97, 100, 108, 120, 126–27, 137, 165, 173, 220, 267 n.36; death, 220; European revolutions of 1848 and, 127

Gandhi, Mahatma, 10, 14, 151, 263
Gardner, Henry, 205, 214
Garnet, Henry Highland, 23, 31–32, 113, 131–32, 133, 178, 235
Garrison, William Lloyd, 15, 49, 65, 67, 73–74, 78, 80, 85, 138, 144, 155, 156, 163, 172, 181–82, 195, 204, 218, 225, 232, 244, 248, 259, 263; on democratic government, 229–31; on the federal government, 223, 228–29; and fugitive slaves, 148, 157; nonresistant ideology of, 92–94, 194; and Transcendentalists, 55, 68, 69, 70, 72, 73, 79; views on workers' movements, 103, 108–10, 125, 129, 140
Garvey, Marcus, 14
Goldman, Emma, 263
Graham, Sylvester, 46, 192
Greeley, Horace, 103, 137, 176, 263
Green, Beriah, 32
Grimké, Angelina, 46, 47, 48

Hale, Sarah Josepha, 209
Hamilton Lyceum, 23, 26, 31–32
Hammond, James Henry, 89, 100, 207

Harbinger, 109, 123, 137
Harris, Charles Torrey, 238
Harvard University, 27, 31, 49
Hawthorne, Nathaniel, 16, 121–22, 220
Hayden, Lewis, 4–5, 55, 82, 132, 142, 193, 214, 215–16, 224, 251, 255–56, 262–64; experiences in slavery, 62–65, 106; protection of fugitive slaves, 134–35, 147, 157, 159, 160, 174–77, 185, 190
Hedge, Frederic Henry, 30
Hegel, Georg Wilhelm Friedrich, 12, 30, 42, 49, 100, 104, 115, 116, 119, 127, 130, 199, 201, 238
Heinzen, Karl, 130–31, 244
Hemingway, Ernest, 222
Heywood, Ezra, 242
Higginson, Thomas Wentworth, 3–4, 11, 63, 75, 98, 110, 112, 168–69, 172–73, 186, 191–92, 200, 203, 206, 220, 221, 247, 269, 261, 267 n.35, 281 n.95, 314 n.8; and John Brown, 215, 217; and resistance to Fugitive Slave Law, 142–46, 159, 160–61, 175–76, 183
Higher Law Ethos, 4, 10–11, 14–15, 17, 18, 66, 104, 144–46, 160, 171, 172, 180, 222, 259, 262, 264
Hildreth, Richard, 98
Hilton, John, 45, 56, 89, 148, 227
Hoar, Samuel, 89, 90
Holley, Sallie, 8, 88, 158, 225, 232
Holmes, Oliver Wendell, 208
Howe, Irving, 12, 66
Howe, Julia Ward, 37, 69, 259, 260
Howe, Samuel Gridley, 124, 214–15, 217, 220, 221
Hugo, Victor, 44, 134
Hume, David, 29, 39, 170
Hutchinson, Francis, 29, 30

Impartial Citizen, 131, 135
intellectual clubs, 26–28, 43–44

Jackson, Francis, 69, 129, 203
James, William, 8, 11, 50, 81, 166, 198, 259, 260, 274 n.131
Jefferson, Thomas, 29
Julian, George, 252

Kansas, 185–86, 187, 214
Kantianism, 12, 34–38, 42, 115, 119, 201, 239; contrasted with Lockeanism, 38–39
Keckley, Elizabeth, 249

Kelly, J. J., 181
Kemp, Henry, 130, 205
King, Martin Luther, Jr., 5, 10, 167, 263–64
Kneeland, Abner, 73
Know-Nothing Party (American Party),
    205–6, 214

Lamartine, Alphonse, 44, 126, 127
Langston, John Mercer, 58, 195, 258
Larcom, Lucy, 7, 113–15, 240
Latimer George, 112, 148–49, 154
Lawrence, Amos, 112, 175
Leroux, Pierre, 135, 137, 138
Liberia, 38
Liberty Party, 15, 95, 98, 113, 138, 149, 180, 214
Lieber, Francis, 38
Lincoln, Abraham, 18–19, 221–25, 233–34,
    237–39; Gettysburg address of, 246
Locke, John, 10, 29–31, 34, 35–36, 38, 107, 115,
    189; contrasted with Kantianism, 38–39
Longfellow, Henry, 208, 286 n.42
L'Ouverture, Toussaint, 25, 190, 193, 248, 264
Loring, Ellis Gray, 124, 149, 183
Lovejoy, Elijah, 4, 73, 190
Lowell, James Russell, 15, 99, 208, 210, 261
Lowell (Massachusetts), 113–14
Lowell Offering, 113–14

Madison, James, 18, 29
Marcuse, Herbert, 119
Marsh, James, 7, 30, 35
Martin, J. Sella, 58, 111, 215, 217, 226, 243, 250
Martin, Sarah, 249
Marx, Karl, 105, 110, 116–17, 122–23, 126, 130,
    133, 244
Massachusetts: Civil War and, 226–27;
    conflated with New England, 209–10; as
    hotbed for reform movements, 9, 206–7;
    politics in, 205–6, 224, 240–42
Massachusetts Quarterly Review, 90, 97–98,
    208
Massachusetts Workingmen's Party, 138–39
May, Samuel J., 35, 70, 79, 97, 98, 149, 173, 184,
    271 n.54, 278 n.22
Mazzini, Giuseppe, 127, 185
McClellan, George, 240
Melville, Herman, 4, 13, 160, 163, 166, 220
Merriam, Francis, 215, 216
Mexican War, 90–91, 150
Michelet, Jules, 126
Mickiewicz, Adam, 126, 127

Mill, John Stuart, 171, 259
Minkins, Shadrach, 174–75
Morris, Robert, 46, 132, 149, 157, 175, 178, 182,
    206, 254
Morton, Samuel, 197, 199, 200
Mott, Lucretia, 3, 80, 84
Muir, John, 263

Nell, William C., 4, 7, 27–28, 59, 74, 82–83,
    86, 89, 92, 154, 193–94, 196, 207, 221, 233,
    247, 251, 256, 259, 260, 262, 264, 275
    nn.145–46, 283 n.179, 284 n.1; Adelphic
    Union and, 45–47, 49, 61, 77; American
    Civil War and, 251; European revolutions
    of 1848 and, 132–33; New England
    nationalist pride and, 212–13; Transcenden-
    talism and, 26, 53–57, 60, 65, 96, 98–99,
    199; Utopian socialism and, 102–4, 120,
    122, 132, 138; vigilance committees and,
    148–49, 157, 159–60, 174–75, 177
New England: anti-Irish sentiment in, 204–5;
    antislavery in, 112, 210; economy of, 103–8,
    162, 207; nationalist pride in, 209–12;
    uniqueness of, 180
New England Freedom Association,
    148–49
New England Non-Resistant Society, 92
newspapers, 28
Niebuhr, Reinhold, 267 n.40
Nietzsche, Friedrich, 14, 71, 162, 172, 189, 296
    n.96
non-resistance, 91–94
Northrup, Solomon, 232
Northampton Association, 1–3, 102, 103, 120,
    122, 124
Nott, Josiah, 197, 199
Noyes Academy, 31–32

Obama, Barack, 5
Oneida Institute, 32, 33, 39
Orvis, John, 94, 98

Palfrey, John G., 90
Parker, Theodore, 4, 5, 19, 30, 39, 45, 55, 59,
    63, 73, 93, 111, 115, 130, 135, 181, 186, 189,
    191, 192, 208, 210, 214, 245, 246, 249, 263;
    abolitionism and, 67–68, 97–98;
    Adelphic Union and, 46, 47, 48; death,
    220; John Brown and, 215, 217–18; racism
    of, 194, 195–99, 202–4, 205–6; religious
    ideas of, 75, 76–77, 79, 80, 83, 86, 87, 88,

232; resistance to Fugitive Slave Act, 142, 147, 151, 156, 157, 159, 164–65, 170–71, 174, 183; socialism and, 103, 109, 110, 124, 129

Pennington, James W. C., 154–55, 162

"People's Party," 213, 240–42

Phillips, Ann Terry, 83

Phillips, Wendell, 2, 4, 47, 55, 65, 69, 72, 75, 94, 130, 142, 151, 153, 154, 172, 185, 195, 206, 207, 211, 213, 218, 225, 227, 229, 234, 236–37, 242, 250, 257, 259, 261, 263, 264, 269 n.57, 308 n.44; Abraham Lincoln and, 224, 235, 245, 253; economic ideas of, 103, 105, 110, 125, 223, 262, 263; Emerson and, 59, 95, 97, 158, 188; political philosophy of, 17–19, 230, 244, 246

Phillips, Moses, 208

Phoenixonian Society, 26, 27, 31, 32–33, 46

Pierpont, John, 260

Pillsbury, Parker, 99, 207

Powell, William P., 110, 133, 227, 229

Proudhon, Pierre-Joseph, 138

Putnam, Caroline, 8, 88

Putnam, George, 141

Putnam, Lewis, 244

Quincy, Edmund, 46, 48, 68, 69, 79, 80, 92, 93, 208–9

Quincy, Josiah, 111–12

Quinet, Edgar, 126–27

racial uplift/elevation ideology, 56–58, 85–86

Radical Club (1867), 259–60, 262

Rael, Patrick, 48

Raynal, Guillaume Thomas François, 67, 278 n.21

Reason, Charles, 58

Reid, Thomas, 29, 30

Republican Party, 185, 213–14, 216, 218, 225–26, 232, 237, 240, 249, 255, 259, 261, 307 n.11

Remond, Charles Lenox, 59, 110, 112, 146, 178–80, 182, 195–96, 218, 232, 251, 252, 254, 255, 257

Ricketson, Daniel, 80

Ripley, George, 2, 11, 73, 79, 93, 102, 104, 110, 116, 121, 122, 125, 137

Robespierre, Maximilien, 134, 217

Robinson, Harriet, 114

Robinson, William, 114, 214

Rock, John S., 4, 111, 132, 225, 227–28, 233, 234, 238, 256–57; criticism of Theodore Parker, 194–97; meaning of American Civil War and, 228, 240, 242–46, 251, 252–53; Supreme Court and, 256–57

Rogers, Nathaniel, 33, 74, 91

Rogers, Seth, 219, 248

Romanticism, 12–13, 37–38, 44, 104, 191, 242

Rorty, Richard, 12

Rose, Erskine, 130

Russell, Charles, 152

Rynders, Isaiah, 100, 155

Ruggles, David, 2, 124, 147

Salem Lyceum, 59

Sanborn, Franklin, 214–15, 217, 237, 259

Sand, George, 127

Sanderson, Jeremiah Burke, 8, 55–56, 82, 92

Santayana, George, 261

Schiller, Friedrich, 11, 26, 31, 49, 70, 119

Schleiermacher, Friedrich, 11, 30

Scottish Common Sense School, 28–31, 107, 115; critique of, 29–31

selfhood, 9, 49–53, 77, 87, 163

Sewall, Samuel, 149, 207, 217

Seward, William Henry, 15, 152, 225, 234

Sidney, Thomas, 7, 26, 31–32, 33–36, 38, 39, 43, 264, 271 n.49

Sims, Thomas, 160, 175, 176, 187, 193

slavery, 3, 4–5, 24, 57, 59–60, 67–68, 81–82, 93, 97, 105–6, 108, 120, 124, 128, 155, 265 n.11, 267 n.29; abolition of, in Washington, D.C., 232–33; fugitives from, 147

Smith, Adam, 115

Smith, Gerrit, 15, 55, 194, 195, 242

Smith, James McCune, 28, 31, 32, 39, 46, 60, 193, 194–95, 199–200, 276, n.175

Snowden, Isaac, 61

Spooner, Lysander, 93

Stanton, Elizabeth Cady, 15, 244

Stearns, Charles, 91

Stearns, George, 215

Stetson, Caleb, 48, 156

Stewart, Maria, 28, 84–86

Stone, James, 214, 237

Story, Joseph, 90

Stowe, Harriet Beecher, 62, 157, 160, 183, 209–10, 213

Strong, George Templeton, 256

Stuart, Moses, 73, 278 n.34

Sumner, Charles, 28, 47, 95, 97, 98, 99, 139, 164, 167, 174, 206, 211, 214, 221, 233–37, 240–42, 246, 252, 256–59; caning of, 180, 185–86
Swedenborg, Emanuel, 77

Tappan, Lewis, 32, 78
Taney, Robert, 178, 194, 212, 256
Taylor, Charles, 75
Taylor, Zachary, 156
Texan annexation, 90
Thatcher, Margaret, 12
Thoreau, Henry David, 11, 13, 63, 81, 93–94, 98, 99, 153, 192–93, 200, 202, 221, 263; abolitionism and, 72, 88, 95, 144; black thinkers and 5, 14, 61, 264; Boston Vigilance Committee and, 158–59, 190; *Civil Disobedience*, 5, 63, 90–91, 169–70; critique of marketplace and industrialization, 117–18, 119, 120; death, 220; John Brown and, 215–18; heroism and, 190–91; ideas about selfhood, 36, 41, 50–51, 167, 171, 188; nature and, 48, 59, 112, 211; *Walden*, 58, 119
de Tocqueville, Alexis, 10, 171, 231
Tolstoy, Leo, 14, 92, 263
Torrey, Charles, 148
Town and Country Club, 9, 55, 98, 99, 139, 173, 214, 221, 224, 283 n.179
Transcendentalist Club, 45, 48, 49, 135, 138
Trask, Henry, 124, 129
Treanor, Bernard, 141, 293 n.226
Trilling, Lionel, 16
Truth, Sojourner, 2, 124
Tubman, Harriet, 193

Uncle Tom's Cabin, 147, 179, 183
Unitarianism, 30, 38, 65, 66, 67, 68, 72–77, 107, 115

Walker, Amasa, 46
Walker, David, 49, 56, 67, 85, 131, 132
Ward, Samuel R., 28, 31, 33, 39, 82, 111, 131, 135, 151, 155, 195
Warren, Robert Penn, 16–17
Washington, D.C., 232–35
Watkins, William, 182–83
Weber, Max, 19, 42
Webster, Daniel, 18, 87, 106, 128, 145, 150–56, 159, 169*f*, 175, 176, 185
Webster, Delia, 62–63
West, Cornel, 14
Whipper, William, 28–29
Whitfield, James Monroe, 60
Whitman, Walt, 6, 13, 50, 51, 83, 144, 160, 192, 219, 226, 236, 239, 274 n.134
Whittier, John Greenleaf, 95, 114, 144, 151, 156, 210, 219
Wightman, Joseph, 225
Willich, August, 244
Wilson, Henry, 184, 205, 207, 214
women's rights, 83–88
Workingmen's Party, 109
Wright, Elizur, 97, 98, 113, 129, 140, 173, 175, 214
Wright, Henry C., 74–75, 80, 92, 163, 204, 214, 278 n.34

Young Men's Literary Society, 61

ACKNOWLEDGMENTS

I did not retreat into the woods like Thoreau to write a book all by myself. Instead, I wrote this with the help and support of too many people to properly thank.

I never would have been able to write a book such as this without the support and mentorship of so many wonderful teachers. At Swarthmore, Bruce Dorsey—who was willing to take a chance on an unexperienced research assistant—inspired in me a love of dusty archives and rickety microfilm readers. When I was applying to grad school, Mike Mullins and my fellow salts encouraged and helped me. At New York University, I couldn't have asked for a more patient and encouraging adviser than Martha Hodes, who was always there to push my analysis further, to demand that my prose be clear and that I be rigorous with my claims. I'll forever be grateful for Thomas Bender's generosity with his time, ideas, and coffee. Linda Gordon modeled what it meant to be a socially committed historian. Both Manisha Sinha and John Stauffer didn't have to take so much time out of their busy schedules to read my dissertation, but I'm so thankful they did.

I was extraordinarily lucky to have found a spectacular group of colleagues in the NYU history department. Members of the exclusive U.S. history "Nerd Club"—Lauren Gutterman, Melissa Milewski, Lilly Tuttle, Dylan Yeats, and Natalie Blum-Ross—read and commented on chapters of this book. As important, they were true friends in a field that so often encourages competition rather than collaboration. Reynolds Richter, Daniel Rodriguez, and David Weinfeld made my years in New York both intellectually interesting and personally rewarding. Finally, my neighbors and colleagues Sam Seeley and Geoff Traugh read chapters and discussed ideas over dinner and drinks (normally drinks) too many times to count. From my brothers and sisters in GSOC-UAW, I learned the heartbreak, struggle, and joy of a fight for justice. The union struggle, more than any graduate seminar itself, was my true education into what power actually looks like in our society.

At the American Academy of Arts and Sciences, I was fortunate to have an amazing crew of colleagues and advisers. Mary Dunn's intellectual and writing advice was invaluable. Hillary Chute, Matt Karp, Lindy Baldwin, Chris Loss, Nicki Skillman, and Francesca Ammon were as insightful readers as they were amazing dancers.

Facing a bleak job market, I was beyond grateful that a political scientist, Gary Herrigel, took a chance on me and hired me to teach in the University of Chicago's Core. At Chicago, I received invaluable feedback and assistance from Jon Levy, Amy Lippert, Emma Stone-Mackinnon, and the U.S. Social History Workshop. I'm especially grateful to the mentorship and assistance of Amy Dru Stanley. There were too many friends and colleagues in the Society of Fellows to name here, but so many contributed to my success. I do want to mention, though, David Egan, who did the best one could patiently trying to explain Kantian metaphysics to me. SEIU Local 73, the national Faculty Forward campaign, and my colleagues on the bargaining committee demonstrated the slow hard work that will someday transform the lives of contingent academic faculty.

I have learned so much from my colleagues at Princeton. Matt Karp, Beth Lew-Williams, Rosina Lozano, Joe Fronczak, Michael Blaakman, Xin Wen, Rob Karl, Rhae Lynn Barnes, and Natasha Wheatley read chapters in reading groups. More important, they became friends who helped me navigate a new institution. Sean Wilentz closely read and commented on the whole book. Keith Wailoo, Yair Mintzker, Phil Nord, Yaacob Dweck, Max Weiss, Tera Hunter, Dan Rodgers, and the members of the Modern American History Workshop read my work and gave me invaluable advice. Andrew Fagel directed me to the autobiography of his ancestor, a friend of Emerson's. This book is so much better because of all the people at Princeton.

Caleb McDaniel was a model reader who offered careful suggestions that improved this book tremendously. James Kloppenberg and Leslie Butler read the manuscript and offered invaluable advice. At the University of Pennsylvania Press, Bob Lockhart was a wonderful editor who always fought to make this the best book it could be. Bryan LaPointe assisted with indexing.

I have been supported and assisted by a number of archives and grants. The American Council of Learned Societies supported a year's worth of writing. The Massachusetts Historical Society, Boston Athenaeum, and Bostonian Society generously funded my research in Boston; their librarians and archivists were patient and kind. The American Antiquarian Society and the Ralph Waldo Emerson Society assisted research in Worcester. In addition, librarians and archivists at the New York Public Library, the Boston Public Library, Howard's Moorland-Spingarn Library, Harvard's Houghton Library, the Newberry Library, and NYU's Bobst Library all contributed to my success.

I can't forget my friends, who made this all so probable. Jared, Aaron, Jake, Katherine, Andy, Amy, Davide, and Jen helped me survive college. New York wouldn't have been New York without Lindsay and Jenny. Finally, of course, I could never step foot back in Mystic if I didn't mention Bates, David, Kris, John, Ian, Shaymus, Maddog, Andy, Steamer, Ryan, and Sam. I owe you all a beer (or more . . .). Thank you, friends. I wouldn't be here if it wasn't for you.

My parents and family supported me so much during this process. Alan and Kristie let me crash on their couch while I slogged through research in Boston. My mother never stopped encouraging me to follow my dreams. And Meg spent hours correcting my typos and listening to me drone on about Transcendentalists. She was an intellectual collaborator and a true partner. When it sometimes seemed as though no one else did, I knew she always believed in me. I love you, Meg.

Finally, this book is dedicated to my father, who brought me to Revolutionary War battlefields when I was a boy and bought me a copy of *Walden* when I was fourteen. From him, I learned to love history, to always mean what you say, and to never respect authority.